ARABIC CORPUS LINGUISTICS

Edited by Tony McEnery, Andrew Hardie
and Nagwa Younis

EDINBURGH
University Press

Edinburgh University Press is one of the leading university presses in the UK. We publish academic books and journals in our selected subject areas across the humanities and social sciences, combining cutting-edge scholarship with high editorial and production values to produce academic works of lasting importance. For more information visit our website: edinburghuniversitypress.com

Edinburgh University Press Ltd
The Tun – Holyrood Road, 12(2f) Jackson's Entry, Edinburgh EH8 8PJ

First published in hardback by Edinburgh University Press 2019

Typeset in 10/12 Ehrhardt by
Servis Filmsetting Ltd, Stockport, Cheshire,

A CIP record for this book is available from the British Library

ISBN 978 0 7486 7737 5 (hardback)
ISBN 978 1 4744 8545 6 (paperback)
ISBN 978 0 7486 7738 2 (webready PDF)
ISBN 978 0 7486 7739 9 (epub)

Contents

Notes on Contributors iv

1 Introducing Arabic Corpus Linguistics 1
Tony McEnery, Andrew Hardie and Nagwa Younis

2 Under the Hood of arabiCorpus 17
Dilworth B. Parkinson

3 Tunisian Arabic Corpus: Creating a Written Corpus of an 'Unwritten' Language 30
Karen McNeil

4 Accessible Corpus Annotation for Arabic 56
Wesam Ibrahim and Andrew Hardie

5 The Leeds Arabic Discourse Treebank: Guidelines for Annotating Discourse Connectives and Relations 76
Amal Alsaif and Katja Markert

6 Using the Web to Model Modern and Qur'anic Arabic 100
Eric Atwell

7 Semantic Prosody as a Tool for Translating Prepositions in the Holy Qur'an: A Corpus-Based Analysis 120
Nagwa Younis

8 A Relational Approach to Modern Literary Arabic Conditional Clauses 143
Manuel Sartori

9 Quantitative Approaches to Analysing COME Constructions in Modern Standard Arabic 170
Dana Abdulrahim

10 Approaching Text Typology through Cluster Analysis in Arabic 201
Ghada Mohamed and Andrew Hardie

Appendix: Arabic Transliteration Systems Used in This Book 229

Index 232

Notes on Contributors

Dana Abdulrahim is a faculty member of the Department of English Language and Literature, University of Bahrain, Bahrain.

Amal Alsaif is a member of the Islamic NLP Studies Research Group, Al-Imam Mohammad Bin Saud University, Saudi Arabia.

Eric Atwell is Professor of Artificial Intelligence for Language, School of Computing, University of Leeds, UK.

Andrew Hardie is Reader in Linguistics at the Department of Linguistics and English Language, Lancaster University, UK.

Wesam Ibrahim is Associate Professor, Faculty of Education, Tanta University, Egypt.

Tony McEnery is Distinguished Professor of English Language and Linguistics at the Department of Linguistics and English Language, Lancaster University, UK.

Karen McNeil is Program Director, Office of Student Veterans and Commissioning Programs, Brown University, USA.

Katja Markert is Professor in the Institut für Computerlinguistik, Heidelberg University, Germany.

Ghada Mohamed is Assistant Professor of Linguistics and Director of the English Language Centre, University of Bahrain, Bahrain.

Dilworth B. Parkinson is Professor of Asian and Near Eastern Languages, Kennedy Center, Brigham Young University, USA.

Manuel Sartori is Professor of Arabic Linguistics and Grammar, Aix-Marseille University, France.

Nagwa Younis is Head of the Department of English, Faculty of Education, Ain Shams University, Egypt.

1

Introducing Arabic Corpus Linguistics

Tony McEnery, Andrew Hardie and Nagwa Younis

1. Introduction

Arabic is a major world language, spoken not only in the Arabian peninsula, but by hundreds of millions of people across northern Africa and western Asia, and more broadly around the world. Corpus linguistics – the analysis of very large amounts of natural language data using computer-assisted methods and techniques – is a major methodology in modern linguistics. Yet, so far, relatively few studies have attempted to apply this major methodology to this major language. We may say, then, that Arabic corpus linguistics as a research endeavour is still in its infancy.[1]

This volume represents an attempt by its authors and editors to help foster its development by bringing together cutting-edge contributions on the data, methods and research foci of this nascent field. Our aim is not merely to place on record present work of this kind but also, we hope, to showcase the intersection of Arabic linguistics and corpus-based methods in such a way as to inspire future work in the area. We feel strongly that this book represents the starting-point for major developments still to come in Arabic corpus linguistics.

Our goal in this introductory chapter is to set the scene for the contributions to follow in the remainder of the book. In doing so, we have attempted to address the perspectives of three main groups of readers who we anticipate will find this book of interest. Researchers and students working in Arabic corpus linguistics are only the first of these groups. We also address here (1) corpus linguists (or those in allied fields such as computational linguistics, natural language processing, or digital humanities) who have little experience of working with Arabic; and (2) Arabic linguists with little experience of corpus methods.

With this in mind, our scene-setting necessarily involves a brief introduction to corpus linguistics on the one hand, and Arabic linguistics on the other. The next section addresses the latter of these goals, and sketches in outline those features of the Arabic language which are most important as background for an understanding of the various chapters in this book. As part of this, we will introduce the transliteration scheme used throughout the volume. This sketch is necessarily short. For readers who wish to learn more, many excellent grammars of Arabic are available, but the ones which are, perhaps, cited most often by the various contributors to this volume are Holes (2004), Ryding (2005) and Abu-Chacra (2007); all are highly recommended as references and background reading for non-speakers of the language.

Subsequently, we present a very cursory overview of the principal ideas and methods that underpin corpus-based analysis of language data. We can hardly do justice to such an extensive field in the space available here, and therefore we focus in particular on the history of corpus linguistics and its application to English on the one hand, and in multilingual research on the other; for readers interested in finding out more, we recommend McEnery and Hardie (2012), especially as it is available in an Arabic translation for those who would prefer to read the book in that language. Also of note is Baker et al. (2006), a short reference volume which contains introductory definitions for key terms and concepts in the field.

We move on to consider the status of Arabic corpus linguistics as an *emerging* field. The use of attested language data in Arabic linguistics goes back to the very origins of the discipline – and yet in spite of that, as we have noted, Arabic has in many respects lagged behind other languages in terms of the spread of applications of the methodology. This is illustrated by means of a fairly simple publication database search. Yet, we argue, the nascent status of Arabic corpus linguistics can be seen as an opportunity, rather than a deficiency, in the context of contemporary Arabic studies. We will conclude this chapter by giving a brief overview of each of the chapters which follow, and finally laying out how we see these various directions of research contributing to a new focus for the application of corpus linguistics to Arabic.

2. The Arabic language: some basic background

Since we anticipate that not all our readers may be fully acquainted with the background of Arabic, we will now provide a brief overview of the most crucial points regarding the social context and the grammar, phonology, and orthography of the language. It goes without saying that, for reasons of space, the following represents an extreme simplification of a very complex picture; we hope that, nevertheless, those readers not familiar with Arabic will find it useful.

Arabic is spoken as a first language by almost 300 million people,[2] as well as having a crucial status as the language of Islam for the even greater number of Muslims who are native speakers of other languages (see Holes 2004: 1–49 for an overview). Three main divisions of Arabic are usually recognised: *Classical Arabic*, the language of the Qur'an and other early texts; *Modern Standard Arabic* (MSA), a revived and modernised variety based on Classical Arabic that is the standard written form of the language, and the most prestigious spoken form, throughout the Arabic-speaking world; and a very wide range of *Colloquial Arabics*, which are for the most part not written, which differ greatly from place to place, and which are not all entirely mutually comprehensible. Contemporarily, then, a state of diglossia exists throughout the Arabic-speaking world between MSA and the regional form of Colloquial Arabic. Of the regional varieties, Egyptian Arabic has most speakers (over 64 million). It is also the most influential

Colloquial Arabic, as 'from the 1950s onwards, the Egyptian media was predominant in the Arabic-speaking world' (Rubin 2012: 239).

Arabic is part of the Semitic branch of the Afro-Asiatic language family, and shares the morphological structure characteristic of that family. Much of both the derivational and inflectional morphology in the language is *nonconcatenative*, in that most root morphemes consist solely of consonants, and the patterns of vowels that are added to the roots to create base words are themselves bound morphemes (see Ryding 2005: 44–9; Abu-Chacra 2007: 78–86, *passim*). In addition to the consonantal roots and vowel patterns, there also exist suffixes, prefixes, and infixes, as well as a wide range of clitics. The most common number of consonants in a root is three, although some roots have two or four consonants. An oft-used example of a root is *k-t-b*, associated with the meanings of 'write/writing'. Different word bases are formed by combining this root with different vowel patterns, for example *kitāb*, 'book' and *kātib*, 'writer'; or with vowel patterns plus additional affixes, for example *katab-a*, 'he wrote' and *ma-ktab*, 'office'. Within a single verbal or nominal lemma, inflectional contrasts may be indicated solely by affixes (for instance, *kitāb*, 'book (singular)' versus *kitāb-ayn*, 'books (dual)') or by affixes alongside yet further differences in the vowel pattern (for instance, *katab-a*, 'he wrote' versus *ya-ktub-u*, 'he writes'; *kitāb*, 'book (singular)' versus *kutub*, 'books (plural)'). While most of the main vocabulary follows this root-and-pattern system, loanwords and many proper nouns exist as unitary underived items, as do a variety of grammatical words generally referred to as *particles*.

Apart from the particles, words follow either verbal inflection (for categories including subject agreement for person, number, and gender; tense or aspect;[3] voice; and mood) or nominal inflection (for the categories of number, gender, case, and definiteness/state). Adjectives follow the same pattern of inflection as nouns and are thus sometimes considered to be a subcategory of nouns rather than a separate major word-class. A significant proportion of this complex inflection has, however, been levelled in whole or part between the classical and contemporary periods, so that Colloquial Arabics in particular do not display all of the categories observed in Classical Arabic.

Arabic syntax has perhaps attracted less attention over the centuries than its highly complex morphology. Arabic shows nominative-accusative alignment (cf. Dixon 1979); clause word order is either VSO or SVO. Adjectives follow nouns, and the language has prepositions rather than postpositions. Famously, nominal possession is indicated with a structure called the *genitive construct* or, in Arabic, *ʾiḍāfah* (lit. 'augmentation'), where the possessed noun appears in the construct state (a third nominal form alongside the definite and indefinite inflections) and the possessor noun follows it in definite form. Object pronouns and possessive pronouns appear as enclitics; many prepositions and conjunctions appear as proclitics.

Computational and corpus-based analyses necessarily address the written form of a language as well as the spoken, and therefore the interaction of Arabic grammar with Arabic's phonology and writing system bears some comment here. The phonology of Arabic is notable for being rich in consonant distinctions, with uvular, pharyngeal, and glottal obstruents all present in the system, as well as a phonemic distinction between so-called 'plain' and 'emphatic' (pharyngealised) dental/alveolar obstruents. Conversely, there are only three distinct vowel qualities (/a i u/), although the number of actual vowels is somewhat greater: each of the three vowels can be long as well as short, and there also exist diphthongs /ai/ and /au/, albeit the latter are often regarded as sequences of /a/ with the glides /j/ and /w/ respectively. Once again, this summary reflects in large part the Classical Arabic situation; the Colloquial Arabics differ widely, and the pronunciation of MSA may vary across the Arabic-speaking world in keeping with the local colloquial variety.

The Arabic alphabet is related most closely to the other Semitic writing systems, notably the Phoenician alphabet from which the Greek, and thus Latin and Cyrillic, alphabets ultimately derive. Like Phoenician, but unlike Greek or Latin, the Arabic alphabet is consonantal: there existed originally no letters for vowels. Over time, two developments added vowels to the system. First, certain consonant letters came to be used to indicate related long vowels as well as their original consonantal value. For instance, the symbol for /w/ is also used to indicate long /uː/. Second, the system came to use a series of diacritic signs which can be placed above or below a consonant letter to indicate the presence of a subsequent short vowel (diacritics are also used to indicate consonant gemination and other features). However – critically – in most types of written Arabic, the most notable exception being the Qur'an, the short vowel diacritics *are not used*. This generates much ambiguity among word-types which must be resolved by the reader's contextual understanding, since several important morphological distinctions are made purely by differences in the vowels, not only in the vowel patterns added to roots but also in affixes. For example, the nominative, accusative, and genitive suffixes are *-u*, *-a*, and *-i* respectively – all three of which are typically absent in the written form.

The phonological and orthographic factors outlined above create certain issues for the transliteration of Arabic into the Latin alphabet (also known as *Romanisation*). First, the large consonant inventory means that additional consonant letters, beyond those used by most European languages, are required; this can be addressed by use of digraphs, by the addition of diacritics to Latin consonants, by using International Phonetic Alphabet symbols for the 'extra' consonants, or by pressing into service otherwise unused letters, punctuation, and so on as the 'extra' consonants. The second issue is thornier. A Romanisation of written Arabic may attempt *either* to map each Arabic character uniquely to a Latin character, *or* to produce an (approximate) representation of the original's pronunciation. (Only an approximate representation is possible because, as noted above, there is much variation across regions in pronunciation of MSA.) Because of the unwritten short vowels, which must normally be absent in a character-to-character mapping but present in a representation of pronunciation, the two forms of Romanisation are typically very different. Targeting unique mapping leads to ambiguity (due to the absence of short vowels) and redundancy (since some phonemes, notably the glottal stop and long /aː/, are represented by multiple, distinct Arabic characters). Conversely, approximating pronunciation leads to the inclusion of matter not in the original (i.e. the short vowels, *inter alia*) and loss of distinctions among different letters that indicate the same sound.

Scholarly transliteration systems tend to be of the latter kind – that is, they approximate the pronunciation, and include short vowels. Several standards for this kind of transliteration exist: the one we adopt for all Arabic words used as examples in this book is that of the Deutsches Institut für Normung, standard no. 31635 (DIN 31635). This standard is distinctive for its use of consonant diacritics, rather than digraphs or phonetic characters, to represent consonant letters that have no simple equivalent in the unadorned Latin alphabet. For instance, the Arabic letter representing the phoneme /x/ is transliterated to <ḫ>, rather than <x> or <kh> as in other systems.

Conversely, transliteration systems designed for use by computer programs tend to be of the former kind – with one-to-one mappings – because this allows unambiguous restoration of the original Arabic form (which DIN 31635 and similar scholarly transliterations do not permit). Computational analysis of Arabic predates the widespread use of the Unicode standard for character encoding; in a pre-Unicode age, linguistic software could most easily operate on Arabic by processing it in the form of an unambiguous transliteration into the ASCII character set. The most well-known such transliteration system is that introduced in the 1990s by Tim Buckwalter for use with his morphological analyser program, but now widely used in Arabic natural language processing and computational linguistics; it is generally referred to as the *Buckwalter transliteration*.[4] While eminently tractable for computer, the Buckwalter transliteration is not easy to read, even for Arabic speakers; most vowels are absent, and in order to avoid the use of non-ASCII characters, many Latin characters (including punctuation) have been pressed into service for Arabic letters whose sounds they do not reflect even remotely. For instance, in the Buckwalter system, <p> represents an Arabic letter that is either silent or else pronounced /t/; <E> represents a pharyngeal fricative; and <*> represents an interdental fricative. Moreover, the Buckwalter system is case sensitive, so that <s> and <S> represent two different Arabic consonants, letters which – in scholarly transliterations – are usually not case sensitive, allowing them to co-exist with the normal functions (e.g. sentence initial) of capitalisation in the Latin writing system as used in European languages.

Our primary use of DIN 31635 transliteration in this volume is motivated by concern for scholarly tradition as well as overall readability. However, at certain points in the text, namely in discussions of the inputs to and outputs from certain software systems that employ Buckwalter transliteration internally, it has been essential to use the Buckwalter transliteration rather than DIN 31635 in order to properly illustrate the operation of the program under discussion. This has, however, been kept to a minimum. Both the DIN 31635 and Buckwalter transliterations are detailed in full in the Appendix.

3. Corpus linguistics

At the heart of corpus linguistics is the challenge of analysing collections of linguistic data – corpora – which are too vast in extent to be approached by the hand-and-eye techniques which linguists use when considering individual example sentences, utterances, passages, or texts. Two primary computer-assisted techniques underpin the many and various components of the corpus linguistic toolbox: the frequency list and the concordance. A *frequency list* is constructed by the computer scanning a corpus progressively to identify all the distinct word forms and how often each of them occurs within that corpus; frequency lists are at the foundation of a plethora of quantitative methods of corpus analysis. Meanwhile, a *concordance* is a listing of all instances in the corpus that match against a query term supplied by the user. Again, the computer scans the corpus, identifying all the matches and displaying them in tabular from – each instance being presented alongside a small amount of the preceding and following text. This concordance display can then be analysed for patterns of meaning, usage, and co-occurrence among linguistic items in the discourse.

Whereas today, these two foundational techniques – as well as the entire methodological apparatus of corpus linguistics that has been erected atop them – are inextricably associated with the affordances of the digital computer, this was not always the case. In the pre-computer era that lasted until the middle of the twentieth century, concordances and frequency lists were indeed compiled from collections of text comparable in nature to modern computer corpora – despite the gargantuan investment of human labour that this necessitated (for an overview, see McEnery and Wilson's 2001: 2–4 account of early corpus linguistics). To grasp the immense practical difficulties of this way of working with language data – not limited merely to the effort required and the consequent prohibitive expense, but also including the susceptibility of humans to making errors – is to understand why, without the computer, corpus analysis remained very much in the realms of what Abercrombie (1965) terms a *pseudo-procedure*: that is, a method that is in principle very useful but which is, in practice, not viable. But even at the time that Abercrombie wrote, the advent of the computer – first in the form of mechanical punch-card devices, and then electronic devices that led to the technology of today – was already beginning to show that corpus-based linguistics could indeed be viable.

In its first stage, this development was situated within a firmly multilingual milieu. As early as the late 1940s, researchers such as Roberto Busa had started to use data processing machinery to carry out concordances of large (by the standards of the time) volumes of data. Similarly, Alphonse Juilland built corpora of hundreds of thousands of words and used computers to explore word frequency in a range of languages, producing frequency lists of Spanish, Romanian, French, and Italian which he published in the 1960s. This pioneering work lies at the historical root not only of corpus linguistics, but also the allied field of *humanities computing*, today usually known as *digital humanities*.

However, despite these multilingual beginnings, from the 1960s and through the 1970s and 1980s corpus linguistics was fostered and developed principally in the context of study of English, by linguists such as Stig Johansson, Geoffrey Leech, Randolph Quirk, John Sinclair, and Jan Svartvik. While some of these scholars, notably Johansson, did also work on other languages, English corpus linguistics was the locus of a number of critical advances in both the methodology and the technology of the corpus approach.

First, by using corpora to build and redefine standard reference resources, notably grammars and dictionaries, these researchers showed that corpus data was an unmatchable source of evidence for such descriptive materials. Second, in order to produce these materials they began to elaborate and explore what would become key concepts in corpus analysis, such as collocation (see Sinclair et al. 2004). Third, to facilitate their work they pioneered the development of new forms of computer analysis of language, for instance reliable automated part-of-speech taggers (see Garside et al. 1987). Fourth, they began to lay down the elements of the design of the basic software tools that corpus linguists use to this day to explore data, notably the concordancer. Fifth, they fostered a now-flourishing enterprise of developing not merely *larger* corpora, but also corpora of an ever-growing range of different *types*.

While it may be convenient in some cases to discuss linguistic corpora as if they are a homogeneous type of resource, they are, in reality, very heterogeneous. This is because different research questions require different types of data. For instance, most early corpora of English consisted of published writing. But if we have research questions that bear on the spoken form of the language, then such corpora are of little use. Spoken corpora were indeed developed, and began to generate deep insights into the differences between these modes of production (see Biber 1988). Similarly, most early corpora of English were what can be termed *snapshot* corpora, which are designed to represent balanced subsets of a particular language at a point in time that are not altered or added to after they have been completed. But over time, research questions emerged which required resources which would not remain static, but would evolve over time to track changes in the language itself. These questions motivated the creation of resources of this kind, known as *monitor* corpora. Another dimension along which corpus resources vary is the degree to which they are annotated when made available to the scholarly community. Corpus *annotation* (see Garside et al. 1997) is the practice of embedding linguistic analyses into the text of the corpus itself; an annotated corpus permits many forms of analysis, particularly in terms of abstract (grammatical, semantic) corpus queries, which are difficult or impossible in an unannotated (or *raw*) corpus. Approaching corpus resources in this spirit of matching the data to the research question has led to very real advances in the study of languages for which we have appropriate corpus resources.

It was over the course of the 1980s that corpus linguistics became once more a truly multilingual enterprise, as multilingual corpora started to allow languages to be contrasted and translation practices to be explored using the techniques of corpus analysis. Two broad types of multilingual corpus can be defined. In a *comparable* corpus, multiple monolingual subcorpora are built according to the same, or very similar, collection procedures. The resulting assemblage of resources is an ideal basis for comparing and contrasting different languages. A *parallel* corpus, on the other hand, consists of a collection of original material in one language and its translations into one or more other languages; such parallel data has become central to the study of translation, among other matters. Both these kinds of multilingual corpus may, moreover, cover one or many modes, genres, or registers of the different languages in question – just as monolingual corpora do. Through the 1990s and into the twenty-first century, researchers began to use these resources and the novel corpus-based methods developed to work with them to explore not only near relatives of English such as German and Norwegian (see Johansson and Oksefjell 1998), but also languages as genetically diverse as Chinese (Xiao and McEnery 2004) and Somali (Biber 1995: 314–58).

4. Arabic corpus linguistics as an emerging field

Neither in the initial emergence of corpus linguistics, nor in the later flowering of multilingual work undertaken using corpora, has Arabic been a major focus of corpus-based research. This is surprising – especially in light of the fact that what Ditters (1990: 130) describes as a kind of corpus linguistics lies at the very root of the Arabic grammatical tradition (see Owens 1990, 1997). Most notably, the Persian linguist Sībawayh[5] (c. 760–96 CE; see Carter 2004) used attested language as the basis of his comprehensive Arabic grammar, the first ever to be written, known as *al-Kitāb* (lit. 'The Book'). Similarly, Sībawayh's teacher al-Ḫalīl wrote the first Arabic dictionary – *al-Kitāb al-ʿAyn*, 'The Book of (the letter) ʿayn' – on the basis of attested language. What was this 'corpus'? Brustad (2016: 148–9) reports that it consisted of 'pre-Islamic poetry, formal speeches, and tribal war (*ayyām*) material [and] is what grammarians and others refer to as "*kalām al-ʿarab*"' (lit. 'talk of the Arabs'); whether this corpus included everyday speech is a point on which Ditters and Brustad disagree. The corpus was, it seems, structured in a linguistically meaningful fashion, differentiating spoken and written materials, and organised into distinct registers. This allowed early Arabic grammarians, for example, to identify features typical of Bedouin usage (Ditters 1990: 129). The terms in which evidence from the corpus were cited by al-Ḫalīl and Sībawayh are at times strikingly modern:

> [Al-Ḫalīl] makes statements on whether certain words and patterns are 'part of the corpus' (*min kalām al-ʿarab*) [. . .] Sībawayh offers frequency judgments for some of the structures he talks about, using phrases such as 'this occurs more than I can describe for you in the corpus,' and 'this rarely/often occurs in the corpus.' Both scholars repeatedly state that a certain word or structure is or is not part of, or occurs rarely or frequently, in the [ʿArabiyyah] or the *kalām al-ʿarab*. (Brustad 2016: 150)[6]

Given the partiality to corpus-based argumentation that is thus embedded in the foundations of the Arabic linguistic tradition, we might expect to see the modern form of the corpus linguistic methodology being applied to the Arabic language both swiftly and enthusiastically – once certain non-trivial technical problems related to the computer storage and rendering of the Arabic writing system had been decisively solved, which happened circa 1990–5. Yet this seems not to have been the case. Far less work has been done within corpus linguistics on Arabic than on other languages that lack any such figure as Sībawayh in their background. Even a very superficial search of the literature is sufficient to make this clear. While any of several relevant academic publication databases could be used to make this point, we will use the openly accessible Google Scholar so that interested readers may replicate or update our findings.

We looked in Google Scholar for the phrase 'arabic corpus', limiting the search to publications from the twentieth century. This search returned 90 results. By contrast, searching for 'english corpus' returned 1,940 papers. It might be argued that the difficulty (or impossibility) of representing the Arabic script on computer in the period c. 1950–90 makes this an unfair comparison. But a very similar ratio of results is found if the Google Scholar query is instead restricted to publications from the twenty-first century: searching for 'english corpus' returns 15,600 results, in contrast to 1,800 for 'arabic corpus'. Of course, this is only an informal test – Google result counts are notoriously approximate, and it may be that the papers on Arabic corpus linguistics are being written in Arabic and are thus invisible to this search, despite the dominance of the English language in academic publishing. Yet if we repeat the exercise for other languages with traditions of non-English academic publishing, we find that Arabic still lags behind, albeit to a lesser degree. Looking just at the twenty-first century in Google Scholar, the query 'chinese corpus' finds 4,150 results and the query 'french corpus' finds 2,320 results. It is difficult to avoid the conclusion that, relative to its demographic and sociocultural importance, Arabic is underrepresented as an object of study within corpus linguistics.

Rather than seeing Arabic's status as relatively underserved by corpus-based study as a deficit, we would prefer to characterise this state of affairs as an opportunity. Arabic corpus linguistics, from this perspective, can be seen as an *emergent* rather than a *deficient* area of study. Moreover, there are many encouraging signs that this nascent field is gaining both momentum and prominence within Arabic linguistics more generally. To give just one example, four of the nine papers in the published proceedings of the 2001 'Annual Symposium on Arabic Linguistics' address Arabic corpus linguistics (Parkinson and Farwaneh 2003). Even the 1,800 results found in Google Scholar themselves evidence the vitality of this nascent (sub)discipline. But to what extent is the persistent relative lack of focus on Arabic in corpus-based studies to date actually a problem? Bluntly, why does it matter?

The ultimate answer to this question is simply that attested language use is a good guide for the linguist. Other guides, notably intuition, are prone to all sorts of biases and can give rise to disagreements based on nothing more than fervently held opinion. Interestingly, a (possibly somewhat mythicised) incident in the biography of Sībawayh serves to demonstrate this. Sībawayh famously engaged in, and lost, a debate with another grammarian, al-Kisaʾi, in the palace of the Caliph Hārūn ar-Rašīd in Baghdad; the historiography of this incident – known as the Question of the Wasp (*al-Masʿalah az-Zunbūriyyah*) – is explored by Brustad (2016: 156ff.). At the peak of the debate, the question at hand was whether a pronoun acting as a subject complement should be in the nominative or accusative case. Sībawayh argued for the nominative. Al-Kisaʾi disagreed and, in a *coup de théâtre*, produced four Bedouins, whom he had bribed in advance, to provide him with their native speaker opinions as to who was right. Thanks to the bribery, the Bedouins agreed with al-Kisaʾi; Sībawayh was humiliated and soon died of grief, though he was posthumously vindicated when one of his students went on to get the better of al-Kisaʾi in a later encounter.

The biases that can derail our analyses if we do not have access to attested language data are typically far less blatant than bribery: they include the bias to prefer data that confirms an already-held belief over data that does not; the bias towards that which is salient by virtual of being marked or unusual over that which is frequent; and other such human failings. Without the kind of window on real language usage that corpus analyses provide, Arabic linguistics may be as prone to the misdescription of Arabic as al-Kisaʾi was. Appropriately compiled and exploited corpus data provide us with relatively objective controls on what we may claim about language, and thus, consulting large collections of attested language use can be a powerful way of resolving exactly the kinds of issues that Sībawayh and al-Kisaʾi debated. It is with this in mind that the research presented in this book has been undertaken and compiled in the present volume.

5. Overview of this volume

The chapters in this volume reflect research presented at one or other of the (to date) two events in the *Workshop on Arabic Corpus Linguistics* (WACL) series. Together, they form a snapshot of the state of the field of Arabic corpus linguistics as it currently stands – its accomplishments across a range of linguistic investigations, but also the problems it has faced and continues to face.

The book is organised into two primary divisions, reflecting what are indeed the two primary concerns of any corpus linguistic endeavour: first, methods for creating, making accessible and analysing the corpora that are to underpin the research (Chapters 2, 3, 4, 5 and 6); and second, the application of these methods and datasets in actual linguistic research (Chapters 7, 8, 9 and 10).

The focus on corpus construction and annotation begins with Chapter 2, by Parkinson. This presents a history of how arabiCorpus.byu.edu – a large, openly available collection of Arabic data, together with an online interface for its analysis – was developed. The account is written in such a way that users of the corpus and interface will better understand its affordances and limitations; but Parkinson also considers the perspective of other developers, who will be able to benefit from understanding how the program was conceived and structured. The corpus is a non-lemmatised, untagged corpus, but the software incorporates techniques to overcome at least some of the limitations imposed by the lack of annotation. The software's web-based user interface is, critically, designed in a way meant to not frighten or drive away non-technical users (i.e. students and researchers with few or no technical skills in the management of corpus data).

The focus shifts slightly in Chapter 3, in which McNeil considers the implication of the variation that exists in (especially Colloquial) Arabic for corpus representativeness. McNeil argues, simply, that because of the many varieties of Arabic, there can never be any single authoritative corpus of the language. Rather, to achieve the best results for language-learning resources and natural language processing, corpora for both the standard language and the spoken varieties are needed. With this background in mind, McNeil presents a project to build a 4-million-word corpus of Tunisian Spoken Arabic – the Tunisian Arabic Corpus (TAC). Many challenges exist in the process of creating Arabic corpora, and these are even more acute when addressing a specific Colloquial Arabic; they include the issues of sources, balance, and parsing. The TAC remains under development; the version described in this chapter consists only of about 881,000 words, within which the issues of balance and parsing have not been completely solved. Nonetheless, the corpus has proved to be a useful resource to Arabic students and researchers, and also constitutes a model for others who wish to create dialectal Arabic corpora.

The next two chapters turn from corpus construction to the related topic of corpus annotation. In Chapter 4, Ibrahim and Hardie address morphosyntactic annotation, otherwise known as part-of-speech (POS) tagging. As characteristic for a Semitic language, Arabic displays a high level of morphological complexity. This, together with the high level of ambiguity present in its written form, makes automated morphological and morphosyntactic analysis highly challenging. There has been much work on Arabic POS tagging; however, the authors' detailed critical review of this work illustrates (1) that there is a very great variety in the analytic schemata used; (2) that many of these schemata focus on matters of morphology as much as or more than morphosyntax; and (3) that these schemata are typically highly complex and not easily accessible to non-technical users. Ibrahim and Hardie present an approach to making corpus annotation for Arabic accessible within the frameworks that corpus linguists typically work in, by taking the output of one widely used system (the MADA system, which operates to disambiguate the output of the Buckwalter morphological analyser) and mapping it to a new format. This format includes a redesigned tagset intended to be more easily usable than the feature-matrix schemata used by many state-of-the-art systems. The transfer of formats involves the addition of a category of auxiliary verbs, which are absent from existing tagsets due in part to the focus of much previous work on the morphology of Arabic at the expense of its syntax.

Chapter 5 by Alsaif and Markert looks at discourse annotation. The usefulness of this form of corpus annotation stems straightforwardly from the observation that a text is not only a sequence of sentences or clauses, it is also a coherent object that has many cohesive devices linking the units within it (e.g. words, clauses, and sentences). One of the critical aspects of this coherence is theoretical relations, or 'discourse relations' as they are also known. Examples of such relations between units of discourse at the clause or sentence level are Explanation or Contrast. Discourse connectives (such as *wa*, 'and' and *lākin*, 'but') are widely used to signal these discourse relations. The Leeds Discourse Arabic Treebank (LADTB v.1) extends the syntactic annotation of the Arabic Treebank Part 1 by incorporating this discourse layer, via annotating all explicit Arabic connectives as well as the associated discourse relations and arguments. It has 6,328 discourse connectives reliably annotated by two annotators using the annotation tool READ, which was specifically developed for this project. The authors' approach to discourse annotation is based on principles for identifying explicit discourse connectives similar to those used in the Penn Discourse Treebank project for English. They conclude the chapter by presenting the guidelines designed to build the LADTB, which is the very first discoursally annotated corpus for MSA.

Chapter 6 concludes the book's exploration of corpus construction and annotation with Atwell discussing the use of the Web to collect and promote data resources for the analysis of Arabic, exemplified across a series of projects. Natural language processing (NLP) research can supply useful text-corpus resources in many domains, resources which are in many cases of critical interest for research in corpus linguistics as well as NLP. Atwell's initial survey found few freely available Arabic corpus resources; but work in the early projects he recounts also found that machine learning could be harnessed to adapt generic NLP techniques to Arabic. This required an Arabic text training set, a need which drove the subsequent project to develop the first freely downloadable Corpus of Contemporary Arabic and Arabic concordance visualisation toolkit. Later projects also developed tools for Modern Arabic text analytics: morphological analysis, stemming, tagging, and discourse analysis. Atwell and colleagues went on to extend analytics techniques to the Classical Arabic of the Qurʾan, addressing question-answering, knowledge representation, and syntactic annotation. The Corpus of Contemporary Arabic and the Qurʾanic Arabic Corpus have been widely reused in Arabic corpus linguistics – not least within two later chapters of this volume – and in NLP research for training and evaluation. Moreover, the Qurʾanic Arabic Corpus website has become a widely used resource, not just by Arabic and Qurʾanic researchers, but also by members of the general public wanting online tools to explore and understand the Qurʾan. Atwell concludes by proposing *Understanding the Qurʾan* as a new 'grand challenge' for computer science, artificial intelligence, and corpus linguistics.

In Chapter 7, Younis begins the book's series of case studies in Arabic corpus linguistic research with an examination of how the differences of semantic prosody expressed by different prepositions in similar contexts is reflected in translation to English. Semantic prosody is the phenomenon of co-occurrence associations between linguistic items (here, prepositions) and the contextual expression of particular pragmatic or attitudinal functions; over the past twenty years or so it has become a central concept in corpus analysis of English, but it has yet to be applied to the study of Arabic in a substantive way. Here, Younis takes a step forward in this process, scrutinising relevant prosodies using a parallel corpus of six translations of the Holy Qurʾan provided in the Qurʾanic Arabic Corpus (Dukes 2012; also introduced in Atwell's preceding survey chapter). In scope is the issue of the translation of prepositions in verb-preposition constructions where the preposition plays a role in the meaning of the verb. Special consideration is given to the prepositions *ʿalā*, 'on'; *ʾilā*, 'to'; and *li-*, 'for'. Younis's results shed light on some linguistic aspects of the translation of prepositions in the Holy Qurʾan, insights which are of importance both to the field of linguistics in general, due to their bearing on the phenomenon, and to translation studies in particular.

The next case study, by Sartori in Chapter 8, is based on a corpus of novels in Modern Standard Arabic published between 1963 and 2005 across the entire Arab world. Sartori explores the hypothesis that hypothetical clauses (that is, broadly speaking, *if . . . then . . .* structures) in this variety of Arabic no longer correspond to the established 'classical' model. Specifically, Sartori demonstrates that grammar books which claim to characterise MSA are, in face of the reality of the texts, descriptively inadequate. His analysis shows how, in the literary register of MSA, there has been created within the conditional clause a kind of sequence of tenses, certainly at least in part due to the influence of European languages such as French and English. Therefore, it is no longer the operator of the hypothetical clause (i.e. *iḏā*, *in* or *law*) that enables the meaning of a conditional clause to be understood, but rather the *relationship* between the operator of the hypothetical clause's protasis and the verbal form of its apodosis. Sartori's approach exemplifies the crucial role that corpus data can play both in challenging established views on grammatical structure and in generating new insights to supplement, or in some cases even replace entirely, such traditional analyses.

Staying on the topic of grammar, Chapter 9 by Abdulrahim presents a study within the framework of Construction Grammar. The author presents a constructionist account of four verbs in MSA which all encode the meaning expressed in English by the verb *come*, namely *atā*, *ǧā'a*, *ḥaḍara*, and *qadima*. These verbs are traditionally treated as synonymous lexical items, since they can appear interchangeably in certain contexts. Upon closer examination, however, each verb is seen to favour a distinct set of constructional features that set it apart from the others. The amount of overlap in the usage of these verbs is therefore restricted. Abdulrahim undertakes a detailed quantitative examination of the lexico-syntactic frames – or *constructions* – that host these verbs, following the methodology proposed by Gries and colleagues (e.g. Gries and Divjak 2009) for quantitative corpus-based examination of (near-)synonymous and polysemous lexical items. This method involves the construction of a data frame in which a large set of corpus examples (of each verb) are annotated for various morphosyntactic and semantic features. This data frame is subsequently explored via two kinds of multivariate statistical technique: Hierarchical Agglomerative Cluster Analysis and Hierarchical Configural Frequency Analysis. Abdulrahim's analyses of the data frame that she compiled illustrate the distinct sets of constructional features that typically associate with each verb; this allows the identification of the prototypical uses of each of these four near-synonyms in MSA.

The final case study, by Mohamed and Hardie in Chapter 10, illustrates a novel approach to the classification of Arabic texts, using multivariate statistical analysis to produce a text-type model that arises from the analysis of corpus data. Although there exist many different approaches to the classification of texts into categories, most such work can be considered *top-down* in orientation, being based on features external to the text. Within such an approach, the categories that emerge are not linguistically defined; texts that belong to the same category are not necessarily similar in their linguistic forms. In *bottom-up* approaches, categorisation is based on features internal to the language of the texts, as notably exemplified by Biber's (1988, 1995) *Multi-Dimensional* (MD) analysis. But even Biber's approach begins by presuming externally defined registers. Mohamed and Hardie demonstrate an alternative methodology which does not require externally defined registers; rather, a text typology based on linguistic form is derived systematically using cluster analysis. The corpus analysed is the Leeds Corpus of Contemporary Arabic (Al-Sulaiti and Atwell 2006, also introduced by Atwell in Chapter 6 of this volume), and the variables used for clustering are the (relative) frequencies of linguistic features with particular functional associations. The findings of the cluster analysis represent a plausible attempt to systematise the study of the diversity of Arabic texts: eight clusters/text-types, which a thorough investigation reveals to be reducible to a more limited number of overall text-types that share linguistic features: *narration*, *exposition*, and *scientific exposition*. Cluster analysis thus proves a powerful tool for structuring the data, if used with caution.

Collectively, the contributions to this volume thus cover the majority of key fronts in the emerging field of Arabic corpus linguistics: corpus creation, research software development, and applications to issues of real and urgent interest to scholars of Arabic language and linguistics. The path ahead for this new area of research focused on the application of corpus-based methodologies to Arabic data will perhaps not always be easy, but it is a direction rich with possibilities. In these studies, and in the future work that we hope this book will help to foster, we see that for Arabic as for other languages, our understanding of the nuances of structure and usage of language can only ever be enhanced by incorporating real, attested data into the heart of our analyses. We like to think that Sībawayh would have approved.

Acknowledgements

Tony McEnery and Andrew Hardie's work on this book was undertaken as part of the ESRC Centre for Corpus Approaches to Social Science (CASS), funded by the UK Economic and Social Research Council: grant reference ES/K002155/1. We gratefully acknowledge this support.

Notes

1. The allied but quite distinct area of *natural language processing* (NLP) has a much more extensive record of engagement with issues of the Arabic language than has corpus linguistics, with many publications and regular workshops and conferences devoted to the Arabic NLP endeavour. Among the contributions to this volume, there are several which present or draw on relevant work in NLP, most notably Atwell.
2. Numbers of speakers quoted in this paragraph are taken from the *Ethnologue*, available at <https://www.ethnologue.com/statistics/size> (last accessed 16 May 2018).
3. There exists controversy over whether it is better to characterise the major verbal distinction (as seen in *kataba*, 'he wrote' versus *yaktubu*, 'he writes') as primarily one of tense or primarily one of aspect; both are found in the literature.
4. See <http://www.qamus.org/transliteration.htm> (last accessed 16 May 2018).
5. Sībawayh's name is alternatively found in the literature as *Sibawayhi*; we follow Brustad (2016) in preferring the former.
6. In this quotation, the term *ʿArabiyyah* refers to the prestigious variety of Arabic exemplified in the Qurʾan and early Arabic poetry (Brustad 2016: 142), that is, more or less the same as the variety we have labelled *Classical Arabic*.

References

Abercrombie, D. (1965), *Studies in Phonetics and Linguistics*, London: Oxford University Press.

Abu-Chacra, F. (2007), *Arabic: An Essential Grammar*, London: Routledge.

Al-Sulaiti, L. and E. Atwell (2006), 'The design of a corpus of contemporary Arabic', *International Journal of Corpus Linguistics*, 11(1): 1–36.

Baker, P., A. Hardie and T. McEnery (2006), *A Glossary of Corpus Linguistics*, Edinburgh: Edinburgh University Press.
Biber, D. (1988), *Variation Across Speech and Writing*, Cambridge: Cambridge University Press.
Biber, D. (1995), *Dimensions of Register Variation: A Cross-Linguistic Comparison*, Cambridge: Cambridge University Press.
Brustad, K. (2016), 'The iconic Sībawayh', in A. Korangy, W. M. Thackston, R. P. Mottahedejh and W. Granara (eds), *Essays in Islamic Philology, History, and Philosophy*, Berlin: de Gruyter, pp. 141–65.
Carter, M. G. (2004), *Sībawayhi*, London and New York: I.B. Tauris.
Ditters, E. (1990), 'Arabic corpus linguistics in past and present', in K. Versteegh and M. G. Carter (eds), *Studies in the History of Arabic Grammar II: Proceedings of the 2nd Symposium on the History of Arabic Grammar, Nijmegen, 27 April–1 May 1987*, Amsterdam: John Benjamins, pp. 129–41.
Dixon, R. M. W. (1979), 'Ergativity', *Language*, 55(1): 59–138.
Dukes, K. (2012), *The Quranic Arabic Corpus*, School of Computing, University of Leeds, <http://corpus.quran.com/> (last accessed 16 May 2018).
Garside, R., G. Leech and T. McEnery (eds) (1997), *Corpus Annotation: Linguistic Information from Computer Text Corpora*, Harlow: Longman.
Garside, R., G. Leech and G. Sampson (1987), *The Computational Analysis of English: A Corpus-Based Approach*, Harlow: Longman.
Gries, S. Th. and D. S. Divjak (2009), 'Behavioral profiles: A corpus-based approach towards cognitive semantic analysis', in V. Evans and S. S. Pourcel (eds), *New Directions in Cognitive Linguistics*, Amsterdam and Philadelphia: John Benjamins, pp. 57–75.
Holes, C. (2004), *Modern Arabic: Structures, Functions and Varieties*, 2nd edn, Washington, DC: Georgetown University Press.
Johansson, S. and S. Oksefjell (eds) (1998), *Corpora and Cross-Linguistic Research: Theory, Method and Case Studies*, Amsterdam: Rodopi.
McEnery, T. and A. Hardie (2012), *Corpus Linguistics: Method, Theory and Practice*, Cambridge: Cambridge University Press.
McEnery, T. and A. Wilson (2001), *Corpus Linguistics*, 2nd edn, Edinburgh: Edinburgh University Press.
Owens, J. (1990), *Early Arabic Grammatical Theory: Heterogeneity and Standardization*, Amsterdam: John Benjamins.
Owens, J. (1997), 'The Arabic grammatical tradition', in R. Hetzron (ed.), *The Semitic Languages*, London and New York: Routledge, pp. 46–58.
Parkinson, D. B. and S. Farwaneh (eds) (2003), *Perspectives on Arabic Linguistics XV: Papers from the Fifteenth Annual Symposium on Arabic Linguistics, Salt Lake City 2001*, Amsterdam: John Benjamins.
Rubin, B. (2012), 'The Egyptian media', in B. Rubin (ed.), *The Middle East: A Guide to Politics, Economics, Society and Culture*, London and New York: Routledge, pp. 239–47.
Ryding, K. (2005), *A Reference Grammar of Modern Standard Arabic*, Cambridge: Cambridge University Press.

Sinclair, J., S. Jones, R. Daley and R. Krishnamurthy (2004), *English Collocational Studies: The OSTI Report*, London: Continuum.

Xiao, X. and T. McEnery (2004), 'A corpus-based two-level model of situation aspect', *Journal of Linguistics*, 40(2): 325–63.

2

Under the Hood of arabiCorpus

Dilworth B. Parkinson

1. Introduction

Several years ago, as free internet interfaces to very large English corpora began to become available (such as those listed at corpus.byu.edu), I began to get a bad case of corpus-envy. I had a never-ending stream of questions about Arabic words and their usage, and nowhere to go to find real data about them. I started to search for available Arabic corpora and found that while several existed (such as the Arabic Gigaword), most were in a form that was intended to be exploited by trained corpus linguists. Not being one of those myself, I made feeble attempts to use these corpora for my purposes, but always found the experience daunting. I did not necessarily need to have all the capabilities that the English sites had (like searching on parts of speech, for example). I simply wanted to be able to go to a website, type in an Arabic word in a basic dictionary form, and have the site return a multitude of authentic examples of that word in all its forms being used in authentic contexts. In talking with other scholars and students, I found similar sentiments. Although we would love to have powerful tools such as those available for English, we would be very content with much less powerful tools as long as they performed those basic functions.

The primary purpose of this chapter is not to show how cleverly the corpus website arabiCorpus.byu.edu was programmed, but rather to demonstrate how a technically untrained person, with limited and self-taught programming skills, was nevertheless able to make something relatively useful for both students and researchers of Arabic. It is also meant as something of a kindly rebuke of more technical corpus researchers, who despite far superior technical skills have not produced products that are accessible to normal students and researchers of the Arabic language. I recognise that this is partially because they were not aiming to produce such a thing, and for a number of other reasons as well, but I still believe that if those with the technical skill were to put their minds to this problem, we would be able to provide the Arabic language community with incredibly useful tools.

2. Description of arabiCorpus

arabiCorpus is a medium-sized (about 100 million words) plain text corpus of Modern Standard Arabic, with a small amount of additional material from medieval Arabic and from Egyptian Arabic. Although it is relatively large, it compares poorly with what one might consider to be the regular standards of corpus creation that inform corpora like the British National Corpus and many others, not only in that it is not lemmatised or part-of-speech tagged, which means that many useful searches cannot be performed, but also in that it was not designed in the first place to be a 'balanced' corpus, with large sections representing a variety of written and spoken genres. The initial principle on which text selection was based can best be characterised as 'take whatever you can get your hands on' and try to fill in the holes later. It is legitimate to ask why this was not taken into account at the beginning and why attempts were not made to comply with the standards of the field in building this corpus. The answer to that is that this project never had the funding or time to be built in that way. I personally am very much in favour of this field, or someone in it, getting the funding to build a very large, very representative and balanced corpus of all varieties of Arabic. The idea of the arabiCorpus project was simply to get a large amount of text out there, available for use by students and researchers, while we wait for the more balanced and adequate corpora of the future.

The fact that the corpus is not lemmatised needs a particular focus. Not lemmatising an English corpus is a minor problem, since different forms of the same word tend to alphabetise together. With Arabic, however, it is a major problem, since any one Arabic word or lemma, whether a noun or a verb, will have potentially hundreds of word forms that appear in the corpus, and these forms alphabetise all over the map. This means that one of the special problems facing Arabic corpus creators is finding a way to get the different forms that are all considered to be examples of the same 'word' together. arabiCorpus uses a technique to accomplish this that may be considered 'quick and dirty', but which provides results that are accurate enough to be helpful.

Crucially, in addition to the corpus itself, arabiCorpus provides a web interface that was designed to be maximally simple for non-technical users, while still allowing for some kinds of more complex searches by users who are more technically proficient.

arabiCorpus is mainly a newspaper corpus, and searches can be limited to only newspapers if desired. We have been able to acquire about 1 million words of Arabic literature, which is very little, but is at least a start, and a half-million words of non-fiction that is not newspaper text. In addition, we have about 2 million words of medieval Arabic, including the Qur'an, the *Thousand and One Nights*, and some books of medieval philosophy, medicine, and grammar. Finally, we have included a small amount of Arabic chat and colloquial Arabic plays for those who want to take a stab at searching colloquial materials. Table 2.1 summarises the total number of words in the various sections of the corpus.

The newspapers represented include two separate full years of *Al-Hayat*, a complete year of *Al-Ahram* and of *Al-Masri Al-Yawm*, and smaller but substantial amounts

Table 2.1 Contents of arabiCorpus (as of October 2013)

Genre	N of word tokens
Newspapers	137,021,439
Modern Literature	1,026,171
Non-fiction	27,945,460
Chat/Colloquial	164,457
Premodern	9,127,331
Total	**175,284,858**

Table 2.2 Newspapers in arabiCorpus

Newspaper	N of word tokens
Al-Hayat 1996 (full year)	21,564,329
Al-Hayat 1997 (full year)	19,473,315
Al-Ahram (Egypt) 1999 (full year)	16,475,979
Al-Masri Al-Yawm (Egypt) 2010 (full year)	13,880,826
Al-Watan (Kuwait) 2002	6,454,411
Al-Tajdid (Morocco) 2002	2,919,782
Al-Thawra (Syria)	16,631,975
Al-Shuruq (Egypt) 2010	2,067,137
Al-Ghad 1 (Jordan) 2011	17,327,087
Al-Ghad 2 (Jordan) 2012	19,628,008
Treebank (various)[a]	598,590
Total	**137,021,439**

Note: [a] A treebank is a parsed corpus.

of *Al-Watan* from Kuwait, *Al-Tajdid* from Morocco, *Al-Thawra* from Syria, *Al-Ghad* from Jordan, and the editorial writers from *Al-Shuruq*. This information in summarised in Table 2.2.

It is aimed primarily at students of Arabic, but can also be useful to researchers, particularly lexicographers, and to other non-technical users. It does not have the capabilities that many technical corpus users would desire, and would thus be somewhat frustrating for them to use.

3. History of arabiCorpus

To help explain why arabiCorpus is the way it is, I am going to present a short history of how it was created. Several years ago, I was commissioned by Cambridge University Press to produce a book of Arabic synonyms as part of their series of synonym books for a variety of languages. One of the features of the books in this series is that they include authentic examples or citations for each entry, as well as some indication of both level of use and frequency of use. None of this information was available to me, so I started searching around for something that might help me. I first purchased some

CDs with two separate years of *Al-Hayat* newspaper. I then started downloading the *Al-Ahram* newspaper site daily until I also had a full year of that newspaper.

Since my newspapers were coming in year units, I thought it would be very intuitive for students to get a rough sense of frequency in a newspaper over time, in other words, if someone read, say, *Al-Ahram* every day for a year, would they see this word about once a month, once a week, or every day?

Since this was before Unicode had taken over the world, and since it is difficult to find text-editing programs that deal adequately with Arabic in a programming environment, I found it useful to change the text files into a transliterated system using simple ASCII characters with a one-to-one correspondence to the original Arabic characters (the Buckwalter transliteration, see Appendix).

I then started using simple Perl scripts with regular expressions to find examples of the words I was working with at any particular time. Since I was learning Perl as I went, this proceeded by fits and starts.

I started by searching for exact forms. For example, if I needed sentences illustrating the use of *dars*, 'lesson', I used the ASCII regular expression <drs>. The extremely simple Perl program I used to find this regular expression in plain text files was:

```
#! /usr/bin/perl
$f = "NAME OF TEXT FILE";
open RF, "<$f" or die "Can't open $f\n";
while (<RF>) {
 print if m/REGULAR EXPRESSION HERE/;
}
```

This gave me the examples I needed and allowed me to proceed with my work, but I soon discovered that it 'over'-found things, giving me many examples of things I did not want, and which I had to wade through to find the things that I did want. This is because such a regular expression finds every example of this string of letters no matter what else surrounds them, even, for example, if the letter directly before them is <y>, indicating that the form would be a present tense verb and not the noun we are looking for. You can see in Table 2.3 a small number of the many unwanted items this expression found.

Table 2.3 Overfinding: examples of unwanted forms found while searching for <drs>, 'lesson'

Translation	ASCII representation	Word
school	<mdrst>	مدرسة
he studies	<ydrs>	يدرس
Anderson	<Andrswn>	اندرسون
Hedersfield	<hdrsfyld>	هدرسفيلد
Sanderson	<sAndrswn>	ساندرسون
teachers	<mdrswn>	مدرسون

I then discovered that I could add word boundaries (\b) to the regular expression to cut out the undesired items, for example:

/\bdrs\b/

This did, in fact, have the result of cutting out all those unwanted items, but I soon discovered that it 'under'-found things, not giving me many of the forms that in fact I *did* want. This is because such a search will find only the bare form, and omit the form with the article, with the attached prepositions and conjunctions, and with pronoun endings. You can see in Table 2.4 a small number of the desired items which this search did not find.

At this point I had to sit down and really figure out how to use regular expressions. Once I did so, I realised that I could specify the full set of forms I wanted to find and only those. For example, the following regular expression to find the noun <drs>, 'lesson', allows for an optional conjunction, for every possible combination of prepositions and the definite article, and for all pronoun endings. Note that it uses the transliteration system used by arabiCorpus, not the one used elsewhere in this chapter and this volume:

/(w|f)?(bAl|kAl|ll|Al|b|k|l)?drs(h|hA|k|y|hm|hn|km|kn|nA|hmA|kmA)?/

This expression finds everything we want, and cuts out most of what we do not want, meaning that I was able to quickly find the examples I was searching for to use in the synonym book without having to spend time wading through unwanted citations. For example, this regular expression will not find present tense verb forms like <ydrs>, 'he studies'.

Of course, I also quickly discovered that no matter how cleverly written the regular expression, 'false hits' are still relatively common. This turns out to be due entirely to the massive natural morphological/graphological ambiguity with which Arabic is blessed. For example, the bare form <drs> can be the noun *dars*, 'lesson', and the verb *darasa*, 'he studied', and only context can differentiate them, since Arabic is written without short vowels. Since these regular expressions are not really up to analysing

Table 2.4 Underfinding: examples of forms *not* found when searching for <drs>, 'lesson', with word boundaries

Translation	ASCII representation	Word
the school	<Aldrs>	الدرس
in the school	<bAldrs>	بالدرس
in a school	<bdrs>	بدرس
in her school	<bdrshA>	بدرسها
a school (acc.)	<drsA>	درسا
to the school	<lldrs>	للدرس
to his school	<ldrsh>	لدرسه
and his school	<wdrsh>	ودرسه

the syntactic context, forms that are ambiguous in and of themselves will always 'slip through the cracks' and create numerous false hits in any search. For my purposes, however, this technique of using regular expressions was still very successful, since it did cut out huge numbers of examples that I then did not need to wade through, and it provided me all the examples I did want to see, with the result that I was able to quickly and efficiently find the citations I needed for the book I was working on.

It should be remembered that I was not using a website for these procedures, but rather was running Perl directly from the UNIX terminal window on my Mac, and saving the results in text files, which I would then examine. After a few weeks of practice, I had developed 'templates' for nouns, adjectives, verbs, and so on in a template file. When I needed to search for a particular word, say a verb, I would copy the appropriate template from the template file into the simple Perl program, change the core at the centre of the template to the word I was looking for, and run the program. This turned out to be a reasonably efficient method, and allowed me to feel comfortable doing the hundreds of searches necessary to do my work.

Once I was done with finding examples for the synonym book, I realised that I had really enjoyed using those programs, and that I had learned a lot about the words I had searched for. In other words, even though I had basically never heard of a corpus before this experience, I was starting to get interested in having and using one, and starting to get a vision of how useful it is to have one. I had one, it turns out, limited as it may have been, and I decided I wanted to give my advanced students access to it. So I tried to show them how to use the templates to find what they wanted. What I discovered is that for the vast majority of students, no matter how 'easy' I tried to make it, and no matter how much time I spent explaining it, if it involved running Perl directly in a UNIX terminal window, and writing and using regular expressions directly, even as templates, they were simply not willing to do it.

It was at that point that I decided that this basic programming could be the basis of a website that would be simple enough and appealing enough that some students might actually use it.

This became the basis of arabiCorpus. It had those regular expressions, the templates, in a Perl core. We then used PHP to design a web interface that allowed users to type in the search string (that would end up in the middle of those regular expressions), to choose which part-of-speech 'filter' was desired, and which part of the corpus they wanted to search. Since the results of many searches created huge amounts of text, we also used MySQL to save the results of the most recent search, so that users could quickly access various parts of those results without having to run the search again. In summary, the structure of arabiCorpus is:

- a Perl core (or 'engine') for query matching
- PHP for Web interface
- MySQL for saving immediate search results so the user can access different parts quickly.

The Perl core of the program accepts from the website the word being searched for, the part-of-speech filter chosen, and the parts of the corpus to be searched. It then starts looking through the corpus line by line. It first strips out all vowels, kashidas (line lengtheners), and Latin letters from the line being searched. It then looks for every example of the string typed in by the user, no matter what is around it. It then sends what it found to the part-of-speech filter to see if it matches any of the patterns. In summary, the functions of the Perl core are:

1. Strip vowels, kashidas, Latin letters.
2. Search for every example of the entered string.
3. Omit from the results those part-of-speech filters that do not fit the morphological patterns for the part of speech chosen (using regular expressions).

So if 'noun' is chosen as the part-of-speech filter, the pattern accepts bare forms and forms with conjunctions like <w> and <f>; prefix prepositions like <b>, <l>, and <k>; the definite article; and pronoun suffixes. If 'adjective' is chosen, on the other hand, only initial conjunctions and the definite article are allowed. If the user wants to find out if this particular adjective ever appears with a preposition or a pronoun ending, they would have to search for it under 'noun', not 'adjective'. It is, of course, tempting for the non-technical user to believe that the program somehow knows whether or not this form is a noun or an adjective, but of course it knows nothing of the kind. It is just looking for a straight morphological match to things that *can* be around adjectives.

Adverbs allow initial conjunctions only, along with the bare form, so if you choose 'adverb', it will not find examples of your form with a definite article. 'Adverb', therefore, can be used to find specific forms of verbs and nouns you want to type in, without finding anything else. For example, if you want to find examples of third person masculine <ydrs>, but not third person feminine/second person <tdrs> or first person plural <ndrs>, then you could search for it using 'adverb'.

The 'verb' choice allows the bare form, initial conjunctions, initial verbal particles, imperfect prefixes, perfect suffixes, and pronoun endings. The user has the choice of adding information about defective verb forms that can make the search for verbs more accurate.

Finally, choosing 'string' means that there is no filter at all. Every single example of the string of letters you type in will be found and displayed.

For example, Tables 2.5 and 2.6 show some of the forms found when <ktb> and <ktAb> are searched for as strings.

The program gathers frequency information about the form searched for. It gives the total number of forms found, and then provides the number per 100,000 words of text (a *normalised frequency*), for comparative purposes. Of course, this number is only accurate to the extent that those false hits caused by graphological ambiguity are not a factor in that particular search.

It also allows the user to compare the frequency of a form over specific genres or subsections of newspapers. As mentioned before, if the individual newspapers for which the corpus contains exactly one year of issues are searched, the student can get a more concrete feel for what the frequency information implies.

Table 2.5 Sample results when using 'string' as the part of speech filter for <ktb>

Translation	ASCII representation	Word
books, he wrote	<ktb>	كتب
the books	<Alktb>	الكتب
his books, he wrote it	<ktbh>	كتبه
in his books	<bktbh>	بكتبه
he is writing	<yktb>	يكتب
he dictated	<Astktb>	استكتب
like donations	<ktbrcAt>	ك تبرعات

Table 2.6 Sample results when using 'string' as the part of speech filter for <ktAb>

Translation	ASCII representation	Word
book	<ktAb>	كتاب
the book	<AlktAb>	الكتاب
in the book	<bAlktAb>	بالكتاب
writing	<ktAbt>	كتابة
dictating	<AstktAb>	استكتاب

The user interface involves fairly rudimentary PHP programming, allowing the user to register, log in, and perform searches.

The following figures show the user interface being used. Figure 2.1 demonstrates that you can search for a form using Arabic script; or you can use a one-to-one transliteration system using Latin characters. This is the most appropriate choice if you are going to do more complex searches using regular expressions.

Note, alongside the search term boxes shown in Figure 2.1, the controls that let you choose the part of speech you want to specify, and the part of the corpus you want to search.

Once the search has been performed, there are several ways to examine the results. First, you can look at the frequency information, where you find out exactly how many citations of the form were found, and how many words per 100,000 words that represents (see Figure 2.2).

If you click on 'citations' in the control bar above the summary of search results, you will be given a view of the actual citations found (in corpus linguistics terminology, a 'concordance'). These are presented 100 at a time, and can be sorted either by the word before the form you were looking for, or the word after it (see Figure 2.3).

Figure 2.1 Searching using Arabic or Latin script

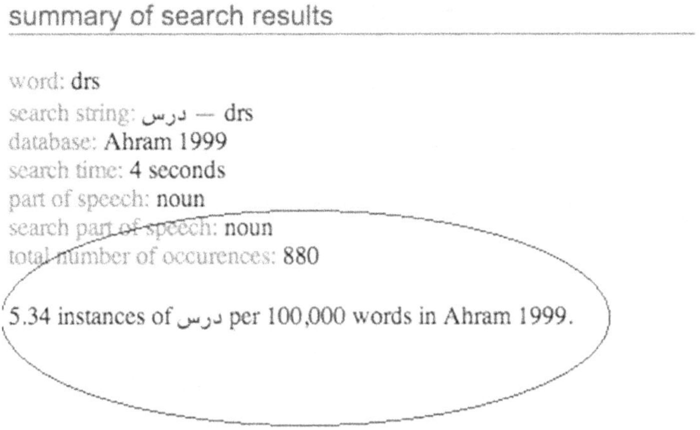

Figure 2.2 Example of frequency information

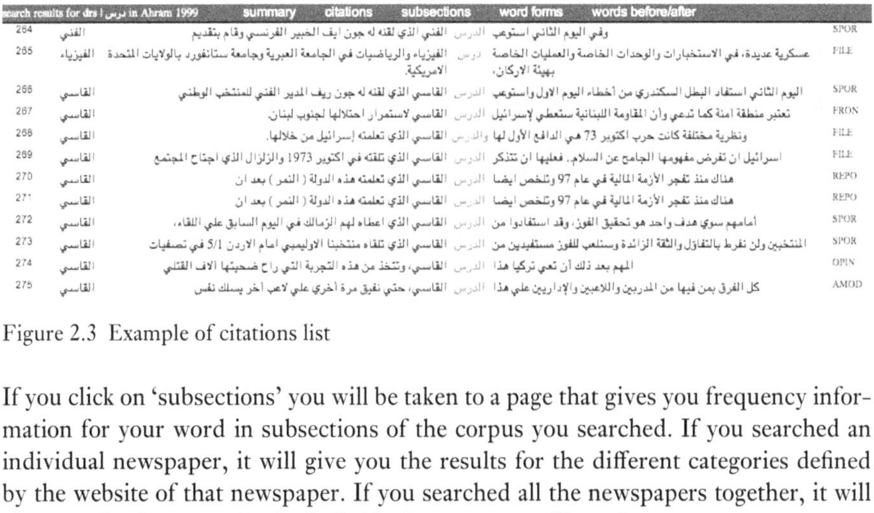

Figure 2.3 Example of citations list

If you click on 'subsections' you will be taken to a page that gives you frequency information for your word in subsections of the corpus you searched. If you searched an individual newspaper, it will give you the results for the different categories defined by the website of that newspaper. If you searched all the newspapers together, it will give you the frequency in the individual newspapers. Since the newspapers represent different countries, and different styles to some extent, this can be useful information (see Figure 2.4).

If you click on 'word forms', you will be taken to a page that displays all the different word forms that made it through your filter for this search (see Figure 2.5). Examining this page can be helpful in spotting false hits, and in designing searches that avoid some of them. If you are interested in the citations of a specific word form, you can click on it and they will be brought up in a new window.

If you click on 'words before/after', you will be given a list of all the word forms that appear directly before and directly after the word in question, listed by frequency (see Figure 2.6); this kind of data is sometimes called a 'frequency breakdown' in corpus linguistics. Again, this can provide useful collocational information. If you are

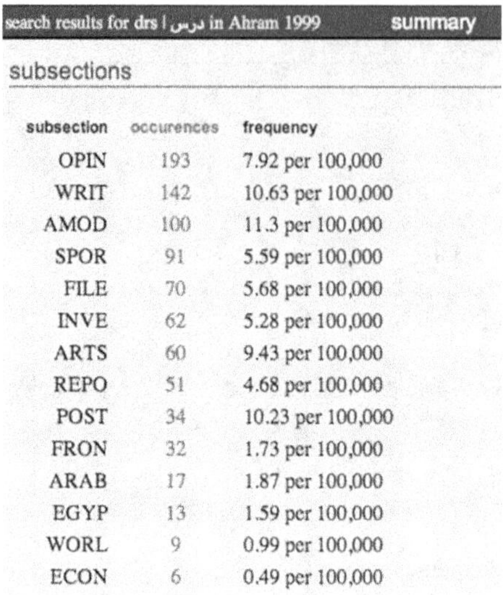

search results for drs | درس in Ahram 1999 summary

subsections

subsection	occurences	frequency
OPIN	193	7.92 per 100,000
WRIT	142	10.63 per 100,000
AMOD	100	11.3 per 100,000
SPOR	91	5.59 per 100,000
FILE	70	5.68 per 100,000
INVE	62	5.28 per 100,000
ARTS	60	9.43 per 100,000
REPO	51	4.68 per 100,000
POST	34	10.23 per 100,000
FRON	32	1.73 per 100,000
ARAB	17	1.87 per 100,000
EGYP	13	1.59 per 100,000
WORL	9	0.99 per 100,000
ECON	6	0.49 per 100,000

Figure 2.4 Example of subsections

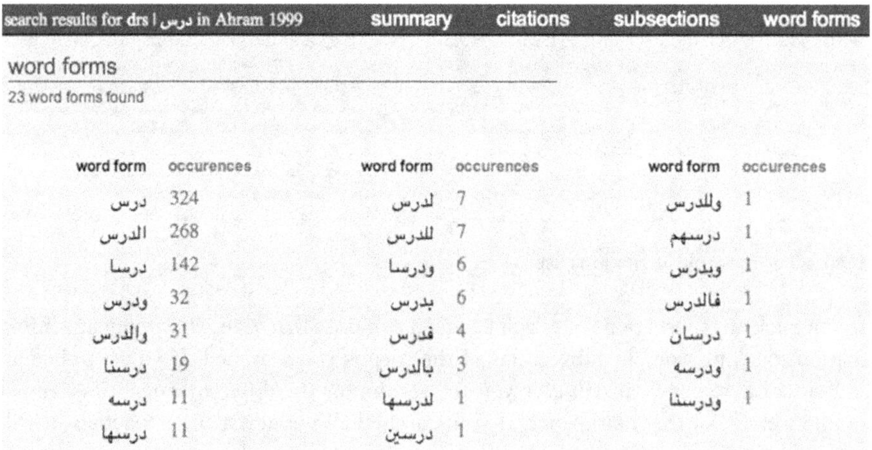

search results for drs | درس in Ahram 1999 summary citations subsections word forms

word forms

23 word forms found

word form	occurences	word form	occurences	word form	occurences
درس	324	لدرس	7	وللدرس	1
الدرس	268	للدرس	7	درسهم	1
درسا	142	ودرسا	6	وبدرس	1
ودرس	32	بدرس	6	فالدرس	1
والدرس	31	فدرس	4	درسان	1
درسنا	19	بالدرس	3	ودرسه	1
درسه	11	لدرسها	1	ودرسنا	1
درسها	11	درسين	1		

Figure 2.5 Example of word forms

interested in the citations related to a specific before or after word, click on it and a new window will open showing you those citations.

Finally, if you click on 'collocations', a similar list will appear, but this time it will be a compilation of all the word forms surrounding the word in question, from 4 words before the word to 4 words after it. This can give a more accurate picture of the actual collocates of a word. (It should be remembered, of course, that since this corpus is not lemmatised, the results you get in 'collocations' and in 'words before/after' will refer to specific word forms, and so to find the results for a particular word base you would need to combine the counts of all the forms that derive from that base.)

search results for drs | درس in Ahram 1999 summary citatio

words before and after

lists of before and after words occuring at least twice
click on the word for citations including that word before or after

word before	occurences	word after	occurences
هذا	39	في	53
من	30	الذي	30
هو	25	من	24
وهو	13	التاريخ	19
وهذا	12	المستفاد	16
حيث	11	خصوصي	15
وقد	10	القاسي	12
الذي	10	جيدا	11
في	10	لكل	10
أنه	10	قاسيا	10
أن	9	الثاني	8
ان	9	الأول	7
يكون	9	التجربة	7
كان	8	هو	6
قد	8	الخصوصي	5
أول	7	فيها	5
ثم	7	عمليا	5
إنه	6	لن	5
هناك	6	مهما	5
	6	يمكن	5
التى	6	الجهاز	5

Figure 2.6 Example of words before/after

A MySQL database is used to keep track of the users, and to temporarily store the results of specific searches so that users can navigate the different sections of the program and get the results without having to do the search again.

Since the programming is based on regular expressions, it was not difficult to allow the user to *search* using regular expressions, to limit and very precisely specify what is being searched for. Users can choose to do a regular search and then add a regular expression which will cut out any results that match it, or they can use regular expressions in the original search.

So if the part-of-speech filters provided are not giving you the accuracy you need in a particular search, you can 'do it yourself', so to speak. You can use the 'word forms' and 'words before/after' lists to identify word forms that you do not want. You can also limit your searches in this way to certain unambiguous subsets of certain lemmata (like the *ya-* form of the imperfect verb). Of course, it is also possible to go through the citations by hand and simply subtract from your numbers any that turn out not to be examples of what you are looking for. If the results are very numerous, you can also use a random number generator to pick out a representative sample of the citations, and go through those by hand, and then apply the resulting ratios to your numbers.

Table 2.7 Sample ambiguous forms

Translation	ASCII representation	Word
my son; build! (to feminine singular)	<Abny>	ابني
books; he wrote; it was written	<ktb>	كتب
and to, governor	<wAle>	والى

As stated before, the program by itself can do nothing to limit inherently ambiguous forms in Arabic. See Table 2.7 for three of the many ambiguous forms you might encounter.

This corpus can, therefore, be used to:

- find examples of specific words and forms
- find examples of morphological and syntactic structures
- find distinct word senses of individual forms
- find collocations and idiomatic uses of words
- find overall frequencies and subfrequencies of words and forms
- compare frequencies and usages between different countries and genres.

4. Discussion

As of the time of writing, there have been over 190,000 distinct queries since arabiCorpus went online, from over 6,200 distinct users. Over 500 of these users accessed the system over 10 times, and over 50 of them have accessed it over 100 times. There has been at least one dissertation completed based on data from the corpus, and others are being completed. Also, a recent book appeared with data from the corpus. It has over 40 references to it listed in Google Scholar. It has settled a number of issues that have arisen on the Arabic-L discussion list, and has provided students with clear examples of difficult usages. In short, I believe that arabiCorpus, despite its many technical limitations, has proven to be very useful to a reasonably large number of users.

It takes a lot of money, time, and effort to develop even a fairly small lemmatised, part-of-speech tagged corpus. In contrast, adding materials to arabiCorpus is fairly simple, straightforward, and cheap, as long as the text is already available in electronic form. I intend to add additional corpora when I have the time, and when people provide me with the texts. For example, I was recently provided with several medieval grammatical texts, and I will be adding them to the corpus in the near future. I have received numerous requests to add more historical depth to the corpus, particularly by adding materials from the nineteenth and first half of the twentieth centuries. This, and other similar requests, are easily fulfilled if the texts are already available in electronic format. Unfortunately, in regard to the Nahḍah era texts, that is not the case. I do not currently have the resources to gather the texts and have them input or OCR scanned, but if someone wants this badly enough to obtain funding for that part of the project, I am very willing to add the resulting texts to the corpus.

5. Conclusion

As a parting note, I would like to point out what an incredible thing it is to have access to a free Arabic corpus with a comprehensible user interface. Countless questions about Arabic and Arabic words that in the past would simply have been wondered about and then forgotten can now be addressed with actual data. As a simple-minded but not unimportant example, take the various uses of the word *wilāyah*, 'state'. American students learn that this word means 'state', but will sooner or later encounter examples where it clearly means something else. They might wonder, as might their teachers and dictionary makers, what the most common modern use of the word is, and how broadly the 'state' meaning applies. A quick look at the before/after section of the corpus confirms that, in fact, the meaning 'term in office' is the most common modern use of the word (despite the fact that this meaning does not even appear in Wehr, Google Translate, or a number of other modern bilingual and monolingual dictionaries), and that the uses meaning 'state' are most common with American states like California and New York rather than any Middle Eastern counterpart to the American concept of 'state'. And finally, they will find that a third common usage involves the collocate *faqīh*, 'legal scholar', and refers to the kind of rule or government that is currently extant in Iran. In short, this is an incredibly rich resource that has the potential to get students excited about words and how they are used.

3

Tunisian Arabic Corpus: Creating a Written Corpus of an 'Unwritten' Language

Karen McNeil

1. Introduction

After learning Standard Arabic at the Defense Language Institute, I learned Egyptian Arabic and a few other varieties (both in classroom settings and on my own), and I found that I very much enjoyed learning about the different varieties of Arabic. Then, in 2007, I decided to study Tunisian Arabic. My experience was that each variety of Arabic I learned made it easier to learn others, so I saw no reason not to branch out into Tunisian. I soon came across significant difficulties, however, when I discovered that – unlike Egyptian – Tunisian was almost entirely bereft of language-learning resources. There was no published dictionary, grammar reference, or basic coursebook similar to what I had used when learning Egyptian. I was nonetheless highly motivated to learn Tunisian (my now-husband is Tunisian and I wanted to be able to communicate with his family), so I persevered in studying it by collecting all the unpublished materials I could find. My frustration with this situation, though, motivated me to create modern, high-quality materials myself. Below I describe the first step of this process, on which all future projects will build: the creation of the first-ever corpus of Tunisian Arabic.

2. Arabic and Tunisian Arabic

As has already been outlined elsewhere in this volume, Arabic is a language of many varieties. The standard form of the language, generally referred to in English as Standard Arabic or Modern Standard Arabic (MSA), is closely related to the language of the Qur'an and classical poetry. It varies very little across the different Arab countries and is highly respected by speakers of Arabic, many of whom believe it to be the most beautiful and perfect form of the language – or of any human language. Almost all written communication, including literature, is conducted in this form of the language, as are formal spoken communications such as news broadcasts and political speeches.

Standard Arabic is an important part of pan-Arab and Muslim identity, as it links Arabic speakers with a cultural past dating to before the revelation of Islam and the beginnings of the Islamic empire in the seventh century CE. The canon of literature dating from that time is written in a variety called Classical Arabic, which is often assumed to be the same thing as the pre-Islamic form of the language (termed here 'Old Arabic'), both spoken and written. This assumption is likely inaccurate; rather, Classical Arabic was likely a high register of Old Arabic, rather than the two terms being synonymous. Even in the time before the expansion of the Islamic empire and the ensuing language contact, there were undoubtedly dialectic differences among Arabic speakers and differences in registers for different situations (see Owens 2006).

When examining the linguistic situation of Arabic, it is helpful that the language has a long and distinguished grammatical tradition, dating back to almost the beginning of the Islamic empire. The earliest Arab grammarians used desert Bedouins as their linguistic informants, claiming that the speech of the urban population, including their own, was corrupted. Later grammarians, such as Ibn Jinni (d. 1002), lamented that even the speech of the Bedouin had become corrupted; from this time on, (Classical) Arabic became a closed corpus and living informants were no longer used for linguistic description (Alhawary 2003). This would suggest that the prestige form of Arabic, Standard Arabic, has not been spoken as a native language for at least a thousand years.

Although nearly all Arabs study Standard Arabic in school (and most would *claim* it to be their native language), most people do not feel comfortable producing it extemporaneously (see Parkinson 1996). Instead, in the vast majority of daily communication, people speak one of the many regional 'dialects', which could all be thought of as the natural modern descendants of Old Arabic. The word 'dialect' is indeed often used to describe the modern spoken varieties of Arabic. I use it here for convenience, since the term 'modern spoken varieties' gets a bit unwieldy. However, I do not believe that the term accurately conveys the linguistic reality, as the dialects are highly divergent from both Standard Arabic and each other in terms of phonology, lexicon, and syntax. Kees Versteegh presents a useful analogy to understand this unusual situation:

> Perhaps the best analogue to the situation in the Arabic-speaking countries would be that of a hypothetical modern France, where all the newspapers and books are written in Latin, speeches in parliament are held in Latin, and in churches the only language used by the priests is Latin. On the other hand, people talking in a bar use French, people at home or among friends use French. In school, the official language of the classroom is Latin, but during the breaks between classes, students use French among themselves, and so do the teachers. (Versteegh 2001: 210)

While this analogy is illustrative, it is important to understand its limitations. First, it should be pointed out that most Arabs would find this comparison deeply offensive, for two reasons. The first is that Latin and French are undoubtedly two different languages, and most Arabs do not consider the different varieties of Arabic to be separate languages. They would insist, rather, that the situation is no different than that between the formal written English (in a book like this, for instance), and the different varieties of colloquial English heard on the street (perhaps admitting that the differences in Arabic are just a bit larger is all). The second source of offence is the fact that Latin is a dead language, and most Arabs would resolutely reject any suggestion that the language of the Holy Qur'an is dead.

A second objection to Versteegh's description is that, while the process that the Arabic varieties are undergoing is the same process which produced the modern Romance languages, it is likely not as far along. Rather than Versteegh's 'hypothetical modern France', it is perhaps more appropriate to compare the Arab world to *actual* medieval France, which spoke several early varieties of French (which were much closer to its Latin parent than modern French), but still wrote and worshiped in Latin. In medieval Europe, the average French peasant would not understand the Latin of the educated classes, and would also have great difficulty understanding the dialect of a Spanish peasant. This scenario would likely be a very close analogue to the Arab world of the recent past (say, during the Ottoman Empire), where the people were largely uneducated and separated greatly by distance, as in medieval Europe.

This does not, however, describe the modern Arab world, since education (especially among the young) has become universal in many Arab countries. Importantly, the majority of Arabs are also constantly exposed to both Standard Arabic and the other dialects of vernacular Arabic through their satellite channels. This is why the question, 'are the varieties mutually intelligible?', is a difficult one to answer for Arabic. Two hypothetical speakers who had never been exposed to anything but their own dialect *would* probably find one another difficult to understand, if not unintelligible. But two such speakers would, in reality, be difficult to find.

As Versteegh's scenario suggests, the spoken dialects are not in linguistic competition with Standard Arabic, but rather in complementary distribution. They are used in all levels of private conversation, in some informal written communications (like internet chat and text messages), and in some broadcast interviews. In many situations which are formal but require extemporaneous speech, like televised interviews, the language used is often not strictly standard or dialect, but rather a kind of 'middle' language. This linguistic situation, with an archaic but revered 'High' language and an ignoble but universally used 'Low' language, is termed diglossia (see Ferguson 1959 for the classic description).

The dialect discussed here is that of the North African country Tunisia, which has a population of nearly 11 million people. While it is common to refer to dialects by the name of a country ('Tunisian Arabic', 'Egyptian Arabic'), linguistic differences do not necessarily follow political borders. In regards to Tunisian, it is important to note that the Arabic spoken in Libya is very similar, showing only minor differences in vocabulary and accent. One could thus speak of this variety as Tunisian–Libyan Arabic, and consider it to be spoken by some 17 million people across the two countries.

3. Arabic and corpora

As a language variety, Tunisian Arabic is sparsely documented. There are currently no language resources – such as dictionaries, reference grammars, or basic coursebooks – commercially available in English for this variety of Arabic. The same could be said for another North African variety, Algerian. In fact, Morocco is the only North African country that has significant language resources available for its dialect of Arabic. So the need for further research and work describing North African varieties of Arabic is clear.

Of course, the first step in producing any of these materials is access to a corpus or corpora that can provide examples of language use. After initially lagging behind other world languages, Arabic has recently made some great strides in the field of corpus linguistics. There are many Arabic corpora currently available, both freely and through paid subscription services like the Linguistic Data Consortium. Although the majority consist of raw text (without part-of-speech tags or other annotations; see Parkinson, this volume), some of them are extensively annotated, like the million-word Penn Arabic Treebank (Maamouri et al. 2003) and the Prague Arabic Dependency Treebank (Hajič et al. 2005). A new and excellent contribution is the International Corpus of Arabic (ICA) (Alansary et al. 2007), a project which launched in February 2014, with a goal of 100 million words, annotated for morphology and part of speech. This corpus is 79 per cent complete (as of this writing) and is available freely to the public for concordance searches.[1]

Yet in spite of the proliferation of these corpora, most of them (even the Arabic 'Gigaword' corpus) are, in a way, very limited: they are excessively focused on formal sources. Many are especially over-dependent on media data: several are composed entirely of collections of newspaper or newswire sources. The Gigaword (Parker et al. 2011), for example, is a massive collection of texts from nine different newswire services. Although these are important resources for certain kinds of linguistic analysis (and especially for research in natural language processing; see Atwell, this volume), they are obviously not balanced representations of the language as a whole.

Even those corpora which are specifically aiming for balance (such as the ICA) suffer from this limitation to a certain extent. To illustrate this, we need only examine the ICA's target genre list (Alansary et al. 2007):

- Strategic Sciences
- Social Sciences
- Religion
- Literature
- Applied Sciences
- Humanities
- Natural Sciences
- Art
- Sports
- Biography
- Miscellanies.

The limitation of this kind of corpus is in the very formal, academic scope of these genres. Common, ordinary topics (like food, sex, family, marriage, friendship, etc.) would not figure at all in these corpora, except incidentally through literature. Of the many likely topics of everyday conversation, 'sports' is the only one that is ever featured in these corpora. This limitation is not a design flaw on the part of the corpus builders, but rather is a result of the diglossic nature of the Arabic language, discussed above.

The compilers of the ICA explicitly stated that one of their goals was 'collecting the texts to convey all regional variations of the Arabic Language', for instance by including newspapers that 'convey a wide range of sources from different countries' (Alansary et al. 2007: 18). But the 'Arabic Language' that they are referring to is solely Standard Arabic, which, in fact, varies little between Arab countries. An example of the variations studied using corpora like this is in the variation of the phrase 'at the same time' between different areas of the Arab world. The two variants studied were:

(1) في نفس الوقت

fī	nafs-i	l-waqt-i
in	same-GEN	DEF-time-GEN

'at the same time'

and

(2) في الوقت نفسه

fī	l-waqt-i	nafs-i-hi
in	DEF-time-GEN	same-GEN-3SG.POSS

'at the same time' (Al-Sulaiti and Atwell 2006: 6)

These differ only in terms of the order of the last two words and the presence of a possessive enclitic in the second. Much of the regional variation observable in MSA is similarly trivial.

To illustrate the difference between the spoken varieties and MSA, however, consider a 2005 study comparing MSA and dialectal Arabic corpora (Kirchhoff and Vergyri 2005). The researchers were developing speech recognition tools for Egyptian Arabic, and were testing whether adding a large MSA corpus to their small Egyptian corpus would improve the error rate of their program. The Egyptian and MSA corpora were based on very different fields (the Egyptian was conversational and the MSA was news-based), so a certain amount of divergence in vocabulary would be expected. The extent of the divergence that the authors found, however, surprised them. To put the results in perspective, they compared them with the overlap between two similarly divergent corpora: one of conversational British English and one of news-based American English. The results, as seen in Table 3.1, were striking. The vocabulary overlap between the two Arabic corpora was less than a quarter that of the English corpora for unigrams, and almost non-existent for bigrams and trigrams.

This likely overstates the differences, to a certain extent, since small differences in spelling would prevent a match. However, such differences in spelling are also likely to represent significant differences in pronunciation (and, of course, the same could be said for the British and American English corpora). In the end, practical usage confirmed the large difference between the two varieties: the researchers found that expanding the Egyptian corpus with an MSA corpus did not significantly improve

Table 3.1 Vocabulary (token) overlap between language varieties

	Conversational Egyptian ∩ Media MSA	Conversational British ∩ Media American
Unigrams	10.3%	44.5%
Bigrams	1%	19.2%
Trigrams	< 1%	5.3%

speech recognition ability, decreasing the error rate just 1.3 per cent on both their development and test sets (Kirchhoff and Vergyri 2005: 49).

In addition to the large difference between the written and spoken varieties, the differences *among* the spoken varieties are also significant. Although conventionally segmented by national boundaries (Egyptian, Iraqi, Lebanese, etc.), the varieties of spoken Arabic actually encompass a graduated dialect continuum extending from Morocco to Iraq, with the dialects at either extreme showing vast differences in phonology, vocabulary, and syntax.

As an illustration of the extent of this difference, consider a 2010 discussion of the popular Egyptian novel, *ʾĀyza ʿatğawwiz* ('I want to get married') on Tunisian radio. When discussing the book's upcoming sequel, *Miš ʾāyza ʿatğawwiz* ('I don't want to get married'), the announcer emphasised the title by translating it into Tunisian Arabic: *Ma nḥabbš nʿarris* ('I don't want to get married'). Below we see this phrase in the two spoken varieties, with MSA added for reference. ('Egyptian' here refers to the prestige variety of the capital Cairo, while the 'Tunisian' Arabic is that of the capital Tunis.)

Egyptian:

(3) مش عايزة أتجوز
miš ʿāyza ʿa-tğawwiz
NEG want.AP.F.SG IPFV.1SG-marry
'I don't want to get married'

Tunisian:

(4) ما نحبش نعرس
ma-n-ḥabb-š n-ʿarris
NEG-IPFV.1SG-like-NEG IPFV.1SG-marry
'I don't want to get married'

MSA:

(5) لا أريد أن أتزوج
lā ʾu-rīd-u ʾan ʾa-tazawwağ-a
NEG IPFV.1SG-want-IND PART IPFV.1SG-marry-SBJV
'I don't want to get married'

It is clear at a glance that the differences between these two varieties are much larger than, say, the differences between British and American English. First, the phonological differences:

1. In Egyptian Arabic, the ǧ is pronounced [g] whereas it would be pronounced [ʒ] in Tunisian Arabic. (The [ʒ] is not actually present in this sample, since Tunisian uses a different word for 'marry', as discussed below. However, the presence of [g] is quite distinctive of Egyptian Arabic.)
2. The Tunisian sample contains many consonant clusters, such as *nḥ-* and *-bbš*, which would be unacceptable in Egyptian Arabic and would require the insertion of an epenthetic vowel. These kinds of consonant clusters are avoided in many varieties of Eastern Arabic (i.e. the varieties of Egypt and West Asia) as well as in MSA, and are in fact distinctive of North African Arabic.

In addition, there are clear lexical differences here:

1. Egyptians use the active participle *ʾāyiz* (m.)/*ʾāyza* (f.) for 'I want', whereas Tunisians use the verb *ḥabb* ('like/love') conjugated for the first person, *nḥabb*. (The phrase 'I want' actually forms a very useful isogloss, delineating nearly all the major varieties of vernacular Arabic.)
2. Tunisian uses the verb *ʾarras* for 'marry', whereas Egyptian uses the verb *ʿitǧawwiz*.

Perhaps even more remarkable, however, are the syntactic differences apparent here:

1. Because Egyptian uses an active participle, *ʿayza*, for 'I want', it requires nominal negation with *miš*. The Tunisian sample uses the verbal negation circumfix, *ma-. . .-š*. Egyptian also uses this structure for verbal negation, but in general the Eastern varieties of Arabic use *mā* before the verb, without the postverbal *š*.
2. The first person singular inflection is *ʿa-* in Egyptian but *n-* in Tunisian. In Egyptian (and historically), *na-* is the first person plural inflection of verbs.

From this simple example, it is clear that the differences between different spoken varieties of Arabic extend far beyond the usual understanding of 'accent' or 'dialect' contrasts. The differences here are more remarkable given the fact that Tunisia and Egypt are relatively close to one another, geographically. A more extreme example could be obtained by comparing two dialects which are separated by vast distances, such as Moroccan and Iraqi. One could argue, however, that the dialects are all closer to one another than any of them are to Standard Arabic.

It is worth noting that there is, of course, language variation within Arabic-speaking countries as well as between them. The variety referred to by the name of the country is usually the prestige variety of the capital city. Thus, 'Egyptian' Arabic is really Cairene Arabic, and 'Tunisian' is the dialect of the capital Tunis, and the coastal cities in general (Sousse, Monastir, Sfax, etc.). The corpus that I introduce below is a corpus of this Tunisian prestige variety, and other varieties feature in it only incidentally. The difference between the urban, prestige variety and the varieties of other (generally rural) parts of the country are not large. The most salient differences are the use of [g], rather than [q], for <q> (letter *qaf*) in the rural accent, and the loss of gender in the second person in the urban dialect.

3.1 Corpora of vernacular Arabic

Because of the heterogeneity of the language, there can never be one authoritative corpus of Arabic. To be of any practical use for either language resources or natural language processing, MSA corpora need to be distinct from the vernacular, and the vernacular corpora will need to be segmented into at least the major dialectal groups. Some efforts in this direction have been undertaken. These are the dialectal corpora currently available from the Linguistic Data Consortium:

- CALLFRIEND Egyptian Arabic (1996)
- CALLHOME Egyptian Arabic Speech (1996)
- BBN/AUB DARPA Babylon Levantine Arabic Speech and Transcripts (2005)
- Fisher Levantine Arabic Conversational Telephone Speech (2005)
- Levantine Arabic QT Training Data Set (2005)
- Gulf Arabic Conversational Telephone Speech (2006)
- Iraqi Arabic Conversational Telephone Speech (2006)
- Levantine Arabic Conversational Telephone Speech (2006).

The drawbacks of these corpora should be immediately clear: most of them are based on telephone conversations, resulting in a limited range of vocabulary. Also, many of them are quite short. Egyptian and Levantine are represented in several corpora, whereas no North African dialect is represented at all.

4. Compilation of the Tunisian Arabic Corpus

To augment this list and address some of these shortcomings, I, together with my colleague Miled Faiza, am working to create a corpus of the spoken Arabic of Tunisia: the Tunisian Arabic Corpus, or TAC. The corpus currently contains approximately 881,000 words at the time of writing and has a final goal of 4 million words. This goal was not chosen at random, but rather with an eye to the eventual use of the corpus to produce a Tunisian–English dictionary covering 25,000 word types. By utilising Zipf's Law (which holds that the frequency of a word is inversely proportional to its rank), we can calculate that, in order for the 25,000th most-common word type to occur at least ten times, we will need approximately 4 million word tokens in the corpus.

Even when it reaches its target word count, the corpus will be relatively small, as corpora go. Unfortunately, this is by necessity. Given the difficulties in compiling dialectal corpora (discussed below), a corpus in the hundreds of millions of words (as is standard for corpora of national or international standard languages) is simply not feasible. Further advances in technology – and specifically in OCR and audio-to-text transcription – would change this situation. These kinds of tools, however, are not on the horizon. Some are available for MSA, with varying degrees of accuracy, but are quite unable to handle dialectal sources. I do not anticipate tools which can accurately transcribe Tunisian audio to be available any time in the near future.

Below, I will describe some of the challenges that we faced in compiling this corpus, many of which would be applicable to any dialectal corpus. I will then discuss what specifically we did to overcome these challenges, and avenues for further work in the future.

4.1 Availability of sources

There are several challenges to developing a corpus of an Arabic dialect. The first challenge is finding sources. Corpora are written resources, and the spoken varieties of Arabic are, by definition, not typically written. (Although, as we will see below, that is not entirely true.) It is therefore very difficult to find written sources to include in the corpus. In the development of the TAC, I have utilised three categories of sources:

1. traditional written sources
2. new written sources
3. transcription of audio sources.

'Traditional written sources' describes the few exceptional types of writing in which dialect has always been used. These include folklore, folk poetry, popular song lyrics, collections of proverbs, and screenplays for movies, television shows, and plays. Of these available sources, we have so far made the most use of folklore (6 per cent of the corpus) and screenplays (24 per cent). In spite of their relatively large size, however, these sources are currently not widely varied. The folklore is entirely from one collection: readings of the popular storyteller ʿAbd al-ʿAzīz al-ʿUrwī. Likewise, the screenplays are made up of only two television series. Having such a large portion of the corpus made up of just three sources is obviously problematic for representativeness and balance; this is an area where we will concentrate future expansion.

The second category of sources is those that were not traditionally written in dialect (or did not exist), but in which the use of dialect has become permissible or possible because of new technology. The best (and, for this project, most useful) example of this is blogs. Traditionally, any kind of published essay, whether on politics or personal matters, never would have been written in dialect; MSA would have been considered the only acceptable language choice. Moreover, any published essay would have gone through at least one (and likely more) layers of editing, in which ensuring that the language was properly correct Standard Arabic would have been a major goal. Publishing an entry in a blog, however, would seem to be different than publishing an essay in a magazine. In Arabic, as in English, blog entries have a style which is much more informal and conversational than traditional formats. In English, this of course affects the language style that the author uses, but in Arabic it goes so far as to affect the language choice of the author as well. Because of this phenomenon, there are many excellent blogs available, either in 'pure' dialectal Arabic, or in a kind of mixed/middle language which could be considered a 'high' register of dialect or a 'conversational' register of MSA. Several Tunisian blogs (87,000 words) of this type are included in the corpus.

In addition to blogs, internet forum postings have proved to be a productive source of dialectal material. These postings, while generally very brief, represent conversations on important everyday topics such as sports, technology, and marriage. Like forums in English, these postings are written in a very informal, conversational style and thus are an excellent source of dialectal Arabic.

The third source strategy utilised for the TAC is transcription. As time-consuming and expensive as it is, there is simply no avoiding the fact that many of the sources needed to make a balanced corpus of vernacular Arabic will not be available in written form. For this part of the corpus, radio broadcasts and podcasts were extensively utilised. They are widely available over the internet, from which they can easily be recorded or downloaded, and they cover a wide range of topics. Because of the difficulty in transcribing these sources, however, they currently represent only a small fraction of the corpus texts. We hope that in the future funding will be available which will allow more of this work to be done.

4.2 Acquiring sources and making them readable

The availability of materials written in dialect is one challenge – acquiring these materials in the digital format suitable for inclusion in the corpus was another.

Some of these sources were easier to access than others. My partner in the project, Miled Faiza, was particularly instrumental in procuring many of the texts, especially the hard copies of written sources that we obtained in Tunisia. The two large screenplays were secured through personal connections, and the collection of Tunisian folklore (published in four volumes) was found after searching public libraries in Tunisia. We also found several plays written in Tunisian Arabic in various bookstores in Tunisia.

Luckily, we received the screenplays in Microsoft Word format so their addition to the corpus was straightforward. The folklore and plays, however, were only available in hard copy. To add these sources to the corpus, we first scanned them in their entirety so that we had them digitally. Unfortunately, there are no OCR programs available which can handle dialectal Arabic with any kind of accuracy, so our only option was to have the scanned pages transcribed by humans. The actual transcription was done either by students in Tunisia whom we hired directly, or by workers on Amazon's Mechanical Turk, a crowdsourcing internet marketplace that connects researchers and other 'requestors' to independent workers to accomplish small, precisely defined tasks.[2] Mechanical Turk is often used by researchers to accomplish small tasks (such as identifying the shapes of galaxies) which computers are very bad at but humans can do very easily.

In contrast to the audio transcription – which was a near-total failure when I tried to use Mechanical Turk, as discussed below – transcribing written texts turned out to be an excellent fit for the format. Mechanical Turk functions best when the job can be broken up into many tiny 'hits', which the Turkers can complete very quickly for a small amount of money. In this case, I submitted the plays as a job, with a 'hit' consisting of just one page. Mechanical Turk allows the employer to review the work done before the worker is paid, so I could quickly skim each page and make sure that the worker had actually made an effort to transcribe the text (and not, as some dishonest workers attempt, simply cut and pasted random text). The texts, once added to the corpus, are then given a quality control check either by Miled or one of the trusted transcribers in Tunisia to catch transcription errors. Using this method, I was able to get all of the plays transcribed in only a couple of weeks, and for a very reasonable sum of money.

We could have used the same method for transcribing al-ʿUrwī's collection of folklore, but by the time we acquired the full text, we had good relationships with student transcribers in Tunisia and so just gave the work directly to them. For some transcribers, we emailed them the scanned pages and they emailed us back the transcribed text, which I added to the corpus. However, I gave two of them direct access to the corpus management tool (discussed in detail below). I supplied them with their own login and password and gave them training on how to use the corpus so that they could log in and input the texts directly. These same trusted transcribers would also log in to the corpus management site to undertake quality control checks on other transcribers' work and to work on housekeeping tasks such as categorisation and identification and removal of duplicate texts.

As alluded to above, the Turkers who did a great job at transcribing individual scanned pages were *not* successful at transcribing audio. The main reason for this is the unsuitability of audio transcription to the Mechanical Turk format. The employers who successfully use Mechanical Turk for audio transcription have accomplished this by breaking their audio up into very short fragments (say, a single sentence), each of which constitutes a 'hit'. But with the long, natural audio I had, this would have been very time-consuming. So I attempted to put entire audio clips (most of which were 3–5 minutes long) to be transcribed as a hit. In spite of the relatively large payment offered for the larger files, very few Turkers attempted the job, and even fewer of those succeeded in the time limit set. The transcription was just too arduous and time-consuming.

Another problem with using Mechanical Turk for the transcription was that the majority of Turkers who attempted the task were Eastern Arabs (mostly Egyptian or Lebanese), and it was clear that they had limited capabilities in Tunisian Arabic. I mentioned above that most Arabs are exposed to dialects other than their own, but I should clarify that this exposure is not equal: everyone is exposed to the most prominent Eastern varieties, but Middle Easterners are exposed very little to North African varieties. Thus, mutual intelligibility between Arabic dialects is asymmetric. This lack of exposure was abundantly clear when the Eastern Turkers attempted to transcribe the Tunisian audio. I ended up rejecting most of the work done by those who finished the task because the transcriptions they produced were completely unusable.[3] Although it was clear that they had exerted great effort, the texts they turned in were largely 'word salad' that, while superficially similar to the audio, did not actually form coherent sentences. It was obvious that they did not understand the Tunisian very well at all.

The only positive result I had was with a Moroccan Turker. Although his transcription still contained many mistakes (there are significant differences between Moroccan and Tunisian), the texts were largely sound and the mistakes could be corrected by the Tunisian quality control checkers. In fact, this experience with Mechanical Turk was not a total loss, since it connected me with this particular transcriber whom I later contacted and employed directly and who is responsible for most of the (admittedly few) audio transcriptions currently available in the corpus.

As mentioned, internet sources such as blogs and forums were important sources for the corpus and ones that, thankfully, did not require transcription. I discovered most of these sources by performing web crawls for typically Tunisian words and phrases using the utility BootCaT (Baroni and Bernardini 2004). Appropriate sources were identified and harvested automatically to be uploaded into the corpus database. Among the metadata attached to each corpus file is a status, such as 'To be transcribed', 'Needs QC [= quality control]', and 'Complete'. The automatically harvested web material was marked to be manually checked to ensure that the language is actually Tunisian, and to remove duplicate entries (this quality control is currently in process, with much still to be done).

A major problem which limits the web sources we can access is the fact that Arabs do not always write Arabic content (especially on the internet) using Arabic characters. Instead, they are often written in internet transcription, often called 'Arabizi', a portmanteau of *ʿarabī* ('Arabic') and *ʾinğlīzī* ('English'). This system, which uses Roman letters and numbers to approximate Arabic sounds, originated when Arab young people were typing messages on primitive phones or computers which did not have input capabilities for Arabic text. Even now, when most phones and computer systems *do* have this capability, many young people still prefer using Arabizi over Arabic script when conversing in dialectal Arabic, for a variety of social and technical reasons (see Yaghan 2008).

As an example of this, the Tunisian band Si Lemhaf publish the lyrics to all their songs on Facebook, but the lyrics look like this:

> bledi gharriiiiiba fi 3alem gharib
> sa7bi ma tefhem chay, chab3a akathib
> 'operation Tounes' al baladoul 3ajib
> boutoulet gregorios fechecha 3an 9arib
> (Lemhaf 2011)

Here you can see distinctive features of Arabizi, such as the use of <3> to represent *ʿayn* [ʕ], <7> to represent *ḥāʾ* [ħ], and <9> to represent *qāf* [q]. We can also see that it is not so much *Arabizi* (Arabic + English) as it is *Arabçais*, since the vowel sounds and some of the consonants (such as <ou> for *wāw* [u:], <ch> for *šīn* [ʃ]) represent

French spelling rather than English. This is hardly surprising, since Tunisia is a Francophone country.

We can also see some of the features that make this kind of text so difficult for automatic processing. The word *ġarībah*, 'strange' is elongated for emphasis to *gharrii-iiiba*. (This difficulty is not restricted to Arabizi: it is not uncommon for internet users writing in Arabic characters to do the same thing, i.e. غريييبة.) There is also French text ('operation Tounes') which cannot be easily separated from the Arabic. In addition, the transcription is ambiguous: the word written *akathib* is actually *ʾakaḏīb*, 'lies'. So not only is <i> used to represent both short and long vowels, but also <th> is used for both *ṯāʾ* [θ] and *ḏāl* [ð].

I currently have no ability to process this kind of text, which is common not only for song lyrics but also for forum posts and Facebook statuses and comments. There are several online tools, such as Yamli, which will convert Arabizi to Arabic script, but, because of the ambiguities inherent in Arabizi writing, the text is processed word by word and the user must select the correct word from a drop-down list.[4] Similar tools from Microsoft and Google function the same way.[5] For this reason, they are not useful for processing large amounts of text. There are computational linguists who have developed programs to convert texts automatically, using a combination of language identification, transliteration mining, and language modelling (Darwish 2013). However, there are as of yet no publicly available tools to do this. If this functionality becomes available in the future, it will open up vast amounts of online sources to the corpus.

4.3 Orthography and other irregularities

Another challenge presented by dialectal Arabic is that of spelling variability. Because it is a (mostly) unwritten language, Tunisian has no established 'correct' spelling. There are, of course, commonly accepted ways of spelling words, but there are many frequent words which have more than one common spelling. For example, the word for 'what' is sometimes written as two separate words (*ʿāš niya*), though most write it as one (*ʿāšniya* or *šniya*). Also, among those who include the beginning *ʿā-*, some write it as an *alif maddah*, some as an *alif* with a *hamzah* on top, and some as a bare *alif*. Likewise, the *a* sound at the end is represented variably as a *tāʾ marbūṭah*, a *hāʾ*, or as an *alif*. A corpus search (using the regular expression `[Aea]?Jny[ahp]`, which is designed to search the data via a slightly modified Buckwalter transliteration) revealed a wide variety of spellings, as shown in Table 3.2.

In Table 3.2 we see that a highly frequent function word, an interrogative pronoun, is represented in the corpus by nine different spellings, three of which are very common. (It is important to note that the ranking in this list cannot be considered representative of Tunisian spelling of this word, due to the balance issues discussed below.)

When the corpus is more complete and ready for more sophisticated analysis, it will be necessary to identify the most commonly used of the spelling variants, which will be used as the 'standard' spelling for our analysis. This spelling will then be correlated with the original spelling as a part of preprocessing in order to get accurate vocabulary frequencies and other metrics (spelling normalisation of this

Table 3.2 Alternative spellings of *ʿāšniya*, 'what', with frequency counts

Wordform	Transliteration	Frequency count
آشنية	ʿāšniya^{t}	78
شنية	šniya^{h}	52
اشنيه	āšniya^{h}	21
شنيه	šniya^{h}	10
آشنيه	ʿāšniya^{h}	7
شنيا	šniyā	6
أشنية	ʿašniya^{t}	5
اشنية	āšniya^{t}	5
أشنيه	ʿašniya^{h}	2

Notes: ^{t} indicates spelling of final *-ah* using *tāʾ marbūṭah*. ^{h} indicates spelling of final *-ah* using *hāʾ*.

sort, it should be noted, is an established procedure for historical forms of European languages such as English; see Baron et al. 2009). However, this will be done without altering the non-standard spelling in the corpus itself, so as to protect the integrity of the corpus for future research.

4.4 The question of balance

Another major problem in creating a corpus of dialectal Arabic is that of balance. It is difficult to imagine how a 'balanced' corpus, in the conventional sense, can be possible. The spoken varieties of Arabic are, to a great extent, in complementary distribution with MSA. Just as media sources are vastly overrepresented in all the MSA corpora, they will be vastly underrepresented in any variety of spoken Arabic. Because of the scarcity of sources, mentioned earlier, I am taking a fairly pragmatic view towards balance. For the time being, I am gathering all the sources I can find, with the hope that the users of the corpus will recognise, and compensate for, its shortcomings.

A larger problem is the fact that, currently, three large works (two screenplays and a collection of folk tales) make up almost a third (29 per cent) of the total text in the corpus. Any search will tend to be skewed towards the language usage in those three works. For instance, the list of various spellings of *ʿāšniya*, 'what', is more likely to be representative of the spellings of these three authors than of Tunisians as a whole. (Indeed, the top spelling *ʿāšniya^{t}* is that used by the author of the longer screenplay, *Ṣāyd arrīm*.) This problem will, hopefully, be ameliorated as more and more varied texts are added to the corpus. While we hope to obtain more screenplays, many of these new texts will come from internet sources. We have not exploited blogs and forums to the full extent possible, and we have not yet exploited Facebook and Twitter at all. So there are still potentially large amounts of text which can be added to the corpus, whenever time is available to do it. These internet sources will create balance issues of their own; however, they have the major benefit of being the work of many authors.

5. Morphologic segmentation and processing

In Arabic, many linguistic units which would be considered separate words in English are written together as one word. Since conjunctions, possessive pronouns, and direct object pronouns are all cliticised, most nouns and adjectives will be inflected in some way. In addition, the complex morphology of the verbs means that each verb may be marked with either a prefix or suffix (or both) to show agreement for person, number, and gender. To get an idea of the extent of morphological inflection, consider the following example from a blog in the corpus:

(6) ثمة شكون تمثّلهم النهضة . . . علاش تقصي فيهم؟ علاش ما تحبهمش يحكيو؟

ṯamma	škun	t-maṯṯal-hum	in-naḥḍa . . .	ʿalaš
there.are	REL	IPFV.3SG-represent-3PL	DEF-renaissance . . .	why

tu-qṣī	fī-him ?	ʿalaš	mā-t-ḥabb-hum-š
IPFV.2SG-exclude	in.PROG-3PL ?	why	NEG-IPFV.2SG-like-3PL-NEG

ya-ḥkiy-ū ?
PRS.3-speak-PRS.3PL ?

'There are people who Ennahda represent . . . Why are you excluding them? Why don't you want them to speak?'

Here we see the definite article prefixed to its noun (as in the name of the political party 'Ennahda', *innaḥḍa*) and object pronouns attaching to both prepositions (*fīhim*) and verbs (*tmaṯṯalhum*). Most strikingly, we see the incredibly complex morphology of verbs, which are not only inflected for person, gender (in the third person), and number of the subject, but also have cliticised direct object pronouns and negation markers (as in *mā tḥabbhumš*). This is problematic for purposes of corpus analysis, since the inflected words would not be included with the uninflected forms for frequency counts, which will aggravate any data scarcity. To address this problem for the TAC, I built a morphological parser which uses a combination of rule-based parsing and statistical measures to achieve a word-level accuracy rate of 89.2 per cent.

A common way of performing morphological parsing in Arabic is using the Buckwalter Arabic Morphological Analyzer (BAMA), a software package developed by Tim Buckwalter and distributed by the Linguistic Data Consortium (Buckwalter 2002). This is the method that the Penn Arabic Treebank (ATB) used to construct their corpus of Standard Arabic, which is annotated for part of speech, morphology, and sentence structure. BAMA (and its newer version, SAMA) uses a group of lexicons (prefixes, suffixes, and stems) as well as tables listing valid morphological combinations in order to produce a list of possible parses for each word. The ATB's project leaders reported a parsing accuracy rate of 98.7 per cent (Maamouri and Bies 2004: 5).

A more sophisticated system that performs contextual disambiguation of possible parses, MADA, is now available for this task. This is the system that Oxford University Press used to analyse their Arabic corpus, the basis of the recently published *Oxford Arabic Dictionary* (OAD). MADA uses the latest version of Buckwalter's morphological analyser (SAMA), combined with Support Vector Machine (SVM) classifiers, to vowel, lemmatise, and part-of-speech tag each token in the corpus (Habbash et al. 2009). Although the Oxford University Press corpus is not publicly available, both I and Miled Faiza worked with this corpus extensively as part of our work on OAD and can attest to its high degree of accuracy (see further Ibrahim and Hardie, this volume).

Unfortunately, these publicly available toolkits will not work for my data. Although Tunisian Arabic and Standard Arabic are closely related languages and share many features, the differences between them in lexicon and syntax are substantial. Modifying SAMA's lexicons of prefixes and suffixes to conform to the grammar of Tunisian would be relatively trivial, but for stems there is no existing lexicon of Tunisian Arabic, and many of the most common words of the language are not present in Standard Arabic.

For this reason, I built a custom parser for the corpus, a rule-based parser similar to Buckwalter's. I built this parser using Python's *pyparsing* module, and a grammar I wrote of valid prefixes, suffixes, and word forms. In this way it is similar to the Buckwalter parser, but – because I do not have a lexicon of valid word stems – it necessarily produces erroneous parses with non-existent stems. However, by applying some statistical methods, I was able to discard many of the erroneous parses and achieve a fairly good accuracy rate.

The steps of this process were:

1. Text normalisation.
2. Create and hand-annotate test data.
3. Parse words using *pyparsing*.
4. Baseline evaluation.
5. Resolve ambiguous cases using Suffix Level Similarity.
6. Re-evaluate.

I will go over each of the steps, as well as the results achieved, in detail below.

5.1 Preprocessing

The first step was to prepare the raw Arabic text for automatic processing. To do this, I first extracted all of the corpus text (which is stored in 2,000 database records, one for each corpus text) to a single text file. I then ran the text through a script I wrote which strips out punctuation and transliterates the Arabic text into a Latin transliteration system. The transliteration system I used is a modified version of the Buckwalter transliteration, adapted for the slightly different phonology of Tunisian Arabic, and modified so that no punctuation or special characters are used. For example, the script would take an Arabic word like وباليد (*wa-b-al-yad*, 'and by/with the hand') and transliterate it into `wbalyd`. Importantly, the script also marks foreign words (which are very common in Tunisian text, especially French words), by testing whether a given character has case or not. All letters in European scripts are either upper case or lower case, but Arabic has no case. I use the presence of a case attribute to identify foreign words among the Arabic text and mark them, preventing them from being included in the morphological parsing.

My next step was to create the data that the parser would be tested against. Because the gold-standard evaluation data had to be hand-parsed, I chose a modest test set of 2,000 tokens (representing about 5.5 per cent of the tokens in the corpus at that time). I selected the test data from different parts of the corpus by adding the last 5 of every 2,000 words to the test data file (and removing them from the training data file to avoid over-training). Miled then marked the segment boundaries manually (with a '+' in between segments).

5.2 Parse words using *pyparsing*

To implement the base parser using the Python tool pyparsing, I wrote a basic grammar describing the morphological rules of Tunisian Arabic. Here is a small portion of the grammar, expressed in Python code:

```
conjunctions = ['w']
prepositions = ['l','b']
def_art = ["al", "l"]
poss_suffixes = ["y", "ya", "na", "k", "km", "w", "h", "ha",
"hm"]
noun_suffix = oneOf (poss_suffixes) + FollowedBy (endOfString)
def_noun = ( Optional (oneOf(conjunctions) ) +
       Optional( oneOf (prepositions) ) +
       oneOf (def_art) ) ("prefix") + \
       SkipTo (endOfString) ("stem")
```

These rules define the suffixes that can attach to a noun as one of a choice of literal strings that can come at the end of the word. Then one of my major word types (definite noun) is defined as a combination of allowable noun-prefixes, and a word stem – which is anything in-between the prefix and the end of the string. (Many word types can also have suffixes, in which case the stem is defined as anything between the prefix and either the suffix or the end of the string.) I then fed the transliterated text, one word at a time, to the parsing function. The parsing function would try the word against the definition of each word type in the grammar (i.e. possessive noun, definite noun, present-tense verb, past-tense verb), and output a list of possible parses, like this:

```
['w', 'b', 'al', 'yd']          # definite noun
- prefix: ['w', 'b', 'al']
- stem: yd
['wbalyd']                      # uninflected word
- stem: wbalyd
['w', 'balyd']                  # conjunction + uninflected word
- prefix: w
- stem: balyd
```

For this word the analyser produced three possible parses, the correct one of which is the first. (The comments on the right indicate which word definition in the *pyparsing* grammar the parse results from.) For my baseline evaluation, I then checked the frequency of the parsed stem in the training data, and selected the parse with the highest stem frequency as the correct parse. To continue the above example, for `wbalyd` three parses are produced with associated stem frequencies:

```
['w','b','al','yd'] , stem: yd , stem frequency: 0.000115
['wbalyd'] , stem: wbalyd , stem frequency: 2.50e-06
['w', 'balyd'] , stem: balyd , stem frequency: 7.50e-06
'w+b+al+yd'
```

Since the stem of the first parse (*yd*) has the highest frequency of the three choices (0.000115), the algorithm selects it as the morphological analysis for this word. In this particular example, the parse chosen is also the correct analysis.

5.3 Baseline evaluation

For each of the parsed words, I transposed the test parse and corresponding gold-standard parse into a string of ones and zeros showing segmentation boundaries (i.e. if the letter is followed by a segment boundary, it becomes a 1; if not, it becomes a 0):

```
w+b+al+yd  11010
w+balyd    10000
```

Since the last letter of the word will always be a boundary that the parser does not have to assign, it was not counted and so each binary string is one character shorter than the input string (as the examples above illustrate). Using the binary string, the program then computed the accuracy, recall, and precision of the parse: if the test parse had a 1 where there was supposed to be a 0, that took a point off precision. If it had a 0 instead of a 1, minus one for recall. While the precision, recall, and combined F-score were scoring per non-final character, the accuracy is per word: whether the entire word is correct or not. So the correct parse `['w','b','al','yd']` would score 1/1 on accuracy, 3/3 on recall, and 2/2 on precision. Had the parse `['w', 'balyd']` been selected instead, it would have scored 0/1 on accuracy, 1/3 on recall, and 1/1 on precision. These scores were then used to compute a cumulative score over every word in the test data, yielding the following baseline results:

```
Recall: 0.4507
Precision: 0.9837
F-Score: 0.6182
Accuracy: 0.6688
```

Or, to put it another way: 45 per cent of the manually annotated breaks were correctly identified by the parser. Of the breaks found, 98 per cent of them were correct (i.e. they matched the manually annotated breaks). Overall, approximately 67 per cent of the words were analysed entirely correctly.

Examining the log of incorrect parses, I found that this method was very likely to select the analysis where the entire word is a single unit, without any internal breaks (as you can see from the excellent precision, at the cost of a very low recall). The words that suffered most from this were common collocations of stem plus affix and/or clitic, such as *bal*ʿ*ks* (`b+al+Cks`, 'in the opposite'):

```
['w', 'bal', 'Cks'] , stem: Cks , stem frequency: 7.28e-05
['wbalCks'] , stem: wbalCks , stem frequency: 2.51e-06
['w', 'balCks'] , stem: balCks , stem frequency: 8.79e-05
'w+balCks'
```

The first parse (`w+b+al+Cks`) is the correct one, but as you can see from the final line of output, the algorithm selected the third parse (`w+balCks`), which indeed had the highest stem frequency (underlined). The problem is that *bal*ʿ*ks* is used to mean 'on the contrary' and is a common discourse marker, much more common than the stem word used in its basic sense of 'opposite' or 'reflection'. So the unparsed stem of `balCks` was the most frequent in the corpus. But even words that were not obvious collocations, such as *a*ṯ*ṯānī* (`alvany`, 'the second'), were affected:

```
['alvan', 'y'] , stem: alvan , stem frequency: 0.0
['al', 'vany'] , stem: vany , stem frequency: 4.50e-05
['alvany'] , stem: alvany , stem frequency: 0.000200
'alvany'
```

I believe that this is due to the simple fact that definite nouns and adjectives are more common than indefinite ones in Arabic (a phrase which is indefinite in English will often need to be translated as definite in the Arabic). This makes the inflected forms of many words more common than the naked stem.

5.4 Affix similarity

To improve on the baseline accuracy, I added some statistical analysis to the parser. The concept of suffix level similarity that I employ here is based on the work of Dasgupta and Ng (2007):

> Suffix level similarity is motivated by the following observation: if a word *w* combines with a suffix *x*, then *w* should also combine with the suffixes that are 'morphologically similar' to *x*. To exemplify, consider the suffix 'ate' and the root word 'candid'. The words that combine with the suffix 'ate' (e.g. 'alien', 'fabric', 'origin') also combine with suffixes like 'ated', 'ation' and 's'. (Dasgupta and Ng 2007: 5)

Using this measure alone, 'candid+ate' would be identified as an inaccurate parse, since there are no instances of 'candidation', 'candidated', and so on. Dasgupta and

Ng also describe another refinement, based on the ratio of a word's frequency to that of its root, but I found that this was not useful for Arabic and actually decreased the accuracy of the parser from the baseline level.

Dasgupta and Ng compute the affix similarity using a probabilistic measure, but that is not necessary for my parser, since I already know which affixes behave similarly, and had defined them as such when writing the grammar. I could then use this information to test the goodness of fit for each word type. To do this, I wrote code that, for example, takes a parse that is supposed to be a present tense verb, and tests if the 'stem' behaves like a verb. It does this by taking the stem and combining it with all of the verb prefixes, except the one in this parse, and computing the average frequency of all those verb forms. For example, for the word *yunẓur* (*ynZr*, 'he sees'), the affix-similarity-based parser would examine each of the possible parses and see if the parse is a good fit for the type of word it is supposed to be:

```
['y', 'nZr'] present verb
['y', 'nZr'] , with present verb score of 0.000435
['ynZr'] uninflected
['ynZr'] , with poss noun score of 0.0
['ynZr'] , with poss vbz score of 0.0
['ynZr'] , with poss vbd score of 4.165e-07
['ynZr'] , with discounted frequency 0.000376
'y+nZr'
```

The parser is evaluating two hypotheses here. The first is that this is a present tense verb. To test this hypothesis, the goodness of fit function tests the proposed stem in combination with all of the verbal prefixes except `y-`, and returns the average frequency of all forms (0.000435). It then tests the second hypothesis, that this word is uninflected and the whole word is the stem. In order to do this, it tests against every kind of word this could be. So it adds all of the nominal affixes to the (non-extant) stem `ynZr` to get an average noun frequency of 0, and does the same for present and past tense verb affixes, assigning to each of these possibilities a score. Of all these possibilities, the parse chosen is the one with the highest goodness of fit score for its word class, in this case `y+nZr`, which is indeed the correct parse.

The affix-similarity method greatly improved the parser's accuracy compared with the baseline:

```
Recall: 0.8736
Precision: 0.9740
F-Score: 0.9211
Accuracy: 0.8924
```

This level of accuracy is fairly good, considering the simplicity of the grammar. In the future, I hope to improve the accuracy of the analyser by accounting for regular spelling changes and connecting it to a database, so that stored parses can be saved and (possibly) corrected manually. In the meantime, though, the existing parser provides useful functionality for the users with reasonable accuracy.

6. Managing the corpus and making it publicly accessible

To organise the corpus materials and optimise workflow, I created a web application using the programming language Python and the web framework Django.[6] A *web framework* is a set of libraries that provide code for most common tasks involved in creating all web applications, such as serving the webpages and validating user input. Django is one of several competing frameworks and is used by major websites like Instagram and *The Washington Times*. One of the greatest advantages of Django is that, once the programmer has defined the database models that the application is based on (in my case, the corpus texts and associated metadata), Django creates an administrative interface more or less automatically. This makes it very easy for someone with limited programming skills to create a usable application for managing corpus texts.

Although building this application required a significant amount of time, it is well worth it in that it has allowed me to manage and organise the corpus files and metadata, and perform basic linguistic processing (such as frequency lists, collocations, and concordancing). In addition, the application acts as a central portal for all the people working on the project (including transcribers working from Tunisia), allowing them to download yet-to-be-completed files, and upload the completed transcripts. The corpus tool allows for a broad range of functionality, including the ability to:

- view a list of all texts in the corpus (Figure 3.1), with links to view the text metadata and full text
- add, delete, and modify corpus texts
- filter texts by date added, category, and/or status
- add, delete, and modify metadata fields such as author and genre.

In addition to the management tool, the web application also provides the public face of the corpus and provides search capabilities to the general public. Visitors are able to search for any word in the corpus (either by surface form or parsed lemma) and bring up concordance results for the word. So a user can search for كرهبة (*karhabah*, 'car') as an 'Exact' search and see all of the results of the word in exactly that form (Figure 3.2).

If they perform the same search, but select 'Stem' as the search type, they will get results showing not only the base form *karhabah*, but also *alkarhabah* ('the car'), *walkarhabah* ('and the car'), and so on. This is particularly useful for verbs: a stem search for كتب (*katab*, 'to write') will also return *yaktab* ('he writes'), *ktabt* ('I wrote'), *naktabū* ('we go'), and so on (Figure 3.3).

The stem search suffers from some of the weaknesses of the parser, however. In a feminine word like *karhabah*, the feminine marker *-ah* changes to a *-t* when a possessive pronoun is added to the word, for example *karhabtī*, 'my car'. A stem search for *karhabah* will not return results like *karhabtī*, though, because the current version of the parser does not take regular spelling changes like this into account. I hope to correct this in the future.

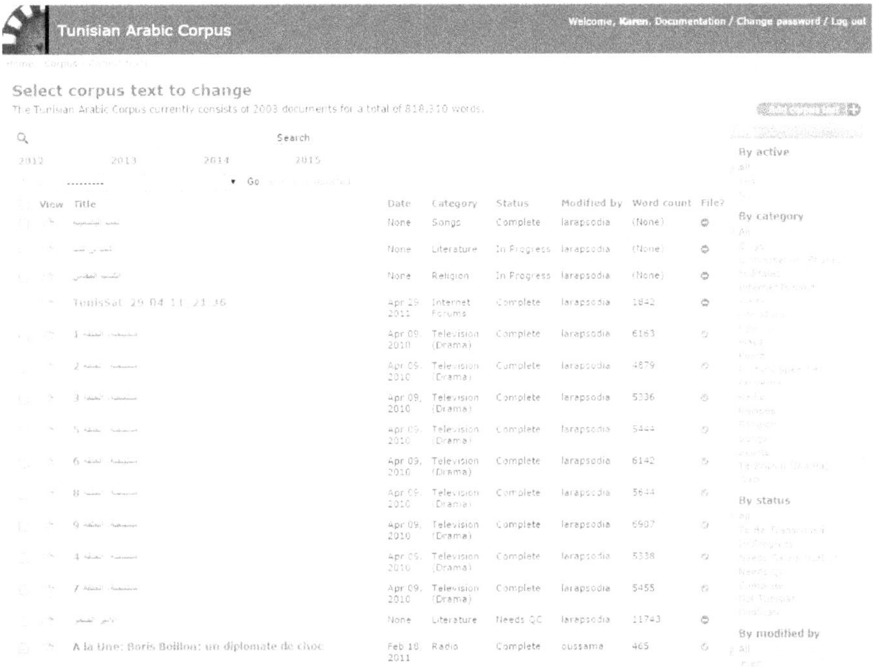

Figure 3.1 The TAC management tool

Figure 3.2 Concordance result from كهربة (*karhabah*), exact search

تسكره بعثها لواحد من اصحابو قال لو راني متضايق وسع	كتب	ننجمش ولا ما عنديش ما يستعرفوش بيها قعد يخمم آه
لو ربي الجنه والصدقه تخفف من الذنوب وتمحي المعاصي وتدفع	وكتب	للضرير وزنوهم جات الخبزه صدقه أثقل من السبعه ليالي معصيه
لو قعد هاك الشايب يخمم ومنها قال تي انا آش	تكتبهو	وربي يواجهو خير هو ومرتو قال لو لا رزقك الكل
الرزق الكل للولد ما خلى لنفسوحتى قنشاره والي عطى رزقو	كتب	مانيش ماش نخلي لو الكل ايا ولدي ما نكفخوش ومشى
الصداق عرس الولد لكن العروسه بنت أكابر وهذاكه براني راجله	تكتب	قنشاره والي عطى رزقو في حياتو طلب الله ولاغالو ايا
الصداق سبعه ايام وسبعه لياليقال لويا سيدي شرط قال لو	تكتب	لو هاو نجيب هولك مشى جاب سي علي حضروا الشهود
أمر في ولاية الجزيره وقال لو ايا اركب بره شد	كتبلو	ايام في السرايه وخلع عليه وعطاه ومنها عيط لباش كاتب
لو الحانوت احنا ما نستحقوا لهاش استنى ومن بعدين ابعث	نكتبوا	ريال باش تعمل صارميه استنى بره ياولد جيب لي الشهود
لك صداقك على خالتي حنيفه ام العروس ونوليوا عايله واحده	يكتبوا	اماله اشنوه تحب تاخذ امرا أخرى قال لو لاآما يزيدوا
الزوز صداقات والله لا يقطع بركه من أمة محمد ووين	كتبوا	كيف عوينات القنفود تحت الزعتر وما خرجوا العدول لا ما
الصداق ولى السلطان كل ليله يتنكر ويمشي لها ويقول خدمتو	تكتب	يا سيدي انا عندي طفله معاك اللي عملت مبروك أيا
تسكره للخادم اللي كانت رضعتو قال لها اعمل مزيه على	كتب	لكن اشكون ماش يبعث لو امو امو عمرها ما ترض
ونتهنى ونربح راحتي مشى جاب العدول وكتب لها كل ما	نكتبهولها	الهدرهوهو يمني فيها حتى قال تي آش ماش نخسر هات
لها كل ما عندو باسمها الدار الهنشير الحانوت الفلانيه المخزن	وكتب	ماش نخسر هات نكتبهولها ونتهنى ونربح راحتي مشى جاب العدول
لها باسمها والشرع يحكم بالظاهر ما عندي ما نقول يا	وكتبتهو	علي الفلوس على خاطر الرزق الكل عمى لي ربي بصيرتي
جواب للوليد يقول له يا امير المؤمنين راهو هرب لي	يكتب	ياسر من اول الدنيا وصل الخبر للحجاج بن يوسف يمشي
جواب لخوه قال لو ابعث لي الراجل ولى سليمان جاوبو	وكتب	وهو ما عندوش مسؤوليات هذي الامور هذيه ما يعرفش قيمتها
لو جواب يقول لو هاني بعثت لك يزيد ومعاه ولد	وكتب	المسلسله الاخرى ولاوا مربوطين في بعضهم وقال يهزوهم لامير المؤمنين

Figure 3.3 Concordance result for كتب (*katab*, 'to write'), stem search

Regular expression searches across the Buckwalter-transliterated form of the corpus text are also supported, allowing users to search for multiple variables of a word. In Figure 3.4, we can see the result from searching for `brJ.`, a search designed to find all of the common spellings of the distinctively Tunisian word *baršah*, 'many, a lot of'. This word, similar to *šniya* discussed above, is spelled alternatively with a *tāʾ marbūṭah* (ة), a *ha*' (ه), or an *alif* (ا).

In addition to seeing the concordance results onscreen, users can download the search results as a comma-delimited file, which they can then open up in any spreadsheet program for further analysis.

Supporting public access to the corpus is a very important part of the project. Although originally conceived to support my own research and future materials on

Figure 3.4 Concordance results for search `brJ.`, 'many, a lot of', which will bring up all variant spellings of *baršah*

Tunisian Arabic, accessible corpora are vital to researchers in a variety of disciplines. Arabists can use this corpus to study particular syntactic features of Tunisian Arabic; sociolinguists can use it to study the usage of French in Tunisian Arabic; in addition, teachers of Tunisian Arabic can use the corpus to find authentic example sentences and see how words and grammatical structures are used in context.

In spite of its incompleteness, the corpus has already proved useful for several pieces of research. Studies in which I am aware it has been used include: a study on referring expressions in Tunisian Arabic; a master's thesis on the progressive aspect in Arabic; and a book on Arabic indefinites, interrogatives, and negators (Wilmsen 2014). As the corpus grows, I intend to keep it available as a public resource.

7. Conclusion

Even though it is not yet complete, the TAC has already proved useful to a variety of scholars all over the world who are studying various aspects of vernacular Arabic. It is hoped that, with the addition of more texts and the further refinement of the morphological parser, it will be even more useful and will constitute an important resource for Arabic researchers in general, and scholars of spoken Arabic in particular. In addition, I hope that this project will serve as a model for the creation of other freely available dialectal corpora, thereby aiding the study of Arabic corpus linguistics and natural language processing in general, and dialectal studies in particular.

Abbreviations

1	first person	NEG	negative
2	second person	PART	particle
3	third person	PL	plural
AP	active participle	POSS	possessive
DEF	definite	PROG	progressive
F	feminine	PRS	present
GEN	genitive	REL	relative
IND	indicative	SBJV	subjunctive
IPFV	imperfective	SG	singular

Notes

1. See <http://www.bibalex.org/ica/en/> (last accessed 17 May 2018).
2. See <https://www.mturk.com/> (last accessed 17 May 2018).
3. In practice, and counter to the general procedure on Mechanical Turk, I did pay several of them, in recognition of the time and effort they had spent, but blocked them from accepting future jobs I posted.
4. See <https://www.yamli.com/arabic-keyboard/> (last accessed 17 May 2018).
5. See <https://www.microsoft.com/en-gb/download/details.aspx?id=20530> and <http://www.google.com/ta3reeb/> (both last accessed 17 May 2018).
6. See <https://www.djangoproject.com/> (last accessed 17 May 2018).

References

Alansary, S., M. Nagi and N. Adly (2007), 'Building an International Corpus of Arabic (ICA): Progress of compilation stage', in *7th International Conference on Language Engineering*, Cairo, Egypt, 5–6 December 2007.

Alhawary, M. (2003), 'Elicitation techniques and considerations in data collection in Arabic grammatical tradition', *Journal of Arabic Linguistics Tradition*, 1:1–24, <http://www.jalt.net/jaltusr/CurrJournals/AlhawaryJalt1.pdf> (last accessed 17 May 2018).

Al-Sulaiti, L. and E. Atwell (2006), 'The design of a corpus of Contemporary Arabic', *International Journal of Corpus Linguistics*, 11(1): 1–36.

Baron, A., P. Rayson and D. Archer (2009), 'Automatic standardization of spelling for historical text mining', poster session presented at Digital Humanities 2009, University of Maryland, 22–9 June 2009, <http://eprints.lancs.ac.uk/42525/> (last accessed 17 May 2018).

Baroni, M. and S. Bernardini (2004), 'BootCaT: Bootstrapping corpora and terms from the Web', in M. T. Lino, M. F. Xavier, F. Ferreira, R. Costa, R. Silva, C. Pereira, F. Carvalho, M. Lopes, M. Catarino and S. Barros (eds), *Proceedings of LREC 2004*, Paris: ELRA, pp. 1313–16.

Buckwalter, T. (2002), *Buckwalter Arabic Morphological Analyzer Version* 1.0, LDC catalog no.: LDC2002L49, Philadelphia: University of Pennsylvania, Linguistic Data Consortium.

Darwish, K. (2013), 'Arabizi detection and conversion to Arabic', arXiv preprint, arXiv:1306.6755.

Dasgupta, S. and V. Ng (2007), 'High-performance, language-independent morphological segmentation', in *Human Language Technologies 2007: The Conference of the North American Chapter of the Association for Computational Linguistics: Proceedings of the Main Conference*, Stroudsburg, PA: Association for Computational Linguistics, pp. 155–63.

Ferguson, C. (1959), 'Diglossia', *Word*, 15(2): 325–40.

Hajič, J., O. Smrž, T. Buckwalter and H. Jin (2005), 'Feature-based tagger of approximations of functional Arabic morphology', in *Proceedings of the Fourth Workshop on Treebanks and Linguistic Theories (TLT 2005)*, Barcelona, Spain, pp. 53–64.

Kirchhoff, K. and D. Vergyri (2005), 'Cross-dialectal data sharing for acoustic modeling in Arabic speech recognition', *Speech Communication*, 64(1): 37–51.

Lemhaf (2011), *Si Lemhaf – Gregorius,* video file, <https://www.facebook.com/video/video.php?v=489544031821> (last accessed 17 May 2018).

Maamouri, M. and A. Bies (2004), 'Developing an Arabic Treebank: Methods, guidelines, procedures, and tools', in A. Farghaly and K. Megerdoomian (eds), *Proceedings of the Workshop on Computational Approaches to Arabic Script-Based Languages*, Stroudsburg, PA: Association for Computational Linguistics, pp. 2–9.

Maamouri, M., A. Bies, H. Jin and T. Buckwalter (2003), *Arabic Treebank: Part 1 v 2.0,* LDC catalog no.: LDC2003T06, Philadelphia: University of Pennsylvania, Linguistic Data Consortium.

Owens, J. (2006), *A Linguistic History of Arabic*, Oxford: Oxford University Press.

Parker, R., D. Graff, K. Chen, J. Kong and K. Maeda (2011), *Arabic Gigaword*, 5th edn, LDC catalog no. LDC2011T11, Linguistic Data Consortium, University of Pennsylvania.

Parkinson, D. B. (1996), 'Variability in Standard Arabic grammar skills', in A. Elgibali (ed.), *Understanding Arabic: Essays in Contemporary Arabic Linguistics in Honor of El-Said Badawi*, Cairo: The American University in Cairo Press, pp. 91–102.

Versteegh, K. (2001), *The Arabic Language*, Edinburgh: Edinburgh University Press.

Wilmsen, D. (2014), *Arabic Indefinites, Interrogatives and Negators: A Linguistic History of Western Dialects,* Oxford: Oxford University Press.

Yaghan, M. A. (2008), '"Arabizi": A contemporary style of Arabic slang', *Design Issues*, 24(2): 39–52.

4

Accessible Corpus Annotation for Arabic

Wesam Ibrahim and Andrew Hardie

1. Introduction

In this chapter, we introduce a process for making the highly complex output of morphosyntactic analysis software for Arabic usable and accessible within a framework that is familiar to (corpus) linguists with minimal technical expertise. Our argument is organised as follows. After a brief exposition of the key premise of our work (section 2), we move on to a review of some of the schemata and systems that have been devised and distributed in recent years for the morphological and/or morphosyntactic annotation of Arabic text (section 3). In section 4, we move on to build an argument for why a new formulation of the output of systems such as those reviewed is necessary for reasons of usability and accessibility within widely used corpus query tools. (Since one of the present authors is the developer of the CQPweb software – see Hardie 2012 – we will refer mainly to CQPweb here.) Our actual implementation of this goal, a system which postprocesses the output of the MADA software (discussed in section 2), is outlined in section 5. Finally, we outline briefly the avenues for further work that this accessible corpus annotation opens up (section 6).

2. The nature of POS tagging in Arabic

In light of the fact that morphology rather than syntax is the locus of much of Arabic's structural complexity (see overview in McEnery et al., this volume), it is perhaps unsurprising that in much computational work on the grammatical analysis of Arabic, morphological considerations have been extremely prominent. In languages such as English, the definitions of morphosyntactic categories for POS tagging rely as often on syntactic criteria as morphological criteria – for instance, the difference between infinitives and present tense in English is entirely syntax-driven, as there is no morphological distinction. For Arabic, by contrast, it has often been the case that POS tagging has not been fully distinguished from morphological analysis: as we will see in the review that follows, Arabic POS tagsets often classify morphemes rather than words, and

Arabic POS taggers likewise often undertake full morphological analysis rather than simply applying a single tag to each word.

While this is understandable, it is in our view not entirely satisfactory on certain linguistic grounds. As we will outline below, for instance, it has been rare in Arabic POS tagging to distinguish main verbs from auxiliary verbs, as these are not morphological categories, even though – on syntactic criteria – auxiliary verbs, traditionally called 'sisters of *kāna*', are easily distinguishable from main verbs. We will return to this precise issue later (section 5.1). First, however, we will review a selection of work within computational linguistics on morphological and/or morphosyntactic analysis of Arabic, with a particular focus on differences in the kinds of tags produced by different systems. (Since the field of Arabic computational linguistics, and/or natural language processing (NLP), is much more established than Arabic corpus linguistics, it is unfortunately not possible to review *every* relevant study here.)

3. Review of existing systems

Arabic presents numerous challenges for computational analysis (Dukes et al. 2013: 40). First, the sheer complexity of the morphology is itself a challenge: Habash et al. (2009: 102) point out that if every possible combination of morphological features leads to one analysis, then there are 'about 333,000 theoretically possible completely specified morphological analyses'. We must add to this the complexity inherent in dealing with the orthographic ambiguities, discussed above. Moreover, as Sawalha and Atwell (2009: 1) point out, in many words phonetic phenomena can obscure the basic structure: with a root such as *k-t-b* the patterns are fairly clear, but if one of the root consonants is a glide (*w* or *y*) the patterns may be much harder to discern as glides may merge in complicated manners with different adjacent vowels.

The centrality of morphological analysis to much computational work has been driven, not only by the complexity of Arabic morphology, but also by the centrality of word structure analysis to traditional Arabic grammar. Some early computational modelling was done within the broadly formalist framework of 'two-level morphology' (Koskenniemi 1983; Beesley 1996, 1998 describes the application of this approach to Arabic). However, more recent work has tended to look to traditional Arabic grammar more than it has to contemporary linguistic theory. This has, naturally, reinforced the focus on matters morphological at the expense of matters syntactic, since traditional Arabic grammar shares with other classical grammatical traditions (e.g. Latin, Greek, Sanskrit) a strong focus on morphology.

For example, Khoja et al. begin their description of a POS tagset for Arabic with the following comment:

> The morphosyntactic tagset that is described here follows the tagging system that has been used for around fourteen centuries by all students of Arabic (both young and old). Arabic grammarians describe Arabic as being derived from three main categories: noun, verb and particle. In fact there is a famous poem that actually starts with the verse: the word or language is one of three, noun, verb and particle. It is from these three main categories that the rest of the language is derived. [. . .] The point is that Arabic grammar has been studied for

> centuries, and the principles of describing the language already exist. Since so much knowledge is readily available, it is logical to derive our tagset from this wealth of information. The alternative to this is to base the Arabic tagset on an Indo-European one, but by doing this we may lose a lot of the information that an Arabic tagset would give us. Also, by moulding Arabic to fit an Indo-European language, we might distort the way Arabic is perceived by its native speakers. (Khoja et al. 2003: 61)

Khoja et al. describe a *hierarchical and decomposable* tagset. That is, the tagset is arranged as a *hierarchy* of categories, beginning with the basic three mentioned in the quote above, and then progressively subdividing those categories at different levels, until the actual categories of the tagset are arrived at. Moreover, the tags that label the categories are *decomposable* in that within a tag, each step in the subdivision process is represented by a single character or short sequence. For instance, Khoja et al. define the tag *NACSgMGD* to represent the following sequence of subdivisions: noun – adjective – singular – masculine – genitive – definite. Likewise, *VISg2MI* represents verb – imperfect – singular – second person – masculine – indicative. We see therefore that the major morphological features included in Khoja et al.'s tagset are, for nouns/adjectives, gender, number, case, and definiteness (but *not* state, as construct state nouns are tagged as indefinite) and, for verbs, tense, mood, person, number, and gender. Clitics receive their own separate tags drawn from the same tagset. Hierarchical-decomposable tagsets have also often been used for English, but in English, there are rarely more than three decomposable elements per tag (e.g. in the CLAWS6 tagset[1]). Khoja et al.'s tagset contains a total of 177 tags.

Subsequently, Khoja (2001, 2003) describes the implementation of a part-of-speech tagger which assigns these tags to text, dubbed *Arabic Part-of-Speech Tagger* or APT. This is a probabilistic tagger using the Viterbi algorithm, an approach based on a hidden Markov model (see DeRose 1988). The transition probabilities (probabilities of one tag following another) used in the Markov model consider only the top-level distinction between noun, verb, and particle plus residuals (e.g. formulae) and punctuation (see Khoja 2001: 6). Typical use of a Markov model would use a full matrix of transition probabilities across all the tags in the tagset. However, the large number of tags in Khoja's tagset would make this difficult to do without a very large training corpus.

Of the approaches reviewed here, that exemplified by Khoja's work is perhaps the one that sticks closest to the model of POS tagsets and POS tagging that is familiar in the literature on English corpus annotation. Sawalha and Atwell's (2013) comprehensive review of Arabic POS tagsets includes several which adopt a similar approach to the tagset as Khoja's, for instance Alqrainy (2008), whose tagset is also decomposable but is less similar to a hierarchy and more similar to a feature matrix (see below). Other approaches embrace more thoroughly the central focus on morphology, in many cases either explicitly or implicitly casting the task to be addressed as one of morphological analysis rather than morphosyntactic categorisation.

One scholar for whom the focus on morphology is explicit is Buckwalter.[2] The Buckwalter Arabic Morphological Analyzer (BAMA; distributed by the Linguistic Data Consortium, see Buckwalter 2004) is a system which operates solely at the word level; that is, it attempts no contextual analysis. Rather, it works out, for any given string of Arabic letters, what combinations of base, prefix, and suffix (where the 'affixes' may also incorporate clitics) represent possible analyses, based on its lexicons of prefixes, suffixes, and bases. The result of a Buckwalter analysis of a given word is then a series of possible morpheme segmentations. Within each analysis, each morpheme is given a tag. It is important to note, however, that tags for morphemes are inherently distinct from tags for words. Let us consider two example Buckwalter analyses to illustrate this point:

```
wa:CONJ+qAl:PV+a:PVSUFF_SUBJ:3MS
```

The word in this example is *waqāla*, 'and he said'. Morpheme breaks are indicated by a +, and each morpheme is connected to its tag with a colon. The tags are not directly designed to be decomposable, but we can in some cases make out distinct elements within the tags. So in *waqāla*, three morphemes are identified: *wa* as a CONJ, i.e. conjunction (a proclitic); *qāl* as a PV, i.e. perfective verb base (Buckwalter uses aspect rather than tense terminology); and *a* as a PVSUFF_SUBJ:3MS, i.e. a suffix for a perfective verb, indicating agreement with a third person masculine singular subject.

Our second example is the word *alʿarabiyyati* 'Arabic (adj.)':

```
Al:DET+Earabiy~:ADJ+ap:NSUFF_FEM_SG+i:CASE_DEF_GEN
```

Four morphemes have been identified here: *al* as DET, i.e. determiner; *ʿarabiyy* as ADJ, i.e. adjective base; *at* as NSUFF_FEM_SG, i.e. a nominal/adjectival suffix marking a word as feminine singular; and *i* as CASE_DEF_GEN, i.e. a genitive case suffix which is marked as definite. As the ADJ tag illustrates, the Buckwalter system does not treat adjectives as a subcategory of nouns as Khoja's schema does, but instead as a distinct category. This example also illustrates how the Buckwalter analysis in some respects does not clearly differentiate categories that apply to words from categories that apply to morphemes. For instance, *al* is tagged as DET although in fact it is not a determiner but is the definite-marking prefix.

When (as is typical) the input text to BAMA does not contain short vowel diacritics, any given Buckwalter analysis necessarily implies the presence of one given pattern of vowels as opposed to any other. Words which are ambiguous as to their short vowels will necessarily have at least two analyses.

The Buckwalter system is an important one because, as we will see, other systems have been based upon it. BAMA itself is published by the LDC, as is the updated SAMA (Standard Arabic Morphological Analyzer) system derived from it; both BAMA and SAMA are available via LDC membership only, but a freely available derivative of an early version of BAMA has been released under the title AraMorph. The Buckwalter tags are utilised within the Penn Arabic Treebank (ATB) and the tagset is documented most fully in publications and supplementary materials associated with that corpus (see Diab 2007). Some work on POS tagging that draws on Penn ATB data has developed alternative software that uses the same tagset schema as does the Buckwalter system (Kübler and Mohamed 2012; Abdul-Mageed et al. 2013).

Buckwalter analyses involve, as we have seen, unitary labels applied to morphemes, which stand in contrast to the hierarchical tagset of Khoja et al. (2003) that we discussed above. One further style of annotation system is prominent in Arabic morphological and morphosyntactic annotation, namely feature matrices.

The most complete and most thoroughly documented feature matrix system for Arabic morphology to our knowledge is the SALMA (Sawalha Atwell Leeds Morphological Analysis) tagset (outlined in a series of papers, most centrally Sawalha and Atwell 2013; Sawalha et al. 2013; see also Sawalha and Atwell 2009, 2010; and see also Atwell, this volume). By labelling it a *feature matrix*, we mean that (1) every tag consists of a string of characters of precisely the same length; (2) each position in the string always indicates the same, single feature in every tag; and (3) each feature can have different values, indicated by different characters, or a 'not applicable' value if that particular feature is not relevant for a given word (or, in this case, morpheme, since SALMA annotates morphemes rather than words).

Twenty-two features are defined for the SALMA system, and therefore every tag consists of twenty-two characters. It is worth listing the features in full; they are as follows (feature descriptors quoted from Sawalha and Atwell 2013: 70, with our own explanatory comments added in *italics*):

1. Main Part-of-Speech
   - *Distinguishes noun, verb, particle, punctuation, other.*
2. Part-of-Speech: Noun
   - *Applies only when the first field indicates a noun; 34 possibilities here distinguish a variety of morphological, morphosyntactic, semantic, or etymological categories of nouns, adjectives, and pronouns.*
3. Part-of-Speech: Verb
   - *As for feature 2, but for verbs; the 3 categories are perfect/imperfect/imperative.*
4. Part-of-Speech: Particle
   - *As for feature 2, but identifies the specific participle in question; 20 options.*
5. Part-of-Speech: Other (Residual)
   - *As for feature 2, but identifies 15 subcategories of the 'other' category; these are all various prefixes and suffixes, although confusingly, two of the category names are actually 'prefix' and 'suffix'; this contrasts with the use of the term 'Residual' in other tagsets, where it usually refers to things such as foreign words, formulae, symbols, and abbreviations, i.e. things which are only marginally words in the language being analysed.*
6. Punctuation marks
   - *As for feature 2, but identifies 12 separate punctuation marks.*
7. Gender
   - *Can be common as well as masculine/feminine.*
8. Number
   - *Distinguishes singular and dual, plus there are several different categories for plurals depending on inflection type and semantics.*
9. Person
   - *Distinguishes the normal first, second, and third.*

10. Inflectional morphology
    - *Indicates whether or not the word is part of a lemma with multiple inflectional forms.*
11. Case or Mood
    - *Using the same set of labels, distinguishes nominative/accusative/genitive on nominals and indicative/subjunctive/jussive on verbs.*
12. Case and Mood marks
    - *Indicates the form of the inflectional affix that marks the category noted in feature 11.*
13. Definiteness
    - *Definite versus indefinite (construct state is not dealt with here; indefinite = absence of the definite prefix, rather than presence of an indefinite suffix).*
14. Voice
    - *Makes the typical active/passive distinction for verbs.*
15. Emphasised and non-emphasised
    - *Distinguishes emphatic versus non-emphatic forms of the non-past tense (or, imperfect aspect); a feature of Classical Arabic and not MSA.*
16. Transitivity
    - *Makes the typical distinction based on number of objects of a verb.*
17. Rational
    - *Distinguishes the semantic feature of words referring to entities with a mind versus entities without a mind (typically human/non-human).*
18. Declension and Conjugation
    - *Distinguishes 8 categories based on the inflectional behaviour of the word, but also in some cases involving criteria of semantics (concrete, abstract) and derivation.*
19. Unaugmented and Augmented
    - *Identifies whether or not the inflection and derivation of the word involves the addition of extra consonants to the fundamental consonantal root.*
20. Number of root letters
    - *That is, in the fundamental consonantal root.*
21. Verb root
    - *Marks distinctions between sets of phonological characteristics in the derivation of a verb lemma from the fundamental consonantal root (30 types).*
22. Noun finals
    - *Distinguishes 6 categories based on phonological characteristics of the derivation of a noun lemma.*

That this is a system for classifying *morphemes*, rather than for classifying *words*, is illustrated by the fact that not only clitics but also some affixes receive their own tags independent of the base to which they are attached. This is illustrated by certain examples cited by Sawalha and Atwell (2013: 68, 71–2). For example, the definite prefix *al* and the feminine suffix *at* receive tags independent of their base. In POS analysis, it is typical to analyse clitics independently (as in English, for instance: clitic auxiliary verbs such as *'d*, *'ll* and the clitic genitive postposition *'s* are most usually tagged as separate elements) but *not* affixes. Thus, from our perspective the use within the SALMA definitions of the term *part-of-speech* is potentially confusing, because POS categories are typically considered to be *morphosyntactic* (apply to words and clitics) rather than *morphological* (apply to all morphemes individually).

Further scrutiny of the SALMA scheme indicates, however, that it is not entirely a scheme for morphological analysis either. As well as elements of both morphological and morphosyntactic categorisation, it incorporates elements of morphophonological analysis (e.g. the final four features) and analysis of purely semantic features (e.g. feature 17, many of the categories within feature 2, etc.). At the same time, distinctions which a morphosyntactic tagset might be expected to emphasise – such as those between open and closed POS categories – are backgrounded. For instance, there is no category for pronoun. Instead, subcategories of the pronoun category appear as direct subordinates of the noun category, and as sisters to both the adjective and noun subcategories.

We can understand the shape of the SALMA tagset more clearly if we note that Sawalha and Atwell's aim is to capture within this schema of analysis most or all of the features included within traditional Arabic grammar, wherein the semantic, the morphophonological, and the morphosyntactic are not rigidly delineated (the central role of traditional Arabic grammar is mentioned by Sawalha and Atwell 2013: 73 and *passim*). This has, of course, certain advantages, particularly when it comes to fine-grained annotation of Classical Arabic texts; the centrality of this application to Sawalha and Atwell's concern is underlined by the fact that they develop mappings between SALMA and the tagset of the Quranic Arabic Corpus (Sawalha and Atwell 2013: 82; see Dukes et al. 2013 for details of that corpus). However, as we will outline below, there are also certain disadvantages.

One other potential weakness in the SALMA system is some inconsistency regarding the choice between a 'lumping' approach to features (devising the scheme so as to minimise the overall number of features) and a 'splitting' approach (adding features to achieve higher granularity). The separate subcategory features for each main POS category (features 2–6) epitomise a 'splitting' approach, as does the SALMA system generally. On the other hand, feature 11 exemplifies a 'lumping' approach: the features of case and mood are conceptually distinct, but are grouped together as a single field in the feature matrix. This is possible because they never overlap in Arabic: any given word has either nominal inflections (and thus case) or verbal inflections (and thus mood) but not both; in other languages, for instance, Latin, mood and case *can* overlap.[3] But the same non-overlap would have made it possible to represent all subcategorisation features (2–6) in a 'lumped' way as a single feature. The treatment of agreement features similarly 'lumps': gender, number, and person are indicated by the same features on the words (nouns and pronouns) that possess these features as on the words (verbs and adjectives) that are marked with these features through agreement with some other word – a 'lumping' common to all feature matrix approaches with which we are familiar (see Sampson 1995: 79–82 for a critique of this practice).

The primary representation of SALMA is as a string of single-character values, which, as noted above, are associated with the correct features by virtue of their position in the string. A more verbose representation of a feature matrix – an unordered set of feature-value pairs – is utilised by the other prominent feature matrix analytic schema, that employed by the MADA system.

Developed at Columbia University, MADA is a system of analysis which builds on BAMA. As we explained previously, BAMA frequently assigns more than one analysis to each word token as a result of limited orthographic distinctness among certain words. MADA reduces the resulting ambiguity by selecting a single analysis which is the most contextually appropriate based on automated statistical calculations. The computational techniques used by MADA are beyond the scope of this review; the reader is referred to Habash et al. (2009). In short, a series of features are extracted from the Buckwalter analyses; the probability of each feature is assessed in its textual context using a separate statistical model (called a *support vector machine*); and the single Buckwalter analysis which matches the set of features judged most probable is selected as the winning analysis. As a result of this process, the MADA output contains all the different features used in the probabilistic selection procedure as a feature matrix; these features include a POS tag, a lemma, a full Buckwalter analysis, and a range of inflectional features.

An example MADA analysis, quoted from the software manual,[4] is as follows:

```
;;WORD yblg
;;SVM_PREDICTIONS: yblg asp:i cas:na enc0:0 gen:m mod:i
      num:s per:3 pos:verb prc0:0 prc1:0 prc2:0 prc3:0
      stt:na vox:a
*0.991246 diac:yabolugu lex:balag-u_1
      bw:ya/IV3MS+bolug/IV+u/IVSUFF_MOOD:I
      gloss:reach;attain pos:verb prc3:0 prc2:0 prc1:0
      prc0:0 per:3 asp:i vox:a mod:i gen:m num:s stt:na
      cas:na enc0:0 rat:na source:lex stem:bolug stemcat:IV
_0.968597 diac:yabolugu lex:balug-u_1
      bw:ya/IV3MS+bolug/IV+u/IVSUFF_MOOD:I gloss:be_eloquent
      pos:verb prc3:0 prc2:0 prc1:0 prc0:0 per:3 asp:i
      vox:a mod:i gen:m num:s stt:na cas:na enc0:0 rat:na
      source:lex stem:bolug stemcat:IV_intr
_0.945947 diac:yuboligu lex:>abolag_1
      bw:yu/IV3MS+bolig/IV+u/IVSUFF_MOOD:I
      gloss:report;inform;notify pos:verb prc3:0 prc2:0
      prc1:0 prc0:0 per:3 asp:i vox:a mod:i gen:m num:s
      stt:na cas:na enc0:0 rat:na source:lex stem:bolig
      stemcat:IV_yu
_0.945947 diac:yubal~igu lex:bal~ag_1
      bw:yu/IV3MS+bal~ig/IV+u/IVSUFF_MOOD:I
      gloss:communicate;convey pos:
      verb prc3:0 prc2:0 prc1:0 prc0:0 per:3 asp:i vox:a
      mod:i gen:m num:s stt:na cas:na enc0:0 rat:na
      source:lex stem:bal~ig stemcat:IV_yu
```

(Habash et al. 2012: 17)

Habash et al. (2012) give detailed guidance on how to read MADA output; this will not be repeated here, but we will point out certain key features of the format which will be important for our subsequent discussion.

Each analysis consists of a series of feature-value pairs, where the abbreviated name of the feature is linked to the value by a colon. So, for example, *per:3* indicates that the *person* feature has the value *3*, i.e. third person. The features which make up a single analysis – derived from one potential Buckwalter analysis – appear on one line. Thus, each line contains a full feature matrix for the features represented within MADA's scheme; although the presentation is very different from SALMA, and the set of features is also different, the underlying idea of a feature matrix analysis is the same. At the start of each line is the probabilistic score given to that analysis by MADA. The top score is preceded by an asterisk (*); other scores are preceded by an underscore (_). The original word is given at the top and flagged by the label *;;WORD*; the line flagged *;;SVM_PREDICTIONS* contains the features judged by the support vector machines to be most likely in context; the highest scoring analysis should be that which matches most closely the SVM_PREDICTIONS (although that analysis may not match the predictions in every detail). As befits a system derived from BAMA, all output appears in the Buckwalter transcription (see Appendix).

In this case, the input word is, in Arabic script, < يبلغ >, i.e. *yblġ*. This word has four possible readings: *yabluġu*, 'he reaches'; the homophonous *yabluġu*, 'he is being eloquent'; *yubliġu*, 'he reports, informs'; and *yuballiġu*, 'he communicates'. All four of these are third person present tense indicative active verbs. In this case, the ambiguity arises because orthographically indistinct forms derive from four different verb lemmata; in other cases, different forms within a single lemma may be the source of ambiguity.

The morphosyntactic features represented within the MADA matrix are POS category, plus (for nominal categories) gender, number, state, and case, or (for verbal categories) tense/aspect, voice, mood, person, gender, and number. All features are always present, but those that are not relevant for a particular word get the value *na* for *not applicable*. This set of features is very similar to that expressed within Khoja's schema, discussed above. However, also present are features for the wordform with short vowel signs added in (*diac*), the lemma (*lex*), the unprocessed Buckwalter analysis (*bw*), and a number of features used internally by the system (*rat*, *source*, *stem*, *stemcat*) in the course of processing the Buckwalter analysis. Finally, five further features (*prc0*, *prc1*, *prc2*, *prc3*, and *enc*) identify the presence or absence of various clitics and affixes.

MADA has gone through multiple versions, using different tagsets for the *pos* feature. Different versions reflect different aspects of the tagging used in two Arabic treebanks that the team behind MADA have worked with, both of which add dependency parsing to the word-level analyses on which MADA operates. These treebanks are the Penn ATB (see Maamouri et al. 2004), on which MADA's statistical model was trained; and the Columbia Arabic Treebank (CATiB; see Habash and Roth 2009; Marton et al. 2013). The POS tagset we discuss here is that of MADA version 3.2. It is based ultimately on the labels used within the Buckwalter analysis. Thus, like the Buckwalter system – but unlike SALMA or Khoja's tagset – the basic POS categories include top-level distinctions between nouns, adjectives, adverbs, prepositions, conjunctions, and so on, rather than the three-way noun/verb/particle split. Although the values of the *pos* feature are in principle unitary category labels, they are in many cases decomposable, creating a hierarchy of category and subcategory. Consider, for instance, the following list of noun and adjective tags:

- noun
- noun_num
- noun_quant
- noun_prop
- adj
- adj_comp
- adj_num.

In each case, the first element in the label is qualified, and a subcategory is created, by the second element; *noun* and *adj* alone thus implicitly signify a 'general' subcategory. Thus, since we have *numeral noun*, *quantifier noun*, and *proper noun*, the unsubcategorised label stands for *common nouns*. Likewise, alongside *comparative adjective* and numeral adjective, *adj* alone by implication means *general adjective*. The other categories behave similarly, for a total of 34 subcategories across 13 top-level categories (Habash et al. 2012: 14). Among these, it is worth noting, are certain categories which, to our knowledge, no other schema discussed here incorporates. One of these is the tag *verb_pseudo*, i.e. pseudo-verb. This category reflects what are traditionally called *sisters of ʾinna*. These are elements (of which the word *ʾinna*, 'indeed' is the prototypical case) which originated as function words, i.e. invariant particles, but which syntactically can appear as the main verb of a clause without acquiring verbal inflection (Ryding 2005: 422–8; Abu-Chacra 2007: 193–5). While *ʾinna*-type particles receive separate categorisation in SALMA, their distinct verbal function is not handled there; its presence within the MADA scheme reflects the greater role that syntactic criteria play for the MADA system as opposed to SALMA. Of course, distinguishing alternative syntactic roles of the same word is one of the traditionally important functions of morphosyntactic (POS) tagging. For example, the C5 tagset for English (used in the British National Corpus) distinguishes between *much* modifying an adjective or adverb (given AV0) and *much* modifying a noun (given DT0). The functional distinction between the two uses of *ʾinna* is parallel.

One other notable feature of the MADA system is its use of a *state* feature, rather than a *definiteness* feature. Treating Arabic nouns as having three states (definite, indefinite, and construct) represents, in our view, a much more efficient approach to the classification of possessor and possessed nouns than using a definite/indefinite distinction and treating construct-state (possessed) nouns as a special case of one or the other.

The foregoing introduction to MADA concludes our survey of POS tagsets for Arabic. Other schemes for part-of-speech are used within Arabic treebank corpora. Several of these have been mentioned already: the Qur'anic Arabic Corpus, CATiB, and Penn ATB. Another important treebank is the Prague Arabic Dependency Treebank (Hajič et al. 2004; Smrž and Hajič 2006). All these treebanks contain multilayered annotation, from morphological to POS to syntactic, and are based on substantial manual analytic work; their tagsets are therefore designed for rather different purposes than those we address here, and we will not review them in detail.

4. The need for accessible annotation

Given the general availability of the different systems we reviewed in the previous section, it is not obvious that a need exists for yet a further schema of POS analysis for Arabic. However, we would argue that all the systems we have reviewed fall short, one way or another, in terms of *accessibility* for one key user group. That user group consists of linguists without an advanced computational background who wish to work on Arabic corpora. Feature matrices such as SALMA or the MADA output format, or morpheme-level formats such as Buckwalter analyses, allow a highly comprehensive analysis. These are very effective when annotations are to be processed by computer. For instance, as Sawalha and Atwell note with reference to SALMA:

> The interpretation of the [SALMA] tag is handled by referring to the attribute value and its position in the tag string. The position of the attribute in the tag string identifies the morphological feature category, while the attribute value is identified by searching the morphological feature category for the specified symbol. Then, all these single interpretations of attributes are grouped together to represent the full tag of the word. The tag is intended to remain readable by linguists. Moreover, the tag is straightforwardly readable by software, for example by a search tool matching specified feature-value(s). (Sawalha and Atwell 2013: 62)

For the purposes of computer science and NLP, the use of a large number of feature fields is a very reasonable response to the challenges created by the high complexity of Arabic morphology. Feature matrices are extremely computationally tractable, as Sawalha and Atwell note. We must, however, respectfully disagree with Sawalha and Atwell on the issue of whether SALMA tags are 'readable by linguists'. It is extremely difficult, for instance, to distinguish by eye the 14th and 15th characters within a 22 character SALMA tag. Moreover the sheer number of distinctions at each position presents a major obstacle to memorability. The more verbose and explicit feature matrix format used by MADA is less subject to potential misreading, but is difficult to read on account of its sheer bulkiness in terms of the extent in characters of each analysis.

For an audience of linguists who are interested in the use of corpora but do not know anything about Arabic NLP, and who thus will need to access tagged corpora via general-purpose software, something else is needed. Our experience, in our own research and when helping students with Arabic corpus data, indicated the following criteria:

- Annotated Arabic data would need to be accessible within a general concordancer – without the need for software specifically designed for a unique feature matrix format. For us, that means Corpus Workbench (CWB) and specifically CQPweb, which is designed to deal with heavily annotated corpora.
- Using more than one type of tag per word is possible (since CWB supports multiple levels of annotation), but each individual type of tag needs to be relatively readable and easy to remember.

- Where tags include more than one piece of information, that information should be structured in the same way found in traditional POS tagsets: that is, not as a feature matrix but as a left-to-right category hierarchy.
- POS tags should be limited to morphosyntactic categorisation and exclude issues of derivation, etymology, semantic category, morphophonemics, and so on.

Hierarchical tagsets consisting of decomposable elements do already exist for Arabic, for example the Khoja et al. tagset (see above). Such tagsets, where a single POS tag indicates major word category, subcategory, and some inflectional information, are more in line with the way that most corpus linguists have traditionally been trained to work than feature matrix systems. We therefore resolved to create *accessible* annotation for Arabic by working with state-of-the-art software but reshaping its output into a form more in line with the expectations of such relatively less technical corpus linguists.

We elected to work with the MADA system for a number of reasons. First, it is a well-documented system described at length in several papers. Second, it is based on the well-known and widely used Buckwalter morphological analyser, but performs contextual disambiguation. Although for many NLP purposes, it is worthwhile to retain ambiguous analyses, our experience is that for purposes of linguistic research, it is easier to work with annotated corpora where a single analysis has been chosen, even if there is an error rate in the choices that have been made, than to work with data where words have potentially many analyses. Third, the MADA system is under active development and has a lively user community.

We proceeded as follows. We developed a piece of 'wrapper' software for MADA which does two separate things. On the input side, it prepares the input text by converting it into the one-sentence-per-line format that MADA requires; it also controls the various options afforded by the MADA software, selecting standard settings in each case. On the output side, it reads in the output data from MADA, and for each word reformats that data into a form which addresses the issues of accessibility. This involves mapping the MADA output into a traditional POS tagset of our devising. The wrapper software also *adjusts* the analyses in a number of ways which will be outlined below (affecting the annotation of pseudo-verbs, auxiliary verbs, and trilateral roots). The result is a CWB vertical input file which can be subsequently indexed within CQPweb and thus made available for linguistic research to a wide range of users who would not otherwise have the necessary technical skills to avail themselves of MADA or any other system of a similar level of complexity.

5. Creating accessible annotation

5.1 From MADA output to a part-of-speech tagset

As described above, the MADA output includes a wide range of features, and we determined to reorganise (some of) them into a hierarchical POS tagset. A new tagset was needed because MADA works from the principle of many top-level POS categories, unlike, for instance, the Khoja et al. tagset, which is based on the traditional grammatical approach where Arabic has only three top-level categories based on morphological criteria (see section 3). We devised a tagset consisting of two-letter tags, where the first letter indicates a major category and the second letter indicates a subcategory. We followed the mnemonics established by the CLAWS tradition of English tagsets, including J for adjective and R for adverb, so that there are not multiple major categories beginning in A, which in our experience is less readable. Some tags consist only of these two letters, for example:

- RR – general adverb
- RQ – interrogative adverb
- VT – pseudo-verb (*particle acting as verb, i.e. 'sisters of ʾinna'*)
- TT – general particle.

Such tags are derived, in principle unproblematically, from particular values of the MADA *pos* feature. In practice, the way in which MADA makes use of the underlying Buckwalter system meant non-straightforward conversions in some cases. For instance, the pseudo-verb category is only present in MADA output when the most recent Buckwalter-type system, SAMA, is used. As we had access only to the somewhat older BAMA system, we added a check to our conversion procedure which overrides the tagging of words such as *ʾinna*, 'indeed, that' as a conjunction (the only analysis available in earlier versions) when MADA's SVM_PREDICTIONS suggest the pseudo-verb category instead. The same procedure was used to allow the SAMA subcategories of *quantifier noun*, *comparative adjective*, and *numeral adjective* to appear in our tagset.

Where, as well as category and subcategory, inflectional features are present, it is necessary to combine different features from the MADA feature matrix into a single POS tag. For nouns and adjectives, these features are straightforward: gender, number, case, and state (we follow MADA in treating state as a single feature with three values – indefinite, definite, and construct – as we consider this the most sensible analysis on linguistic grounds). We use one-letter abbreviations for each of these to produce a further four-letter block which is added to the base tag. To aid readability – since a six-letter string already approaches the limits of what the human eye can grasp at a glance – a colon separates the first two characters and the last four. This yields tags such as the following:

- NN:FDND – definite nominative dual feminine common noun (e.g. *al-bintāni*, 'the (two) girls')
- NP:MSXI – indefinite singular masculine proper noun, indeterminate case (e.g. *muḥammad*)
- JJ:MPAI – indefinite accusative plural masculine general adjective (e.g. *mustaqilīn*, 'independent').

Case is often indeterminate (indicated as X) because the case affixes are short vowels and thus unwritten (and often also unspoken in Modern Standard and Colloquial Arabic). Indefinite state can sometimes be counter-intuitive, as in the example above, where a man's name *muḥammad* is tagged as indefinite; however, definiteness is deemed to be determined by the presence of the definite prefix *al*, which is absent from such personal names.

The situation with verbs is somewhat more complicated, as there are two sets of relevant inflectional features. First, there are the subject agreement features: person, gender, and number. But there are also the features of tense, mood, and voice. In feature matrix systems, these are typically treated as three separate features. In the MADA system, there are three 'aspects' ('command', i.e. imperative; 'imperfective', i.e. present tense; 'perfective', i.e. past tense) and three moods (indicative, jussive, subjunctive). Future tense is marked entirely separately by MADA: the future-marking prefix *sa* is handled by the features that indicate the presence of clitics. However, tense and mood do not vary independently. Notably, the past and future tenses do not show mood variation; the indicative/jussive/subjunctive distinction is only found in the present tense. These different moods are indicated by distinct suffixes applied to the present tense base; but the future and imperative are *also* indicated in that same way, by affixes on the present tense base. The future has no mood distinctions, and the imperative has no tense distinctions. We thus determined that a simpler model could be arrived at by merging tense and mood (indicating voice separately). Our verb tags simply contain a single letter that indicates one of six tense-moods, as follows, with examples from the third person masculine singular paradigm of *kataba*, 'he wrote':

- P – past tense (*kataba*)
- I – indicative present tense (*yaktubu*)
- F – future tense (*sayaktubu*)
- J – jussive (*yaktub*)
- S – subjunctive (*yaktuba*)
- C – imperative (C for 'command') (*uktub* (2nd person)).

The traditional treatment of these six verbal forms via multiple features appears to be driven by morphological considerations; for instance, it seems that the *kataba/yaktubu* (past/present) distinction is treated differently from the *yaktubu/sayaktubu* (present/future) distinction because the morphological phenomena that mark the difference are formally distinct. However, part of the purpose of a POS tagset is to abstract away from form to considerations of category.

As well as the inflectional features, verbs also have an important subcategory division between main verbs and auxiliary verbs. Auxiliary verbs are traditionally called 'sisters of *kāna*' after the prototypical auxiliary verb, also a copula and translated 'be'. Like the English primary auxiliaries *do*, *be*, and *have*, the sisters of *kāna* can be main verbs in their own right, but when followed by a main finite verb they function as auxiliaries, creating complex tense-aspect constructions. We consider this distinction an important one to facilitate grammatical research. However, it is not present in BAMA or MADA (nor in SALMA, nor the Khoja et al. tagset), probably because it corresponds to no morphological distinction. We therefore added a very simple rule to distinguish auxiliary from main verbs. Any verb token whose lemma is on a list of eight possibly auxiliary verbs is given the base tag VX (as opposed to VV for main verb). In addition, any verb token whose lemma is on a separate list of three verbs which are only auxiliary when they follow a negative word or proclitic are tagged VX if that condition is fulfilled. Subsequently, once a full sentence is tagged, any token tagged VX is converted *back* to VV if there is no main verb in the following context (that is, between the auxiliary verb and the next punctuation mark, subordinating conjunction, or sentence break). While far from foolproof, this simple procedure captures a majority of cases.

As with nouns, the inflection features are joined to the rest of the tag with a colon. Some overall examples of POS tags for verbs are as follows:

- VVAS:3FS – active main verb, subjunctive, third person feminine singular (*taktuba*)
- VVAP:1MP – active main verb, past tense, first person plural (*katabnā*)
- VXAJ:3MS – active auxiliary verb, future tense, third person masculine singular (*sayakūnu*, 'he will be').

One feature of the MADA output that the POS tags reflect is that inflections where gender is neutralised (e.g. the first person) are labelled masculine; this is illustrated by the second of the example tags above. The POS tags for verbs do not include any indication of object person, number, or gender, since these are indicated via clitic pronouns, rather than by direct inflection of the verb (the same clitic pronouns appear as possessive clitics on nouns and on prepositions). We discuss our strategy for dealing with clitics in the following section. Independent pronouns, on the other hand, are fairly straightforward; they have nominal inflections added to a category/subcategory tag, as in the following examples:

- PP1:MPNI – indefinite nominative plural first person personal pronoun (*naḥnu*, 'we')
- PD:FSXI – indefinite unknown case singular feminine demonstrative pronoun (*hāḏihi*, 'this')
- PR:MPXI – indefinite unknown case plural masculine relative pronoun (*allaḏīna*, 'who').

Pronouns are never marked by the definite prefix *al* and so are never definite, according to the definitions in use here. As with proper nouns, this is to a degree counter-intuitive, especially with personal and demonstrative pronouns. Some relative pronouns, including *allaḏīna* in the third example above, do in fact begin with *al*. Ryding (2005: 322) describes these as 'definite relative pronouns', and notes that they 'have a component that resembles the definite article'. However, in the Buckwalter analysis, pronouns such as *allaḏīna* are considered to be monomorphemic and in consequence MADA does not analyse them as definite.

5.2 Other attributes drawn from the MADA output

The POS tagset described above does not exhaust the information present in the MADA output, which – as outlined above – also includes the wordform with vowel diacritics added, the lemma, the Buckwalter analysis, and a translation. We determined to make all this information available in an accessible way as well. Because we targeted the CQPweb platform, we were able to make use of the CWB data model (Evert and Hardie 2011). This allows multiple layers of word-level annotation, or *attributes*, to be applied to a single token sequence by representing each layer as a separate column in the input file. We could, in fact, have mapped the MADA feature matrix directly to a large set of CWB attributes. But to have a system with *many* attributes or features where each feature contains just one piece of information is counter to the way in which most corpus linguists have been trained to work, so we designed the tagset with such users in mind, as outlined above. However, for each of the vowelised wordform, the lemma, the Buckwalter analysis, and the translation, adding a separate attribute column seemed the best way to make this additional information available; the virtue of CWB and CQPweb is that these further attributes are invisible unless specifically requested. The vowelised wordform, lemma, and raw wordform are all recoded from Buckwalter encoding into Arabic script by the conversion procedure.

We also added three more attributes that are not directly present in the MADA output. First, there is a simple POS. The POS tagset described above is very fine-grained, although many theoretically possible combinations of features do not in practice occur: one 5 million word corpus we tagged has 717 different tags, of which 585 occur more than twice (the rest may possibly indicate BAMA or MADA errors; we have yet to investigate this). It is possible to work at a higher level of abstraction by referring to the first letter of each tag only: N, V, P, T, and so on. However, to make this yet easier, and also to assist cross-linguistic comparison, we added a further POS tag to each word that indicates only major word-class, using the tagset designed for the XML edition of the BNC by Oxford University Computing Services.[5] The categories of this 'simple POS' are ADJ, ADV, ART, CONJ, INTERJ, PREP, PRON, STOP, SUBST, UNC, and VERB. Some of these are not useful for Arabic (e.g. ART, 'article') and some Arabic categories require minor shoehorning to fit in this schema (e.g. particles are folded into the ADV class). However, used carefully, this simplified tagset offers the user additional analytic possibilities.

Second, we add the trilateral root of the word's lemma (so, for instance, for the token *al-kutub*, 'the books' the lemma is *kitāb* but the root is *ktb*). While not present in the MADA output, roots *are* contained in the BAMA lexicon, where lemmata are listed under their roots. We automatically reversed the BAMA lexicon to create a lexicon which maps lemmata to roots, and added a procedure to our program which looks up each lemma and adds its root as a new attribute.

Third, we add an attribute listing the clitics present on the token. MADA uses a set of five features to note the presence of clitics, including some morphemes (definite *al*, future *sa*) which we consider prefixes rather than proclitics, and which are, therefore, covered by the main POS tagset. The clitics *not* so covered, such as proclitic prepositions and conjunctions and enclitic object/possessive pronouns, could in theory have been split apart from the tokens they appear with and given their own, separate tags. This is the usual course for clitics in English (*'ve*, *'ll*, *n't*, etc.), and the MADA distribution includes a program called TOKAN which performs exactly this kind of retokenisation. However, we did not adopt this course, because discussion with our prospective end users made it clear that this would run contrary to the expectations of Arabic-speaking linguists and make the final annotated corpora harder to use. Instead, we combined all the MADA clitic flags into a single field, separating them with pipe symbols < | > to allow easy access using certain CQP-syntax operators.

6. Future work

The system of accessible annotation for Arabic outlined here is now part of the infrastructure of the UCREL research centre at Lancaster University and is in use by researchers at UCREL and collaborating scholars. To support users, we have developed a simple manual of the tagset and other fields within our CQPweb-indexed Arabic corpora, which also explains how these fields can be accessed via the query syntax, mostly by means of presenting example queries (see 'Supplementary material' below). In future work, we hope to expand this guidance documentation, for instance by providing video walkthroughs.

We have already applied the annotation pipeline to the Leeds Corpus of Contemporary Arabic (Al-Sulaiti and Atwell 2006), one of the major openly available corpora of Arabic; this is available to all users of our CQPweb server. Other corpora, under more restrictive licences, are not so widely available. Two further future directions are (1) to make available more general-purpose Arabic corpora in annotated form; and (2) to make it possible for CQPweb users to run their own corpora through the annotation pipeline, thus making not only the annotation output but the software itself widely accessible.

One final obvious direction of future work is to evaluate the accuracy of the output of our system. The performance of MADA has, of course, been reported in the literature (between 86 per cent and 96 per cent depending on which morphological features are included in the evaluation: Habash et al. 2009: 104). However, it remains to be seen to what extent the accuracy rate is affected by the mappings we perform. In principle we would expect the accuracy to remain within the range reported for MADA, but this has yet to be confirmed. A full assessment of the nature of the errors that occur most frequently would also, we anticipate, be useful to end users.

Although, as shown here, there is further work that could be done on the annotation, we are now able to begin work on the (especially: grammatical) investigations that the accessible Arabic annotation facilitates.

Supplementary material

A full account of the annotations described in this chapter is available online at <http://www.lancs.ac.uk/staff/hardiea/arabic-supplementary.html> (last accessed 17 May 2018).

Notes

1. See <http://ucrel.lancs.ac.uk/claws6tags.html> (last accessed 17 May 2018).
2. See <http://www.qamus.org/morphology.htm> (last accessed 17 May 2018).

3. For example, the Latin gerundive is case-marked, since it is a nominalised (actually adjectivised) verb form, but being gerundive is a form of modal marking.
4. Two versions of this manual are available. All quotations here are from the 2012 version (Habash et al. 2012), not the original 2010 version.
5. See this section of the BNC User Reference Guide: <http://www.natcorp.ox.ac.uk/docs/URG/codes.html#klettpos> (last accessed 17 May 2018).

References

Abdul-Mageed, M., M. Diab and S. Kübler (2013), 'ASMA: A system for automatic segmentation and morpho-syntactic disambiguation of Modern Standard Arabic', in G. Angelova, K. Bontcheva and R. Mitkov (eds), *Proceedings of the International Conference Recent Advances in Natural Language Processing RANLP 2013*, Shoumen, Bulgaria: INCOMA, pp. 1–8.

Abu-Chacra, F. (2007), *Arabic: An Essential Grammar*, London: Routledge.

Ali, N. (1988), *Computers and the Arabic Language*, Cairo: Al-Khat Publishing Press, Ta'reep.

Alqrainy, S. (2008), *A Morphological-Syntactical Analysis Approach for Arabic Textual Tagging*, Leicester: De Montfort University.

Al-Sulaiti, L. and E. Atwell (2006), 'The design of a corpus of Contemporary Arabic', *International Journal of Corpus Linguistics*, 11(1): 135–71.

Beesley, K. R. (1996), 'Arabic finite-state morphological analysis and generation', in *Proceedings of the 16th Conference on Computational Linguistics, Volume 1*, Stroudsburg, PA: Association for Computational Linguistics, pp. 89–94.

Beesley, K. R. (1998), 'Arabic morphology using only finite state operations', in M. Rosner (ed.), *Proceedings of the Workshop on Computational Approaches to Semitic Languages*, Montreal: Association for Computational Linguistics, pp. 50–7.

Buckwalter, T. (2004), *Buckwalter Arabic Morphological Analyzer Version 2.0*, LDC catalog no.: LDC2004L02, Philadelphia: University of Pennsylvania, Linguistic Data Consortium.

DeRose, S. J. (1988), 'Grammatical category disambiguation by statistical optimization', *Computational Linguistics*, 14(1): 31–9.

Diab, M. (2007), 'Towards an optimal POS tag set for Modern Standard Arabic processing', in G. Angelova, K. Bontcheva, R. Mitkov, N. Nicolov and N. Nikolov (eds), *Proceedings of Recent Advances in Natural Language Processing* (RANLP), pp. 157–61.

Dukes, K., E. Atwell and N. Habash (2013), 'Supervised collaboration for syntactic annotation of Quranic Arabic', *Language Resources and Evaluation*, 47(1): 33–62.

Evert, S. and A. Hardie (2011), 'Twenty-first century Corpus Workbench: Updating a query architecture for the new millennium', in *Proceedings of the Corpus Linguistics 2011 Conference*, Birmingham: University of Birmingham, <http://www.birmingham.ac.uk/documents/college-artslaw/corpus/conference-archives/2011/Paper-153.pdf> (last accessed 29 June 2018).

Habash, N., O. Rambow and R. Roth (2009), 'MADA+TOKAN: A toolkit for Arabic tokenization, diacritization, morphological disambiguation, POS tagging, stemming and lemmatization', in *Proceedings of the 2nd International Conference on Arabic Language Resources and Tools (MEDAR)*, pp. 102–9, <http://www.elda.org/medar-conference/pdf/24.pdf> (last accessed 17 May 2018).

Habash, N., O. Rambow and R. Roth (2012), *MADA+TOKAN Manual*, Center for Computational Learning Systems technical report #CCLS-12-01, New York: Columbia University.

Habash, N. and R. Roth (2009), 'CATiB: The Columbia Arabic Treebank', in *Proceedings of the ACL-IJCNLP 2009 Conference Short Papers*, Suntec, Singapore, pp. 221–4.

Hajič, J., O. Smrž, P. Zemánek, J. Šnaidauf and E. Beška (2004), 'Prague Arabic Dependency Treebank: Development in data and tools', in *Proceedings of the NEMLAR International Conference on Arabic Language Resources and Tools*, Cairo, Egypt.

Hardie, A. (2012), 'CQPweb – combining power, flexibility and usability in a corpus analysis tool', *International Journal of Corpus Linguistics*, 17(3): 380–409.

Khoja, S. (2001), 'APT: Arabic Part-of-Speech Tagger', in *Proceedings of the Student Workshop at the Second Meeting of the North American Chapter of the Association for Computational Linguistics (NAACL2001)*, Pittsburgh, PA: Carnegie Mellon University, pp. 20–5.

Khoja, S. (2003), 'APT: An Automatic Arabic Part-of-Speech Tagger', unpublished PhD thesis, Lancaster University.

Khoja, S., R. Garside and G. Knowles (2003), 'A tagset for the morphosyntactic tagging of Arabic', in A. Wilson, P. Rayson and T. McEnery (eds), *A Rainbow of Corpora: Corpus Linguistics and the Languages of the World*, Munich: Lincom, pp. 59–72.

Koskenniemi, K. (1983), *Two-Level Morphology: A General Computational Model for Word-Form Recognition and Production*, Helsinki: University of Helsinki.

Kübler, S. and E. Mohamed (2012), 'Part of speech tagging for Arabic', *Natural Language Engineering*, 18(4): 521–48.

Maamouri, M., A. Bies, T. Buckwalter and W. Mekki (2004), 'The Penn Arabic Treebank: Building a large-scale annotated Arabic corpus', in *Proceedings of the NEMLAR International Conference on Arabic Language Resources and Tools*, Cairo, Egypt, pp. 466–7.

Marton, Y., N. Habash and O. Rambow (2013), 'Dependency parsing of Modern Standard Arabic with lexical and inflectional features', *Computational Linguistics*, 39(1): 161–94.

Ryding, K. C. (2005), *A Reference Grammar of Modern Standard Arabic*, Cambridge: Cambridge University Press.

Sampson, G. (1995), *English for the Computer: The SUSANNE Corpus and Analytic Scheme*, Oxford: Clarendon Press.

Sawalha, M. and E. Atwell (2009), 'Linguistically informed and corpus informed morphological analysis of Arabic', in *Proceedings of the 5th International Corpus Linguistics Conference CL2009*, Liverpool, <https://www.birmingham.ac.uk/Documents/college-artslaw/corpus/conference-archives/2005-journal/Compilingacorpus/CLPaper.doc> (last accessed 29 June 2018).

Sawalha, M. and E. Atwell (2010), 'Fine-grain morphological analyzer and part-of-speech tagger for Arabic text', in N. Calzolari, K. Chooukri, B. Maegaard, J. Mariani, J. Oodijk, S. Piperidis, M. Rosner and D. Tapias (eds), *Proceedings of the Language Resource and Evaluation Conference LREC 2010*, Valleta, Malta, pp. 1258–65.

Sawalha, M. and E. Atwell (2013), 'A standard tag set expounding traditional morphological features for Arabic language part-of-speech tagging', *Word Structure*, 6(1): 43–99.

Sawalha, M., E. Atwell and M. A. M. Abushariah (2013), 'SALMA: Standard Arabic Language Morphological Analysis', in *Proceedings ICCSPA International Conference on Communications, Signal Processing, and Their Applications*, pp. 1–6.

Smrž, O. and J. Hajič (2006), *The Other Arabic Treebank: Prague Dependencies and Functions*, *Arabic Computational Linguistics: Current Implementations*, Stanford, CA: CSLI Publications.

5

The Leeds Arabic Discourse Treebank: Guidelines for Annotating Discourse Connectives and Relations

Amal Alsaif and Katja Markert

1. Introduction

In the last two decades, advanced discourse studies have tended to use annotated corpora to obtain a complete empirical view of contemporary usage of the language. In addition, these corpora have been used as a basis for the automatic discovery of discourse relations, especially for English. However, discourse annotation remains an attractive but challenging field for the natural language processing (NLP) community when it comes to widely used languages other than English. One such language is Arabic.

Arabic remains a challenging language in many respects for linguistic and computational linguistic studies. Arabic has a complex morphology, many local dialects, and free word order. It allows the construction of a full clause or sentence using only one token.

Existing Arabic corpora include collections of unannotated written texts and/or spoken scripts, such as the Arabic Gigaword (Parker et al. 2011) or the King Saud University Corpus of Classical Arabic (KSUCCA);[1] corpora with syntactic and/or morphological annotation, such as the Arabic Treebank (Maamouri et al. 2004); and resources for lexical and semantic relationships (Arabic WordNet). However, none of these include annotation of the discourse features of discourse units.

We present the first empirical attempt to annotate Arabic text with discourse features, namely the Leeds Arabic Discourse Treebank (LADTB). This corpus contains annotations for all of the explicit discourse connectives in the Penn Arabic Treebank Part 1 (Maamouri et al. 2004), their arguments, and the discourse relations they convey.

We base our annotation guidelines for the LADTB on the same principles as the (English) Penn Discourse Treebank but adapt and expand the annotation to take into account properties specific to Arabic. Using similar principles for annotation allows us to advance comparative studies and thus our understanding of the two languages. *Discourse relations* are semantic relations, such as causality, contrast, and temporality, which connect two textual units, typically clauses or sentences. The textual units connected should express *abstract objects*, such as events, actions, facts, or beliefs, and are called *arguments* of the discourse relation. There are two types of discourse relations: (1) relations that are signalled explicitly via so-called *discourse connectives*, such as coordinating or subordinating conjunctions or discourse adverbials (explicit relations); and (2) relations that can be inferred from the context without any explicit signalling (implicit relations). Both are illustrated in the example below.

(1)
(a) John didn't go to the party$_{cl1}$ **because** he was tired$_{cl2}$. **Instead**, he went to bed$_{cl3}$.
(b) John didn't go to the party. He was tired.

In (1a) the connective *because* in the second clause establishes explicitly that the reason for John being absent from the party is that he was tired: a causal relationship. The connective *instead* in the third clause contrasts going to bed with going to the party: a contrast relation. The connective *because* therefore takes clause 1 and clause 2 as its arguments, whereas *instead* takes the non-adjacent units clause 1 and clause 3 as its arguments. In (1b) the second sentence gives a potential reason for the event in the first sentence: there is a causal relationship between the two arguments. This relation is inferred from the context with no explicit connectives.

Discourse relations are widely studied in theoretical linguistics, where a number of different relational taxonomies have been developed. As a result of these, different inventories have been used in annotating English corpora for discourse relations. These schemas also differ in other respects, such as whether they prescribe a tree, a graph, or a flat structure for discourse annotation (Carlson et al. 2002; Wolf and Gibson 2005; Halliday and Hasan 1976).

Discourse connectives are likewise intensively studied in theoretical linguistics, and have a wide range of applications in computational linguistics. For example, in automatic text generation, it is necessary to use the right connectives in the right places in the generated text. Moreover, in text summarisation, text segments offering mainly elaboration of related text segments – often identifiable via the presence of discourse connectives – might be ignored. In machine translation, discourse connectives need to be translated correctly to ensure coherence of translated text. Similarly to our work on the LADTB for Arabic, interest in discourse relations has recently spread from English into other languages, such as Turkish, Hindi, and Chinese; for each of these languages, corpora have been annotated with that language's own inventory of discourse relations and connectives (see section 2 for an in-depth discussion).

But despite the LADTB project, discourse processing remains a challenging field for the Arabic NLP community due to a lack of resources, such as annotated corpora and tools, and a lack of reliable algorithms for Arabic tagging and parsing.

The remainder of the chapter is structured as follows. Section 2 reviews relevant recent work on discourse guidelines and annotating discourse corpora. Section 3 presents a brief summary of the syntactically annotated corpus on which we base our discourse annotation to build the LADTB. We discuss in section 4 the basic annotation principles for discourse connectives in Arabic, and illustrate also the potential discourse connectives and how we collected them. Section 5 outlines some special cases that arise when annotating discourse connectives for Arabic. Our discourse relation inventory and the techniques we used to assist annotators in disambiguating discourse connectives in context are discussed in section 6. Section 7 presents an annotation tool, READ, that we developed for the purpose of annotating Arabic discourse connectives. Then, we summarise the properties of our final gold standard LADTB version 1 in section 8. Finally, we conclude with a summary of our contribution and an outlook on future work.

Examples in this chapter are presented according to the following conventions: (1) explicit (but not implicit) discourse connectives are bold-faced and underlined; (2) the text span which is introduced by the discourse connective and expresses an abstract object (Arg2) is marked in bold; and (3) the text span which expresses the other abstract object (Argl) is marked in italics, for English translations only. Note that, for Arabic examples, the discourse connectives and their arguments are marked in the main Arabic and English text, but not in the Arabic transliteration or the morpheme-by-morpheme glosses. The discourse relation that applies in an example is specified in parentheses after the example number. The exact inventory of relations is described in section 6.

2. Related work

Our guidelines for Arabic discourse annotation follow principles similar to the ones used to annotate explicit discourse connectives in the Penn Discourse Treebank project (PDTB, Prasad et al. 2008a). The latest version of the Penn Discourse Treebank, PDTB2, contains annotations of a wide variety of discourse relations and their arguments on the 1 million words in the Penn Treebank. The PDTB annotation principles for discourse relations are almost theory-neutral, with clear predefined relations that link adjacent and non-adjacent arguments. Thus, unlike other theories of discourse structure, such as the RST (Carlson et al. 2002) and graph theories (Wolf and Gibson 2005), the PDTB allows crossing dependencies, and grants annotators the flexibility to assign more than one relation between arguments.

The relation inventory is a hierarchical taxonomy of coarse-grained and fine-grained relations and contains mostly informational discourse relations, with a few pragmatic relations.

Annotated discourse relations are seen as predicate-argument relations whose predicates are mainly from explicit/implicit discourse connectives, and whose arguments are textual units expressing abstract objects (AOs), such as events, facts, opinions, and propositions.

Discourse relations in the PDTB may be signalled explicitly by discourse connectives, such as subordinating or coordinating conjunctions or discourse adverbials. Implicit relations are also annotated, but only between adjacent text spans. In the latter case, the implicit inferable relations are annotated by inserting a so-called *implicit connective* that best expresses the inferred relation.

In (2), an example from the PDTB, the subordinating conjunction *since* is an explicit connective indicating a temporal relation between the event of the earthquake hitting and a state where no music is played by a certain woman.

(2) (TEMPORAL.Asynchronous)
She hasn't played any music since **the earthquake hit**. (WSJ text 0766)

An example of a relation inferred due to adjacency is given in (3), where the Causal relation between the AOs denoted by the two adjacent sentences is annotated with *because* as the implicit connective.

(3) (CONDITION.Cause)
Also unlike Mr. Ruder, Mr. Breeden appears to be in a position to get somewhere with his agenda. Implicit = BECAUSE (CAUSE) **As a former White House aide** [. . .], **he is savvy in the ways of Washington**. (WSJ text 0955)

In addition, annotators are allowed to annotate relations signalled by expressions not defined as discourse connectives, such as *Alternative Lexicalization* relations which use non-connective lexical expressions to link adjacent sentences, Entity relations, and Attribution. The PDTB is used in developing algorithms for discourse parsing and automatic identification of discourse relations (Webber et al. 2011).

Good inter-annotator agreement was reported when annotating discourse relations for English in the PDTB2 (Prasad et al. 2008a) and for other languages in comparable projects including the METU Turkish Discourse Bank (Zeyrek and Webber 2008), the Hindi Discourse Relation Bank (Prasad et al. 2008b), and the Chinese Treebank (Xue 2005), all of which were annotated using similar annotation principles to the PDTB. In the LADTB, we annotate explicit discourse relations in Arabic, following similar annotation principles to the PDTB, after applying all required Arabic-specific adaptations. Using similar guidelines for annotating discourse relations will open the door to shared use of resources in discourse linguistics and computational linguistics studies.

3. The Penn Arabic Treebank

The LADTB extends the Penn Arabic Treebank (ATB) Part 1 v.1 (Maamouri et al. 2004) with discourse relation information. The Penn ATB Part 1 was released in January 2003 and consists of 734 files with roughly 166,000 words of written Modern Standard Arabic newswire text from Agence France Presse (AFP), with an English translation of some files. Each sentence is manually tagged and syntactically parsed. The part-of-speech (POS) tags are based on Tim Buckwalter's morphological analysis (Maamouri et al. 2004; Maamouri and Bies 2004) as used in the BAMA system.

The Penn ATB has been used in different studies and applications in Arabic NLP, such as tokenisation, diacritisation, POS tagging, morphological disambiguation, phrase chunking, and semantic role labelling (Habash and Rambow 2004; Habash and

Roth 2009; Dukes and Buckwalter 2010; Sadat and Habash 2006; Chiang et al. 2006). In addition to the general benefits of using a standard resource, we use the Penn ATB because tagging can make discourse connectives easier to identify, as they often belong to specific parts of speech such as conjunctions. Moreover, the parse trees provide informative features for the automatic identification of discourse connectives, relations, and argument boundaries (Alsaif 2012; Lin et al. 2012).

4. Basic annotation principles for discourse connectives in Arabic

There was no existing large-scale list of discourse connectives in the Arabic literature. We therefore used different strategies to collect potential discourse connectives. First, we collected as many as possible from existing Arabic textbooks and grammars (e.g. Ryding 2005; Alansari 1985; Alfarabi 1990). Second, we manually analysed fifty Arabic texts from the Penn ATB to identify further connectives. Third, we undertook automatic collection from the Penn ATB by searching for the POS tags of the potential discourse connectives in our list, and verifying the output in context.

We used a similar definition of discourse connectives to that used in the PDTB (Prasad et al. 2008a) in order to distinguish discourse use and non-discourse use of potential discourse connectives in context. For example, one potential discourse connective, the conjunction *wa*, 'and' is not a discourse connective in *āḥmad wa sārā ḏahabā llḥadīqah*, 'Ahmad and Sara went to the park'. Discourse connectives in context are any 'lexical expressions that relate two text segments [arguments] expressing abstract objects such as events, beliefs, facts or propositions' (Asher 1993). A connective should indicate one or more discourse relations, such as Elaboration, Exemplification, Contrast, Temporal, Exception, Causal, or simply Conjunction.

The collection process ended with a list of 107 discourse connectives overall. The complete list of discourse connectives is given in Appendix A.

The discourse connectives come from different syntactic categories and can be simple (*lākin*, 'but') or paired (*āḏā . . . fa . . .*, 'if . . . then . . .'). Our collection also includes so-called *modified* forms of discourse connectives. These are forms extended from another connective, such as English *even though* as a modified form of the connective *though*. An Arabic example is *biālruġum min*, 'although' as a modified form of *ruġma*, 'despite'. As in the PDTB, we annotate multiple connectives that occur adjacent to one another, such as *wa*, 'and' and *lākin*, 'but', separately as two independent connectives, although they might share one or two arguments.

However, we agree with Prasad et al. (2010) that discourse connectives are not a closed set and that the category can be expanded to cover all expressions used to link discourse arguments. Thus the syntactic categories of discourse connectives in Arabic go beyond the predominant syntactic categories of English connectives (conjunctions, subordinators, adverbial and prepositional phrases) to include nouns: (1) simple nouns such as *buġyah*, 'desire' and *natīyğata*, 'result', or (2) combined nouns with a preposition such as *faḍlān*, 'as well as'. In addition, discourse connectives in Arabic can be clitics as they are often attached to other words. The clitics can be attached to pronouns such as *lākin*, 'but' in *lākinhu*, 'but-he'; to verbs such as *fa*, 'then' in *faqāla*, 'then-said'; or to nouns such as *li*, 'for' in *lilḥadi*, 'for-limiting'. The clitic connectives have different syntactic categories, which determines what words they can be attached to. There are no end-of-sentence connectives in Arabic, in contrast to English.

Arguments can be simple clauses or sentences, sequences of sentences, or nominalisations (*al-maṣdar* nouns, see section 5). Both arguments must express AOs and be related explicitly via a connective (note that *implicit* connectives and discourse relations are *not* annotated in the LADTB). If this is not the case, we do not annotate the potential connectives as discourse connectives in context. The arguments might be adjacent or non-adjacent, with no restrictions on position or order. The only restriction is that Arg2 is always the argument that is introduced by the connective. We also apply in our annotation scheme the so-called minimality principle introduced by Prasad et al. (2008a), in that only the stretch of text representing the AO is considered as a valid argument. However, the argument should also include any necessary complements to the AO, such as temporal adverbs.

Our analysis of the potential discourse connectives shows that the order of the connective DC and its arguments Arg1 and Arg2 might occur in the text following one of these canonical forms:

<Arg1. DC+Arg2>
<Arg1, DC+Arg2>
<Arg1+DC+Arg2>
<DC+Arg2, Arg1>
<DC+Arg2+Arg1>
<Arg1+DC+Arg2+Arg1>
<DCP1+Arg2+DCP2+ Arg1>
<DCP1+Arg2, DCP2 +Arg1>

For example, the connective *ba'da*, 'after' in (4) follows the order <DC+Arg2, Arg1>. In the table, DCP1 and DCP2 are the first and second parts of the connective if it is a paired connective such as *āḏā . . . faāna . . .*, 'if . . . then . . .'. The second argument Arg2 is syntactically introduced by the connective DC or DCP1, while the first argument Arg1 can occur prior to (often) or after (rarely) the second argument Arg2 in the text. In addition, it is not essential to have punctuation as clause-separators to determine the argument boundaries, especially as sentence-internal punctuation in MSA can be infrequent.

(4) (TEMPORAL.Asynchronous and CONTINGENCY.Cause.Reason) the canonical form <DC+Arg2, Arg1>:

بعد رحيلي عن القرية، لم اشعر بالسعادة مجدداً

ba'da raḥīlī 'an al+qaryah, lam aš'ur bi+al+sa'ādah muğadadan
After myleaving from DEF+village, i-were-not feel on+DEF+happiness again
'**After I left my home village**, *I never was happy again*'

In this version of our guidelines, we focused on relations explicitly signalled via discourse connectives. We collected the discourse relations during text analysis of the potential discourse connectives. Our definition of discourse relations can be mapped to the discourse relation hierarchy used in the PDTB (Prasad et al. 2008a) with a few adaptations. Section 6 presents our formalisation of Arabic discourse relations and the adaptations we applied to the discourse relation hierarchy.

5. Adaptations for specific discourse connectives and argument types

5.1 The Connective *wa*, 'and'

The conjunction *wa*, 'and' is the most frequent potential connective in Arabic texts. It is a very flexible conjunction, used in Arabic to join nouns, numbers, adjectives, prepositional phrases, clauses, sentences, paragraphs, and other connectives. It can also signal any discourse relation. Thus, unsurprisingly, the connective *wa* is the most ambiguous of all connectives, presenting the most difficulty when it comes to determining discourse function or discourse relations.

The annotators on the LADTB project were encouraged to pay more attention when dealing with the connective *wa*, 'and', in order to distinguish discourse and non-discourse connective instances and to identify its arguments correctly. One particular case stands out: *wa* is used to introduce almost every paragraph and sentence in newswire text (of which our corpus consists) in order to produce a coherent report. In many such cases, no explicit connective would be used in English. In the case of such *beginning of a paragraph* (BOP) occurrences, all prior propositions in the text could in principle be valid arguments to be linked with the argument introduced by the connective *wa*. Therefore, it was decided that instances of *wa* at BOP should be seen as relating to the closest proposition and a Conjunction relation was assigned, unless clearer discourse relations were explicitly indicated.

5.2 The connective *ḥayṯu*, 'where, since, when'

The potential connective ***ḥayṯu***, 'where, since, when' is often used to refer to a place or time in prior text, as in (5). In these cases, it is a relative pronoun without discourse function. However, it sometimes has a discourse function, relating two AOs as in (6), where it relates the change and how this change happened. A special case study was designed with several examples of ***ḥayṯu***, 'where, since, when' as discourse connective and others showing it as non-discourse connective in context.

(5) (no discourse relation)

كان محتشمي شغل في الثمانينات منصب سفير ايران في دمشق **حيث** اصيب بجروح خطيرة في انفجار استهدفه عام 1982

kāna	muḥtašimī	šaġala	fī	al+ṯamānīnāt	manṣib	safīr
was	Mohteshmi	held	in	DEF+eighties	position	ambassador

āyrān fī dimašq ḥayṯu āuṣība bi-ğurūḥ ḫaṭīrah
Iran in Damascus **where** injured wounded serious

fī āinfiğār astahdafa+hu ʿām 1982
in explosion his+attack year 1982
'Mohteshmi held the position as Iran's ambassador in Damascus in the eighties, **where** he was seriously wounded in a bomb attack in 1982'

(6) (EXPANSION.Reformulation)
طرأ تعديل على نادي اللاعبات **حيث ارتقت الاسبانية ارانشا مرتبة واحدة و تبادلت المركزين التاسع و العاشر مع الالمانية انكه**

ṭrāʾ taʿdīl ʿalā nādī al+lāʿbāt **ḥayṯu** irtaqat al+āsbāniyah
occur change on club DEF+players **where** raised DEF+Spanish

ārānšā martabah wāḥidah wa tabādalat al+markazayn āl+tāsʿ wa
Arancha position one and exchange DEF+positions DEF+ninth and

al+ʿāšr maʿ al+ālmāniyah ānkah
DEF+tenth with DEF+German Anke
'*There was a change to the club of female players* **where the Spanish Arancha rose one rank and swapped ninth and tenth places with the German Anke**'

5.3 *Al-maṣdar* nouns as arguments

Al-maṣdar is a well-known category of noun that expresses events without tense (Ryding 2005). The closest equivalent term in English is *nominalisation*. However, *al-maṣdar* nouns do not correspond exactly to one grammatical or morphological category in English; they might correspond to a gerund, nominalisation, or non-nominalised noun. Table 5.1 gives some examples of *al-maṣdar* nouns which are translated into different categories in English. The events expressed by *al-maṣdar* nouns are eligible to be arguments of discourse relations, according to our definitions. As a result, because they are often followed by *al-maṣdar* nouns, prepositions are potential discourse connectives in Arabic.

Table 5.1 Examples of *al-maṣdar* nouns, roots, and patterns with English correspondences (Alsaif 2012)

Root	Morph. pattern	*Al-maṣdar* noun	English
سبح/sabaḥa	فعالة/fiʿālah	سباحة/sibāḥah	swimming
عكس/ʿakasa	انفعال/ainfiʿāl	انعكاس/ainʿikās	reflection
جرب/ğaraba	تفعلة/tafʿilah	تجربة/tağribah	experiment
حَرَبَ/ḥaraba	فَعْل/faʿl	حَرْبْ/ḥarb	war
دفع/dafaʿa	فعال/fiʿāl	دفاع/difāʿ	defence

Al-maṣdar nouns are generated, using well-defined morphological patterns (which patterns are, by the tradition of Arabic grammar, always referred to by the form they take in conjunction with the root of the verb *fa ʿala*), from three or four letter-roots. The patterns can attach suffixes to the root and insert consonant or vowel letters or diacritics into the root. More than sixty morphological patterns can be used to generate *al-maṣdar* nouns (Abdl al latif et al. 1997; Ryding 2005; Alansari 1985). Some patterns used with trilateral roots use only diacritics, without addition of any letters. Identifying *al-maṣdar* nouns requires the linguistic ability to check whether a noun after the potential connective fits one of the *al-maṣdar* patterns. Some patterns are listed in Appendix B.

Al-maṣdar nouns can be the full argument either alone or with additional complements. They can be arguments for any connective type. In particular, preposition connectives are always followed by *al-maṣdar* nouns (with the negator intervening if the *al-maṣdar* argument is negated). The *al-maṣdar* argument is therefore usually located at the first or second place in Arg2. It is also possible for both arguments Arg1 and Arg2 to be *al-maṣdar* nouns. In (7), *tablīġ*, 'informing' is the *al-maṣdar* form of *balaġa*, 'inform', which acts as an argument for the preposition connective *li*, 'for'. In (8), *āinʿidām*, 'lack' is the *al-maṣdar* form of *ʿadama*, 'reduce' and the argument of the prepositional phrase connective *bisababi*, 'because of'.

(7) (CONDITION.Cause)

ذهبنا الى مركز الشرطة للتبليغ **عن فقدان وثائق الشركة الرسمية**

ḏahabnā	ālā	markaz	al+šurṭah	**li+tablīġ**	ʿan	fuqdān
gone	to	centre	DEF+police	**for+informing**	about	loss

waṯāʾīq	al+šarikah	al+rasmīyah
documents	DEF+company	DEF+official

'*We went to the police station* in order to **inform about the loss of the company's official documents**'

(8) (CONDITION.Cause)

ان كبسولة الانقاذ لم تتمكن من الالتحام بالغواصة بسبب **انعدام الرؤية**.

ān	kabsūlah	al+ānqāḏ	lam	tatamakn	min	al+āltiḥām	bi+al+ġawaṣah
that	capsule	DEF+rescue	was-NEG	able	from	DEF+attach	by+DEF+submarine

bisabab	ānʿidām	al+rwʾuyah
because+of	lack	DEF+vision

'*The rescue capsule could not be attached to the submarine* because of **the lack of visibility**'

6. Discourse relations in Arabic

In common with the English PDTB and the projects based on other languages, our discourse relation taxonomy has a hierarchical structure for more flexibility and reliability. We share with others (Prasad et al. 2008a, 2008b; Zeyrek and Webber 2008; Xue 2005) the main four classes: TEMPORAL, CONTINGENCY, COMPARISON, and EXPANSION. Each class has a number of fine-grained relation types, some of which have further subtypes for yet more detailed relations. Fine-grained relations are notated with a dot expansion after the coarse-grained type: for example, EXPANSION. Reformulation stands for the fine-grained discourse relation Reformulation which is a subtype of the main class EXPANSION.

From the text analysis that we had previously done to collect Arabic discourse connectives, we realised that most of the discourse relations in the PDTB also exist in Arabic text. After running a pilot annotation, we determined what were the frequently used relations in our news corpus. This led us, for example, to merge some rarely used fine-grained relations that would confuse annotators and lead to low agreement among them.

In particular, we exclude the List relation from our EXPANSION relations inventory, and use a sequence of Conjunction relations instead. In addition, we merge the three fine-grained relations EXPANSION.Reformulation.Specification, EXPANSION.Reformulation.Generalization, and EXPANSION.Reformulation. Equivalence, keeping only the superordinate relation EXPANSION.Reformulation. We also exclude the Pragmatic Contrast relation, as it rarely occurred in the LADTB. The Conjunction relation is assigned if, and only if, there is no other relation indicated by the connective, due to the misleading behaviour of some Conjunctions. The final hierarchy of Arabic discourse relations is shown in Figure 5.1.

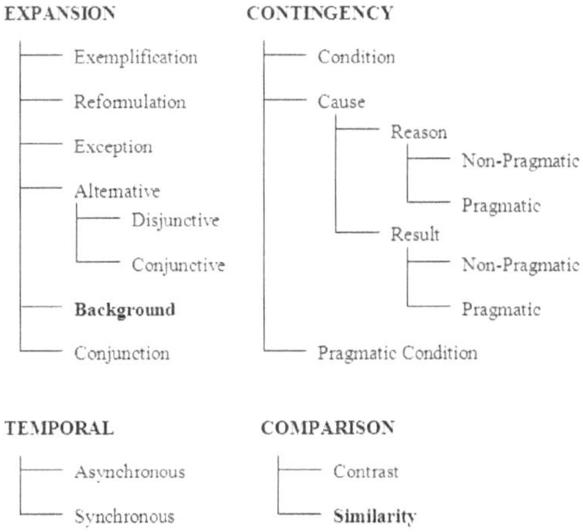

Figure 5.1 The hierarchy of discourse relations for Arabic in the LADTB (Alsaif and Markert 2010). The two relations Background and Similarity have been newly introduced for Arabic (see section 6.1) and are therefore shown in bold

6.1 The introduction of two novel relations

Two new relations, EXPANSION.Background and COMPARISON.Similarity, were introduced during our analysis of discourse connectives in the LADTB.

6.1.1 EXPANSION.Background

The type EXPANSION.Background applies when Arg2 describes a situation related to a prior situation in Arg1 such that Arg2 provides background information in order to give the reader a wider view of the situation in Arg1. For example, Arg2 in (9) presents information about the war in Iraq and how it began. Similarly in (10), Arg2 gives information about the task of the Lebanese delegation. In both examples, the relation is more than simply a combination of TEMPORAL.Asynchronous and CONTINGENCY.Cause.Reason. Rather, Arg2 gives background information for a full understanding of the argument in Arg1.

(9) (EXPANSION.Background)

غادر الرئيس جورج بوش العراق بخيبة أمل من إيجاد حل سياسي للحرب على الإرهاب في العراق. **<u>وقد</u> بدأت الحرب في العراق عام 2005 اثر مزاعم امريكية بنية العراق امتلاك سلاح نووي.**

ġādar	al+raʾīs	ǧūrǧ	būš	al+ʿirāq	bi+ḫaybah	ʾāmal	min
left	DEF+president	George	Bush	DEF+Iraq	in+disappointed	hope	from

ʾāyǧād	ḥal	sīāsī	li+l+ḥarb	ʿalā	al+ʾārhāb	fī
having	solution	political	for+DEF+war	on	terrorism	in

al+ʿirāq.	**wa+qad**	badʾāt	al+ḥarb	fī	Al+ʿirāq	ʿām	2005
DEF+Iraq.	**and+where**	starts	DEF+war	in	DEF+Iraq	year	2005

āṯrʾa	mazāʾim	āmrīkīh	bi+nīt	al+ʾrāq	āmtilāk	silāḥ	nawawī.
after	allegations	American	of+intention	DEF+Iraq	acquiring	weapon	nuclear.

'*President George Bush left Iraq disappointed not to have found a political solution to the war on terrorism in Iraq.* **(<u>and</u>) The war in Iraq began in 2005 after US allegations that Iraq had the intention of acquiring nuclear weapons'**

(10) (EXPANSION.Background)

ان الطائرة التي تقل الوفد اللبناني الرسمي وصلت اليوم الثلاثاء الى طرابلس. **و<u>كان</u> قد اتى الوفد لاصطحاب الرهينة اللبنانية ماري ميشال معربس المحتجزة في الفلبين**

āna	al+ṭaʾyrah	al+tī	tuqil	al+wafd	al+lubnānī
that	DEF+plane	DEF+which	carrying	DEF+delegation	DEF+Lebanese

al+rasmī	waṣalt	al+yawm	al+ṯulāṯāʾ	āilā	ṭarāblus.
DEF+official	arrive	DEF+today	DEF+Tuesday	to	Tripoli.

wa+kāna	qad	ātā	al+wafd	li+āṣṭiḥāb	al+rahīnah
and+was	that	come	DEF+delegation	to+accompany	DEF+hostage

al+lubnānīh	mārī	al+muḥtağazah	fī	al+filibīn
DEF+Lebanese	Marie	DEF+hostage	in	DEF+Philippines

'*The plane, which was carrying the official Lebanese delegation, arrived in Tripoli on Tuesday*. **(<u>and</u>) The delegation came to accompany the Lebanese hostage Marie, who was held in the Philippines**'

6.1.2 COMPARISON.Similarity

The type COMPARISON.Similarity applies when the connective indicates that the two arguments express similar abstract objects. It is therefore a complement to the COMPARISON.Contrast relation. The discourse connective in (11) establishes a similarity relation between how one feels when one misses one's home country (in Arg1) and missing a small child (in Arg2).

(11) (COMPARISON.Similarity)

انك تتألم من فراق الوطن **<u>كما</u> تتألم الأم على فقد رضيعها**

āinaka	tataʾālam	min	firāq	al+waṭan	**kamā**	tataʾālam
you	suffering	from	leaving	DEF+homecountry	**as**	suffering

al+āʾumu	ʿalā	faqdi	raḍīʿi+hā
DEF+mother	on	losing	child+her

'*You are suffering from leaving your home country* <u>**as**</u> **a mother suffers from losing her child**'

We believe that the relation COMPARISON.Similarity exists in English as well via connectives such as 'just as' or 'like' and that its non-inclusion in the PDTB is an oversight.

6.2 A special case: Temporal and causal relations

Causal relations, whether to do with reason or result, imply a temporal sequence of their abstract objects (as a cause must precede its effect in time). Thus, there is normally no need to annotate both temporal and causal relations when annotating primarily causal connectives such as *bisababi*, 'because'. However, connectives that are usually used to indicate the temporal order of AOs, such as *qabla*, 'before', *ba'da*, 'after' and *'aqiba*, 'shortly after', should be dealt with differently if they indicate a causal relation as well in a specific context. In these cases, both relations should be assigned to those instances, as multiple relations. In (12), travelling away from the person's home village is the (implied) reason for never being happy again. The relation here is a combination of TEMPORAL.Asynchronous and CONTINGENCY.Cause. Reason.Non-Pragmatic.

(12) (TEMPORAL.Asynchronous and CONTINGENCY.Cause.Reason. Non-Pragmatic)

<u>بعد</u> رحيلي عن القرية، لم اشعر بالسعادة مجدداً

ba'da raḥīl+ī 'an al+qaryah, lam aš'ur bi+as+sa'ādah muğadadan
After leaving+my from DEF+village, NEG feel on+DEF+happiness again
'**<u>After</u> I left my home village**, *I never was happy again*'

6.3 Techniques for disambiguating discourse connectives

We have developed some techniques to assist annotators in disambiguating discourse connectives in context correctly according to our annotation scheme.

6.3.1 First technique: Connective substitution

The connective substitution technique is used to disambiguate the function of potentially ambiguous discourse connectives. Such connectives are tested for the possibility of substitution with a *less ambiguous* connective indicating a clear relation. If the two connectives indicate the same relation in a given context, then this relation is assigned to the original connective. We designed the ordered list in Table 5.2, to be used in disambiguating some unclear connectives during the annotation process.

We exclude the highly ambiguous relations EXPANSION.Conjunction and EXPANSION.Background from the substitution technique, as they are often signalled by broadly ambiguous connectives such as *wa*, 'and', which might indicate *any* relation in our taxonomy.

6.3.2 Second technique: Decision tree for expansion relations

The most ambiguous instances in the pilot annotation were those of Expansion relations. We designed a sequence of questions in a binary tree structure to help the annotator make a decision between different expansion relations. The flowchart is presented in Figure 5.2. It starts with the easily identifiable relation EXPANSION.Exception and ends with EXPANSION.Conjunction relation as the last alternative.

Table 5.2 A sequence of substitutions for disambiguating discourse connectives in terms of relations

	Substituted connective(s)	Discourse relation
1	في المقابل, *fī al+muqābil*, 'in contrast'	COMPARISON.Contrast
2	لذا, *liḏā*, 'for that'/ نتيجة لذلك, *natyğah liḏalika*, 'as a result'/ بالتالي, bi+tālī, 'consequently/so/thus'	CONTINGENCY. Result. Try also no. 4 if the original connective has a temporal meaning
3	بسبب, *bisababi*, 'because of'/ لأن, *li'āna*, 'because'	CONTINGENCY. Reason
4	بعد, *ba'da*, 'after'/ ثم, *ṯuma*, 'then'	TEMPORAL.Asynchronous
5	خلال, *ḫilāla*, 'during'/ بالتزامن, *bi+ātazāmun*, 'at the same time'	TEMPORAL.Synchronous
6	باستثناء, *bi+'āistiṯnā*, 'except'/ إلا, *āilā*, 'except'	EXPANSION.Exception
7	أو, *āw*, 'or'/ كبديل, *kabadīl*, 'as alternative'	EXPANSION.Alternative
8	على سبيل المثال, *ālā sabīl al+miṯāl*, 'for example'	EXPANSION.Exemplification
9	خصوصا, *ḫuṣuwṣan*, 'specially'/ عموما, *'umuwman*, 'generally'/ بعبارة أخرى, *bi+'ibārah āuḫrā*, 'in other words'	EXPANSION.Reformulation

7. The READ tool: A discourse annotation tool for English and Arabic

The READ tool has been developed in response to the challenges of supporting specific features of Arabic. This is the first tool that can be used to annotate explicit discourse connectives for Arabic and English, by pre-highlighting potential discourse connectives. First, the annotator decides whether each highlighted potential connective is a discourse connective in the particular context at hand; if so, they must mark its arguments and relations. Figure 5.3 shows a screenshot of the tool. The READ tool can also be adapted to work for other languages, as it uses Unicode format. The tool is available online free of charge for non-commercial use.[2]

8. Evaluation

The discourse annotation in the LADTB covers three main tasks:

- **Task 1:** Identification of explicit Arabic discourse connectives in context.
- **Task 2:** Disambiguation of discourse connectives by annotating the discourse relations they convey.
- **Task 3:** Annotation of the two arguments linked by each particular connective.

The manual annotation was conducted by two well-trained Arabic native speakers, with a good linguistic background, on 537 news files from the Penn Arabic Treebank

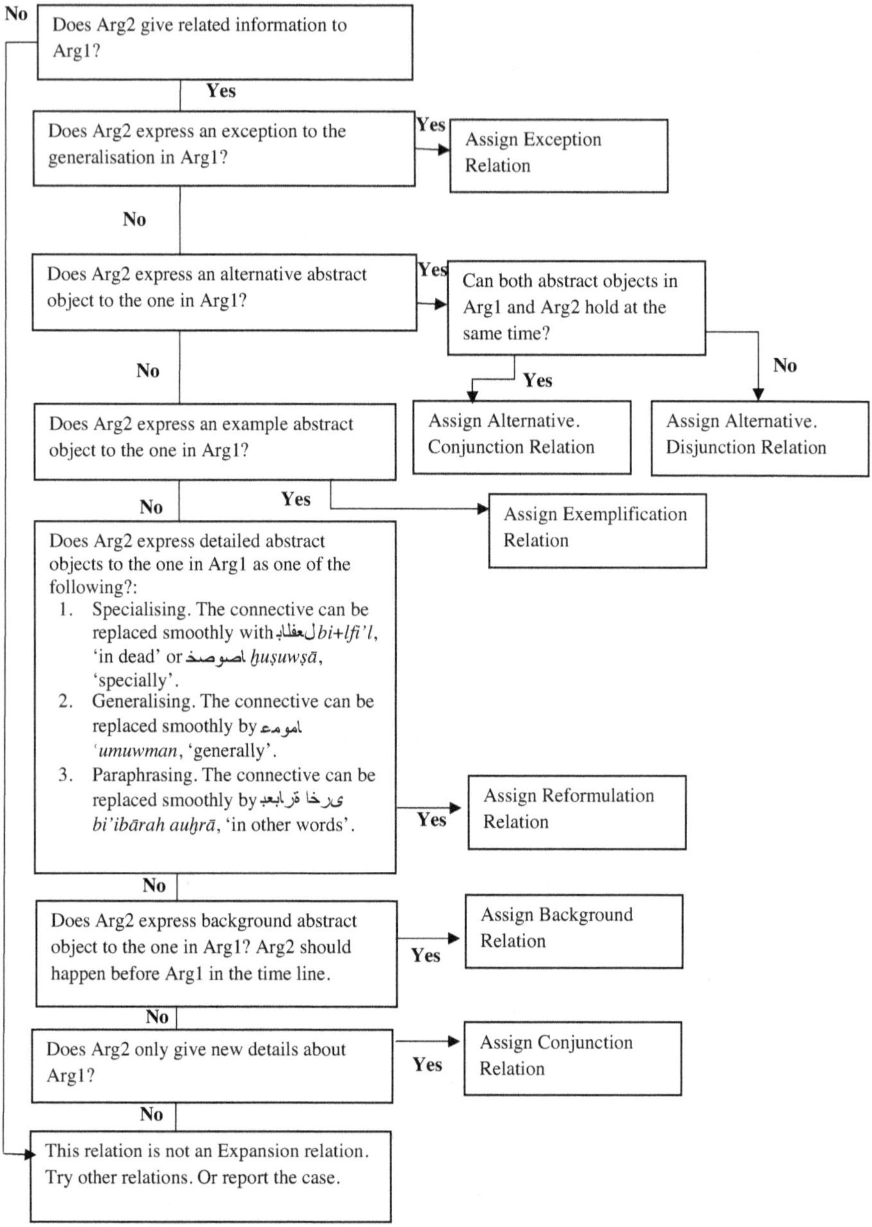

Figure 5.2 A decision flowchart for different expansion relations in Arabic

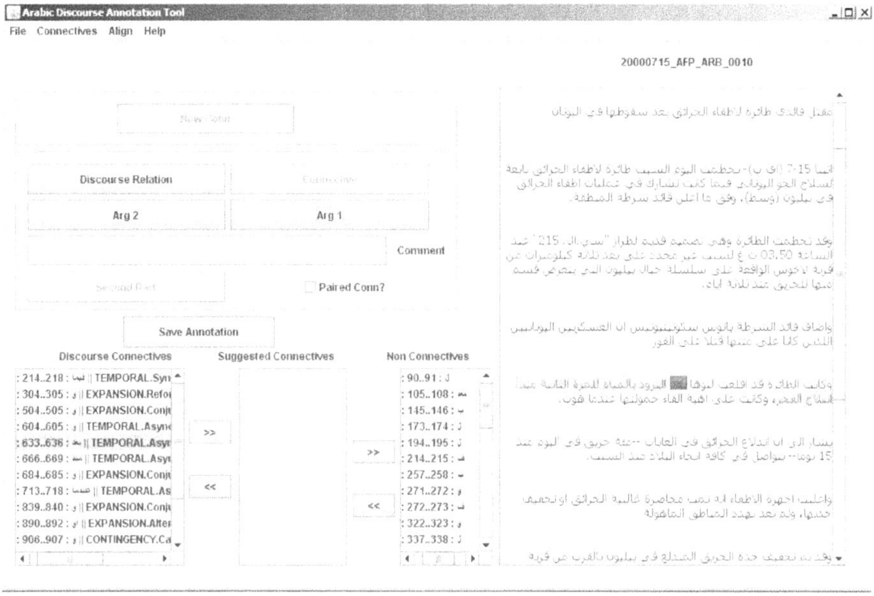

Figure 5.3 A screenshot of the READ annotation tool. The potential connectives are annotated either as discourse connectives (left list) or non-discourse connectives (right list). Arg1 is shaded to the right of the first line while Arg2 is shaded to the left of the first line and right of the second line in the text.

Part 1, including 126,394 tokens (after Treebank clitic segmentation). The gold standard of the LADTB includes 6,328 annotated explicit connective tokens belonging to 80 explicit connective types, and 55 distinct discourse relations (17 single relations). Most of the discourse connectives (95 per cent) were annotated with a single relation; 5 per cent were annotated with two relations. These statistics are summarised in Table 5.3. We found that 70 per cent of the sentences in news texts within the LADTB are introduced by a connective. This highlights the importance of annotating discourse connectives in Arabic (Alsaif 2012).

Our inter-annotator agreement studies show that the identification of discourse connectives, and their arguments and the determination of the discourse relations they convey, are reliable. Agreement on Task 1 (identifying connectives) is highly reliable (percentage agreement of 95 per cent, kappa of 0.88). Agreement on Task 2 (relation assignment) is relatively reliable, especially if we exclude the most ambiguous connective *wa*, 'and' when it occurs at beginning of the paragraph (percentage agreement of 74 per cent, kappa of 0.70). Of the sentences in our news corpus, 39 per cent are introduced by *wa*, mostly without a clear discourse relation being conveyed. Agreement on Task 3 (argument labelling) is highly reliable on Arg2 (95 per cent), as this is introduced by the discourse connective. We also achieve good agreement on Arg1 (78 per cent), though not as high as on Arg2, because Arg1 could be any proposition prior to the discourse connective. Further details of our inter-annotator agreement studies are discussed in Alsaif (2012).

Table 5.3 Statistics of the final gold standard corpus LADTB

Total tagged tokens		126,394
Files		534
Total paragraphs		3,312
Total sentences		3,607
Total potential discourse connectives	**20,312**	**100%**
• Discourse connective in context	6,328	31%
• Not a discourse connective	13,984	69%
Discourse connective types		**80**
Discourse relation types	**55**	**100%**
• Single relations	17	31%
• Combined relations	38	69%
Total discourse connective tokens	**6,328**	**100%**
• Single relation tokens	6,039	95%
• Combined relation tokens	289	5%

9. Conclusion

We have developed the first guidelines for identifying Arabic discourse connectives in context and annotating them for the relation they convey as well as the arguments they relate. As part of this work, we have also presented the first large collection of potential Arabic discourse connectives as well as an annotation tool specifically developed for Arabic discourse annotation. We have discussed issues specific to Arabic, in particular the ordering of arguments and discourse connectives; handling the ubiquitous connective *wa*, 'and'; and the frequent use of *al-maṣdar* nouns as arguments. We have also extended the Penn Discourse Treebank inventory of discourse relations with two new relations, Background and Similarity. In our annotation study on a newspaper corpus, we used a decision tree approach to guide annotators through the relation hierarchy, and we have shown that there was good agreement on all subtasks of the annotation process. The resulting corpus is the first Arabic corpus that is reliably annotated for discourse relations. In the future, we would like to extend our work to different genres, as well as cover implicit relations.

Appendix A: Inventory of Arabic discourse connectives

The process of collecting discourse connectives resulted in a list containing 91 basic Arabic discourse connectives, enhanced with 16 modified forms, yielding 107 discourse connectives overall. This number is comparable to the 100 distinct English connectives in the PDTB. The connectives are categorised by syntactic category as annotated in the ATB, and are presented in Tables 5.5–5.12. The connective type might be *Simple* (one token), *Clitic* (attached to a word), or *MoreThanToken* (two or more tokens). The position of the connective, given in the third column, is either the beginning of a sentence (BOS) or the middle of a sentence (MOS). In contrast to English, there are no end-of-sentence connectives in Arabic. The POS tags in the last column are according to version 2 of the Penn ATB Part 1, and may have been

Table 5.4 Coordinating conjunction connectives in the LADTB

Discourse connective	Type	Position	ATB POS
اذ, *āiḏ*, 'as'	Simple	B/MOS	CONJ
او, *āw*, 'or'	Simple	MOS	CONJ
ف, *fa*, 'then'	Clitic	B/MOS	CONJ
لكن, *lākin*, 'but'	Simple, Clitic	B/MOS	CONJ, NO_FUNC
و, *wa*, 'and'	Simple, Clitic	B/MOS	CONJ

Table 5.5 Subordinating conjunction connectives in the LADTB

Discourse connective	Type	Position	ATB POS
اذا, *āiḏā*, 'if'	Simple	B/MOS	CONJ
الا, *āilā*, 'except'	Simple	MOS	EXCEPT_PART
الا اذ, *āilā āiḏā*, 'except if'	MoreThanToken	MOS	EXCEPT_PART+CONJ
الا ان, *āilā ān*, 'but'	MoreThanToken	MOS	EXCEPT_PART+Func_ word
الا بعد, *ālā ba'da*, 'expect after'	MoreThanToken	MOS	EXCEPT_PART+PREP, PREP+PREP
اما, *āimā*, 'while'	Simple	BOS	PREP
انما, *āinamā*, 'but'	Simple	B/MOS	CONJ
بسبب, *bisababi*, 'because of'	Simple	B/MOS	PREP, PREP+NOUN
بعدما, *ba'damā*, 'after that'	Simple	B/MOS	CONJ, RELuADV
بل, *bal*, 'but'	Simple	B/MOS	CONJ
بمعنى آخر, *bima'nā 'āḫr*, 'in other words'	MoreThanToken	B/MOS	PREP+NOUN
بينما, *bīnamā*, 'while'	Simple	B/MOS	CONJ, REL_ADV
عندما, *'indamā*, 'when'	Simple	MOS	CONJ, REL_ADV
غير ان, *ġayra āna*, 'however'	MoreThanToken	B/MOS	NEG_ PART+FUNC_ WORD
حيث, *ḥayṯu*, 'where, when, since'	Simple	MOS	CONJ, REL_ADV
كأن, *kā'na*, 'as'	Simple	MOS	CONJ
كلما, *kulamā*, 'whenever'	Simple	B/MOS	CONJ
كما, *kamā* 'as'	Simple	B/MOS	CONJ
كي, *kayi*, 'to'	Simple	MOS	CONJ
لذا, *liḏā*, 'for this'	MoreThanToken	B/MOS	CONJ
لاسيما, *lāsīamā*, 'particularly'	Simple	B/MOS	NEG_PART+ADV
لأن, *liāna*, 'because'	Simple, Clitic	B/MOS	CONJ
لكي, *likay*, 'for/in order to'	Simple	B/MOS	CONJ
لو, *law*, 'if (in past)'	Simple	MOS	CONJ
لولا, *lawlā*, 'if not'	Simple	B/MOS	PREP
طالما, *ṭālamā*, 'as long as'	Simple	BOS	CONJ
وقبل, *waqabla*, 'and before'	MoreThanToken	BOS	NONE

Table 5.6 Noun connectives (single and modified nouns) in the LADTB

Discourse connective	Type	Position	ATB POS
اضافة الى, *āiḍāfhan āilā*, 'in addition to'	MoreThanToken	MOS	NOUN+PREP
بغية, *buġyah*, 'desire/to'	Simple	MOS	NOUN, PREP
بيد, *bayda*, 'but'	Simple	B/MOS	NOUN
بيد ان, *bayda āna*, 'but'	MoreThanToken	B/MOS	NOUN+FUNC_WORD
فضلاعن, *faḍlan 'an*, 'as well as'	MoreThanToken	B/MOS	NOUN+PREP
حينها, *ḥīnahā*, 'when that'	MoreThanToken	B/MOS	NOUN+POSS_PRON
نتيجة, *natīǧah*, 'result of'	Simple	MOS	NOUN
قبيل, *qubayla*, 'shortly before'	Simple	MOS	NOUN, PREP
رغم, *ruġma*, 'though'	Simple	B/MOS	NOUN, PREP
رغم ان, *ruġma āna*, 'although'	MoreThanToken	B/MOS	NOUN+FUNC_WORD, PREP+FUNC_WORD
خلافا ل, *ḫilāfān l*, 'unlike'	MoreThanToken	B/MOS	NOUN+PREP
نظرا ل, *naḍarān l*, 'because of'	MoreThanToken	B/MOS	NO_FUNC+PREP, NOUN+NO_FUNC, NOUN+PREP

Table 5.7 Adverbial connectives in the LADTB

Discourse connective	Type	Position	ATB POS
ايضا, *āyḍan*, 'also'	Simple	B/MOS	ADV
حال, *ḥāl*, 'when'	Simple	B/MOS	NONE
حتى, *ḥatā*, 'until'	Simple	B/MOS	ADV, CONJ, PREP
حتى لو, *ḥatā lw*, 'even if'	MoreThanToken	B/MOS	ADV+CONJ
حين, *ḥīna*, 'when'	Simple	B/MOS	ADV
كذلك, *kaḏalika*, 'and that'	Simple	B/MOS	ADV, NOUN
لذلك, *liḏalika*, 'for that'	MoreThanToken	B/MOS	ADV
من ثم, *min ṯama*, 'then'	MoreThanToken	MOS	PREP+ADV, PREP+NOUN
ثم, *ṯuma*, 'then'	Simple	MOS	ADV
خصوصا, *ḫuṣūṣān*, 'specially'	Simple	B/MOS	ADV

Table 5.8 (Preposition + relative pronoun) connectives in the LADTB

Discourse connective	Type	Position	ATB POS
فيما, *fīmā*, 'while'	MoreThanToken	B/MOS	CONJ, PREP+REL PRON
مما, *mimā*, 'which' (+ past verb)	MoreThanToken	MOS	CONJ, PREP+REL_PRON, REL_PRON

Table 5.9 Preposition connectives in the LADTB

Discourse connective	Type	Position	ATB POS
اثر, *āiṯra*, 'after'	Simple	MOS	PREP
ب, *bi*, 'by'	Clitic	B/MOS	PREP
بعد, *ba'da*, 'after'	Simple	B/MOS	PREP
عقب, *'aqib*, 'shortly after'	Simple	B/MOS	PREP
جراء, *ğara'*, 'because'	Simple	MOS	PREP
ل, *li*, 'for'	Clitic	MOS	EMPHATIC_PARTICLE, PREP, RuCuP, SUBJUNC
منذ, *munḏu*, 'since'	Simple	B/MOS	CONJ, NOuFUNC, PREP
قبل, *qabla*, 'before'	Simple	B/MOS	PREP
قبل ان, *qabla ān*, 'before that'	MoreThanToken	B/MOS	PREP+FUNC_WORD
خلال, *ḫilāla*, 'during'	Simple	MOS	PREP

Table 5.10 Prepositional phrase connectives in the LADTB

Discourse connective	Type	Position	ATB POS
بالمقابل, *bi+almuqābil*, 'in contrast'	MoreThanToken	B/MOS	PREP+NOUN
بفضل, *bifaḍli*, 'thanks to'	Simple	MOS	PREP+NOUN
بهدف, *bihdaf*, 'in order to'	MoreThanToken	MOS	PREP+NOUN
برغم, *biruğmi*, 'although'	Simple	B/MOS	PREP+NOUN
بالاضافة الى, *bi+ālāiḍāfah āilā* 'in addition to'	MoreThanToken	B/MOS	PREP+NOUN
بالرغم من, *bi+alruğmi min*, 'although'	MoreThanToken	B/MOS	PREP+NOUN
بالتالي, *bi+altālī*, 'consequently'	MoreThanToken	B/MOS	ADV, PREP+NOUN
على الرغم, *'alā alruğmi*, 'although'	MoreThanToken	B/MOS	PREP+NOUN
في المقابل, *fī al+muqābil*, 'in contrast'	MoreThanToken	B/MOS	PREP+NOUN
في حال, *fī ḥal*, 'in case'	MoreThanToken	B/MOS	PREP+NOUN
في حين, *fī ḥīn*, 'while'	MoreThanToken	B/MOS	PREP+ADV, PREP+NOUN
في ظل, *fī ḍil*, 'under'	MoreThanToken	B/MOS	PREP+NOUN

slightly modified in newer versions of the ATB. The Arabic connectives are ordered alphabetically within the tables. Two connectives (listed in Table 5.8) consist of a preposition plus a relative pronoun, and do not fit into any of the syntactic classes in section 4.

Table 5.11 Discourse connectives in MSA that do not occur in the Penn ATB Part 1

Discourse connective	Type	Position	Syntactic class
على العموم, *'alā al+ 'umūm*, 'in general'	MoreThanToken	BOS	Adverbial
مثلا, *maṯalān*, 'for example'	Simple	B/EOS	Adverbial
باختصار, *biāiḫtiṣār*, 'briefly/ in sum'	MoreThanToken	BOS	Adverbial, prepositional phrase
بالاساس, *bi+lāsās*, 'basically'	MoreThanToken	M/EOS	Adverbial, prepositional phrase
بالاضافة, *bi+al+āiḍāfah*, 'in addition to'	MoreThanToken	BOS	Adverbial
بالفعل, *bi+lfi'l*, 'indeed'	MoreThanToken	B/M/ EOS	Adverbial, prepositional phrase
بحجة أن, *biḥuğah āna*, 'because of'	MoreThanToken	B/MOS	Subordinating conjunction
بعد ذلك, *ba'da ḏalik*, 'after that'	MoreThanToken	BOS	Subordinating conjunction
جدير بالذكر, *ğadīrun bi+lḏkr*, 'it should be noted'	MoreThanToken	BOS	Subordinating conjunction
ختاما, *ḫitāmān*, 'finally'	Simple	BOS	Adverbial
خلاصة, *ḫulāṣah*, 'to sum up'	Simple	BOS	Adverbial
دليلا على, *dalīlān 'alā*, 'evidence for'	MoreThanToken	MOS	Adverbial
ذلك ان, *ḏalik āna*, 'that because'	MoreThanToken	BOS	Subordinating conjunction
علاوة على, *'al āwh 'alā*, 'in addition to'	MoreThanToken	BOS	Adverbial
على العكس, *'alā al+ 'aks*, 'by opposite'	MoreThanToken	BOS	Prepositional phrase
على النقيض, *'alā al+nqīḍ*, 'in contrast'	MoreThanToken	BOS	Prepositional phrase
على سبيل المثال, *'alā sabīl al+miṯāl*, 'for example'	MoreThanToken	BOS	Prepositional phrase
عموما, *'umūmān*, 'generally'	Simple	BOS	Adverbial
فعلا, *fi'lān*, 'indeed'	Simple	M/EOS	Subordinating conjunction
في الواقع, *fī al+wāqi'*, 'of course/in fact'	MoreThanToken	BOS	Subordinating conjunction
في أعقاب, *fī ā'qābi*, 'after all'	MoreThanToken	MOS	Prepositional phrase
في هذه الاثناء, *fī haḏihi al+āṯnā'*, 'in the meantime'	MoreThanToken	BOS	Subordinating conjunction
كدليل, *kadalīlin*, 'as an evidence'	MoreThanToken	EOS	Adverbial
لاجل, *liāğli*, 'for'	MoreThanToken	B/MOS	Subordinating conjunction
لهذا السبب, *lihaḏā al+sabab*, 'for this reason'	MoreThanToken	BOS	Subordinating conjunction
لئلا, *li'ylā*, 'for not'	MoreThanToken	MOS	Subordinating conjunction
نتيجة ل, *natīğahin li*, 'resulted by'	MoreThanToken	B/MOS	Subordinating conjunction
وفي الختام, *wa fī al+ḫitām*, 'finally'	MoreThanToken	BOS	Prepositional phrase

Appendix B: Morphological patterns of *al-maṣdar* nouns

Table 5.12 presents some morphological patterns of *al-maṣdar* nouns that are used by the automatic Arabic morphological analyser Alkulil Morpho Sys, developed by KACST and ALECSO.[3]

Table 5.12 Examples of some morphological patterns of *al-maṣdar* nouns

Morphological pattern/ الوزن	Example/ مثال	Morphological pattern/ الوزن	Example/ مثال
فَعَل, *fa ʿal*	فرح, *faraḥ*, 'happiness'	فَعْل, *fa ʿl*	نوم, *nawm*, 'sleep'
فَعَالة, *fa ʿālah*	فصاحة , *faṣāḥah*, 'eloquence'	فُعُول, *fu ʿūl*	قدوم, *qudūm*, 'arrival, coming'
فِعَال, *fi ʿāl*	جماح, *ğimāḥ*, 'fantasy'	فَعَال, *fa ʿāl*	ثراء, *ṯarāʾ*, 'richness'
فَعِيل, *fa ʿīl*	صهيل, *ṣahīl*, 'neighing'	فَعَلان, *fa ʿalān*	غليان, *ġalayān*, 'boiling'
فُعُولة, *fu ʿūlah*	سهولة, *suhūlah*, 'easiness'	فَعْلَة, *fa ʿlah*	رحمة, *raḥmah*, 'mercy'
فُعَال, *fu ʿāl*	سعال, *su ʿāl*, 'cough'	فُعْل, *fu ʿl*	حسن, *husn*, 'niceness'

Acknowledgements

The construction of the LADTB was funded by a PhD scholarship from the Imam Muhammad Ibn Saud University, Saudi Arabia, to Amal Alsaif. We thank the British Academy for additional funding for the annotation study via Grant SG51944. Moreover, the development of the READ annotation tool is funded by King Abdulaziz City for Science and Technology (KACST). We would also like to acknowledge the contributions of the annotators Latifa Alsulaiti and Abdul-baqi Sharif in the annotation of the main corpus and Basmah Al-Soli, Boshra Al-shyban, and Maryam Al-Gawi in the pilot annotation. A special thank you goes to Dr Hussein Abdul-Raof for linguistic advice on the collection of discourse connectives as well as to Prof. Bonnie Webber and other members of the PDTB team for useful discussions. Any errors and omissions are, however, the authors' own.

Notes

1. See <https://www.sketchengine.eu/corpus-of-classical-arabic-ksucca/> (last accessed 29 June 2018).
2. Accessible via <https://readannotationtool.sourceforge.io> (last accessed 21 May 2018).
3. See <http://www.econtent.org.sa/Projects/InitiativeProjects/Lists/Initiative Projects/DispForm.aspx?ID=25>.

References

Alansari, I. H. (1985), *Mogny Alabib En Kutb AlAEareb*, Lebanon: Dar Alfekur.

Alfarabi, H. (1990), *Ketab Alhroof*, Lebanon: Dar Almashreg.

Alsaif, A. (2012), 'Human and Automatic Annotation of Discourse Relations for Arabic', unpublished PhD thesis, University of Leeds.

Alsaif, A. and K. Markert (2010), 'The Leeds Arabic Discourse Treebank: Annotating discourse connectives for Arabic', in N. Calzolari, K. Choukri, B. Maegaard, J. Mariani, J. Odijk, S. Piperidis, M. Rosner and D. Tapias (eds), *Proceedings of the Seventh Conference on Language Resources and Evaluation Conference (LREC) 2010*, Paris: ELRA, pp. 2046–53.

Asher, N. (1993), *Reference to Abstract Objects in Discourse*, Boston: Kluwer.

Carlson, L., D. Marcu and M. E. Okurowski (2002), *RST Discourse Treebank*, LDC catalog no.: LDC2002T07, Philadelphia: University of Pennsylvania, Linguistic Data Consortium.

Chiang, D., M. Diab, N. Habash, O. Rambow and S. Shareef (2006), 'Parsing Arabic dialects', in F. Keller and G. Proszeky (eds), *Proceedings of EACL-06*, pp. 369–76.

Dukes, K. and T. Buckwalter (2010), 'A dependency treebank of the Quran using traditional Arabic grammar', in *7th International Conference on Informatics and Systems*, Cairo, Egypt.

Habash, N. and O. Rambow (2004), 'Extracting a tree adjoining grammar from the Penn Arabic Treebank', in *Proceedings of Traitement Automatique du Langage Naturel (TALN-04)*, Fez, Morocco, <https://pdfs.semanticscholar.org/7b70/bd48c25a1418edf19897a081a03ea771ca3f.pdf> (last accessed 29 June 2018).

Habash, N. and R. M. Roth (2009), *CATiB: The Columbia Arabic Treebank*, Technical Report CCLS-09-01, New York: Columbia University, Center for Computational Learning Systems.

Halliday, M. A. K. and R. Hasan (1976), *Cohesion in English*, London: Longman.

Lin, Z., H. T. Ng and M.-Y. Kan (2012), 'A PDTB-styled end-to-end discourse parser', *Natural Language Engineering*, 20(2): 151–84.

M. Abdl al latif, A. Umar, M. Zahran and D. A. Al-Arabi (1997), *Alnhw AlAsAsi*, Stanford, CA: Stanford University, Center for the Study of Language and Information.

Maamouri, M. and A. Bies (2004), 'Developing an Arabic Treebank: Methods, guidelines, procedures, and tools', in A. Farghaly and K. Megerdoomian (eds), *Proceedings of the Workshop on Computational Approaches to Arabic Script-Based Languages*, Stroudsburg, PA: Association for Computational Linguistics, pp. 2–9.

Maamouri, M., A. Bies, T. Buckwalter and W. Mekki (2004), 'The Penn Arabic Treebank: Building a large-scale annotated Arabic corpus', in *Proceedings of the NEMLAR International Conference on Arabic Language Resources and Tools*, Cairo, Egypt, pp. 466–7.

Parker, R., D. Graff, K. Chen, J. Kong and K. Maeda (2011), *Arabic Gigaword*, 5th edn, LDC catalog no. LDC2011T11, Linguistic Data Consortium, University of Pennsylvania.

Prasad, R., N. Dinesh, A. Lee, E. Miltsakaki, L. Robaldo, A. Joshi and B. Webber (2008a), 'The Penn Discourse TreeBank 2.0', in N. Calzolari, K. Choukri, B. Maegaard, J. Mariani, J. Oodijk, S. Piperidis, M. Rosner and D. Tapias (eds), *Proceedings of the 6th International Conference on Language Resources and Evaluation* (LREC 2008), Marrakech, Morocco, pp. 2961–8.

Prasad, R., S. Husain, D. Mishra Sharma and A. Joshi (2008b), 'Towards an annotated corpus of discourse relations in Hindi', in J. H. Lee (ed.), *Third International Joint Conference on Natural Language Processing*, India, pp. 73–80.

Prasad, R., A. Joshi and B. Webber (2010), 'Realization of discourse relations by other means: Alternative lexicalizations', in C.-R. Huang and D. Jurafsky (eds), *Proceedings of COLING 2010*, Beijing, pp. 1023–31.

Ryding, K. C. (2005), *A Reference Grammar of Modern Standard Arabic*, Cambridge: Cambridge University Press.

Sadat, F. and N. Habash (2006), 'Combination of Arabic preprocessing schemes for statistical machine translation', in N. Calzolari, C. Cardie and P. Isabelle (eds), *Proceedings of the 21st International Conference on Computational Linguistics and 44th Annual Meeting of the Association for Computational Linguistics*, Sydney, Australia, pp. 1–8.

Webber, B., M. Egg and V. Kordoni (2011), 'Discourse structure and language technology', *Natural Language Engineering*, 18(4): 437–90.

Wolf, F. and E. Gibson (2005), 'Representing discourse coherence: A corpus-based study', *Computational Linguistics*, 31(2): 249–87.

Xue, N. (2005), 'Annotating discourse connectives in the Chinese Treebank', in A. Meyers (ed.), *Proceedings of the ACL 2005 Workshop on Frontiers in Corpus Annotation: Pie in the Sky II*, Ann Arbor, MI, pp. 84–91.

Zeyrek, D. and B. Webber (2008), 'A discourse resource for Turkish: Annotating discourse connectives in the METU Corpus', in *Proceedings of IJCNLP-2008*, Hyderabad, India, pp. 65–72.

6

Using the Web to Model Modern and Qur᾿anic Arabic

Eric Atwell

1. Introduction

This chapter is not about a specific Arabic corpus, nor about the use of a corpus in an Arabic linguistics research project. I work in the School of Computing within the Faculty of Engineering at Leeds University, and engineers build things for others to use; so our contribution to Arabic corpus linguistics has been to develop a range of Arabic-language resources – corpora and software tools – for as wide a range of users as possible, including not just linguists but also computing and artificial intelligence researchers, religious scholars, and the general public.

In the School of Computing at Leeds University, we are not Arabic linguists, but we enjoy working with Arabic linguists. To explain our motivation for contributing to Arabic corpus linguistics, I will outline some examples of artificial intelligence and corpus linguistics research where we have worked with end users across interesting and challenging domains. We may have little or no expertise in a domain, but nevertheless we can apply machine learning to textual data from the domain to produce useful results.

Next I explain what I mean by the phrases 'using the Web', 'to model', 'modern (Arabic)', and 'Qur᾿anic Arabic'. This leads into a summary of the web-based software and corpus datasets developed by Leeds University researchers, covering Modern Standard Arabic and the Classical Arabic of the Qur᾿an.

I conclude with some ideas for further development of Arabic corpus linguistics resources. Most Arabic linguistic research focuses on Modern Standard Arabic and modern Arabic dialects. However, modern Arabic linguists, lexicographers, and language teachers need to recognise and deal with the religious terms and quotations from Qur᾿anic Arabic that can appear in modern Arabic texts. Furthermore, while Qur᾿anic Arabic corpus research may be a minority interest in linguistics, it has huge potential for impact on society and the general public including Muslims worldwide who want to study and understand the Qur᾿an.

2. Artificial intelligence for corpus linguistics

I like the definition of artificial intelligence (AI) currently provided by the Google web search system: 'the theory and development of computer systems able to perform tasks normally requiring human intelligence, such as visual perception, speech recognition, decision-making, and translation between languages'.[1] Much early AI research involved trying to encode human expert knowledge as sets of formal rules in expert systems or knowledge-based systems (e.g. Atwell 1993a, 1993b). However, most current AI theory and systems incorporate the techniques of machine learning, wherein the goal of the scientist is to create algorithms that can learn from data – the source of knowledge in the system is thus the data, rather than a priori knowledge inserted explicitly by the scientist. A corpus is a collection of texts, representing a language use, topic, or task; corpus linguists study some specific feature of a language using a corpus to provide empirical evidence of the language feature. A corpus is also useful as a training and/or test dataset for machine learning, particularly if annotated or tagged with linguistic information by linguists. An example of the trend towards machine learning relevant to corpus linguistics is development of part-of-speech (POS) taggers. POS taggers based on explicit grammar rules written by linguists, such as TAGGIT (Greene and Rubin 1971) or Constraint Grammar taggers (Karlsson et al. 1995), have largely been supplanted by POS taggers based on machine learning models trained with a POS-tagged corpus, for example CLAWS, the Constituent Likelihood Automatic Word-tagging System (Leech et al. 1983a, 1983b; Garside and Smith 1997).

An example use of machine learning to learn from a corpus is for classifying cause of death in verbal autopsies (Danso et al. 2013). In some developing countries, when someone dies a doctor may not be available to diagnose and certify cause of death. A verbal autopsy can be used as a proxy to ascertain likely cause of death via an interview with a close relative of the deceased, for example a mother after her baby has died. Bodies such as the World Health Organization use verbal autopsies to gather statistics on major causes of death, to inform health policies. Danso et al. (2013) worked with a corpus of 11,741 verbal autopsies from Ghana, which had been sent to the London School of Hygiene and Tropical Medicine, where doctors diagnosed the likely cause of death. Thus, each text in the verbal autopsy corpus was tagged with its class: the cause of death. A machine learning classifier was used to learn patterns linking features of each verbal autopsy to cause of death. This classifier can in principle be used to predict cause of death in future verbal autopsy datasets, without need for doctors; the classifier is not good enough to use in front-line health care, to confidently diagnose each individual case, but its overall predictions of the prevalence of major causes of death may be sufficiently accurate to guide health funding policy, for example. Another case of machine learning applied to a corpus is for classifying 'suspiciousness' of texts. The project Detecting Terrorist Activities: Making Sense (Brierley et al. 2013) aimed to develop systems to better manage data collected in connection with alleged terrorist plots. Very few of the texts collected from subjects of interest are actually suspicious; therefore the task can be characterised as looking for threads (rather than needles) in a haystack – machine learning aims to find 'interesting' texts from the corpus, and 'threads' linking them. To train a machine learning classifier, we used a training corpus in which 'interesting' texts are marked or tagged.

In the School of Computing at Leeds University, we are not Arabic linguists; so how can we be involved in Arabic corpus linguistic research? Machine learning requires data tagged and classified by experts to train an automated classifier algorithm. We do not have to 'understand' the data or the tagging to apply machine learning; we just work with the experts to provide classifiers, and then leave the experts to evaluate the accuracy and usefulness of the results. Of course, I want to work in application areas I find interesting, challenging, and useful. I am not a clinician, but maybe machine learning can help classify cause of death in verbal autopsies; and assisting the World Health Organization to target life-threatening diseases is surely worthwhile. I am not a counter-terrorism expert, but maybe machine learning can help detect terrorist threads in data, and detecting terrorist activities is a fascinating challenge of national and international importance. Similarly, Arabic is a major international language, yet has fewer computational and corpus linguistic resources than major European languages such as English, French, German, or Spanish; this invites research on Arabic corpus resource development. An initial survey (Atwell et al. 2004) found few publicly available Arabic language computing resources; but we found that machine learning could be used to adapt generic natural language processing (NLP) techniques to Arabic (Abu Shawar and Atwell 2005a, 2005b). The Classical Arabic of the Qur'an is of even wider interest than modern Arabic, since Muslims worldwide want to understand the Qur'an as the key source text of their religion; corpus resources developed for the Qur'an will be useful not only to linguists but to a much broader user community.

3. Using the Web to model modern Arabic and Qur'anic Arabic

The Web is a very useful resource for Arabic corpus linguistics, as a source of Arabic corpus data. For example, the Corpus of Contemporary Arabic (Al-Sulaiti and Atwell 2006) was collated by selecting the genres to be included, and then scouting for websites with appropriate data. A more recent trend in corpus linguistics is to use a web-crawler tool such as BootCaT (Baroni and Bernadini 2004) to automate harvesting of webpage text. At Leeds, Sharoff (2006) harvested large corpora in many languages from webpages, including the 176 million word Arabic Internet Corpus, which was then automatically lemmatised as a case-study in high-performance computing (Sawalha and Atwell 2013a) to enable concordance and collocation analysis by Arabic lemma.

Another use of the Web is to annotate a corpus, via crowdsourcing. The morphological and syntactic tagging of the Qur'anic Arabic Corpus (which will be discussed in detail below) was achieved by starting with an automated tagger, putting the results online, and then inviting website users to report mistakes and propose corrections. Volunteers can build a shared resource if they have a common interest, and the Qur'an attracts many more interested volunteers than other online corpus resources. For Arabic corpus tagging projects which are not as 'interesting' to volunteers, researchers can hire and manage online annotators via websites such as Amazon Mechanical Turk.

A third use of the Web is to publicise and promote reuse of corpora. Often corpus linguists collect a corpus with their own research questions in mind, and then at the end of their project may (or may not) consider how to make the corpus reusable by others. There are a range of options, with pros and cons: donating to an established web-based corpus repository, such as ICAME, ELRA, or the LDC; depositing with a conference website repository, such as the LREC language resources map; setting up a project website and adding a corpus download page; setting up a customised corpus website for users, with search and corpus use tools, such as the Qur'anic Arabic Corpus website; donating the corpus to an existing specialist corpus website already hosting other related corpora, such as the ArabiCorpus website (see Parkinson, this volume); donating to an academic corpus-user website with resources for a wider range of languages, such as Intellitext (Wilson et al. 2010); and donating to a commercial corpus-user website catering for the language technology industry as well as academics, such as Sketch Engine (Kilgarriff et al. 2014a). To achieve widest reuse of a corpus (and maximise subsequent citations), it is best to devote time to what machine learning researchers call an 'ensemble' approach, combining several methods.

Arabic corpus and tool builders can use the Web in these three ways, to build, annotate, and promote new Arabic corpus resources. But probably the most common use of the Web by individual Arabic corpus linguists is not to create new corpora, but to find and use existing online Arabic corpora and analysis tools. Early surveys (Atwell et al. 2004; Al-Sulaiti and Atwell 2006) found few freely available online Arabic corpus resources; but today a Google search for 'Arabic corpus' produces thousands of results including many links to free-to-use online resources.

In the title of this chapter, I use the verb *model* in the sense 'to do a computer representation or scientific description of a situation or event' (as per one definition provided by the *Longman Dictionary of Contemporary English*). This covers use of a corpus to guide development of linguistic theories or models, as well as use of a corpus as training data for machine learning of a language analysis model. Traditional Arabic grammar descriptions in classical textbooks can be modelled in computer representations. In the Qur'anic Arabic Corpus, narrative text descriptions of the grammar of each verse have been taken from tafsirs (*tafsīr*, lit. 'explanation, clarification'), Islamic scholarly textbooks of commentary and analysis of the Qur'an, and this narrative text has been modelled using formal syntax tree diagrams, to produce a Classical Arabic treebank. Similarly, the SALMA morphological analysis toolkit (discussed below) implements a computational model based on traditional Arabic morphological theory from established Arabic grammar and morphology textbooks.

Most of the chapters in this book deal with corpora of various modern forms of Arabic, including Modern Standard Arabic and modern dialects; and researchers can find a growing range of modern Arabic corpora, including news text, web corpora, dialect data, and even corpora of quite specialised genres such as the 'Dark Web' terrorism corpus (Chen 2012). This reflects the importance of Arabic as a modern international language. The Qur'an, the core holy text of Islam, is written in Classical Arabic of around 1,400 years ago, a time when Latin was still widely used in Europe and the modern languages of Europe had yet to emerge. Despite its antiquity, Qur'anic Arabic is of immense importance even in the modern world, because all Muslims (about one quarter of the world's population) are required to learn and memorise the Qur'an in its original language. Words, phrases, and quotes from the Qur'an and related Classical Arabic Islamic texts can readily be found in modern Arabic corpora, in effect a kind of 'code switching'. Moreover, Qur'anic vocabulary and quotations even crop up in other language corpora: this is because Muslims with mother tongues other than Arabic are also required to study the Qur'an in its Classical Arabic form, in case some of the meaning is lost in translation.

4. Arabic corpus linguistics research at Leeds University

Leeds University is unique in its range of departments and research units active in Arabic corpus linguistic research, including Languages, Cultures and Societies; Computing; Arabic, Islamic and Middle Eastern Studies; Translation Studies; Linguistics and Phonetics; and the Institute for Artificial Intelligence and Biological Systems. This broad range of expertise has led to interdisciplinary collaboration and cross-fertilisation of ideas, resulting in a range of Arabic corpus linguistics research projects.

4.1 ABC: Arabic By Computer

Arabic corpus linguistic research collaboration at Leeds University started with a project to collect Modern Standard Arabic texts for use in computer-aided Arabic language teaching, the ABC: Arabic By Computer project to develop an Arabic text database and glossary system for language students (Brockett et al. 1989). At the time, a major challenge was editing and display of Arabic text, requiring specialist Apple Macintosh hardware and software. Another practical challenge was giving students access to the ABC resources; the University computing provision did not include language teaching, as computers were assumed to be used only for science and engineering research. This inspired us to investigate methods for free, open access to Arabic corpus linguistic resources for teaching and research.

4.2 Arabic corpus-trained chatbots

An unusual use of corpora was to train web-based machine-learning chatbot systems (Abu Shawar and Atwell 2005a), and using a corpus-trained chatbot system as a tool to animate and explore the corpus (Abu Shawar and Atwell 2005b). Our system could be trained to chat in the language of a given training corpus; as an example, we trained the chatbot with the Qur'an, resulting in a web-based Arabic chatbot producing answers from the Qur'an (Abu Shawar 2005). Another version of the chatbot was trained on an Arabic computing FAQ (frequently asked questions) corpus (Abu Shawar and Atwell 2009).

4.3 The Corpus of Contemporary Arabic

Machine learning can be applied to adapt generic NLP techniques to Arabic. This requires an Arabic text training set, so we developed the first freely downloadable million-word Corpus of Contemporary Arabic (CCA, Al-Sulaiti and Atwell 2006). The CCA was designed to be comparable to the million-word LOB and Brown corpora of contemporary published texts in British English and American English (Leech et al. 1983a); but rather than slavishly copying the exact set of genres in LOB and Brown, we surveyed potential users in Arabic language teaching and Arabic text analytics, to identify user preferences for the distribution of genres to be included. The CCA has been used for research, for example in learning Arabic spelling and vocabulary (Erradi et al. 2012); Arabic lexical profiling (Attia et al. 2011); the translation of culturally bound metaphors in the genre of popular science articles (Merakchi and Rogers 2013); lexical differences in world affairs and sports sections in Arabic newspapers (Abdul Razak 2011); and corpus-based sociolinguistics (Friginal and Hardy 2014).

4.4 The aConCorde concordancer for Arabic

We realised that the concordance tools available at the time were not designed to handle the unusual properties of the Arabic script, including the non-Roman character set, several rival encoding standards, contextual variant character shapes, the frequent omission of vowels resulting in spelling variations, varying use of punctuation, and notably the flow of text from right-to-left not left-to-right which requires the 'before' and 'after' windows typically provided by concordance software to be swapped. So we developed aConCorde, a freely downloadable, open-source, extendable concordance program specifically for Arabic corpus linguistics (Roberts et al. 2006). A review of concordancing software at the time praised aConCorde for:

> providing comprehensive support for working with Arabic texts. This is reflected on several levels: the user interface can be switched to Arabic, the character encoding supports Unicode as well as specific Arabic fonts and text orientation can be mirrored vertically. (Wiechmann and Fuhs 2006: 118)

Most other concordancers still do not handle Arabic text well; so aConCorde is still used for Arabic corpus linguistic research, for example exploration of common lexical patterns in Arabic text (Ali 2012), extraction of key words and phrases (El-Haj et al. 2015), and identification of patterns from an Arabic crime news report corpus (Alruily 2012).

4.5 Corpus-based Arabic language teaching

We have been able to experiment with the use of web-based corpora, concordances, and chatbots in the teaching of Arabic (Al-Sulaiti and Atwell 2005; Al-Sulaiti et al. 2007), for example corpus-based vocabulary lists for language learners (Kilgarriff et al. 2013b). We had access to students as well as language teachers in the department of Arabic at Leeds University, keen to use Arabic corpus linguistic resources in their learning and teaching. The local Muslim community ran a Saturday school for children to learn Arabic to read and understand the Qur'an, and they enjoyed the novelty of a web-based, corpus-trained chatbot giving answers in Qur'anic Arabic (Abu Shawar 2005).

4.6 Arabic Web-as-Corpus

The British National Corpus (BNC) became an established gold standard for English corpus linguistics in the 1990s; but for other languages, funding and expertise were not then available for a large, general corpus of the size of the BNC (100 million words). But then the Web-as-Corpus approach was developed (Baroni and Bernardini 2004). In essence, this requires you to select a representative list of words in your target language; then use these in a corpus-harvester program (e.g. BootCaT), which sends subsets of the words as search-terms to Google, Yahoo, Bing, or some other web search engine. The program downloads the hit webpages, scrapes the text, and collates the results into a corpus. At Leeds, Sharoff (2006) used the Web-as-Corpus method to collect internet corpora for Arabic, Chinese, French, German, Italian, Spanish, Polish, and Russian, freely accessible via a concordance and collocation search interface.[2] This includes the 176 million word Arabic Internet Corpus.

We later collected a smaller World Wide Arabic Corpus, analogous to the World Wide English Corpus (Atwell et al. 2007), comprising 200,000 word subcorpora from each country, to capture country-by-country dialect variation. This was used to study Arabic dialect variation in connectives (Hassan et al. 2013), and variation in Arabic and Arab English in the Arab world (Atwell et al. 2009). We also used the Web-as-Corpus approach to collect a specialised 'corpus' of texts for university-level teaching about Islam (Atwell et al. 2011).

4.7 Arabic corpus part-of-speech tagging and morphological analysis

Some years ago, I worked on the LOB Corpus tagging project (Leech and Garside 1982; Leech et al. 1983b), and I wanted to apply my experience of English tagging to Arabic (Atwell 2008; Atwell et al. 2008), that is, to develop Arabic corpus annotation software for POS tagging, morphological analysis, and more. A first step was a comparative evaluation of existing Arabic morphological analysers and stemmers, by hand-analysis of small, gold standard samples of the Qur'an and modern news text, to compare and evaluate the outputs of automated analysers (Sawalha and Atwell 2008). We also compared linguistically informed and corpus-informed approaches to morphological analysis of Arabic (Sawalha and Atwell 2009). This guided the development of a new, fine-grained morphological analyser and POS tagset and tagger software for Arabic (Sawalha and Atwell 2010a): the SALMA tagger. The name SALMA could stand for either 'Sawalha Atwell Leeds Morphological Analysis' (Sawalha and Atwell 2013a), or 'Standard Arabic Language Morphological Analysis' (Sawalha et al. 2013), although it originated as a suggested name for a granddaughter!

The SALMA tagger is part of a broader Arabic corpus analysis toolkit, including a standard tagset expounding traditional morphological features for Arabic POS tagging (Sawalha et al. 2013). Developing this involved formal analysis of traditional

Arabic grammarians' theoretical research applied to POS tagging, giving a detailed and comprehensive ontology of established Arabic word-structure theory. Several other Arabic POS tagsets have been developed for specific tasks, but generally are adapted from English models, and/or cover only a limited subset of traditional treatises on Arabic morphology. We provided an online benchmark for comparison and evaluation of task-specific POS tagsets. This work will enable Arabic corpus POS tagging research to be grounded on established traditional Arabic linguistic theory. The SALMA tagset and tagging software are complemented with a broad-coverage Arabic lexicon derived from open-source, online lexical resources and traditional Arabic dictionaries (Sawalha and Atwell 2010b), and tools for visualisation of Arabic morphology (Sawalha and Atwell 2012). To verify its robustness for processing large corpora, we applied the SALMA tagger to the Arabic Internet Corpus (Sawalha and Atwell 2013b). The SALMA corpus analysis toolkit has been used for corpus linguistic research, for example in developing vocabulary lists for Arabic language learners (Kilgarriff et al. 2014b), learning Arabic spelling and vocabulary (Erradi et al. 2012), Arabic grammatical analysis (Rabiee 2011), and analysis of Arabic social media (El-Beltagy and Ali 2013).

4.8 Discourse treebank for Modern Standard Arabic

A different sort of tagging is required for Arabic discourse analysis. Alsaif and Markert (2010; this volume) describe the development of the Leeds Arabic Discourse Treebank, a corpus of 537 news texts in which all 5,651 discourse connectives are identified and annotated with the discourse relations they convey as well, as with the two arguments they relate.

4.9 Arabic Learner Corpus

The Arabic Learner Corpus (ALC) is a freely downloadable resource for Arabic language teaching (Alfaifi and Atwell 2013; Alfaifi et al. 2014), comprising a collection of written and spoken materials from learners of Arabic in Saudi Arabia. The ALC data was captured in 2012 and 2013. It comprises 282,732 words across 1,585 texts (written and spoken), produced by 942 students of 67 nationalities and 66 different first-language backgrounds. The corpus metadata, in English and Arabic, enables researchers to identify characteristics of each transcribed text and its producer, adding more depth to the data analysis. We also developed a new tagset for error annotation of the Arabic Learner Corpus (Alfaifi et al. 2013). This was informed by error tagsets used in other learner corpus projects, but adapted to the specific types of errors made by learners of Arabic.

4.10 Arabic phonetic and prosodic tagging

Another sort of tagging is phonetic transcription of texts to be read out loud, such as the Qur'an. Phonetics researchers use the International Phonetic Alphabet (IPA) to transcribe spoken texts in any language; as the Arabic script is not entirely phonetic, there is not a simple one-to-one mapping between Arabic written characters and IPA symbols. We therefore developed a verified mapping between Arabic script and the IPA, for automated Arabic phonetic transcription; this was informed by analysis of Qurʾanic recitation, traditional Arabic linguistics, and modern phonetics (Brierley et al. 2016; Sawalha et al. 2014). The traditional source text of the Qurʾan also includes prosodic symbols denoting several types of pause or phrase boundary. Muslims are required to follow *tajweed* when reading aloud verses from the Qurʾan. The term *tajweed* (*taǧwīd*, lit. 'improvement') refers to the rules governing pronunciation and prosody during recitation of the Qurʾan. The IPA mapping and prosodic symbols were used in phonetic and prosodic annotation of the Qurʾan, to produce the Boundary-Annotated Qurʾan Corpus (Brierley et al. 2012a). This prosodically tagged Arabic corpus can help non-Arabic-speakers to learn correct Qurʾanic recitation; it can also be used to train a prosodic tagger for other Arabic texts, including those in Modern Standard Arabic (Sawalha et al. 2012a, 2012b).

4.11 Corpus-based comparison of English and Arabic

Given my background in English corpus linguistics (e.g. Leech et al. 1983a, 1983b), I am interested in corpus-based comparisons of English and Arabic. These include: Arabic influences on Arab English, the variety of English in use in the Arab world (Atwell et al. 2009); comparing morphological and POS tagsets for English and Arabic (Atwell 2008; Sawalha and Atwell 2013c); and visualisation of prosody in English and Arabic corpora (Brierley et al. 2012b).

4.12 The Qurʾanic Arabic Corpus

Since the open-access release of the Corpus of Contemporary Arabic, discussed above, a growing number and variety of open-access modern Arabic corpora have appeared. However, the Qurʾan and Classical Arabic have attracted much less interest, at least among corpus linguists. The best known Classical Arabic project is the Qurʾanic Arabic Corpus (Dukes et al. 2013), a collaboratively constructed linguistic resource initiated at the University of Leeds, with multiple layers of annotation including POS tagging, morphological segmentation (Dukes and Habash 2010), syntactic analysis using dependency grammar (Dukes and Buckwalter 2010; Dukes et al. 2010), word-by-word English glosses, several parallel verse-by-verse English translations, audio recordings of recitations, and an ontology of Qurʾanic concepts. The motivation behind this work is to produce a resource that enables further analysis and understanding of the Qurʾan. The Qurʾan benefits from a large body of existing historical grammatical analysis, in traditional commentaries by Islamic scholars. Thus, this project contrasts with other Arabic treebanks in its provision of a linguistic model based on the historical traditional grammar known as *ʾiʿrab*, 'nominal declension'. By adopting this well-known canon of Qurʾanic grammar, it is possible to encourage online annotation by Arabic linguists and Qurʾanic experts. This new approach to linguistic annotation of an Arabic corpus consists of automatic rule-based tagging, initial manual verification, and online supervised collaborative proofreading. The Qur'anic Arabic Corpus morphological tagging project relied on approximately a hundred unpaid volunteer annotators, each suggesting corrections to existing linguistic annotations. A small number of expert annotators had a supervisory role, allowing them to review or veto suggestions made by other collaborators. The challenges of annotating Qur'anic Arabic online required a custom-built software platform to aid collaborative annotation: LAMP, the Linguistic Analysis Multimodal Platform (Dukes and Atwell 2012). The Qur'anic Arabic Corpus has been used as a gold standard resource for a range of research on Classical Arabic, including word stemming (Yusof et al. 2010), grammatical analysis (Mohammed and Omar 2011; Rabiee 2011), stylometrics (Alqurneh et al. 2016), coherence analysis in Arabic translation studies (Tabrizi and Mahmud 2013), summarisation (El-Haj et al. 2015), and oral-formulaic analysis (Bannister 2014). It has also had significant social impact: the million visits a year to the corpus's website include non-Arabic-speakers, gaining a deeper insight into the original Classical Arabic text through the linguistic annotations.

4.13 QurAna: Qur'an pronoun anaphoric co-reference

QurAna (Sharaf and Atwell 2012a) is a large-scale annotation of the Qur'an as a corpus, where each personal pronoun is tagged with its antecedent, that is, the word or phrase it refers to in the preceding (or occasionally following) text; and also with its 'meaning', that is, the person, entity, or concept that pronoun and antecedent stand for in a Qur'anic *ontology* (a schema of people, entities, and concepts). QurAna includes a comparatively large number (over 24,500) of pronouns tagged with antecedent information; and an ontology of over a thousand persons, entities, and concepts, all nouns or phrases which are referred to by personal pronouns. Deciding on the reference of a personal pronoun is not always straightforward, but for the Qur'an, we can use scholarly commentaries (tafsirs; see above) to guide the annotator. In uncertain cases, we followed the coreference analysis in the tafsir of Ibn Kathir, a highly trusted and acclaimed Islamic reference work; we have at least as much confidence in this as in the alternative of relying on inter-annotator agreement between two casual-worker annotators. The anaphoric reference annotation is first freely downloadable corpus annotation of its kind for Arabic in general as well as Classical Arabic specifically.

4.14 QurSim: Qur'an verse similarity

QurSim (Sharaf and Atwell 2012b) is another layer of linguistic annotation for the original Qur'anic text, in which semantically similar or related verses are linked together. This corpus is a freely downloadable resource for corpus linguists investigating similarity, relatedness, and paraphrasing in short texts. In our QurSim related-verse dataset, we relied again on Ibn Kathir. As his commentary on each verse points to the related verses, we text-mined his tafsir to extract cross-references, producing over 7,600 pairs of related verses. The QurSim dataset is incorporated into a website where users can visualise, for a given verse, a network of all directly and indirectly related verses.[3] Experiments showed that only 33 per cent of related verse pairs share word roots, indicating that relatedness goes beyond lexical matching, and involves semantics and domain knowledge. QurSim can be used for extraction and visualisation of topics in the Qur'an (Panju 2014). Ibn Kathir's commentary relates to the Classical Arabic source text of the Qur'an, but the verse-relations can also apply to translations: two verses should be 'related' in any language. Hence, QurSim is potentially a resource for research on textual similarity and relatedness in any language that has a translation of the Qur'an.

4.15 Qurany: Qur'an annotated with verse topics

Qurany (Abbas 2009; Abbas and Atwell 2013) is a bilingual (English–Arabic) web-based search tool for the Qur'an that enhances recall and precision when searching for concepts. This is achieved by a combination of corpus annotations. Each verse in the Qur'an is annotated with semantic conceptual information, extracted from *Mushaf Al Tajweed* (*muṣḥaf at-tağwīd*, 'edition of [correct] pronunciation'), a respected Qur'an commentary which includes an index of nearly 1,100 concepts or topics. The *Mushaf Al Tajweed* index, showing the verses each concept or topic appears in, was transformed into an ontology represented as a tree data-structure; on the Qurany website, users can navigate the ontology tree to find their chosen concept, then follow the link to a list of verses tagged with this concept. Each Arabic verse is also annotated with eight alternative English translations from popular published sources; thus, a verse can be found via English keyword-search if any of the translations contains the keyword(s). Also, the user can opt to see WordNet synonyms of keywords, to broaden the search-terms and hence improve recall. The Qurany dataset is downloadable in HTML format.

4.16 King Saud University Corpus of Classical Arabic

Lexical patterns in the Qur'an can be studied using an Arabic-friendly concordancer such as aConCorde. However, linguists and lexicographers generally need much larger corpora to study collocations and concordance patterns: the BNC is 100 million words, while the Qur'an comprises only about 50,000 words (depending on how word-boundaries are counted). For research on distributional lexical semantics, we need a reasonably large number of examples of each word or collocation to be studied; but many words and phrases in the Qur'an occur only a handful of times. We therefore collaborated with researchers at King Saud University to collect a 50 million word corpus of Classical Arabic texts from the same period as the Qur'an, producing the King Saud University Corpus of Classical Arabic (KSUCCA) (Alrabiah et al. 2013, 2014a, 2014b). This allows us to select a word from the Qur'an and then find many more examples of its use in context in Classical Arabic. The KSUCCA corpus is downloadable from the KSUCCA website,[4] and is also searchable online via Sketch Engine (Kilgarriff et al. 2014a). KSUCCA is crucial to the corpus-based study of Arabic historical linguistics (Alrabiah et al. 2014b) and the distributional lexical semantics of the language of the Qur'an (Alrabiah et al. 2014a).

4.17 Ontologies and semantic tagging for the Qur'an

As outlined above, across a number of projects we have added linguistic tagging to the Qur'an at several levels: POS tags, morphology, anaphoric references, phonetic transcription, prosodic phrase boundaries, syntactic phrase structure, and dependency structure. We also have several types of annotation representing the 'knowledge' in the Qur'an: an ontology of nominal entities referred to by personal pronouns; verse topics and verse similarities; and translations into English at word and verse levels. We aim to combine or unify these linguistic annotations and ontologies (Abbas et al. 2013; Abbas and Atwell 2013), to produce a knowledge-representation formalism for semantic tagging of the Qur'an (Sharaf and Atwell 2009; Alrehaili and Atwell 2013, 2014).

5. Conclusion

Natural language processing (NLP) is a subfield of computer science and artificial intelligence which uses corpora for computational modelling. This computational focus is not always attractive to linguists: as Adam Kilgarriff put it in a post to the *Corpora* online discussion list, 'NLP/computational linguistics has come into the field like a schoolyard bully, forcing everything that's not computational into submission, collusion or the margins.'[5] However, we believe Arabic NLP can be harnessed to produce useful resources for Arabic corpus linguistics. Researchers at Leeds University have developed a series of online datasets and software packages for use in Arabic corpus linguistic research. Our resources are open-source and accessible via the Web, rather than commercial; we hope this will help make them widely reused, compared with some resources kept in-house by other research groups. These resources include some in various types of modern Arabic – the Corpus of Contemporary Arabic, the Arabic Internet Corpus, the World Wide Arabic Corpus, the Arabic Discourse Treebank, the Arabic Learner Corpus – as well as some in Classical Arabic, namely the Qur'an, and the King Saud University Corpus of Classical Arabic. We have tackled various levels of linguistic analysis, including POS tags, morphology, anaphoric references, named entities, learner errors and error-types, phonetic transcription, prosodic phrase boundaries, syntactic phrase structure, dependency structure, discourse connectives and relations, parallel English translations, topics, and distributional lexical semantics. In so doing, we have developed a range of software tools for Arabic corpus research, including tagging and annotation tools for these layers of analysis, and also corpus exploration via search, concordance, chatbot, and visualisation tools.

A challenging area for further research is how to tag and represent semantics and 'knowledge' in Arabic texts, and in particular the Qur'an and other religious texts. Atwell et al. (2010) proposed *Understanding the Qur'an* as a 'Grand Challenge' for computer science and AI research, with twin objectives: to represent Qur'anic 'knowledge' in an AI formalism, as an extra layer of semantic tagging in the Qur'anic corpus; and thus to use AI to help Muslims and non-Muslims to better understand the lessons of the Qur'an. Understanding Islam is a major societal issue. Western schools, universities, and the general public need a high-quality, online, knowledge-based corpus of the Qur'an to learn about Islam. Non-Arabic-speaking Muslims also want to better understand the meanings in the Qur'an, beyond oral recitation. Current systems can search for words, and even answer basic factual questions, for example 'are angels male?'. However, we need a new tagset/formalism for the representation of religious knowledge, one capable of capturing the subtle complexities of the religious discourse contained within the Qur'an.

Moreover, machine learning research needs a gold standard corpus, that is, one where each text is classified and marked up correctly by experts, so the learning algorithm can learn the classification. The Qur'an is an excellent gold standard, since many expert analyses already exist, which can be used to train machine learning algorithms. Subsequently, Qur'anic scholars can verify the results from machine learning to ensure that knowledge-based systems based on the Qur'an are logically consistent and correct. Huge worldwide interest in the Qur'an means we can harness volunteers for crowdsourcing analysis, following the approach used successfully in the Qur'anic Arabic Corpus: initial automatic analysis, then proofreading and correction by many volunteers.

In sum, understanding the Qur'an is a grand challenge for society, for western public education, for Muslim-world education, for knowledge representation and reasoning, for knowledge extraction from text, and for online collaboration. In consequence, understanding the Qur'an is a grand challenge for Arabic corpus linguistics.

Notes

1. At time of writing, this was the result for a Google query for *define artificial intelligence* (last accessed 3 May 2015).
2. Available at <http://corpus.leeds.ac.uk/internet.html> (last accessed 21 May 2018).
3. See <http://TextMiningTheQuran.com> (last accessed 22 May 2018).
4. See <https://www.sketchengine.eu/corpus-of-classical-arabic-ksucca/> (last accessed 29 June 2018).
5. This post is available at <http://mailman.uib.no/public/corpora/2007-January/003842.html> (last accessed 22 May 2018).

References

Abbas, N. (2009), 'Quran Search for a Concept Tool and Website', unpublished MRes thesis, University of Leeds.

Abbas, N., L. Aldhubayi, H. Al-Khalifa, Z. Alqassem, E. Atwell, K. Dukes, M. Sawalha and M. Sharaf (2013), 'Unifying linguistic annotations and ontologies for the Arabic Quran', in E. Atwell and A. Hardie (eds), *Abstracts for the Second Workshop on Arabic Corpus Linguistics*, Lancaster: Lancaster University, p. 14.

Abbas, N. and E. Atwell (2013), 'Annotating the Arabic Quran with a classical semantic ontology', in E. Atwell and A. Hardie (eds), *Abstracts for the Second Workshop on Arabic Corpus Linguistics*, Lancaster: Lancaster University, pp. 55–6.

Abdul Razak, Z. (2011), 'Modern Media Arabic: A Study of Word Frequency in World Affairs and Sports Sections in Arabic Newspapers', unpublished PhD thesis, University of Birmingham.

Abu Shawar, B. (2005), 'A Corpus Based Approach to Generalising a Chatbot System', unpublished PhD thesis, University of Leeds.

Abu Shawar, B. and E. Atwell (2005a), 'Using corpora in machine-learning chatbot systems', *International Journal of Corpus Linguistics*, 10(4): 489–516.

Abu Shawar, B. and E. Atwell (2005b), 'A chatbot system as a tool to animate a corpus', *ICAME Journal*, 29: 5–24.

Abu Shawar, B. and E. Atwell (2009), 'Arabic question-answering via instance based learning from an FAQ corpus', in M. Mahlberg, V. González-Díaz and C. Smith (eds), *Proceedings of Corpus Linguistics 2009*, Liverpool University, <http://ucrel.lancs.ac.uk/publications/cl2009/402_FullPaper.doc> (last accessed 21 May 2018).

Alfaifi, A. and E. Atwell (2013), 'Arabic Learner Corpus v1: A new resource for Arabic language research', in E. Atwell and A. Hardie (eds), *Abstracts for the Second Workshop on Arabic Corpus Linguistics*, Lancaster: Lancaster University, pp. 9–13.

Alfaifi, A., E. Atwell and G. Abuhakema (2013), 'Error annotation of the Arabic Learner Corpus: A new error tagset', in I. Gurevych, C. Biemann and T. Zesch (eds), *Language Processing and Knowledge in the Web*, *Lecture Notes in Computer Science*, vol. 8105, Berlin: Springer, pp. 14–22.

Alfaifi, A., E. Atwell and I. Hedaya (2014), 'Arabic Learner Corpus (ALC) v2: A new written and spoken corpus of Arabic learners', in S. Ishikawa (ed.), *Learner Corpus Studies in Asia and the World, Vol. 2, Papers from LCSAW2014*, Kobe: Kobe University, pp. 77–89.

Ali, I. (2012), 'Application of a mining algorithm to finding frequent patterns in a text corpus: A case study of Arabic', *International Journal of Software Engineering and Its Applications*, 6(3): 127–34.

Alqurneh, A., A. Mustapha, M. Murad and N. Sharef (2016), 'Stylometric model for detecting oath expressions: A case study for Quranic texts', *Digital Scholarship in the Humanities*, 31(1): 1–20.

Alrabiah, M., N. Alhelewh, A. Al-Salman and E. Atwell (2014a), 'An empirical study on the Holy Quran based on a large classical Arabic corpus', *International Journal of Computational Linguistics*, 5(1): 1–13.

Alrabiah, M., A. Al-Salman and E. Atwell (2013), 'The design and construction of the 50 million words KSUCCA King Saud University Corpus of Classical Arabic', in E. Atwell and A. Hardie (eds), *Abstracts for the Second Workshop on Arabic Corpus Linguistics*, Lancaster: Lancaster University, pp. 6–10.

Alrabiah, M., A. Al-Salman, E. Atwell, and N. Alhelewh (2014b), 'KSUCCA: A key to exploring Arabic historical linguistics', *International Journal of Computational Linguistics*, 5(2): 27–36.

Alrehaili, S. and E. Atwell (2013), 'Linguistics features to confirm the chronological order of the Quran', in E. Atwell and A. Hardie (eds), *Abstracts for the Second Workshop on Arabic Corpus Linguistics*, Lancaster: Lancaster University, pp. 63–6.

Alrehaili, S. and E. Atwell (2014), 'Computational ontologies for semantic tagging of the Quran', in C. Brierley, M. Sawalha and E. Atwell (eds), *Proceedings of LRE-Rel 2: 2nd Workshop on Language Resource and Evaluation for Religious Texts*, pp. 19–23.

Alruily, M. (2012), 'Using Text Mining to Identify Crime Patterns from Arabic Crime News Report Corpus', unpublished PhD thesis, De Montfort University.

Alsaif, A. and K. Markert (2010), 'The Leeds Arabic Discourse Treebank: Annotating discourse connectives for Arabic', in N. Calzolari, K. Choukri, B. Maegaard, J. Mariani, J. Odijk, S. Piperidis, M. Rosner and D. Tapias (eds), *Proceedings of the Seventh Conference on Language Resources and Evaluation Conference (LREC) 2010*, Paris: ELRA, pp. 2046–53.

Al-Sulaiti, L. and E. Atwell (2005), 'Extending the Corpus of Contemporary Arabic', in *Proceedings of Corpus Linguistics 2005*, Birmingham University, <http://www.birmingham.ac.uk/Documents/college-artslaw/corpus/conference-archives/2005-journal/Compilingacorpus/CLPaper.doc> (last accessed 21 May 2018).

Al-Sulaiti, L. and E. Atwell (2006), 'The design of a Corpus of Contemporary Arabic', *International Journal of Corpus Linguistics*, 11(1): 135–71.

Al-Sulaiti, L., A. Roberts, B. Abu Shawar and E. Atwell (2007), 'The use of corpus, concordancer and chatbot in the teaching of contemporary Arabic', in *Abstracts from Corpus Linguistics 2007*, Birmingham University, <http://ucrel.lancs.ac.uk/publications/CL2007/abstract/277_Abstract.pdf> (last accessed 21 May 2018).

Attia, M., P. Pecina, L. Tounsi, A. Toral and J. Van Genabith (2011), 'Lexical profiling for Arabic', in I. Kosem and K. Kosem (eds), *Proceedings of eLex 2011 Electronic Lexicography in the 21st Century*, pp. 23–33.

Atwell, E. (1993a), 'The HEFC's knowledge based systems initiative', *AISBQ: Artificial Intelligence and Simulation of Behaviour Quarterly*, 83, pp. 29–34.

Atwell, E. (ed.) (1993b), *Knowledge at Work in Universities: Proceedings of the Second Annual Conference of the Higher Education Funding Council's Knowledge Based Systems Initiative*, Leeds: Leeds University Press.

Atwell, E. (2008), 'Development of tag sets for part-of-speech tagging', in A. Lüdeling and M. Kytö (eds), *Corpus Linguistics: An International Handbook*, vol. 1, Berlin; Walter de Gruyter, pp. 501–26.

Atwell, E., N. Abbas, B. Abu Shawar, L. Al-Sulaiti, A. Roberts and M. Sawalha (2008), 'Mapping Middle Eastern and North African diasporas', in *Abstracts of BRISMES 2008*, British Society for Middle Eastern Studies, <https://www.researchgate.net/publication/262198736_Mapping_Middle_Eastern_and_North_African_diasporas_Arabic_corpus_linguistics_research_at_the_University_of_Leeds> (last accessed 29 June 2018).

Atwell, E., L. Al-Sulaiti, S. Al-Osaimi and B. Abu Shawar (2004), 'A review of Arabic corpus analysis tools', in *Proceedings of TALN '04*, University of Mohamed bin Abdullah, Fez, Morocco, pp. 229–34, <https://www.researchgate.net/publication/268522847_A_review_of_Arabic_corpus_analysis_tools_-_Un_Examen_d'Outils_pour_l'Analyse_de_Corpus_Arabes> (last accessed 29 June 2018).

Atwell, E., L. Al-Sulaiti and S. Sharoff (2009), 'Arabic and Arab English in the Arab world', in M. Mahlberg, V. González-Díaz and C. Smith (eds), *Proceedings of Corpus*

Linguistics 2009, Liverpool University, <http://ucrel.lancs.ac.uk/publications/cl2009/406_FullPaper.doc> (last accessed 21 May 2018).

Atwell, E., J. Arshad, C. Lai, L. Nim, N. Rezapour Asheghi, J. Wang and J. Washtell (2007), 'Which English dominates the World Wide Web, British or American?', in M. Davies, P. Rayson, S. Hunston and P. Danielsson (eds), *Proceedings of the Corpus Linguistics Conference CL 2007*, University of Birmingham, <http://ucrel.lancs.ac.uk/publications/CL2007/paper/268_Paper.pdf> (last accessed 21 May 2018).

Atwell, E., C. Brierley, K. Dukes, M. Sawalha and A. Sharaf (2011), 'An artificial intelligence approach to Arabic and Islamic content on the internet', in *Proceedings of NITS'2011 3rd National Information Technology Symposium*, Riyadh, <http://www.kokannews.org/wp-content/uploads/2014/05/An-Artificial-Intelligence.pdf> (last accessed 21 May 2018).

Atwell, E., K. Dukes, A. Sharaf, N. Habash, B. Louw, B. Abu Shawar, A. McEnery, W. Zaghouani and M. El-Haj (2010), 'Understanding the Quran: A new grand challenge for computer science and artificial intelligence', research proposal, <https://www.researchgate.net/publication/215442740_Understanding_the_Quran_A_New_Grand_Challenge_for_Computer_Science_and_Artificial_Intelligence> (last accessed 29 June 2018).

Bannister, A. (2014), *An Oral-Formulaic Study of the Quran*, New York: Lexington Books.

Baroni, M. and S. Bernardini (2004), 'BootCaT: Bootstrapping corpora and terms from the Web', in M. T. Lino, M. F. Xavier, F. Ferreira, R. Costa and R. Silva (eds), *Proceedings of LREC 2004*, Paris: ELRA, pp. 1313–16.

Brierley, C., E. Atwell, C. Rowland and J. Anderson (2013), 'Semantic pathways: A novel visualization of varieties of English', *ICAME Journal*, 37: 5–36.

Brierley, C., M. Sawalha and E. Atwell (2012a), 'Open-source Boundary-Annotated Corpus for Arabic speech and language processing', in N. Calzolari, K. Choukri, T. Declerck, M. U. Dogan, B. Maegaard, J. Mariani, A. Moreno, J. Odijk and S. Piperidis (eds), *Proceedings of LREC 2012 Language Resources and Evaluation Conference*, Paris: ELRA, pp. 1011–16.

Brierley, C., M. Sawalha and E. Atwell (2012b), 'Visualisation of prosody in English and Arabic speech corpora', in *Abstracts of AVML 2012, Advances in Visual Methods for Linguistics*, York: University of York, pp. 29–30.

Brierley, C., M. Sawalha, B. Heselwood and E. Atwell (2016), 'A verified Arabic–IPA mapping for Arabic transcription technology, informed by Quranic recitation, traditional Arabic linguistics, and modern phonetics', *Journal of Semitic Studies*, 61(1): 157–86.

Brockett, A., E. Atwell, O. Taylor and M. Page (1989), 'An Arabic text database and glossary system for students', in *Proceedings of the Seminar on Bilingual Computing in Arabic and English*, Cambridge: University of Cambridge, pp. 154–62.

Chen, H. (2012), *Dark Web: Exploring and Data Mining the Dark Side of the Web*, New York: Springer.

Danso, S., E. Atwell, O. Johnson, A. ten Asbroek, S. Soromekun, K. Edmond, C. Hurt, L. Hurt, C. Zandoh, C. Tawiah, J. Fenty, S. Etego, S. Agyei and B.

Kirkwood (2013), 'A semantically annotated verbal autopsy corpus for automatic analysis of cause of death', *ICAME Journal*, 37: 37–69.

Dukes, K. and E. Atwell (2012), 'LAMP: A multimodal web platform for collaborative linguistic analysis', in N. Calzolari, K. Choukri, T. Declerck, M. U. Dogan, B. Maegaard, J. Mariani, A. Moreno, J. Odijk and S. Piperidis (eds), *Proceedings of LREC 2012 Language Resources and Evaluation Conference*, Paris: ELRA, pp. 3268–76.

Dukes, K., E. Atwell and N. Habash (2013), 'Supervised collaboration for syntactic annotation of Quranic Arabic', *Language Resources and Evaluation*, 47(1): 33–62.

Dukes, K., E. Atwell and A. Sharaf (2010), 'Syntactic annotation guidelines for the Quranic Arabic dependency treebank', in N. Calzolari, K. Choukri, B. Maegaard, J. Mariani, J. Odijk, S. Piperidis, M. Rosner and D. Tapias (eds), *Proceedings of the Language Resources and Evaluation Conference (LREC) 2010*, Paris: ELRA, pp. 1822–7.

Dukes, K. and T. Buckwalter (2010), 'A dependency treebank of the Quran using traditional Arabic grammar', in *Proceedings of INFOS'2010 7th Informatics and Systems*, IEEE, <http://ieeexplore.ieee.org/document/5461810/?part=1> (last accessed 21 May 2018).

Dukes, K. and N. Habash (2010), 'Morphological annotation of Quranic Arabic', in N. Calzolari, K. Choukri, B. Maegaard, J. Mariani, J. Odijk, S. Piperidis, M. Rosner and D. Tapias (eds), *Proceedings of the Language Resources and Evaluation Conference (LREC) 2010*, Paris: ELRA, pp. 2530–6.

El-Beltagy, S. and A. Ali (2013), 'Open issues in the sentiment analysis of Arabic social media: A case study', in *Proceedings of IIT 2013, Innovations in Information Technology*, IEEE, <http://ieeexplore.ieee.org/document/6544421/> (last accessed 21 May 2018).

El-Haj, M., U. Kruschwitz and C. Fox (2015), 'Creating language resources for under-resourced languages: Methodologies, and experiments with Arabic', *Language Resources and Evaluation*, 49(3): 549–80.

Erradi, A., S. Nahia, H. Almerekhi and L. Al-kailani (2012), 'ArabicTutor: A multimedia m-Learning platform for learning Arabic spelling and vocabulary', in *Proceedings of ICMCS 2012 International Conference on Multimedia Computing and Systems*, IEEE, <http://ieeexplore.ieee.org/document/6320220/> (last accessed 21 May 2018).

Friginal, E. and J. Hardy (2014), *Corpus-Based Sociolinguistics: A Guide for Students*, London: Routledge.

Garside, R. and N. Smith (1997), 'A hybrid grammatical tagger: CLAWS4', in R. Garside, G. Leech and A. McEnery (eds), *Corpus Annotation: Linguistic Information from Computer Text Corpora*, London: Longman, pp. 102–21.

Greene, B. and G. Rubin (1971), *Automatic Grammatical Tagging of English*, technical report, Providence, RI: Brown University, Department of Linguistics.

Hassan, H., N. Daud and E. Atwell (2013), 'Connectives in the World Wide Web Arabic corpus', *World Applied Sciences Journal*, 21(4): 67–72.

Karlsson, F., A. Voutilainen, J. Heikkila and A. Anttila (eds) (1995), *Constraint Grammar: A Language-Independent System for Parsing Running Text*, Berlin and New York: Mouton de Gruyter.

Kilgarriff, A., V. Baisa, J. Bušta, M. Jakubíček, V. Kovář, J. Michelfeit, P. Rychlý and V Suchomel (2014a), 'The Sketch Engine: Ten years on', *Lexicography*, 1(1): 1–30.

Kilgarriff, A., F. Charalabopoulou, M. Gavrilidou, J. Jonannessen, S. Khalil, S. Johansson-Kokkinakis, R. Lew, S. Sharoff, R. Vadlapudi and E. Volodina (2014b), 'Corpus-based vocabulary lists for language learners for nine languages', *Language Resources and Evaluation*, 48(1): 121–63.

Leech, G. and R. Garside (1982), 'Grammatical tagging of the LOB Corpus: General survey', in S. Johansson and K. Hofland (eds), *Computer Corpora in English Language Research*, Bergen: NAVF, pp. 110–17.

Leech, G., R. Garside and E. Atwell (1983a), 'Recent developments in the use of computer corpora in English language research', *Transactions of the Philological Society*, 81(1): 23–40.

Leech, G., R. Garside and E. Atwell (1983b), 'The automatic grammatical tagging of the LOB Corpus', *ICAME Journal*, 7: 13–33.

Merakchi, K. and M. Rogers (2013), 'The translation of culturally bound metaphors in the genre of popular science articles: A corpus-based case study from Scientific American translated into Arabic', *Intercultural Pragmatics*, 10(2): 341–72.

Mohammed, M. and N. Omar (2011), 'Rule based shallow parser for Arabic language', *Journal of Computer Science*, 7(10): 1505–14.

Panju, M. (2014), 'Statistical Extraction and Visualization of Topics in the Quran Corpus', unpublished MMath thesis, University of Waterloo.

Rabiee, H. (2011), 'Adapting standard open-source resources to tagging a morphologically rich language: A case study with Arabic', in I. Temnikova, I. Nikolova and N. Konstantinova (eds), *Proceedings of the Second Student Research Workshop associated with RANLP 2011*, pp. 127–32.

Roberts, A., L. Al-Sulaiti and E. Atwell (2006), 'aConCorde: Towards an open-source, extendable concordancer for Arabic', *Corpora*, 1(1): 39–57.

Sawalha, M. and E. Atwell (2008), 'Comparative evaluation of Arabic language morphological analysers and stemmers', in D. Scott and H. Uszkoreit (eds), *Proceedings of the 22nd International Conference on Computational Linguistics (COLING'2008), Companion Volume (Posters)*, Manchester: University of Manchester, pp. 107–10.

Sawalha, M. and E. Atwell (2009), 'Linguistically informed and corpus informed morphological analysis of Arabic', in M. Mahlberg, V. González-Díaz and C. Smith (eds), *Proceedings of Corpus Linguistics 2009*, Liverpool: Liverpool University, <http://ucrel.lancs.ac.uk/publications/cl2009/168_FullPaper.doc> (last accessed 21 May 2018).

Sawalha, M. and E. Atwell (2010a), 'Fine-grain morphological analyzer and part-of-speech tagger for Arabic text', in N. Calzolari, K. Choukri, B. Maegaard, J. Mariani, J. Odijk, S. Piperidis, M. Rosner and D. Tapias (eds), *Proceedings of the Language Resources and Evaluation Conference (LREC) 2010*, Paris: ELRA, pp. 1258–65.

Sawalha, M. and E. Atwell (2010b), 'Constructing and using broad-coverage lexical resource for enhancing morphological analysis of Arabic', in N. Calzolari, K. Choukri, B. Maegaard, J. Mariani, J. Odijk, S. Piperidis, M. Rosner and D. Tapias (eds), *Proceedings of the Language Resources and Evaluation Conference (LREC) 2010*, Paris: ELRA, pp. 282–7.

Sawalha, M. and E. Atwell (2012), 'Visualization of Arabic morphology', in *Abstracts of AVML 2012, Advances in Visual Methods for Linguistics*, York: University of York, pp. 41–2.

Sawalha, M. and E. Atwell (2013a), 'Accelerating the processing of large corpora: Using grid computing for lemmatizing the 176 million words Arabic Internet Corpus', in E. Atwell and A. Hardie (eds), *Abstracts for the Second Workshop on Arabic Corpus Linguistics*, Lancaster: Lancaster University, pp. 81–2.

Sawalha, M. and E. Atwell (2013b), 'A standard tag set expounding traditional morphological features for Arabic language part-of-speech tagging', *Word Structure*, 6(1): 43–99.

Sawalha, M. and E. Atwell (2013c), ' Comparing morphological tag-sets for Arabic and English', in A. Hardie and R. Love (eds), *Corpus Linguistics 2013 Abstract Book*, Lancaster: UCREL, pp. 261–4.

Sawalha, M., E. Atwell and M. Abushariah (2013), 'SALMA: Standard Arabic Language Morphological Analysis', in *Proceedings ICCSPA'2013 International Conference on Communications, Signal Processing, and Their Applications*, IEEE, <http://ieeexplore.ieee.org/document/6487311/> (last accessed 21 May 2018).

Sawalha, M., C. Brierley and E. Atwell (2012a), 'Predicting phrase breaks in Classical and Modern Standard Arabic text', in N. Calzolari, K. Choukri, T. Declerck, M. U. Dogan, B. Maegaard, J. Mariani, A. Moreno, J. Odijk and S. Piperidis (eds), *Proceedings of LREC 2012 Language Resources and Evaluation Conference*, Paris: ELRA, pp. 3868–73.

Sawalha, M., C. Brierley and E. Atwell (2012b), 'Prosody prediction for Arabic via the open-source Boundary-Annotated Qur'an Corpus', *Journal of Speech Sciences*, 2(2): 175–91.

Sawalha, M., C. Brierley and E. Atwell (2014), 'Automatically generated, phonemic Arabic–IPA pronunciation tiers for the Boundary-Annotated Qur'an dataset for machine learning', in C. Brierley, M. Sawalha and E. Atwell (eds), *Proceedings of LRE-Rel 2: 2nd Workshop on Language Resource and Evaluation for Religious Texts*, pp. 42–7.

Sharaf, A. and E. Atwell (2009), 'A corpus-based computational model for knowledge representation of the Quran', in M. Mahlberg, V. González-Díaz and C. Smith (eds), *Proceedings of Corpus Linguistics 2009*, Liverpool: Liverpool University, <http://ucrel.lancs.ac.uk/publications/cl2009/169_FullPaper.doc> (last accessed 21 May 2018).

Sharaf, A. and E. Atwell (2012a), 'QurAna: Corpus of the Quran annotated with pronominal anaphora', in N. Calzolari, K. Choukri, T. Declerck, M. U. Dogan, B. Maegaard, J. Mariani, A. Moreno, J. Odijk and S. Piperidis (eds), *Proceedings of LREC 2012 Language Resources and Evaluation Conference*, Paris: ELRA, pp. 130–7.

Sharaf, A. and E. Atwell (2012b), 'QurSim: A corpus for evaluation of relatedness in short texts', in N. Calzolari, K. Choukri, T. Declerck, M. U. Dogan, B. Maegaard, J. Mariani, A. Moreno, J. Odijk and S. Piperidis (eds), *Proceedings of LREC 2012 Language Resources and Evaluation Conference*, Paris: ELRA, pp. 2295–302.

Sharoff, S. (2006), 'Open-source corpora: Using the net to fish for linguistic data', *International Journal of Corpus Linguistics*, 11(4): 435–62.

Tabrizi, A. and R. Mahmud (2013), 'Issues of coherence analysis on English translations of Quran', in *Proceedings of ICCSPA'2013 International Conference on Communications, Signal Processing, and Their Applications*, IEEE, <http://ieeexplore.ieee.org/document/6487276/> (last accessed 21 May 2018).

Wiechmann, D. and S. Fuhs (2006), 'Concordancing software', *Corpus Linguistics and Linguistics Theory*, 2(1): 107–27.

Wilson, J., A. Hartley, S. Sharoff and P. Stephenson (2010), 'Advanced corpus solutions for humanities researchers', in R. Otoguro, K. Ishiwaka, H. Umemoto, K. Yoshimoto and Y. Harada (eds), *Proceedings of PACLIC 24*, Sendai: Tohoku University, pp. 769–78.

Yusof, R., R. Zainuddin, M. Baba and Z. Yusoff (2010), 'Quranic words stemming', *Arabian Journal for Science and Engineering*, 35(2): 37–49.

7

Semantic Prosody as a Tool for Translating Prepositions in the Holy Qur'an: A Corpus-Based Analysis

Nagwa Younis

1. Introduction

One of the most challenging aspects of translating the Holy Qur'an is reflecting the shades of meaning conveyed by the use of certain prepositions in the Arabic text. Prepositions are used in the Holy Qur'an not only as a syntactic requirement but also for a semantic and rhetorical function. It is the hypothesis of this research that there is a 'semantic prosody' related to the use of one preposition versus another in a certain linguistic context. This semantic prosody makes it inaccurate for the translator to make consistent use of the same English word as a translation equivalent for a given verb when the verb is followed by more than one preposition in various linguistic contexts.

The aim of this chapter is twofold, and is hence of importance to the field of corpus-based translation studies in general and to the translation of the Holy Qur'an in particular. First, this chapter investigates the semantic prosody related to the use of certain prepositions (*'alā*, 'on'; *'ilā*, 'to'; and *li-*, 'for') in verb-preposition constructions by examining the collocational patterns in which they occur. This corpus-based analysis will, hopefully, help translators to render the Arabic text into the target language while keeping the same semantic effect conveyed by the original preposition. As we will see, the use of two different prepositions with the same verb may result in two different meanings. This contradicts the notion held by some Arab grammarians, for example the Kufi School, that some prepositions in Arabic can be substituted for one another without a change in meaning (see, for example, Hassan 1974). Second, this chapter analyses the strategies adopted by translators to overcome these problems, with a view to providing translators with insights on dealing with the semantic prosodies of such patterns.

More specifically, the chapter is an attempt to answer the following questions:

1. How are specific semantic prosodies related to the use of certain prepositions in the Holy Qur'an, especially in verb-preposition constructions?
2. In what way can this be detected through corpus analysis?

3. How can semantic prosody help translators achieve maximum quality by selecting an equivalent that has the nearest shade of meaning to the word in the original text?

The chapter is organised in the following fashion. In section 2, the concept of 'semantic prosody' is introduced by surveying it in the domain of corpus linguistics. Attempts to characterise the semantic prosody of prepositions in the Holy Qur'an, as a special genre, are indicated in section 3 in the light of previous work done by some Arab thinkers. The research method is described in section 4. The Qur'anic parallel corpus developed by Dukes (2012) will be the major tool used in this study for analysing the translation of prepositions in the Holy Qur'an, together with consultation of the *Qur'an* section of arabiCorpus (Parkinson 2012) to examine broader concordances of some of the verb-preposition constructions in the Holy Qur'an. Section 5 presents and discusses the results. The semantic prosodies of *'alā*, *'ilā*, and *li-* in verb-preposition constructions are detected in context. Six translations will be compared and contrasted to see to what extent the prepositions and their semantic prosodies are evident in the translations. The different strategies developed by translators to render Arabic prepositions into English will also be touched upon in the light of the semantic prosodies discovered. Some concluding remarks will be given, and some implications considered, in section 6.

2. Semantic prosody

Though the term *semantic prosody* was introduced by Louw (1993), who also provided it with its first definition, John Sinclair is considered the concept's real father since it appeared in his early writings (Sinclair 1987, 1991) and was developed in his later work (Sinclair 2004).[1] Whereas Partington (2004) associates semantic prosody explicitly with a binary distinction between positive and negative attitudinal meanings, Sinclair finds it difficult to assign a specific characterisation, or attitudinal discourse function, to a semantic prosody. In Sinclair's usage, *semantic prosody* refers to attitudinal meanings of all kinds, not just positive and negative evaluative meanings (as becomes apparent from Sinclair's various examples of semantic prosody, e.g. a prosody of 'informal invitation' which he posits for *PLACE* as a noun, and more specifically for the phrase *my place*, see Sinclair 1996: 92–3), and is, despite its name, 'on the pragmatic side of the semantics/pragmatics continuum' (Sinclair 2004: 34). As Baker et al. (2006: 145) remark, '[e]xamination of concordances generally helps to reveal the existence of semantic prosodies'.

A distinction is made between semantic prosody and connotation. McEnery and Hardie explain that:

> [t]he key difference from the traditional notion of connotation is that the semantic prosodies are not necessarily accessible to intuition, which is often used to make judgements about the connotations of a word. Rather, a semantic prosody can *only* be discovered by analysis of a concordance, as Louw (1993: 159) argues. (McEnery and Hardie 2012: 136)

In an earlier study on translating different morphological forms of the same verb in the Holy Qur'an (Younis 2012), I proposed that semantic prosody is a mechanism through which two layers of solution can be provided for the translation of different morphological forms in the Holy Qur'an. The first layer is the semantic significance associated with the realisation(s) of the verb form itself. The second layer is related to the contextual use of each form. This typically applies to sets of verb forms that have the same root, such as the difference between *kasaba* and *'iktasaba* (both translated as 'earn'); or to complete versus elided forms of the same verb, such as the distinction between *tawaffāhum* and *tatawaffāhum* (both translated as '(to) take (someone) into death').

3. Prepositions in the Holy Qur'an

In Arabic, much research has been done on the significance of using certain prepositions in specific lexical contexts to convey a certain meaning. In the following section, a brief survey is made of the opinions of three non-traditional early Arab grammarians and rhetoricians who tackled the semantics of prepositions in the Holy Qur'an. These Arab thinkers are 'ibn-ğinni (lived 932–1002 CE) (in *'al-ḫaṣā'iṣ*), 'al-zamaḫšari (lived 1074–1143) (in *'al-kaššāf*), and 'ibnul-qayyim (lived 1292–1349) (in *'at-tafsīr ul-qayyim*).

'ibn-ğinni was an Arab phonetician and a pioneer in the field of Arabic semantics. In the tenth century, 'ibn-ğinni produced his *'al-ḫaṣā'iṣ*, 'The Particularities' (n.d.), in which he included a chapter on 'Using prepositions in place of one another'. 'ibn-ğinni criticised the traditional view of some Arab grammarians (e.g. the Kufi School) that two prepositions in Arabic can be used interchangeably with the same shade of meaning. One of the examples usually quoted in this respect is:

. . . من أنصاري إلى الله . . .
. . . *man 'anṣāri 'ila-llāh* . . . (3:52)
'Who are my supporters for Allah?'

Some grammarians claimed that *'ilā* in this context is the semantic equivalent of *ma'a*, 'with'. 'ibn-ğinni tried to specify a connotation added by *'ilā* that would not be present if it were replaced by another preposition. He postulated that there is a deep meaning in this verse which suggests another verb (e.g. *yahdi*, 'guide'), one which collocates with *'ilā*. This is directly equivalent to how Louw states semantic prosody works: the meaning of the characteristic collocates of a word is present when that word is used in a context without those characteristic collocates.

Another example often given by the Kufi School and quoted by 'ibn-ğinni is:

هل لك إلى أن تزكى
hal laka 'ilā 'an tazakkā (79:18)
'Would you [be willing to] purify yourself?'

Here, the surface meaning requires the preposition *fi*, which habitually collocates with the phrase *hal laka*, 'would you'. 'ibn-ğinni says that the contextual meaning is that Moses (the speaker in this verse) is inviting Pharaoh (the addressee) to accept his (Moses') guidance, using *'ahdiyaka*, 'I guide you', which collocates with the preposition *'ilā*, and does in fact occur in the broader context. The semantic necessity of using ʾ*ilā* here emerges, in ʾibn-ǧinni's view, from the neighbouring collocates of this preposition in the following verse. Or, to put it more briefly, ʾibn-ǧinni argues that *hal laka* would normally collocate with *fi*, and the fact that ʾ*ilā* is used instead brings in the connotation of a verb from the broader context which does collocate with ʾ*ilā*, namely, ʾ*ahdiyaka*.

ʾal-zamaḫšari likewise addresses the linguistic interpretation of the Holy Qurʾan. In ʾ*al-kaššāf*, 'The Spotlight', he explains the distinction in the use of two different prepositions with the same verb. The example he gives is the verb ʾ*irzuqūhum*, 'sustain them' followed on one occasion by the preposition *min*, 'out of, from', and on another by the preposition *fi*, 'in/from', in verses (4:5) and (4:8) respectively. ʾal-zamaḫšari says that the difference is semantic and contextual, and that each preposition has a distinct function. He argues that the use of the preposition *fi* in verse (4:5) is semantically suggested by the context, which indicates that the addressee is a guardian of orphans. Guardians should invest the orphans' money, and hence sustain them out of the profits, so that the capital itself remains untouched:

(4:5) وَلَا تُؤْتُوا۟ ٱلسُّفَهَآءَ أَمْوَٰلَكُمُ ٱلَّتِي جَعَلَ ٱللَّهُ لَكُمْ قِيَٰمًا وَٱرْزُقُوهُمْ فِيهَا وَٱكْسُوهُمْ وَقُولُوا۟ لَهُمْ قَوْلًا مَّعْرُوفًا

Sahih International: And do not give the weak-minded your property, which Allah has made a means of sustenance for you, but ***provide for*** them ***with*** it and clothe them and speak to them words of appropriate kindness.
Pickthall: Give not unto the foolish (what is in) your (keeping of their) wealth, which Allah hath given you to maintain; but *feed* and clothe them *from* it, and speak kindly unto them.
Yusuf Ali: To those weak of understanding Make not over your property, which Allah hath made a means of support for you, but *feed* and clothe them ***therewith***, and speak to them words of kindness and justice.
Shakir: And do not give away your property which Allah has made for you a (means of) support to the weak of understanding, and ***maintain them out*** of (the profits of) it, and clothe them and speak to them words of honest advice.
Mohsin Khan: And give not unto the foolish your property which Allah has made a means of support for you, but *feed* and clothe them ***therewith***, and speak to them words of kindness and justice.
Ghali: And do not bring the foolish ones your riches that Allah has made for keeping you up, (i.e., as a means of support) and ***provide for*** them ***out of it***, and give them raiment, and speak to them beneficent words.

In verse (4:8), by contrast, the context describes dividing the inheritance of a dead person. The meaning is that if the poor attend this division, money should be given to them *from* the main stock of property:

(4:8) وَإِذَا حَضَرَ ٱلْقِسْمَةَ أُو۟لُوا۟ ٱلْقُرْبَىٰ وَٱلْيَتَٰمَىٰ وَٱلْمَسَٰكِينُ **فَٱرْزُقُوهُم مِّنْهُ** وَقُولُوا۟ لَهُمْ قَوْلًا مَّعْرُوفًا

Sahih International: And when [other] relatives and orphans and the needy are present at the [time of] division, then ***provide for*** them [something] ***out of*** the estate and speak to them words of appropriate kindness.

Pickthall: And when kinsfolk and orphans and the needy are present at the division (of the heritage), ***bestow on*** them ***therefrom*** and speak kindly unto them.
Yusuf Ali: But if at the time of division other relatives, or orphans or poor, are present, *feed* them *out of* the (property), and speak to them words of kindness and justice.
Shakir: And when there are present at the division the relatives and the orphans and the needy, ***give*** them (something) ***out of*** it and speak to them kind words.
Mohsin Khan: And when the relatives and the orphans and AlMasakin (the poor) are present at the time of division, ***give*** them ***out of*** the property, and speak to them words of kindness and justice.
Ghali: And when the near of kin (Literally: endowed with kinship, 'nearness') and the orphans and the indigent are present at the division, then ***provide for*** them ***out of*** it, and say to them beneficent saying.

So using the preposition *fi* after the verb *ʾirzuqūhum* gives a different meaning than using the preposition *min* after the same verb. Consequently, these two constructions should be rendered by two different equivalents in English, since as demonstrated they carry different meanings. However, both Shakir's translation of the Holy Qurʾan and Ghali's, for example, use the English verb-preposition construction 'provide . . . out of' for both cases, giving the impression that the two meanings are the same.

ʾibnul-qayyim (n.d.: 68–9) holds the view that each lexical item and even each letter in the Holy Qurʾan has a meaning such that it can never be substituted by any other. He gives the example of the preposition *ʿan*, 'out of, from' as used in the verse *wa mā yanṭiqu ʿan-ilhawā* (53:3), 'nor does he speak from [his own] inclination'. In Arabic the verb *yanṭiq*, 'speak' habitually co-occurs with the preposition *bi-*, 'in' (as in *hāḏa kitābuna yanṭiqu ʿalāykum b-ilḥaqq* (45:29), 'This, Our record, speaks about you in truth'); but the use of *ʿan* instead in verse (53:3) is appropriate to the meaning of that particular case (that the Prophet does not speak from his own whim). In terms of semantic role, we would characterise the prepositions as marking two different types of adverbial with different semantic roles (manner with *bi-* as in 'in truth' versus motive with *ʿan* as in 'from inclination'). ʾibnul-qayyim proposes that the particular preposition *ʿan* is the only possible word that could be used in (53:3) because the adverbial (*ʿan-ilhawā*) is about a motive (a negated motive in this case).

ʾibnul-qayyim also draws attention to the difference in meaning between *ʿalā* and *li-* in the following two Qurʾanic expressions:

سَلَٰمٌ عَلَيْكُم بِمَا صَبَرْتُمْ فَنِعْمَ عُقْبَى ٱلدَّارِ
salām-un ***ʿalā****-ykum bimā ṣabartum faniʿma ʿuqbā d-dār* (13:24)
'Peace be ***on*** you for what you patiently endured. And excellent is the final home.'

فَسَلَٰمٌ لَّكَ مِنْ أَصْحَٰبِ ٱلْيَمِينِ
fa-salām-un ***la****-ka min ʾaṣḥābi l-yamīn* (56:91)
'Peace *for* you; [you are] from the companions of the right.'

ʾibnul-qayyim says that in the first expression, the word *salām*, 'peace' is said as a greeting from the angels to those who gain Paradise, so it is followed by *ʿalā*, making up a phrase meaning 'peace on you'. The second expression means 'peace is granted for you' (i.e. as a reward for patience). 'ibnul-qayyim notes that whenever the word *salām* is mentioned as a greeting it is followed by the preposition *'alā*, as in:

سَلَٰمٌ عَلَىٰ نُوحٍ فِي ٱلْعَٰلَمِينَ
salām-un ***'alā*** *nūḥ-in fī l-'ālamīn* (37:79)
'Peace be ***on*** Noah among the worlds'

سَلَٰمٌ عَلَىٰٓ إِبْرَٰهِيمَ
salām-un ***'alā*** *'ibrahīm* (37:109)
'Peace be ***on*** Ibrahim'

In like manner, 'ibnul-qayyim differentiates between *li-* (and its allomorph *la-*) and *'alā*:

وَٱلَّذِينَ يَنقُضُونَ عَهْدَ ٱللَّهِ مِنۢ بَعْدِ مِيثَٰقِهِۦ وَيَقْطَعُونَ مَآ أَمَرَ ٱللَّهُ بِهِۦٓ أَن يُوصَلَ وَيُفْسِدُونَ فِي ٱلْأَرْضِ أُوْلَٰٓئِكَ لَهُمُ ٱللَّعْنَةُ وَلَهُمْ سُوٓءُ ٱلدَّارِ
wa-allaḏīna yanquḍūna 'ahda l-lahi min ba'di mīṯāqihi wayaqṭa'ūna mā 'amara l-lāhu bihi 'an yūṣala wayufsidūna fī l-'arḍi ulāika ***la****-humu-lla'natu walahum sū'u d-dār* (13:25)
'But those who break the covenant of Allah after contracting it and sever that which Allah has ordered to be joined and spread corruption on earth – ***for*** them is the curse, and they will have the worst home.'

إِنَّ ٱلَّذِينَ كَفَرُواْ وَمَاتُواْ وَهُمْ كُفَّارٌ أُوْلَٰٓئِكَ عَلَيْهِمْ لَعْنَةُ ٱللَّهِ وَٱلْمَلَٰٓئِكَةِ وَٱلنَّاسِ أَجْمَعِينَ
'inna allaḏīna kafarū wamātū wahum kuffārun 'ulāika ***'alāy****-him la'natu-llāhi wal-malā'ikati wan-nāsi 'ajma'īn* (2:161)
'Indeed, those who disbelieve and die while they are disbelievers – ***on*** them will be the curse of Allah and of the angels and the people, all together.'

'ibnul-qayyim argues that the use of *li-* emphasises the occurrence of the action because it is added to the noun using the genitive preposition *la-* (an allomorph of *li-*), which also means possession or gaining; whereas the use of *'alā* gives the meaning of 'added on' or 'upon' in verse (2:161), meaning an additional punishment that may not have occurred yet.

In a nutshell, these Arab scholars were of the view that prepositions in Arabic are not freely interchangeable and that every preposition has its own peculiar meaning that cannot be expressed by another preposition, even if they are preceded by the same verb – which is, of course, entirely in line with the modern linguistic view that no language ever has two *perfectly* synonymous items and that different prepositions express different semantic roles for verbal arguments and adjuncts. However, although Arab grammarians and exegetes have exerted effort in drawing attention to the semantic properties that 'colour' the use of one preposition versus another, there are still untrodden areas that remain problematic to translators.

4. Research method

This study employs the Qur'anic Corpus (Dukes 2012), which comprises multiple English translations of the Qur'an as well as the original Arabic text. The translations of the verb-preposition structures were carefully compared in the six aligned translations, namely Sahih International (1997), Mohsin Khan (1996), Pickthall (1930), Yusuf Ali (1934), Shakir (1999), and Ghali (1997) (see Appendix for full source details). The Qur'an section of arabiCorpus was also consulted, to identify and quantify collocates of verbs which occur alongside more than one preposition.

An analysis of the prepositional structures in the six translations was undertaken in order to explore whether the translators paid due attention to the prepositions in the translation process, and whether they appear to have adopted a particular linguistic strategy to translate the different shades of meaning of the Arabic prepositions into English. To keep the study manageable, only three prepositions, *ʿalā*, *ʾilā*, and *li-*, were included. Pairs of verb-preposition constructions in which the same verb is used alongside more than one of these prepositions were paid special attention in the analysis, to see whether they are translated the same or not.

Using the *Qur'an* section of arabiCorpus (Parkinson 2012; this volume), I scrutinised a number of verbs, including specific forms of the lemmata *kataba*, *ʾistamaʿa*, *ʾanzala*, *ṣabar*, *ʾawḥa*, and *hada*, which occur in combination with at least two of the prepositions under investigation. These particular verbs were chosen for investigation on the basis that my knowledge of the relevant texts suggests that they manifest a multiplicity of potential semantic prosodies that are inextricably intertwined with the preposition that follows. By analysing the concordance lines, the collocates of each verb were identified, and themselves examined using arabiCorpus, to discover the different shades of meaning related to each preposition. I then looked up the translation of the lexical verb itself, examining the translations given for all its Qur'anic contexts by Dukes' (2012) *Qur'an Dictionary*.[2] Then, using the parallel Qur'anic Corpus, the six translations were carefully scrutinised and compared, to identify similarities and differences in the rendering of the source verb-preposition construction into English. The semantic prosody of each preposition was identified by studying the concordance lines and, in particular, its collocates. Occasional reference was made to concordances from the Collins COBUILD corpus, to check on the shades of meaning and syntactic and collocational behaviour of the verbs used in the English translations.[3]

5. Results and discussion

5.1 *kataba+li-/ʿalā*

The verb *kataba*, 'write' combines with two prepositions in the Holy Qur'an, namely *li-* and *ʿalā*, resulting in two different shades of meaning.

The concordances in Figures 7.1 and 7.2 show that the lexical items that collocate with *kataba+li* are words denoting a gift or something granted[4] (by Allah; *kataba* here is used in the derived sense of 'decree, prescribe' rather than 'write'), such as

Following co-text	word	Preceding co-text
في هذه الدنيا حسنة وفي الآخرة إنا هدنا إليك قال	واكتب لنا	
به عمل صالح إن الله لا يضيع أجر المحسنين	كتب لهم	يطؤون موطئا يغيظ الكفار ولا ينالون من عدو نيلا إلا
ليجزيهم الله أحسن ما كانوا يعملون	كتب لهم	ولا ينفقون نفقة صغيرة ولا كبيرة ولا يقطعون واديا إلا
وترغبون أن تنكحوهن والمستضعفين من الولدان وأن تقوموا لليتامى بالقسط	كتب لهن	عليكم في الكتاب في يتامى النساء اللاتي لا تؤتونهن ما

Figure 7.1 Sample concordance of *kataba+li-* as found in arabiCorpus (Qur'an section)

Following co-text	word	Preceding co-text
الذين من قبلكم لعلكم تتقون	كتب على	يا أيها الذين آمنوا كتب عليكم الصيام كما
نفسه الرحمة ليجمعنكم إلى يوم القيامة لا ريب فيه الذين	كتب على	قل لمن ما في السماوات والأرض قل لله
إذا حضر أحدكم الموت إن ترك خيرا الوصية للوالدين والأقربين	كتب عليكم	
القتال وهو كره لكم وعسى أن تكرهوا شيئا وهو خير	كتب عليكم	
القتال ألا تقاتلوا قالوا وما لنا ألا نقاتل في سبيل	كتب عليكم	لنا ملكا نقاتل في سبيل الله قال هل عسيتم إن
القصاص في القتلى الحر بالحر والعبد بالعبد والأنثى بالأنثى فمن	كتب عليكم	يا أيها الذين آمنوا
الصيام كما كتب على الذين من قبلكم لعلكم تتقون	كتب عليكم	يا أيها الذين آمنوا

Figure 7.2 Sample concordance of *kataba+ 'alā* as found in arabiCorpus (Qur'an section)

ḥasanatan, 'good'; *'amalun ṣāliḥ*, 'a good deed'; or *'aḥsani ma kānu ya'malūn*, 'the best of what they were doing'; verse (9:51), given below, illustrates this.

On the other hand, the lexical items that collocate with *kataba+'alā* in the Holy Qur'an usually denote an obligation or commitment, usually something hard or done with difficulty, such as *'al-qitāl*, 'fighting'; *'aṣ-ṣiyām*, 'fasting'; and *'al-qiṣāṣ*, 'legal retribution'. This is even evident in examples where this construction is associated with Allah, for example in verse (6:12), also given below.

Looking at the translations of each of these verb-preposition constructions, it is evident that *some* translators resort to the same equivalent to render both these constructions (consisting in Arabic of the same verb and a different preposition) into English. But no *single* strategy was adopted by all the translators for these constructions:

(9:51) قُل لَّن يُصِيبَنَآ إِلَّا مَا كَتَبَ ٱللَّهُ لَنَا هُوَ مَوۡلَىٰنَاۚ وَعَلَى ٱللَّهِ فَلۡيَتَوَكَّلِ ٱلۡمُؤۡمِنُون

Sahih International: *Say*, 'Never will we be struck except by what Allah ***has decreed for*** us; He is our protector.' And upon Allah let the believers rely.
Pickthall: Say: Naught befalleth us save that which Allah ***hath decreed for*** us. He is our Protecting Friend. In Allah let believers put their trust!
Yusuf Ali: *Say*: 'Nothing will happen to us except what Allah ***has decreed for*** us: He is our protector': and on Allah let the Believers put their trust.
Shakir: Say: Nothing will afflict us save what Allah ***has ordained for*** us; He is our Patron; and on Allah let the believers rely.

Mohsin Khan: Say: '*Nothing* shall ever happen to us except what Allah ***has ordained for*** us. He is our Maula (Lord, Helper and Protector).' And in Allah let the believers put their trust.
Ghali: *Say*, 'Never will anything afflict us except what Allah ***has prescribed for*** us; He is our Supreme Patronizer; and on Allah let the believers then put their trust.'

قُل لِّمَن مَّا فِي ٱلسَّمَٰوَٰتِ وَٱلۡأَرۡضِۖ قُل لِّلَّهِۚ كَتَبَ عَلَىٰ نَفۡسِهِ ٱلرَّحۡمَةَۚ لَيَجۡمَعَنَّكُمۡ إِلَىٰ يَوۡمِ ٱلۡقِيَٰمَةِ لَا رَيۡبَ فِيهِۚ ٱلَّذِينَ خَسِرُوٓاْ
أَنفُسَهُمۡ فَهُمۡ لَا يُؤۡمِنُونَ (6:12)

Sahih International: Say, 'To whom belongs whatever is in the heavens and earth?' Say, 'To Allah.' He ***has decreed upon*** Himself mercy. He will surely assemble you for the Day of Resurrection, about which there is no doubt. Those who will lose themselves [that Day] do not believe.
Pickthall: Say: Unto whom belongeth whatsoever is in the heavens and the earth? Say: Unto Allah. He hath ***prescribed for*** Himself mercy, that He may bring you all together to the Day of Resurrection whereof there is no doubt. Those who ruin their souls will not believe.
Yusuf Ali: Say: 'To whom belongeth all that is in the heavens and on earth?' Say: 'To Allah.' He hath ***inscribed for*** Himself (the rule of) Mercy. That He will gather you together for the Day of Judgment, there is no doubt whatever. It is they who have lost their own souls, that will not believe.
Shakir: Say: To whom belongs what is in the heavens and the earth? Say: To Allah; He ***has ordained*** mercy ***on*** Himself; most certainly He will gather you on the resurrection day – there is no doubt about it. (As for) those who have lost their souls, they will not believe.
Mohsin Khan: Say (O Muhammad SAW): 'To whom belongs all that is in the heavens and the earth?' Say: 'To Allah.' He ***has prescribed*** Mercy ***for*** Himself. Indeed He will gather you together on the Day of Resurrection, about which there is no doubt. Those who destroy themselves will not believe [in Allah as being the only Ilah (God), and Muhammad SAW as being one of His Messengers, and in Resurrection, etc.].
Ghali: Say, 'To whom (belongs) whatever is in the heavens and the earth?' Say, 'To Allah.' He ***has prescribed for*** Himself (the) mercy. Indeed He will definitely gather you to the Day of the Resurrection; there is no suspicion about it. The ones who have lost their (own) selves; so they do not believe.

Table 7.1 summarises the translations used for *kataba+li-* and *kataba+ ʿalā* in verses (6:12) and (9:51).

Looking at COBUILD, we see that the verb *ordain*, used by Mohsin Khan to translate *kataba li-* and by Shakir for both *kataba li-* and *kataba ʿalā*, collocates with *monk*, *priest*, and *staff person*, and behaves syntactically in most cases as a transitive verb in the passive voice. This verb has strong religious connotations in English because, as the concordance shows, it is nearly always used to refer to the process of a person becoming a (typically but not always Christian) priest, rather than with its basic, literal meaning of 'arrange/prepare/set up/plan/appoint' (see Figure 7.3).

The verb *decree* is used by Sahih International for *kataba*, alongside 'upon' as equivalent to *ʿalā*, and 'for' as equivalent to *ʾilā*. In COBUILD we observe that the verb *decree* is not followed by prepositions but rather, in most cases, by a *that*-clause. It col-

Table 7.1 A comparison of the translations of *kataba*+ *ʿalā* and *kataba*+*li*- in verses (6:12) and (9:51) in the parallel corpus of the Holy Qurʾan (Dukes 2012)

Translation	*kataba*+ *ʿalā*	*kataba*+*li*-
Sahih International	has decreed upon	has decreed for
Mohsin Khan	has prescribed . . . for	has ordained for
Pickthall	hath prescribed for	has decreed for
Yusuf Ali	has inscribed for	has decreed for
Shakir	has ordained . . . on	has ordained for
Ghali	has prescribed for	has prescribed for

He was *ordained* as a priest in 1992, after ten years' training.
But if there is a crisis, the answer is not to pull out; priests like him, trained in Depth Psychology, have work to do, he thinks. Lights blazed in a crowded Glasgow church, awash with flowers: James Lutomski was being *ordained*, and was bedecked in priestly robes.
The first of the Westerners to join Ajahn Chah, in 1967, was a newly *ordained* American monk, the Venerable Sumedho.
I know, for example, they'll be celebrating like mad Wednesday's decision' – the Anglican vote to *ordain* women as priests.
The last Guru died in 1708, having *ordained* that from then on the ultimate spiritual authority for the Sikhs would rest in the Guru Granth Sahib.

Figure 7.3 Sample concordance of *ordain* as found in the COBUILD corpus

A Jacobin *decree* that every man has the right to hunt transformed the practice into a lower-class activity far removed from the aristocratic origins of hunting in Britain.
Israel *decreed* a state of emergency in the north on the Lebanese border last night and gave the army broad powers in anticipation of possible new air raids on Lebanon.
Their faith in this concept was dislodged the moment that it was *decreed* that political donations should be put to a shareholder vote and corporate contributions rapidly dried up.
Unless on a very low income, people will have to pay court fees for issuing divorce proceedings and obtaining a final *decree* – some £180.
In Wales, Rhondda's miners did not feel moved to vote for the uninspiring candidate whom Mr Blair *decreed* should be first minister of a glorified talking-shop in Cardiff.

Figure 7.4 Sample concordance of *decree* as found in the COBUILD corpus

locates with words in the semantic field of obligation, such as *right*, *state of emergency*, and *should* (see Figure 7.4).

The verb *prescribe*, in the expression 'has prescribed for', is used both by Mohsin Khan and Pickthall as an equivalent for *kataba ʿalā*, whereas Ghali uses the same verb as a translation of both *kataba ʿalā* and *kataba li*-. Looking at *prescribe* in COBUILD, we notice that it is used both transitively and intransitively, and is sometimes followed by *for*. The verb mostly collocates with lexical items related to *medicine*, such as *drug*, *doctor*, *practitioner*, and *(serious) illness* (see Figure 7.5).

He searched diligently for drugs, both ***prescribed*** and proscribed, anything which would suggest nerves stretched close to breaking point, but found nothing more than a bottle of paracetamol and a child's cough mixture.
Within two months of taking up his new job he had been ***prescribed*** Prozac and some of the behaviour could have been caused by the side-effects of the drug.
Thus, there is no universally ***prescribed*** time limit for surgery.
An epileptic who was left brain-damaged after he was ***prescribed*** an overdose of drugs by Harold Shipman, the serial killer, was awarded compensation of £225,000 at the High Court in Manchester yesterday.
His lawyers, paid for by the Medical Defence Union, admitted that the doctor had been negligent to ***prescribe***, in November 1989, to

Figure 7.5 Sample concordance of *prescribe* as found in the COBUILD corpus

There were two PE manuals, one on athletics coaching, the other on sports injuries, both ***inscribed*** Jane Maguire, South Essex College of Physical Education.
It was ***inscribed***, To Jane, going out into the world, with love and best wishes, Maddy.
Casey manoeuvred his wheelchair to a door adjacent to the bar counter and, pushing it open, made his way down a black and white tiled corridor to another door with his name ***inscribed*** on it in gold lettering.
At the end of that evening I gave Eric the bat I had used on the 1986/87 tour to Australia and he presented me with a Fender Stratocaster ***inscribed*** with the words: 'To brother Beefy'.

Figure 7.6 Sample concordance of *inscribe* as found in the COBUILD corpus

The verb *inscribe* is used as an equivalent for *kataba ʿalā* only by Yusuf Ali. The concordance shows that the verb is transitive, and used in both active and passive voices. The verb collocates with words related to writing (and, as the wider context reveals, specifically writing carved into an object) such as *manual*, *gold lettering*, *name*, *words*, and *reads* (see Figure 7.6).

Comparing the semantic prosodies of the two Arabic verb-preposition constructions *kataba li-* and *kataba ʿalā*, and those of the English equivalents used by the six translators, it is notable that the verb *decree* is close in its semantic prosody to *kataba ʿalā*, since they both collocate with words in the semantic field of obligation. The verb *ordain*, by contrast, collocates with words that give the meaning of *granting*, which is closer to *kataba li-*. However, it is strongly associated with the *granting* of status as a (Christian) priest, and only secondarily with *granting* in general. This gives it strong religious connotations, which may explain why Shakir and Mohsin Khan selected it for use in the Qurʾanic context.

5.2 *yastamiʿ + ʾilā/li-*

In some verses, the verb *yastamiʿ*, 'listen' occurs with a direct object; in others, it is followed by a preposition *ʾilā* or *li-*. Figure 7.7 is a sample of the concordance of *yastamiʿ ʾilā* and *yastamiʿ li-* in the Holy Qurʾan.

Following co-text	word	Preceding co-text
إليك وجعلنا على قلوبهم أكنة أن يفقهوه وفي آذانهم وقرا	يستمع	ومنهم من
إليك حتى إذا خرجوا من عندك قالوا للذين أوتوا العلم	يستمع	ومنهم من
إليك وإذ هم نجوى إذ يقول الظالمون إن تتبعون إلا	يستمعون	نحن أعلم بما يستمعون به إذ
له وأنصتوا لعلكم ترحمون	فاستمعوا	وإذا قرئ القرآن
له إن الذين تدعون من دون الله لن يخلقوا ذبابا	فاستمعوا	يا أيها الناس ضرب مثل

Figure 7.7 Sample concordance of *yastamiʿ* + *ʾilā* and *yastamiʿ*+*li*- as found in arabiCorpus (Qurʾan section)

In translation, 'listen to' is given as equivalent to both prepositional constructions. Exceptionally, Pickthall's translation renders *yastamiʿ* + *ʾilā* and *yastamiʿ*+*li*- as 'give ear to' and 'hearken unto' respectively. The translations of verses (17:47) and (20:13) exemplify this:

(17:47) نَّحْنُ أَعْلَمُ بِمَا يَسْتَمِعُونَ بِهِ إِذْ يَسْتَمِعُونَ إِلَيْكَ وَإِذْ هُمْ نَجْوَىٰ إِذْ يَقُولُ الظَّالِمُونَ إِن تَتَّبِعُونَ إِلَّا رَجُلًا مَّسْحُورًا

Sahih International: We are most knowing of how they ***listen to*** it when they listen to you and [of] when they are in private conversation, when the wrongdoers say, 'You follow not but a man affected by magic.'
Pickthall: We are Best Aware of what they wish to hear when they ***give ear to*** thee and when they take secret counsel, when the evil-doers say: Ye follow but a man bewitched.
Yusuf Ali: We know best why it is they listen, when they ***listen to*** thee; and when they meet in private conference, behold, the wicked say, 'Ye follow none other than a man bewitched!'
Shakir: We know best what they listen to when they ***listen to*** you, and when they take counsel secretly, when the unjust say: You follow only a man deprived of reason.
Mohsin Khan: We know best of what they ***listen to***, when they listen to you. And when they take secret counsel, behold, the Zalimun (polytheists and wrong-doers, etc.) say: 'You follow none but a bewitched man.'
Ghali: We know best what (intention) it is that they ***listen with*** as they listen to you, and as they have private conferences, as the unjust (of them) say, 'Decidedly you are following (none) except a man bewitched.'

(20:13) وَأَنَا ٱخْتَرْتُكَ فَٱسْتَمِعْ لِمَا يُوحَىٰٓ

Sahih International: And I have chosen you, so ***listen to*** what is revealed [to you].
Pickthall: And I have chosen thee, so ***hearken unto*** that which is inspired.
Yusuf Ali: 'I have chosen thee: ***listen***, then, ***to*** the inspiration (sent to thee).'
Shakir: And I have chosen you, so listen to what ***is revealed***:
Mohsin Khan: 'And I have chosen you. So listen to that which ***is inspired to*** you.'
Ghali: And I, Ever I, have chosen you; so listen to whatever ***is revealed***.

Table 7.2 A comparison of the translations of *yastami*ʿ+ ʾ*ilā* and *yastami*ʿ+*li-* in verses (17:47) and (20:13) in the parallel corpus of the Holy Qurʾan (Dukes 2012)

Translation	*yastami*ʿ+ ʾ*ilā*	*yastami*ʿ+*li-*
Sahih International	listen to	listen to
Mohsin Khan	listen to	listen to
Pickthall	give ear to	hearken unto
Yusuf Ali	listen to	listen to
Shakir	listen to	listen to
Ghali	listen to	listen to

Though the semantic behaviour of the object of the preposition with *yastami*ʿ+ ʾ*ilā* differs from that with *yastami*ʿ+*li-*, the English equivalent is the same in all the translations except Pickthall's. *yastami*ʿ+ ʾ*ilā* has a person (or a personal pronoun) as an object, with the semantic prosody of delivering a speech or a saying. *yastami*ʿ+*li-*, on the other hand, has the thing that is said as its object, with the semantic prosody of assigning something. In this case, the English preposition *to* marks two different kinds of participant for the verb *listen* (either the *source* or the *content* of the speech), whereas in Arabic a different preposition is used for each type of participant. The same applies to *give ear to* and *hearken unto*: these are both archaisms for *listen to*. Table 7.2 summarises the various translations of *yastami*ʿ+ ʾ*ilā* and *yastami*ʿ+*li-*.

5.3 ʾ*anzala*+ ʾ*ilā*/ ʿ*alā*

Moving to the verb ʾ*anzala*, 'send down', the verb-preposition constructions ʾ*anzala* ʾ*ilā* and ʾ*anzala* ʿ*alā* vary in their semantic context, but are not distinguished in translation. ʾ*anzala* ʾ*ilā* collocates with contexts that indicate the action of delivering something to someone, where the entity delivered is some representation of knowledge, such as *nūrān mubīnā*, 'a clear light'; *kitāban*, 'a book'; or ʾ*ayātim bayyināt*, 'verses of clear evidence', as shown in Figure 7.8.

On the other hand, ʾ*anzala* ʿ*alā* collocates with words that denote a burden, difficulty, or commitment to a hard task (namely, in these instances, conveying the message of Allah), including *litašqā*, 'that you be distressed' and *bāḫi*ʿ*un*, 'would be killing' (see Figure 7.9).

Verses (2:136) and (3:84), given below, include a stretch of text that is more or less identical except for the preposition following ʾ*anzala*. Searching for the semantic and

Following co-text	word	Preceding co-text
نورا مبينا	وأنزلنا إليكم	يا أيها الناس قد جاءكم برهان من ربكم
كتابا فيه ذكركم أفلا تعقلون	أنزلنا إليكم	لقد
آيات مبينات ومثلا من الذين خلوا من قبلكم وموعظة للمتقين	أنزلنا إليكم	ولقد

Figure 7.8 Sample concordance of ʾ*anzala*+ ʾ*ilā* as found in arabiCorpus (Qurʾan section)

Following co-text	word	Preceding co-text
الكتاب يتلى عليهم إن في ذلك لرحمة وذكرى لقوم يؤمنون	أنزلنا عليك	أولم يكفهم أنا
الكتاب للناس بالحق فمن اهتدى فلنفسه ومن ضل فإنما يضل	أنزلنا عليك	إنا
المن والسلوى كلوا من طيبات ما رزقناكم وما ظلمونا ولكن	وأنزلنا عليكم	وظللنا عليكم الغمام
لباسا يواري سوءاتكم وريشا ولباس التقوى ذلك خير ذلك من	أنزلنا عليكم	يا بني آدم قد
القرآن لتشقى	أنزلنا عليك	ما
الكتاب إلا لتبين لهم الذي اختلفوا فيه وهدى ورحمة لقوم	أنزلنا عليك	وما

Figure 7.9 Sample concordance of *ʾanzala+ʿalā* as found in arabiCorpus (Qurʾan section)

pragmatic contexts of the *neighbouring* verses, I found that (3:84) occurs in a series of verses assigning burdens and commitments to the Prophet, while in (2:136), it is instead a description of the stance of believers as opposed to non-believers: there is, in context, no reference to the assignment of obligations:

قُولُوٓاْ ءَامَنَّا بِٱللَّهِ وَمَآ أُنزِلَ إِلَيۡنَا وَمَآ أُنزِلَ إِلَىٰٓ إِبۡرَٰهِـۧمَ وَإِسۡمَٰعِيلَ وَإِسۡحَٰقَ وَيَعۡقُوبَ وَٱلۡأَسۡبَاطِ وَمَآ أُوتِيَ مُوسَىٰ وَعِيسَىٰ وَمَآ
أُوتِيَ ٱلنَّبِيُّونَ مِن رَّبِّهِمۡ لَا نُفَرِّقُ بَيۡنَ أَحَدٖ مِّنۡهُمۡ وَنَحۡنُ لَهُۥ مُسۡلِمُونَ (2:136)

Sahih International: Say, [O believers], 'We have believed in Allah and what *has been revealed to* us and what *has been revealed to* Abraham and Ishmael and Isaac and Jacob and the Descendants and what was given to Moses and Jesus and what was given to the prophets from their Lord. We make no distinction between any of them, and we are Muslims [in submission] to Him.'
Pickthall: Say (O Muslims): We believe in Allah and that which *is revealed unto* us and that which *was revealed unto* Abraham, and Ishmael, and Isaac, and Jacob, and the tribes, and that which Moses and Jesus received, and that which the prophets received from their Lord. We make no distinction between any of them, and unto Him we have surrendered.
Yusuf Ali: Say ye: 'We believe in Allah, and the revelation *given to* us, and to Abraham, Isma'il, Isaac, Jacob, and the Tribes, and that given to Moses and Jesus, and that *given to* (all) prophets from their Lord: We make no difference between one and another of them: And we bow to Allah (in Islam).'
Shakir: Say: We believe in Allah and (in) that which *had been revealed to* us, and (in) that which *was revealed to* Ibrahim and Ismail and Ishaq and Yaqoub and the tribes, and (in) that which was given to Musa and Isa, and (in) that which was given to the prophets from their Lord, we do not make any distinction between any of them, and to Him do we submit.
Mohsin Khan: Say (O Muslims), 'We believe in Allah and that which *has been sent down to* us and that which *has been sent down to* Ibrahim (Abraham), Isma'il (Ishmael), Ishaque (Isaac), Ya'qub (Jacob), and to Al-Asbat [the twelve sons of Ya'qub (Jacob)], and that which has been given to Musa (Moses) and 'Iesa (Jesus), and that which has been given to the Prophets from their Lord. We make no distinction between any of them, and to Him we have submitted (in Islam).'
Ghali: Say (O Muslims), 'We have believed in Allah, and whatever *has been sent down to* us, and whatever *was sent down to* Ibrahîm, and Shuaayb, and Ishaq and Yaaqûb (Abraham, Ishmael, Isaac and Jacob, respectively) and the Grandsons, (i.e., the Tribes) and

whatever was brought down to Mûsa and Isa, (Moses and Jesus, respectively) and whatever was brought to the Prophets from their Lord. We make no distinction between any of them, and to Him we are Muslims.'

قُلْ ءَامَنَّا بِٱللَّهِ وَمَآ **أُنزِلَ عَلَيْنَا** وَمَآ **أُنزِلَ عَلَىٰٓ** إِبْرَٰهِيمَ وَإِسْمَٰعِيلَ وَإِسْحَٰقَ وَيَعْقُوبَ وَٱلْأَسْبَاطِ وَمَآ أُوتِيَ مُوسَىٰ وَعِيسَىٰ
وَٱلنَّبِيُّونَ مِن رَّبِّهِمْ لَا نُفَرِّقُ بَيْنَ أَحَدٍ مِّنْهُمْ وَنَحْنُ لَهُۥ مُسْلِمُونَ (3.48)

Sahih International: Say, 'We have believed in Allah and in what **was revealed to** us and what **was revealed to** Abraham, Ishmael, Isaac, Jacob, and the Descendants, and in what was given to Moses and Jesus and to the prophets from their Lord. We make no distinction between any of them, and we are Muslims [submitting] to Him.'
Pickthall: Say (O Muhammad): We believe in Allah and that which **is revealed unto** us and that which **was revealed unto** Abraham and Ishmael and Isaac and Jacob and the tribes, and that which was vouchsafed unto Moses and Jesus and the prophets from their Lord. We make no distinction between any of them, and unto Him we have surrendered.
Yusuf Ali: Say: 'We believe in Allah, and in what **has been revealed to** us and what was revealed to Abraham, Isma'il, Isaac, Jacob, and the Tribes, and in (the Books) given to Moses, Jesus, and the prophets, from their Lord: We make no distinction between one and another among them, and to Allah do we bow our will (in Islam).'
Shakir: Say: We believe in Allah and what **has been revealed to** us, and what was revealed to Ibrahim and Ismail and Ishaq and Yaqoub and the tribes, and what was given to Musa and Isa and to the prophets from their Lord; we do not make any distinction between any of them, and to Him do we submit.
Mohsin Khan: Say (O Muhammad SAW): 'We believe in Allah and in what **has been sent down to** us, and what was sent down to Ibrahim (Abraham), Isma'il (Ishmael), Ishaque (Isaac), Ya'qub (Jacob) and Al-Asbat [the twelve sons of Ya'qub (Jacob)] and what was given to Musa (Moses), 'Iesa (Jesus) and the Prophets from their Lord. We make no distinction between one another among them and to Him (Allah) we have submitted (in Islam).'

Table 7.3 compares the six translations of *ʾanzala ʾilā* and *ʾanzala ʿalā* in verses (2:136) and (3:84) respectively. It shows that almost all translators (except for Yusuf Ali and Ghali) use the same English equivalent for both. However, Yusuf Ali's translation does not clarify the shades of meaning related to the preposition *ʿalā*, for example, as he

Table 7.3 A comparison of the translations of *ʾanzala+ ʿalā* and *anzala+ ʾilā* in verses (2:136) and (3:84) in the parallel corpus of the Holy Qurʾan (Dukes 2012)

Translation	*ʾanzala+ ʿalā*	*ʾanzala+ ʾilā*
Sahih International	was revealed to	has been revealed to
Pickthall	is revealed unto	is revealed unto
Yusuf Ali	has been revealed to	given to
Shakir	has been revealed to	has been revealed to
Mohsin Khan	has been sent down to	has been sent down to
Ghali	has been sent down on	has been sent down to

Following co-text	word	Preceding co-text
ما يقولون وسبح بحمد ربك قبل طلوع الشمس وقبل غروبها	فاصبر على	
ما يقولون واذكر عبدنا داوود ذا الأيد إنه أواب	اصبر على	
ما يقولون وسبح بحمد ربك قبل طلوع الشمس وقبل الغروب	فاصبر على	
ما يقولون واهجرهم هجرا جميلا	واصبر على	
ما أصابك إن ذلك من عزم الأمور	واصبر على	يا بني أقم الصلاة وأمر بالمعروف وانه عن المنكر

Figure 7.10 Sample concordance of ʾiṣbir+ʿalā as found in arabiCorpus (Qurʾan section)

Following co-text	word	Preceding co-text
ربك فإنك بأعيننا وسبح بحمد ربك حين تقوم	واصبر لحكم	
ربك ولا تكن كصاحب الحوت إذ نادى وهو مكظوم	فاصبر لحكم	
ربك ولا تطع منهم آثما أو كفورا	فاصبر لحكم	

Figure 7.11 Sample concordance of ʾiṣbir+li- as found in arabiCorpus (Qurʾan section)

chooses 'has been revealed to' (also used by Sahih International and Shakir) for *ʾanzala ʾilā*. Though Ghali uses the same verb 'has been sent down', he adds two prepositions that have the same 'colouring' as the Arabic ones, namely, *on* for *ʿalā* and *to* for *ʾilā*.

5.4 *ʾiṣbir+li-/ʿalā*

The corpus analysis of *ʾiṣbir*, 'be patient' shows that the difference in the semantic prosody of *ʿalā* and *li-* in the verb-preposition constructions *ʾiṣbir+ʿalā* and *ʾiṣbir+li-* is in accordance with the previous analysis of the distinction between *kataba ʿalā* and *kataba li-*.

Let us compare *ʾiṣbir ʿalā ma yaqūlūn*, 'endure patiently what they say' (in the first four examples in Figure 7.10, and verse (68:48) below) with *fa-ṣbir li-ḥokmi rabbika*, 'wait patiently for the judgement of your Lord' (all three examples in Figure 7.11, and verse (73:10) below). We find that the context of *ʾiṣbir ʿalā ma yaqūlūn* suggests something hard to bear or tolerate, whereas the context of *fa-ṣbir li-ḥokmi rabbika* suggests something that is destined for one's future. More generally, the preposition *li-* identifies a positive future thing that the person is being patient for, whereas *ʿalā* identifies a negative present thing which must be endured or forborne until it ends in the future. This is the same positive/negative distinction that was identified, earlier in this analysis, for *li-* versus *ʿalā* when used with *kataba*. In English, the same contrast is most directly conveyed by 'be patient for (positive future thing)' versus 'be patient with (negative present thing)'. As the example verses show and as Table 7.4 summarises, three of the translations do indeed use *for* versus *with* (or *over*) to capture this contrast in semantic prosody. The other three do not use *with*, but rather switch to a verb lemma (*bear*, *endure*) which possesses the negative semantic

Table 7.4 A comparison of the translations of *ʾiṣbir+li-* and *ʾiṣbir+ ʿalā* in verses (68:48) and (99:5) in the parallel corpus of the Holy Qurʾan (Dukes 2012)

Translation	*ʾiṣbir+li-*	*ʾiṣbir+ ʿalā*
Sahih International	be patient for	be patient over
Mohsin Khan	wait with patience for	be patient with
Pickthall	wait . . . for	bear with patience
Yusuf Ali	wait with patience for	have patience with
Shakir	wait patiently for	bear patiently
Ghali	endure patiently	endure patiently

prosody of *ʿalā*. Among the latter three, Ghali, peculiarly, makes no differentiation at all and uses *endure* for *ʾiṣbir* in both cases; thus this translation does not at all reflect the shades of meaning inferred from the semantic prosody of the preposition, and may be misleading:

(68:48) فَاصبِر لِحُكمِ رَبِّكَ وَلا تَكُن كصَاحِبِ الحُوتِ إذ نَادَى وَهُوَ مَكظُوم

Sahih International: Then ***be patient for*** the decision of your Lord, [O Muhammad], and be not like the companion of the fish when he called out while he was distressed.
Pickthall: But ***wait*** thou ***for*** thy Lord's decree, and be not like him of the fish, who cried out in despair.
Yusuf Ali: So ***wait with patience for*** the Command of thy Lord, and be not like the Companion of the Fish,– when he cried out in agony.
Shakir: So ***wait patiently for*** the judgment of your Lord, and be not like the companion of the fish, when he cried while he was in distress.
Mohsin Khan: So ***wait with patience*** for the Decision of your Lord, and be not like the Companion of the Fish, when he cried out (to Us) while he was in deep sorrow.
Ghali: So ***(endure) patiently*** under the Judgment of your Lord, and do not be as the Companion of the Whale (Prophet Yûnus 'Jonah') as he called out, as he (was) made to choke (inwardly).

(73:10) وَاصبِر **على** مَا يَقُولونَ واهجُرهُم هَجرًا جَمِيلا
Sahih International: And ***be patient over*** what they say and avoid them with gracious avoidance.
Pickthall: And ***bear with patience*** what they utter, and part from them with a fair leave-taking.
Yusuf Ali: And ***have patience with*** what they say, and leave them with noble (dignity).
Shakir: And ***bear patiently*** what they say and avoid them with a becoming avoidance.
Mohsin Khan: And ***be patient*** (O Muhammad SAW) **with** what they say, and keep away from them in a good way.
Ghali: And ***(endure) patiently*** what they (The disbelievers) say, and forsake them with a becoming forsaking.

5.5 ʾawḥā+ ʾilā/li-

The verb *ʾawḥā*, 'reveal' collocates with *ʾilā* and *li-* with two different semantic prosodies. With *ʾilā* it collocates with words like *ʾan-naḥl* ('the bees'), *nūḥ* ('Noah'), and *ʾal-ḥawariyyīn* ('the disciples'), that refer to recipients of divine communication through a medium (e.g. an angel); verse (17:39) is an example. Thus, it suggests communicating an illuminating idea; the nearest English verb would be 'inspire' or 'reveal'. The verb-preposition combination *ʾawḥā+li-*, on the other hand, occurs only once in the Holy Qurʾan, in verse (99:5), where it is followed by a pronoun that references the earth (and, more broadly, the earthquake that is the overall topic of chapter 99). The meaning is that the subject of *ʾawḥā* (i.e. *rabbaka*, 'your Lord') has assigned an order to the earth (to quake). The translation of Sahih International is the one that most closely conveys this point. The others do not consistently distinguish the two verb-preposition constructions. Table 7.5 presents a comparison of translations in the two verses:

(17:39) ذَٰلِكَ مِمَّآ **أَوۡحَىٰٓ إِلَيۡكَ** رَبُّكَ مِنَ ٱلۡحِكۡمَةِۗ وَلَا تَجۡعَلۡ مَعَ ٱللَّهِ إِلَٰهًا ءَاخَرَ فَتُلۡقَىٰ فِي جَهَنَّمَ مَلُومٗا مَّدۡحُورًا

Sahih International: That is from what your Lord ***has revealed to*** you, [O Muhammad], of wisdom. And, [O mankind], do not make [as equal] with Allah another deity, lest you be thrown into Hell, blamed and banished.

Pickthall: This is (part) of that wisdom wherewith thy Lord ***hath inspired*** thee (O Muhammad). And set not up with Allah any other god, lest thou be cast into hell, reproved, abandoned.

Yusuf Ali: These are among the (precepts of) wisdom, which thy Lord ***has revealed to*** thee. Take not, with Allah, another object of worship, lest thou shouldst be thrown into Hell, blameworthy and rejected.

Shakir: This is of what your Lord ***has revealed to*** you of wisdom, and do not associate any other god with Allah lest you should be thrown into hell, blamed, cast away.

Mohsin Khan: This is (part) of Al-Hikmah (wisdom, good manners and high character, etc.) which your Lord ***has inspired to*** you (O Muhammad SAW). And set not up with Allah any other ilah (god) lest you should be thrown into Hell, blameworthy and rejected, (from Allah's Mercy).

Table 7.5 A comparison of the translations of *ʾawḥā+li-* and *ʾawḥā + ʾilā* in verses (17:39) and (99:5) in the parallel corpus of the Holy Qurʾan (Dukes 2012)

Translation	*ʾawḥā +li-*	*ʾawḥā + ʾilā*
Sahih International	has commanded	revealed to
Pickthall	inspireth	hath inspired
Yusuf Ali	will have given inspiration	has revealed to
Shakir	had inspired	has revealed to
Mohsin Khan	has inspired	inspired to
Ghali	has revealed to	has revealed to

Ghali: That is of (the) Wisdom your Lord ***has revealed to*** you; and do not make up with Allah another god, (or) then you will be cast in Hell blamed (and) rejected.

بِأَنَّ رَبَّكَ أَوْحَىٰ لَهَا (99:5)

Sahih International: Because your Lord ***has commanded*** it.
Pickthall: Because thy Lord ***inspireth*** her.
Yusuf Ali: For that thy Lord ***will have given*** her ***inspiration***.
Shakir: Because your Lord ***had inspired*** her.
Mohsin Khan: Because your Lord ***has inspired*** it.
Ghali: That your Lord has ***revealed to*** it.

5.6 *yahdi+ ʾilā/li-*

The verb *yahdi*, 'guide' is sometimes transitive, followed by a direct object, sometimes followed by the preposition *ʾilā*, and sometimes by the preposition *li-*. In all the various translations in Dukes' *Qurʾan Dictionary*, all three structures are translated with the English verb 'guide' or the nominalised form 'guidance'. Verse (10:35), in which both *yahdi+ʾilā* and *yahdi+li-* occur, illustrates this (see below: the first and third examples in the verse are with *ʾilā*, the second is with *li-*). Ghali translates *yahdi li-* into 'guides to'; *yahdi ʾilā* is translated into 'gives guidance towards'. However, in the second example of *yahdi ʾilā* in the same verse, he uses the English equivalent he previously used to translate *yahdi li-*, i.e. 'guides to'. Like Ghali, Yusuf Ali uses both 'to' and 'towards' to translate *ʾilā*; however, unlike Ghali, it is 'towards' rather than 'to' that he uses for *li-*. The other translators do not attempt to distinguish the constructions. Sahih International and Shakir use 'guides to' to render both structures into English. Similarly, 'leads to' is used by Pickthall for both *yahdi ʾilā* and *yahdi li-* (see Table 7.6):

قُلْ هَلْ مِن شُرَكَآئِكُم مَّن **يَهْدِيٓ إِلَى** ٱلْحَقِّۚ قُلِ ٱللَّهُ **يَهْدِي** لِلْحَقِّۗ أَفَمَن **يَهْدِيٓ إِلَى** ٱلْحَقِّ أَحَقُّ أَن يُتَّبَعَ أَمَّن لَّا يَهِدِّيٓ إِلَّآ أَن
يُهْدَىٰۖ فَمَا لَكُمْ كَيْفَ تَحْكُمُونَ (10:35)

Sahih International: Say, 'Are there of your "partners" any who ***guides to*** the truth?' Say, 'Allah ***guides to*** the truth. So is He who ***guides to*** the truth more worthy to be followed or he who guides not unless he is guided? Then what is [wrong] with you – how do you judge?'
Pickthall: Say: Is there of your partners (whom ye ascribe unto Allah) one that ***leadeth to*** the Truth? Say: Allah ***leadeth to*** the Truth. Is He Who ***leadeth to*** the Truth more deserving that He should be followed, or he who findeth not the way unless he (himself) be guided. What aileth you? How judge ye?
Yusuf Ali: Say: 'Of your "partners" is there any that can ***give*** any ***guidance towards*** truth?' Say: 'It is Allah Who ***gives guidance towards*** truth, is then He Who ***gives guidance to*** truth more worthy to be followed, or he who finds not guidance (himself) unless he is guided? what then is the matter with you? How judge ye?'

Table 7.6 A comparison of the translations of *yahdi+li-* and *yahdi+ ʾilā* in verse (10:35) in the parallel corpus of the Holy Qurʾan (Dukes 2012)

Translation	*yahdi li-*	*yahdi ʾilā*
Sahih International	guides to	guides to
Pickthall	leadeth to	leadeth to
Yusuf Ali	gives guidance towards	gives guidance towards/gives guidance to
Shakir	guides to	guides to
Mohsin Khan	guides to	guides to/gives guidance to
Ghali	guides to	gives guidance towards/guides to

Shakir: Say: Is there any of your associates who ***guides to*** the truth? Say: Allah ***guides to*** the truth. Is He then Who ***guides to*** the truth more worthy to be followed, or he who himself does not go aright unless he is guided? What then is the matter with you; how do you judge?
Mohsin Khan: Say: 'Is there of your (Allah's so-called) partners one that ***guides to*** the truth?' Say: 'It is Allah Who ***guides to*** the truth. Is then He, Who ***gives guidance to*** the truth, more worthy to be followed, or he who finds not guidance (himself) unless he is guided? Then, what is the matter with you? How judge you?'
Ghali: Say, 'Is there any of your associates (Those things associated with Allah) who ***gives guidance towards*** the Truth?' Say, 'Allah ***guides to*** the Truth. Then is He who ***guides to*** the Truth (worthier) to be closely followed or he who finds no guidance (for himself or others) unless he is guided? What (plea) have you; how do you judge?'

5.7 Summary

Based on the above discussion, the most accurate English equivalent of the verb--preposition combinations in the six translations under investigation may be summarised as shown in Table 7.7.

6. Conclusion

This study has attempted to use the corpus-based approach to translation studies by assuming that the concept of semantic prosody can be a tool that raises the level of accuracy in selecting a translation equivalent. This can be done by studying the concordance and collocational behaviour of the source word as well as the target word in a corpus of each language. The pivotal idea of this chapter, demonstrated in detail by the preceding analyses, is that different semantic prosodies may be associated with a single verb in the Holy Qurʾan when it is followed by different prepositions; this should thus affect how they are most effectively rendered into English. This analysis would not be possible if we confined semantic prosody to only the three possibilities positive/neutral/negative. Rather, it was necessary to follow the broader sense of semantic prosody as expounded by Sinclair (2004). By examining the collocations of *ʿalā* and *ʾilā*, I have arrived at the conclusion that the semantic prosody that seems to

Table 7.7 Summary of preferred translations for verb-preposition constructions under study

Verb-preposition combination	Best English equivalent	Translation(s) using the best equivalent
kataba+ʿalā	*has decreed upon*	Sahih International
kataba+li-	*has decreed for*	Sahih International; Pickthall; Yusuf Ali
yastamiʿ+ʾilā	*give ear to*	Pickthall
yastamiʿ+li-	*hearken unto*	Pickthall
ʾanzala+ʿalā	*has been sent down on*	Ghali
ʾanzal+ʾilā	*has been sent down to*	Mohsin Khan; Ghali
ʾiṣbir+li-	*wait with patience/patiently for*	Mohsin Khan; Yusuf Ali; Shakir
ʾiṣbir+ʿalā	*bear/endure patiently/with patience*	Pickthall; Shakir; Ghali
ʾawḥa+ʾilā	*revealed to*	Sahih International
ʾawḥa+li-	*has commanded*	Sahih International
yahdi+ʾilā	*gives guidance towards*	Yusuf Ali; Ghali
yahdi+li-	*guides to*	Sahih International; Mohsin Khan; Shakir; Ghali

be associated with *ʿalā*, on the one hand, is something that is hard or difficult or done with effort, something that denotes or implies commitment or obligation; on the other hand, the semantic prosody that seems to be associated with *ʾilā* is the delivering of something that is usually good. The collocates of *li-* suggest a semantic prosody of 'assigning something'; especially in cases where it contrasts with *ʿalā*, *li-* often indicates something good or positive.

I have demonstrated that a careful reading of the concordance lines of both the source lexical item and the equivalent used by the translator(s) in the target language, alongside a comparison of the collocational behaviour of both, can easily be a tool for selecting the translation equivalent that has the closest shade of meaning. Thus, analysis of semantic prosody can help translators achieve the best possible translation with the highest possible degree of accuracy.

In most cases, the meaning conveyed in the source text by the use of one preposition versus another was not clearly conveyed in the translated text. As for the strategies used by translators to render these verb-preposition constructions into English, the meaning of the preposition was in most cases neglected in favour of the verb. This is illustrated by the numerous cases where the translators gave the same translation to two structures consisting of the same verb but followed by different prepositions. This illustrates concretely how corpus research can give translators greater insight into the most contextually appropriate means of rendering into another language Arabic texts in general and the Qurʾan in particular.

Appendix: Translations of the Qurʾan in the parallel corpus

- *The Qur'an: Arabic Text with Corresponding English Meanings* (Sahih International). Almunatada Alislami, Abul Qasim Publishing House (1997).
- *The Meaning of the Glorious Koran* (Mohammed Marmaduke Pickthall). Reprinted by Plume (1997). First published 1930.
- *The Holy Qur'an: Translation and Commentary* (Yusuf Ali). Reprinted by Islamic Vision (2001). First published 1934.
- *The Holy Qur'an Translated* (M. H. Shakir). Tahrike Tarsile Qur'an (1999).
- *The Noble Qur'an in the English Language* (Mohsin Khan). King Fahd Printing Complex, Madinah, Saudi Arabia (1996).
- *Towards Understanding the Ever-Glorious Qur'an* (Muhamed M. Ghali). Dar Elnashr Li-lgame'aat (1997).

Acknowledgements

For their valuable questions, comments, and suggestions, I would like to extend my thanks to Eric Atwell, Andrew Hardie, Tony McEnery, Dilworth Parkinson, Marc Van Mol and the audience at the Workshop on Arabic Corpus Linguistics held at Lancaster University in the spring of 2011. Special thanks are due to Paul Thompson, Director of the Centre for Corpus Research, University of Birmingham, for his encouragement and patience in reading early drafts of this chapter. I would also like to express my gratitude to Susan Hunston, Wolfgang Teubert, Michael Toolan, and all the members of the Department of English, University of Birmingham, who helped and encouraged me to start research in corpus linguistics during my academic visit in the year 2009–10. It goes without saying that any mistakes or shortcomings in this chapter are entirely my responsibility.

Notes

1. For a full discussion of the definitions of the term *semantic prosody* and its history and development, see Stewart (2010).
2. See <http://corpus.quran.com/qurandictionary> (last accessed 22 May 2018).
3. Note that all COBUILD examples quoted in this chapter are from the **BR (British) Written** section of the corpus (*Collins COBUILD Advanced Learner's English Dictionary* 2006).
4. I am grateful to Marc Van Mol for drawing my attention to an Arabic proverb which illustrates this point, *ʾaddonya yawmān yawmun* ***laka*** *wa-yawmun* ***ʿalāyka***, 'life is two days, one **for** you and one **against** you', which links the second person pronoun to the good time with the preposition *li-* and to the hard time with *ʿalā*.

References

Baker, P., A. Hardie and T. McEnery (2006), *A Glossary of Corpus Linguistics*, Edinburgh: Edinburgh University Press.

Collins COBUILD Advanced Learner's English Dictionary (2006), CD-ROM, London: HarperCollins.

Dukes, K. (2012), *The Quranic Arabic Corpus*, School of Computing, University of Leeds, <http://corpus.quran.com/> (last accessed 16 May 2018).

Hassan, A. (1974), *Al-Nahw Al-Wafii*, Cairo: Daar-Al-Maarif Bi-Misr.

ʾibn-ǧinni (n.d.), *ʾal-ḫaṣāʾiṣ*, 'The Particularities', Beirut: dār il-kutub il-ʿilmiyyah.

ʾibnul-qayyim (n.d.), *ʾat-tafsīr ul-qayyim*, 'The Precious Exegesis', Beirut: dār il-kutub il-ʿilmiyyah.

Louw, B. (1993), 'Irony in the text or insincerity in the writer? – The diagnostic potential of semantic prosodies', in M. Baker, G. Francis and E. Tognini-Bonelli (eds), *Text and Technology: In Honour of John Sinclair*, Amsterdam: Benjamins, pp. 157–76.

McEnery, T. and A. Hardie (2012), *Corpus Linguistics: Method, Theory and Practice*, Cambridge: Cambridge University Press.

Parkinson, D. (2012), *arabiCorpus*, Brigham Young University, <http://arabicorpus.byu.edu> (last accessed 22 May 2018).

Partington, A. (2004), '"Utterly content in each other's company": Semantic prosody and semantic preference', *International Journal of Corpus Linguistics*, 9(1): 131–56.

Sinclair, J. M. (ed.) (1987), *Looking Up: An Account of the COBUILD Project in Lexical Computing and the Development of the Collins COBUILD English Language Dictionary*, London and Glasgow: Collins.

Sinclair, J. M. (1991), *Corpus, Concordance, Collocation*, Oxford: Oxford University Press.

Sinclair, J. M. (1996), 'The search for units of meaning', *Textus*, 9: 75–106.

Sinclair, J. M. (2004), *Trust the Text: Language, Corpus and Discourse*, London: Routledge.

Stewart, D. (2010), *Semantic Prosody: A Critical Evaluation*, New York: Routledge.

Younis, N. (2012), 'Through lexicographers' eyes: Does morphology count in making Qur'anic bilingual dictionaries?', in E. Atwell, C. Brierley and M. Sawalha (eds), *Proceedings of the International LREC 2012-Rel Language Resources and Evaluation for Religious Texts*, Paris: ELRA, pp. 94–101.

8

A Relational Approach to Modern Literary Arabic Conditional Clauses

Manuel Sartori

1. Introduction

The issue of the conditional in Classical Arabic (CA) is treated in the classic Arabic grammars, be the authors Arab, both traditional such as *Awḍaḥ al-Masālik* by Ibn Hišām (1989) (d. 761 AH/1360 CE) and modern such as *Ǧāmiʿ al-Durūs al-ʿArabiyya* by al-Ġalāyīnī ([1912] 2000) (1886–1944), or foreign (Arabist), for instance Blachère and Gaudefroy-Demombynes (1975), Fischer (1987), or the work dedicated by Peled (1992) to this question. Using the novel *Al-Zaynī Barakāt* by Ǧamāl al-Ġiṭānī as a starting point, I identified many deviations from the rules of Classical Arabic. The question then arose of how we express the conditional in Modern Arabic. Assuming that the answer must be found in Modern Standard Arabic (MSA) grammars, I intended to compare what we saw in different contemporary literary texts with what these grammars say on the subject. Yet the study of the literary texts shows that these grammars are descriptively inadequate. My purpose here will be to study only the literary register of MSA, highlighting at the same time the descriptive inadequacy of the MSA grammars and the *relationship* existing between the operator of the conditional clause and the apodosis of the hypothetical clause in question.

This chapter is structured as follows. Section 2 presents the literary corpus used in the study, some methodological reflections, and some first observations about hypothetical clauses in MSA. Section 3 goes on to illustrate how, in face of the reality of the texts, 'Modern' Arabic grammars are shown to be descriptively inadequate on this particular point. Supporting data will be presented in detail in section 4 and analysed in section 5 leading to the conclusion that MSA conditional clauses are best characterised by the relational approach proposed here.

2. Literary corpus, methodology, and first observations

In order to achieve a realistic description, I chose a linguistic approach based on corpus methods. I have thus reviewed hypothetical clauses *in extenso* in a corpus made up of various contemporary literary works. Diachronically, my sample covers the period from 1963 to 2005. These are therefore novels by authors born after the 1930s, that is, well after the second generation of the *Nahḍa* (Arabic Renaissance) and its effects on the Arabic language, and at a time when the influence of modern European languages on Arabic must have been already widely felt. Geographically speaking, my corpus ranges from Syria to Morocco. The list of works is as follows: Kanafānī, *Riǧāl fī al-Šams* (2002) and *Al-ʿĀšiq* (1987); Zafzāf, *Ḥiwār Layl Mutaʾaḫḫir* (1970); Ġīṭānī, *Al-Zaynī Barakāt* (1974: 225–345/Ghitani 1985: 211–316); Tāmir, *Al-Numūr fī al-Yawm al-ʿĀšir* (1981); Misʿidī, *Ḥaddaṯa Abū Hurayra qāla . . .* (1997); Ibrāhīm, *al-Laǧna* (1997), *Ḏāt* (1998/Ibrahim 1993), and *Warda* (2000/Ibrahim 2005); Ben Haddūqa, *Al-Ǧāziya wa-l-darāwīš* (1991); al-Kūnī, *Malakūt ṭiflat al-Rabb* (2005). It is clear that what we are taught by both Arab and Arabist Classical Arabic grammars inadequately reflects modern usage. We should also note that these novel modern usages do not sufficiently shock modern translators who, otherwise, would perhaps not have failed to report them. This is a direct result of the fact that this new syntax is familiar to speakers of European languages, since it is more or less ours.

For my study, then, I identified all of the conditional clause operators (meaning 'if') present in the novels mentioned, that is, both the two 'classical' particles *in* and *law* (and its derivatives, including *law-lā*, 'if not'), and the time adverbial (*ẓarf zamān*) *iḏā*, 'when' (and its derivatives, including *iḏā mā*, 'as soon as, hardly'). From this set, I naturally chose to keep only truly hypothetical clauses (where the protasis *p* (conditional clause) logically implies the apodosis *q* (main clause)), thus excluding concessive clauses (marked by *wa-law*, *ḥattā law*, *ḥattā wa-law*, *ḥattā iḏā*, *wa-in*, etc., meaning 'even if'). Of the remaining examples, I then retained only the hypothetical clauses that are doubly verbal and assertive. 'Doubly verbal', by which I refer to a hypothetical clause composed of two verbs, one in the main clause and one in the conditional clause, excludes: (1) examples that have a protasis introduced by *law anna*, 'if + *noun*' or *law-lā*, 'if not'; (2) examples that are not fully conditional (i.e. cases of protasis without apodosis due to truncation, optation, and frozen uses, like *law samaḥta*, 'please' or *in šāʾa llah*, 'if God wills'); and (3) examples whose apodosis is a nominal or existential sentence (like *lā budda an*, 'it is necessary that'; *ʿalay-hi an*, 'he has to'; *bi-wusʿi-hi an*, 'he can'). However, this distinction retains the apodoses which are phrases made up of initial NP/report where the report is itself a verbal sentence (like *inna-hu faʿala/yafʿalu*, 'the fact is that he did/does'. I note here that the affirmative apocopate does not affect clauses with *iḏā* or *law* (see Alosh 2005: 271 and examples pp. 195, 218), as confirmed by the following example: *iḏā ǧunna yasʾalūna-hu ʿannī* (*Ḥaddaṯa*: 69), 'When he gets mad, they ask him about me'. The apocopate seems still to be in use in clauses with *in*; see example (11) below. 'Assertive' excludes the imperative, the negative imperative, and the interrogative. From this first selection, out of the entire corpus, we get 402 examples of hypotheticals. Of this total, I will only analyse the 283 relevant *if p q* sequences (which represent 70.4 per cent of the total, while *q if p* sequences only represent 29.6 per cent), to assess the possible importance of *fa-* in Potential clauses and of *la-* in Counterfactual clauses (the relevance of these verbal prefixes is explained below).

Potential and Counterfactual are different meanings that a hypothetical clause may have. *Potential* refers to what is possible. This type of hypothetical indicates that the speaker does not know about the actuality of the condition, but asserts that if one proposition is fulfilled then the linked action is or will be possible; for example, 'if the weather is nice [but I don't know if it is or will be], I (will) go out'. *Counterfactual*, on the other hand (also termed *Unreal* or contrary to fact), refers to what is impossible. In this type of hypothetical, the speaker knows that the condition is or was not fulfilled and therefore that the linked action is or was not possible, as in 'if the weather were nice [but it is not], I would go out' (Present Counterfactual) or 'if the weather had been nice [but it was not], I would have gone out' (Past Counterfactual).

In Postclassical Arabic, that is, from the fourth/tenth century AH/CE, the classic distinction between operators *iḏā* and *law* allowed the verbs within hypothetical clauses generally to be interpreted as neutral from a temporal point of view regardless of their form, which would mainly be perfect, as in *iḏā faʿala . . . faʿala* and *law faʿala . . . faʿala*. The first of these structures, due to the presence of *iḏā*, is interpreted as marking the Potential and the second, due to the presence of *law*, as marking the Counterfactual.

In Classical Arabic as well as Postclassical Arabic, if the verb of the main clause of a hypothetical construction with *in* or *iḏā* does not have the required tense form, it has to be introduced by the prefix *fa-*. Clauses of this sort mark the Potential, that is, they indicate that the content of the main clause is possible (e.g. 'If the weather's nice, [it is possible that] I'll go out'). Similarly, when the hypothetical uses the particle *law*, the main clause has to be introduced by the verbal prefix *la-*. Clauses of this type indicate the Counterfactual, that is to say that the content of the main clause is or was not actual because of the unreal status of the conditional clause (e.g. 'If the weather was nice [but it is not], I would go out' and 'If the weather had been nice [but it was not the case], I would have gone out'). The third alternative sense of a conditional is Factual (or Real or Temporal), because when the conditional clause is true then the main clause necessarily is too (e.g. 'When it rains, the roof tops are [necessarily] wet').

In this context, we must consider the fact that in languages like French, the phrase *s'il faisait beau, je sortirais* can be interpreted either as Potential ('If the weather is nice I will go out') or as Present Counterfactual ('If the weather were nice, I would go out'). There is therefore ambiguity that only the context can remove. The intrinsic difference between Potential and Counterfactual lies in the *necessary* existence of an implicit *but* in the case of the Counterfactual ('but the weather is not/will not be nice' for the Present Counterfactual and 'but the weather was not nice' for the Past Counterfactual). This implicit *but* makes it possible to differentiate the two meanings of the phrase 'If the weather was nice, I would go out': the meaning it has in *direct speech*, with existence of an implicit *but*, which is indeed a Present Counterfactual, and of the meaning it has in *reported speech*, where the syntactic form of Past Counterfactual occurs for narrative reasons and because of agreement of tenses, and where in the absence of the implicit *but*, the meaning is Potential. Let us consider the following sequence happening at night or in a closed room without knowledge of the weather: A: 'If the weather is nice, I will go out' (Potential); B: 'What did A say?'; C: 'He said that if the weather was nice he would go out' (Potential, because there is no implicit *but* that could make this sentence Counterfactual). On the difference between direct speech and reported speech, see among others Abi Aad (2001: esp. 49–72).

Table 8.1 The hypothetical clause in grammars of Postclassical Arabic

Protasis		Apodosis	Meaning of the hypothetical
iḏā	*fa ʿala*	*fa ʿala*	Past Factual
iḏā	*fa ʿala*	*fa ʿala / yafʿalu*	Present Factual
iḏā	*fa ʿala*	*fa ʿala*	Potential[a]
law	*fa ʿala / kāna yafʿalu*	*(fa-)yafʿalu / (la-) fa ʿala*	Present Counterfactual[b]
law	*fa ʿala / kāna fa ʿala*	*fa ʿala*	Past Counterfactual

Notes: [a] Past Factual and Potential can only be distinguished by examining the context.
[b] This line reads in pairs of words: *law fa ʿala . . . (fa-)yafʿalu* or *law kana yafʿalu . . . (la-)fa ʿala* as proposed by Larcher (2003b). It is also noteworthy that Moïnfar (qtd in Abi Aad 2001: 107) suggests distinguishing between the Present Counterfactual in *law yafʿalu . . . yafʿalu* (*law tadrusu tanǧaḥu*, 'If you were studying you would succeed') and the Past Counterfactual in *law fa ʿala . . . la-fa ʿala* (*law darasta la-naǧaḥta*, 'If you had studied you would have succeeded'). However, it was impossible for me to verify this assertion.

In Postclassical Arabic, Arabic hypothetical clauses can be schematised as shown in Table 8.1, which illustrates the possible verbal forms, both in protasis and apodosis, and also the hypothetical meaning of each structure. In Table 8.1, and subsequently, I formalise the verbal forms of protases and apodoses as follows: *māḍī* (perfect) = *fa ʿala*, *muḍāriʿ marfūʿ* (imperfect indicative) = *yafʿalu*, *muḍāriʿ manṣūb* (imperfect subjunctive) = *yafʿala* and *muḍāriʿ maǧzūm* (imperfect apocopate) = *yafʿal*.

Within the 283 relevant examples, we first observe the near absence of *in*: the latter has only 16 occurrences, that is, 5.7 per cent of the total. Thus, our purpose will be to focus primarily on the two remaining operators, *iḏā* and *law*.

We then observe the overwhelming usage of the perfect form for the protasis verb (97.2 per cent). Only 8 examples with *law* have an imperfect protasis verb.

Considering the apodoses, we find, next to the expected *fa ʿala*, the *yafʿalu* verbal form. We also observe structures that tolerate a verb like *sa-yafʿalu* in the apodosis, in 28.6 per cent of *iḏā* examples and 13.8 per cent of *law* examples. We are thus dealing with three possible forms in the apodosis both for *iḏā* and *law*: *yafʿalu*, *sa-yafʿalu* and *fa ʿala*. Although there may be true ambiguous cases, as in Classical Arabic, the principle of non-synonymy requires examining the three forms used in the apodosis (*yafʿalu*, *sa-yafʿalu*, and *fa ʿala*) for three distinct conditional meanings.

It appears, moreover, that some examples of clauses with *iḏā fa ʿala . . . fa ʿala*, classically linked to Factual and Potential, are here indeed linked to both and thus describe a status complying with that described in Classical Arabic grammars. But many of these *iḏā fa ʿala . . . fa ʿala* examples denote instead the Present Counterfactual! And if we add to this the fact that Badawi et al. (2004: 647) indicate that *law* can be synonymous with *in*, what then becomes of the strict classical dichotomy based on the operators: *iḏā / in*-Potential vs *law*-Counterfactual?

From our corpus, we also note that the 'segmentator' *fa-* (for more on the 'segmentator' expression and Charles Bally's introduction into Arabic studies of the notion of segmentation, see Larcher 2006), far from being systematic (which seems to corroborate Taha 1995: 180–2, qtd in Ryding 2005: 671), occurs in only 36.7 per cent of the apodoses with *(sa-)yaf'alu*; apodoses that should require *fa-*, according to the canons of classical grammar. Thus, *fa-* seems no longer to indicate a simultaneous syntactic and semantic break, as it did in Classical Arabic (on the presence of *fa-* in CA, see among others Ibn Hišām 1989: IV, 113 ff.; al-Zamaḫšarī 1999: 417; Larcher 2000; Ayoub 2003), but rather occurs mainly for contrastive reasons, indicating that what follows is indeed the beginning of the apodosis.

As for *la-*, it also now appears, possibly in imitation of the usage of *law*, to indicate the Counterfactual in *iḏā* clauses. However, it is not systematic in Counterfactual clauses, representing only 52.4 per cent of the apodoses with *fa'ala*. It should nevertheless be noted that while quasi-systematically absent from Counterfactual clauses with *iḏā*, it is quasi-systematically present in the case of the Past Counterfactual with *law*. This is regrettable because, as we will see, it would have allowed differentiation between two types of *iḏā fa'ala . . . fa'ala* clause, which only the context can disambiguate: the Past Factual and the Present Counterfactual. Like *fa-*, *la-* may, when present, indicate the beginning of the apodosis; but this is not systematic.

In summary, it appears (1) that various verb forms in the apodoses (*yaf'alu*, *sa-yaf'alu*, and *fa'ala*) appear in the hypothetical clauses with *iḏā* as with *law*; (2) that the dichotomy between *iḏā/in*-Potential and *law*-Counterfactual is no longer as strict as it was; and (3) that *fa-* is not obligatory in cases classically thought to require it, just as *la-* alongside *law* seems now to be optional. What do the Modern Arabic grammars say about all of this?

3. What Modern Arabic grammars show and what they do not: the grammars' descriptive inadequacy

As we can see, the situation outlined above contrasts in a very singular way with what is taught (and then learned and reproduced and taught again . . .). That customarily taught description is 'expected' in the case of the presentation of the normalised expression of the conditional put forward by *modern* grammars of Classical Arabic, like Haywood and Nahmad (2001: 290–300). These mention the classic dichotomy between *in/iḏā*-Potential and *law*-Counterfactual, indicate that *in* predominates over *iḏā*, and note, in regard to the verbal forms, the exclusive presence of the perfect in *law* clauses (or very rarely of the imperfect indicative) while noting the classical verbal possibilities in the case of *in* (for a look at the possible verbal combinations alongside the classical operator *in*, see al-Zamaḫšarī 1999: 416). This applies to Moïnfar, as quoted by Abi Aad (Moïnfar 1973: 123, 129) (see note *b* to Table 8.1), Kouloughli (1994), Neyreneuf and Al-Hakkak (1996), and moreover, as expected, the latest French teaching manual for Arabic, *Kullo Tamâm* (Tahhan 2007), which maintains a classical presentation and whose perspective is more prescriptive than descriptive. What is strange is that the phenomena outlined above are more or less unknown in *modern* grammars of *Modern* Arabic, grammars that aim to be more *descriptive* of a modern, concrete state.

Beeston (2006: 94–7) does record the replacement of *in* by *iḏā*. For him Arabic conditional clauses are not marked by the verb form, but by the particle used. Therefore, he sticks with the classical dichotomy. Without mentioning *in*, he only exemplifies perfects or jussives and reports the systematic use of *fa-* in the case of structurally broken examples, that is, when the form of the apodosis is not the normal and expected one. For *law*, he once again only records perfects, noting the ambiguity between the Present and Past Counterfactual. Finally, *la-* is presented as optional.

Holes (2004: 292–9) seems to note, but without making it systematic, that *iḏā* accepts in apodosis verbal forms other than the simple and classical *fa ʿala* (Holes 2004: 296–7). According to him, 'The salient features of conditional sentences in MSA are the sequence of verb forms used and the particles used to introduce the conditional clause (the protasis) and, in some types of sentences, the answering clause (the apodosis)' (Holes 2004: 293). Nevertheless, Holes continues: 'But, unlike English, the type of condition – real, possible or counterfactual – is signaled chiefly by the particle used to introduce the conditional clause, rather than verb form *per se*' (Holes 2004: 293). He then concludes: 'Thus the different shades of probability of a conditional clause being fulfilled are signaled in written Arabic by the choice of particle and not, as in English, by the form of the verb' (Holes 2004: 294). Yet he is no longer speaking here of MSA but of Classical Arabic. Going back to MSA, he states that 'the reality is different' (Holes 2004: 295). He does record that *in* is now mainly used in concessive clauses (*wa-in*) or subordinate clauses like . . . *in fa ʿala / lam yafʿal* . . . (Holes 2004: 295). Therefore, *iḏā* replaces *in* in the expression of Potential ('open' conditionals, in Holes's terminology), maintaining the classic dichotomy between *iḏā / in*-Potential and *law*-Counterfactual (Holes 2004: 296). However, he records, alongside *iḏā*, apodoses in *fa ʿala*, *yafʿalu*, and *fa-sawfa-yafʿalu*, which is rarely the case in other grammars; and he links this to the Arabic dialects. He notes that in the modern vernacular dialects, (a) the dialectal reflex of *in* has almost disappeared, relegated to expressions such as *in šāʾa llāh*, to the benefit of the dialectal reflex of *iḏā*; and (b) the verbal sequence of Potential clauses is almost always *fa ʿala* . . . *yafʿalu*, which is ambiguous without a context (Holes 2004: 298).

Schulz et al. (2008: 362–76) record the relegation of *in* to second place after *iḏā*, and retain the classic dichotomy between *iḏā*-Potential (Schulz et al. 2008: 362 ff.) and *law*-Counterfactual (Schulz et al. 2008: 366 ff.). Furthermore, although they record structures such as *fa-sa / sawfa-yafʿalu* occurring in the apodoses of *iḏā* clauses, they only mention perfects in the case of *law*. Their presentation then systematises the emergence of *fa-* in the classic cases where it has to occur in the Classical language (i.e. before *lan*, *qad*, *laysa*, *sa- / sawfa*, and *inna* + *[pro]name*) (Schulz et al. 2008: 363–4), but they also show the non-systematic nature of *la-* in the case of *law*. Their examples seem mostly invented rather than authentic.

Buckley (2004: 540, 668, 731–50) also presents the classic dichotomy between *in / iḏā*-Potential and *law*-Counterfactual, but he paraphrases some *iḏā fa ʿala* . . . *fa ʿala* clauses in the Present Counterfactual. Moreover, he records for the *iḏā* clauses apodoses of varied verbal forms (*yafʿalu*, *sa-yafʿalu*, and *fa ʿala*), and points, by use of an example, to the occurrence of *la-* in an *iḏā* clause (Buckley 2004: 737). Concerning *law*, he only gives examples of *law fa ʿala* . . . *fa ʿala* clauses (except for two *law yafʿalu* . . . *la-fa ʿala*, one paraphrased in the Present Counterfactual, and the other in the Past Counterfactual), but nevertheless specifies that *la-* is not systematic in these cases.

Furthermore, his translations reproduce the usual ambiguity between the Present Counterfactual and the Past Counterfactual. It is only in a section devoted to the presence of *fa-* that the author offers three examples of apodosis of *law* clauses that are not in *fa ʿala*: one is in *fa-lan yafʿala*, the second is in *fa-sawfa yafʿalu*, and the last is in *fa-inna-hu sa-yafʿalu*. Alongside *law*, no apodosis in *yafʿalu* is therefore reported. Finally, the appearance of *fa-* conforms to classical rules on the issue, but it is perceived by Buckley as non-systematic (Buckley 2004: 748).

Badawi et al. (2004: 40, 623–4, 632–70) note the disappearance of *in* to the benefit not only of *iḏā* but also of *law*; these authors say that 'CA *law* "if (unreal)" has expanded to cover some of the functions of *in* "if (real)" as the latter falls increasingly into disuse' (Badawi et al. 2004: 636, 647). Moreover, they record the use of *iḏā* in syntaxes imitating that of *law*. Badawi et al. assert that *iḏā* then has the 'same syntax and sense as *law*' (Badawi et al. 2004: 656). Nevertheless, as we will see thanks to the data provided by my corpus, this statement is true only if we add 'when considered in Classical Arabic where *law fa ʿala . . . la-fa ʿala* is neutral as to meaning between Present and Past Counterfactual' or if we specify 'has the same syntax as the Classical Arabic Counterfactual's *law* and the same sense as the MSA Present Counterfactual's *law*'. In doing so, the authors add nuance to the classic dichotomy. In *law* clauses linked to the Counterfactual, the verbal forms given by authors for the protasis and apodosis are imperfect. Thus, they have the *law fa ʿala . . . fa ʿala* syntax retain its classic ambiguity between Present and Past Counterfactual (Badawi et al. 2004: 645). However, concerning the *law* clauses that are 'synonymous with *in*', the apodoses can be paraphrased in *(fa-)sa-yafʿalu* (Badawi et al. 2004: 647). The authors therefore present two verbal forms for *law*: *fa ʿala* and *(fa-)sa-yafʿalu*. For *iḏā*, they offer three different verb forms for the apodosis: *fa ʿala*, *yafʿalu*, and *sa-yafʿalu* (Badawi et al. 2004: 653–4). *Fa-* is presented as quasi-systematic alongside *iḏā* under the same conditions as with the classical *in*. *La-* is, according to the authors, generally present in *law* clauses.

Alosh (2005: 270–2) reproduces the classic dichotomy between *iḏā*/*in*-Potential and *law*-Counterfactual, noting that *iḏā* should be followed by a perfect verb and that its apodosis can be either *fa ʿala* or *yafʿalu*. The author paraphrases the two syntaxes in the same way (Alosh 2005: 218). No mention is made of *fa-*. As for *law*, the structure is presented as fixed in the form *law fa ʿala . . . la-fa ʿala* with obligatory *la-*. Thus the author does not record apodoses in *sa-yafʿalu*, neither for *iḏā* nor for *law*.

Ryding (2005: 671–6) also remains very 'classic' in her presentation of the traditional dichotomy between *iḏā*/*in*-Potential and *law*-Counterfactual. She writes that 'Arabic uses *different particles* to express possible conditions and impossible conditions' (Ryding 2005: 671) with supporting references in her footnotes that are not really up-to-date: Peled, Cantarino, Blachère and Gaudefroy-Demombynes, Fischer, and so on (Ryding 2005: 671). She only offers, for *law*, *fa ʿala*/*lam yafʿal* structures in the protasis as well as in the apodosis (Ryding 2005: 675). She indicates the general, but not the systematic, nature of *la-*. Nothing is said about the negation of the apodosis, nor about the presence or not of *la-* in this case. *Iḏā* is presented as having nowadays replaced *in*. Concerning *iḏā*, whose protasis is in *fa ʿala*, she specifies that a switch (see Ryding 2005: 672) may appear in the apodosis, i.e. a tense other than *fa ʿala*. However she only gives three examples: a defensive, an injunctive, and a prepositional phrase introduced by *fa-* (*fa-ʿalay-ka an*). In doing so, she does not present, for *iḏā*, apodoses in *yafʿalu* or in *sa-yafʿalu*.

Hassanein (2006: 98–100) registers a syntax *iḏā faʿala . . . fa-sa-yafʿalu*, but translates it in the same manner as *iḏā faʿala . . . faʿala*. In addition to replicating the strict dichotomy between *iḏā/in*-Potential and *law*-Counterfactual, she does not mention, in the case of *law*, any apodosis in *yafʿalu* nor in *sa-yafʿalu*. She contents herself with saying that *law* is followed by a perfect verb (in the protasis), but does not specify anything for the apodosis; her examples only show *faʿala* in the apodosis. Still in the case of *law*, *la-* is presented as necessary before a perfect verb and as optional before a negative form, which, according to her, must be in *mā faʿala*, not in *lam yafʿal*. Finally, *fa-* is presented as systematically used when the apodosis is neither a perfect nor a jussive, and as obligatory when there is no perfect verb with *iḏā* (Hassanein 2006: 98–9). We should note that her examples do not seem genuine.

McCarus (2007: 149–52) does not record the apodosis as having any verbal form other than *faʿala* alongside *iḏā/in* and *law*, and adheres to the strict dichotomy between *iḏā/in*-Potential and *law*-Counterfactual. Like other authors, he notes that *iḏā* has taken over *in*; the former signifies more realisable conditions, while *in* would suggest a hypothesis in the true sense of the word. Again, McCarus's examples are not authentic.

Three conclusions can be drawn from this survey. The authors of these Modern Arabic grammars (1) most often retain the classical dichotomy between *iḏā/in*–Potential and *law*-Counterfactual; (2) show, in the vast majority of cases, apodoses only with *faʿala* and almost never with *yafʿalu* or *sa-yafʿalu*; or, if *yafʿalu* or *sa-yafʿalu* are given, it is almost never for *law*, but only for *iḏā*; and (3) report, more generally, that *la-* is not used systematically and that *fa-*, by contrast, appears in cases where the verb of the apodosis is neither a perfect nor a jussive introduced by the *lam* of negation. Among these grammars, Buckley and Badawi et al. especially stand out due to the number and authenticity of their examples, which allow us to see a reality that is far more complex than any of the others depict. Most authors other than Buckley and Badawi et al. are content simply to record the replacement of *in* by *iḏā*, without offering any descriptively adequate account of the reality of the usage. Nonetheless, even Buckley and Badawi et al. do not actually organise these structures into a coherent system; thus, they are forced to interpret identical structures in various different ways.

Thus, for example, in Buckley (2004: 739–40), the structure *law faʿala . . . faʿala* is classically interpreted as a case containing ambiguity between the Present Counterfactual and the Past Counterfactual; here we see only, in what emerges from my study, a Past Counterfactual. Alternatively, there is the structure *iḏā faʿala . . . faʿala* interpreted as Present Counterfactual and Potential (Buckley 2004: 734, 737) where I do not interpret it as Potential.

We thus see that the initial observations from our corpus do not correspond to the majority of descriptions of hypothetical clauses in Arabic given by recent grammars of the Modern Standard language. We will now detail our observations, in order to outline a system that seems to us coherent.

4. Discussion of data

4.1 The Factual

For the Factual, *iḏā* (33 cases out of 37), with *iḏā mā* (4 out of 37), is indeed the most common operator; thus, *iḏā* still expresses the Factual as was the case classically.

4.1.1 Present Factual: iḏā faʿala . . . yafʿalu

To demonstrate that this syntax indicates the Factual, let us consider a first example with *iḏā mā*, which operates in the same way as *iḏā*, *iḏā mā faʿala . . . yafʿalu* being equivalent to *ʿinda-mā yafʿalu . . . yafʿalu*, which is only interpretable as a Factual (*ʿinda-mā* means 'when'):

(1) *wa-**iḏā mā faʿala** aḥadu-hum, fa-inna-hu **yuḍṭarru** bi-l-ṭabʿi ilā rtiqāʾi l-daraği, wa-**ʿinda-mā yabluġu** l-ṭābiqa l-aḫīra **takūnu** ḫuṭuwātu-hu qad abṭaʾat mina l-taʿabi* (*Al-Lağna*: 53)

'**As soon as** one of them **does/has done** it, then he is naturally obliged to climb the stairs, and **when he reaches** the top floor, his steps **are** slowed with fatigue'

(2) ***iḏā ʿalā** ṣawtu rağulin yaṭlubu l-isrāʿa li-talbiyati ṭalabi-hi, huna **yanẓuru** ilay-hi **wa-yušīru** bi-raʾsi-hi išaratan wāḥidatan mūgazatan: "–mšī . . ."* (*Al-Zaynī*: 240)

'**If/when** someone raises his voice, urging him to serve him, he **looks** at him at once **and makes** a simple gesture of the head: "Back off . . . !"'

(3) *ammā **iḏā qārabati** l-intihāʾa **fa-inna** l-šarikata **taqūmu** bi-iʿādati taʿbiʾati-hā dāḫila akyāsin taḥmilu -sma-hā wa-taʾrīḫa iʿādati l-taʿbiʾati* (*Ḏāt*: 271)

'And **when** they **are close** to being outdated, the company **repackages** them in bags bearing its name and the date of the repackaging'

(4) *wa-**iḏā fuṣila** l-hindī **lā yaškū** wa-inna-mā yabḥaṯu fī hudūʾin ʿan ʿamalin āḫara* (*Warda*: 17)

'And **when** the Indian **is dismissed**, he **does not complain** but simply searches quietly for another job'

(5) ***iḏā tašāğarat** imraʾatun maʿa zawği-hā **lā taqṣidu** bayta ahli-hā šākiyatan inna-mā talğaʾu ilay-ka wāṯiqatan bi-anna mā laḥiqa bi-hā min ẓulmin sa-yazūlu* (*Al-Numūr*: 33)

'**When** a woman **quarrels** with her husband, she **does not go** to her parents complaining, but she takes refuge with you, confident that the injustice towards her will pass'

(6) ***iḏā takallamat tanfatiḥu*** *l-nafsu kulliyyatan* (*Al-Ğāziya*: 70)

'**When she speaks**, the soul **opens up** completely'

Not only do Badawi et al. note the existence of this syntax, they also suggest that its meaning is not obvious. Thus, they translate this syntax both as a Potential (Badawi et al. 2004: 654) and as a Factual (Badawi et al. 2004: 661). For some of their examples, we would have opted for a Factual. This is particularly the case with *maʿa ḏālika* (*sic*) ***iḏā ḫaraǧa*** *minhā fī riḥlatin aw ziyāratin ilā makānin mā min al-ʿālami* ***narāhu*** *lā yaḫšā l-iḫtināqa ka-asmāki l-baḥri min hāḏā l-ḫurūǧi*, translated by Badawi et al. as 'however, **if he leaves** it for traveling or to visit any place in the world **we find** [lit. "**see**"] that he does not fear being stifled like the fish of the sea do in this way' (Badawi et al. 2004: 653–4). We would translate it as follows: 'however, **when he leaves** it for travelling or to visit any place in the world, **we see** that he does not fear being stifled, like the fish of the sea do'. Nevertheless, of the 35 examples with *iḏā* whose apodosis has a verb in *(fa-)yafʿalu* form, 22 actually mark the Factual, but 13, i.e. 37.1 per cent, mark the Potential. It seems here that only context can help to distinguish between *iḏā faʿala . . . yafʿalu* for the Present Factual and *iḏā faʿala . . . yafʿalu* for the Potential.

4.1.2 Past Factual: iḏā faʿala . . . faʿala

Before considering the main syntax for expressing the Past Factual, and to link this point to the previous point, it should be noted that this expression can be formed, as in Classical Arabic, with the syntax of a Present Factual used with a perfect auxiliary verb (most commonly *kāna*). This is shown by the following example, where *iḏā* is used along with *ʿinda-mā* but, this time, in a *q if p* sequence:

(7) *wa-kānati l-bahǧatu* ***tušiʿʿu*** *fī kiyānī* ***ʿinda-mā yaqaʿu*** *naẓarī ʿalay-hā wa-****yaǧtāḥu****-nī l-yaʾsu* ***iḏā lam aǧid****-hā* (*Warda*: 56)

'Delight **would irradiate** in my being **whenever** my eye **fell** on her and despair **would overwhelm** me **when I could not find** her'

Another example, this time from Badawi et al., also puts into play *kāna* and its 'sisters' (other auxiliaries) to express habitual actions: ***kuntu iḏā waṣaltu*** *ilā l-munḥanā ʿinda furni l-ḥaǧǧi Nāṣif* ***altafitu*** *ilā l-ḫalfi*, '**whenever I would reach** the corner at Hajj Nasif's bakery **I would look** behind me' (Badawi et al. 2004: 662). Now let us consider the alternative Factual constructions present in the examples from the corpus:

(8) *raʾaytu-hum yuzīḥūna l-aṯqāla ʿan dawābbi-him kulla-mā tawaqqafa bi-him al-sabīlu l-abadī ḥattā* ***iḏā faraġū*** *min dawābbi-him wa-ṭmaʾannū ʿalā ḏawī-him* ***habbū*** *li-naǧdati aqraba man ǧāwara-hum li-yuʿīnū ʿalā amri-hi* (*Malakūt*: 130)

'I saw them removing the loads from their animals at each time they encountered an interruption along the Everlasting Way. So much so that, **when they had finished** with their cattle and were assured of their relatives, **they rose** to rescue the nearest neighbour and help him with his business'

(9) *wa-kāna* ***iḏā arāda*** *l-ṭaʿāma* ***taṭahhara*** *la-hu ka-taṭahhuri-hi li-l-iḥrāmi* (*Ḥaddaṯa*: 96)

'And **when he wanted** food, **he would purify** himself for it as he would for the state of ritual consecration'

In (9) the auxiliary verb *kāna* provides the interpretation of the Past Factual.

(10) ***iḏā taḥaddaṯa*** *l-sukkānu ʿan buṭūlati-him* ***taḥaddaṯū*** *bi-basāṭatin wa-tawāḍuʿin muḏhilayni ! maʿa anna-hum samaw bi-buṭūlati-him ilā mustawā l-maṯali l-sāʾiri* (*Al-Ǧāziya*: 37)

'**When** people **spoke** of their heroism, they **spoke** with disconcerting simplicity and humility! And this despite the fact that they have raised their heroism to a proverbial level!'

The context of example (10) is of a narrative in the past:

maʿa anna l-qaryata kāfaḥat, ṣamadat, waqafat fī waǧhi l-ẓulmi, baytan baytan, fardan fardan, lākin bi-dūni ḥiqdin. Al-šāmbiṭu nafsu-hu ʿinda-mā umira bi-l-istiqāli -staqāla. Wa-lammā ǧāʾa l-istiqlālu wa-umira bi-l-ʿawdati ʿāda . . . Iḏā taḥaddaṯa l-sukkānu . . .

'despite the fact that the village fought, resisted, stood up in front of the oppression, house after house, individual after individual, but without hatred. The constable himself when ordered to resign resigned. And when independence came and they ordered him to return he returned . . . When people were speaking . . .'

In Modern Arabic, however, the emergence of new usages does not necessarily cancel out the previous ones. Moreover, interpretation of data remains difficult and some *iḏā faʿala . . . faʿala* may be interpreted as Present Factual. Thus, Badawi et al. interpret ***iḏā aʿǧaba-nī*** *kitābun* ***tamannaytu*** *law iqtanaytu-hu* as a Present Factual: '**if** a book **pleases me I wish** I owned it' (Badawi et al. 2004: 653); I would have read it in the past: '**When** a book **pleased me, I would wish** I owned it' (as we shall see, it could also be interpreted as a Present Counterfactual, meaning 'If I liked *a book*, I would wish *I owned it*'). Similarly, they interpret as Present Factual both *iḏā faʿala . . . yafʿalu* and *iḏā faʿala . . . faʿala*: ***iḏā ḫaraǧati*** *l-asmāku mina l-baḥri* ***tamūtu*** *bi-l-iḫtināqi*, '**when** the fish **come out** of the sea **they die** of asphyxiation' (Badawi et al. 2004: 661) and ***iḏā samiʿa*** *aḏāna l-faǧri fī hudūʾi l-layli* ***ṭariba*** *l-qalbu*, '**when he hears** the dawn prayer call in the calm of the night his heart **rejoices**'. I would have interpreted the latter as having a Past Factual meaning: '**Whenever he heard** the dawn prayer call in the calm of the night his heart **would rejoice**'.

4.2 The Potential: iḏā faʿala . . . (fa-)sa-yafʿalu and law faʿala . . . yafʿalu

In, despite a tentative incursion into the Past Counterfactual, continues to express only the Potential, regardless of the syntax of the verb forms that follow it. It is the presence of *in*, and not the form of the verb in the apodosis, that determines the nature of these constructions as Potential. But the fact is that the construction with *in* only represents 19.2 per cent of Potential examples; *iḏā*, as was pointed out long ago, is now the most common means to express the Potential (68.0 per cent of instances). However, what is to our knowledge almost never mentioned, except quite remarkably by Badawi et al., is the significant appearance of *law* in this hypothetical sense (12.8 per cent).

4.2.1 In: variable syntax

The syntax remains classical, with *faʿala/lam yafʿal* or *yafʿal/lā yafʿal* (not seen, however, in my corpus; the only positive apocopate found in my corpus is in apodosis, see example (11) below) in protasis as well as in apodosis and with the appearance of *fa-* in the beginning of the apodosis as it appeared in Classical Arabic, except that an innovation has shown up: an apodosis in *sa-yafʿalu* and its negative counterpart *lan yafʿala* both juxtaposed with the protasis without being separated from the latter by *fa-*. This innovation is certainly an imitation of the syntax of European languages:

(11) ***in tazawwağtu** bi-ki **u ʿṭi**-ki kulla mā yumkinu an yaḍumma qalbī min ḥubbin* (*Al-Ğāziya*: 71) = *in faʿala . . . yafʿal*

‘**If I marry** you, **I'll give** you all the love my heart can contain’

(12) *wa-**in lam yastaṭiʿ** kabīru l-baṣṣāṣīna l-ʿuṯmānliyyīna hāḏā **fa-lā yastaḥiqqu** manṣiba-hu* (*Al-Zaynī*: 230) = *in faʿala . . . fa-yafʿalu*

‘And **if** the Ottoman Grand Master **cannot** do this, **then he does not merit** his title’

(13) *yataḫallā ʿani l-dunyā li-anna-hu **in lam yataḫalla** ʿani l-dunyā fa-inna l-dunyā **sawfa tataḫalla** ʿan-hu* (*Malakūt*: 61) = *in faʿala . . . fa-inna-hu sa-yafʿalu*

‘He gives up life for **if he does not give** it **up, it will give** him **up**’

(14) *fa-**in lam yataḥaqqaqi** l-amalu hullu-hu baʿda ḏālika **fa**-l-masīratu **lam tantahi*** (*Ḥaddaṯa*: 31) = *in faʿala . . . fa-inna-hu faʿala*

‘**If** all hope **is not realised** after that, **then** the march **is not over**’

In example (14), the *fa-*, while also acting to focalise the logical subject of the verb, blocks the interpretation of that verb in a future sense. If it had been *lam tantahi l-masīratu*, the meaning would have been ‘the march will not end’; but with *fa-lam tantahi l-masīratu* or *fa-l-masīratu lam tantahi*, the meaning must be ‘the march is not over’.

(15) ***in arkaba** bna-hu ʿalā bağlatin uḫrā **fa-lā yaʾmanu** ʿalay-hi min ʿaṯratin aw šayʾin yuḫīfu-hā fa-taqfiza wa-tarmiya bi-hi ilā l-hāwiyati* (*Al-Ğāziya*: 189)

‘**If he lifts** his son onto another mule, then **nothing prevents** it stumbling or being frightened by something, and then falling and tipping him into the abyss’

(16) ***in nağā*** *ʿinda bābin* ***lan yanğuwa*** *ʿinda l-abwābi l-uḫrā llatī taḥrusu-hā l-fataḥātu l-mawğūdatu ʿinda l-abwābi l-tāliyati la-hā* (*Warda*: 36) = *in faʿala . . . sa-yafʿalu* where *fa-* does not occur.

'**If he escapes** from one door, **he will not escape** from the others which are guarded by the loopholes that are at the doors which follow them'

(17) ***in ḏahaba*** *huwa* ***sa-yaʾtī*** *man yaḫlufu-hu* (*Al-Ğāziya*: 187) = *in faʿala . . . sa-yafʿalu* where *fa-* does not occur.

'**If he goes,** there **will come** one who will succeed him'

4.2.2 iḏā: iḏā faʿala . . . (fa-)sa-yafʿalu

Although Badawi et al. clearly show that *iḏā* can be a 'pure conditional', that is, a Potential, they suggest only a single pattern, *iḏā faʿala . . . faʿala* (Badawi et al. 2004: 653). However, in my corpus, I have already reported that *iḏā faʿala . . . faʿala* may indicate, depending on the context, either the Past Factual or the Present Counterfactual. Thus, none of the examples placed by Badawi et al. under the heading '*iḏā* "if" as a pure conditional' account for what I see in my corpus, and these examples should, I believe, be reinterpreted as Present Counterfactual (see below). But in the following section of Badawi et al., entitled 'variant forms of verb in apod.', we find two other patterns, *iḏā faʿala . . . yafʿalu* and *iḏā faʿala . . . sa-yafʿalu*, which also are paraphrased by Potentials. While *iḏā faʿala . . . yafʿalu* does indeed express the Potential 37.1 per cent of the time, it especially expresses the Present Factual (62.9 per cent of the time), as already demonstrated above. But Badawi et al. (2004: 653–4) give only one example which is actually a Potential and whose English translation accurately reflects this. This example also happens to use the *iḏā faʿala . . . sa-yafʿalu* pattern, in accordance with what my corpus has allowed me to demonstrate: *wa-****iḏā sa'alta****-nī l-āna li-māḏā wāṣaltu l-taradduda ʿalā ʿiyādati-hi baʿda an ṣāraḥa-ni bi-ḏālika wa-li-māḏā lam aḏhab l-ʿiyādata ṭabībin āḫara* ***sa-yakūnu*** *ğawābī* . . ., 'and **if you ask** me now why I continued to go to his clinic after he clearly told me about that and why I did not go to some other doctor's clinic, my answer **will be** . . .'; I agree with this translation.

(18) *wa-****iḏā tağāhala-hu fa-la-sawfa yaʿrifu*** *kayfa yahtadī ilā awwali l-ṭarīqi ka-mā htadā l-kaṯīrūna* (*Riğāl*: 46)

'And **if he pretends to ignore it, then he will necessarily find** how to reach the beginning of the road as did so many others'

In example (18), note the presence of an infix *lām* between *fa-* and the future particle *sawfa*. This *lām* probably has a corroborative value (*lām al-tawkīd*)

(19) *wa-****iḏā ṯabata*** *anna-hu ẓalama maḫlūqan,* ***sa-yaqbalu*** *ayya qiṣāṣin yaqaʿu ʿalay-hi ka-ayyi maḫluqin* (*Al-Zaynī*: 249)

'And **if it turns out** that he has been unjust towards anyone, **he will be ready** to pay for it as a simple mortal'

Note that in examples (18) and (19), the *wa-* prefixed to *iḏā* does not indicate a concessive clause, because the wider context forces an interpretation of this *wa-* as a coordinating conjunction between two hypothetical statements: 'If Zakariyā helped him it would be better, and if he pretends to ignore it . . .'.

(20) *wa-**iḏā kunta** ṭayyiban **fa-sa-tarḍā*** (*Al-ʿĀšiq*: 40)

'And **if you're** good, then you'll love'

(21) ***iḏā ḏahabtumā** l-laylata li-taḫrībi qabri l-waliyyi wa-šağarati-hi **fa-sa-yaḥkumu** ʿalay-kumā bi-l-maḥqi* (*Al-ʿĀšiq*: 92)

'**If you two go** tonight to destroy the tomb of the saint and his tree, **then he will condemn** you to death'

(22) *wa-**iḏā lam taḏhabi** l-āna **fa-sa-aṭlubu** mina l-mumarriḍi an yulqiya bi-ka ilā l-šāriʿi* (*Al-Lağna*: 117)

'And **if you do not leave** now, **I'll ask** the nurse to put you out on the street'

(23) ***iḏā aradtum** tarkanā **lan aʿtariḍa*** (*Warda*: 313)

'**If you want** to leave, **I will not be** opposed to it'

(24) ***iḏā lam taʿtarif sa-aḍribu**-ka bi-l-ḥiḏāʾi wa-aḍribu ahla ḥārati-ka* (*Al-Numūr*: 37)

'**If you do not confess, I will smite** thee with the shoe and beat the people of your neighborhood'

In example (24), note that the second verb, also interpreted as a future, is not marked by a future particle, as it is governed by the future particle on the first verb, to which the second verb is coordinated by *wa-*.

(25) ***iḏā lafafta**-hu ḥawla ʿunqi-ka **sa-yakūnu** rāʾiʿan* (*Ḥiwār*: 26)

'**If you tie** it around your neck, **it will be** great'

In the following examples, the hypothetical clause is placed after a past tense verb:

(26) *awhama-hu baʿḍu l-sukkāni anna l-Ğāziyata sa-taḥḍuru l-zaradata, wa-anna-hā **iḏā raʾati** bna-hu **sa-taʿšaqu**-hu fī l-ḥāli* (*Al-Ğāziya*: 26)

'Some residents made him believe that Al-Ğāziya would be present at the party, and that **if she saw** her son, **she would fall in love** with him immediately'

(27) *fa-l-buyūtu fī sīrati-hā l-ūlā lam tanhaḍ ʿani l-arḍi li-tataṭallaʿa ilā l-samāwāti li-takūna muğarrada maʾwan li-anna-hā **iḏā faqadat** huwiyyata-hā l-aṣliyyata llatī anwī an uḥaddiṯa-kum ʿan-hā **fa-lan yakūna** bayna-hā wa-bayna l-maṯwā farqun* (*Malakūt*: 99)

'The houses in their early development did not rise from earth to aspire to heaven to be simple shelters, because **if they lost** their original identity, about which I want to talk to you, **there would be no** difference between them and a mere dwelling-place'

4.2.3 Law: law fa'ala . . . yaf'alu

Badawi et al. note, in a dedicated section, that *law* may now have, in Modern Written Arabic, the meaning of Potential: '*law* "if" can occur with the sense of *in* "if", thus losing its Counterfactual quality' (Badawi et al. 2004: 647–8). But of their five examples, I exclude the first, which is not doubly verbal and therefore not relevant for my purposes. In the remaining four, the following patterns are exemplified: (1) *law fa'ala . . . fa-lan yaf'ala*, (2) *law fa'ala . . . lan-yaf'ala*, (3) *law fa'ala . . . yaf'alu*, and (4) *law fa'ala . . . la-fa'ala*. In other words, there are three verbal forms of apodosis: *(fa-)sa-yaf'alu*, *yaf'alu*, and *fa'ala*. However, only examples (1) and (2) are actually paraphrased as Potential, while examples (3) and (4) are paraphrased as Present Counterfactual. I agree with Badawi et al. regarding their examples (1) and (2), although I shall insist that the *law fa'ala . . . (fa-)sa-yaf'alu* syntax is ambiguous between the Potential and the Present Counterfactual (see Table 8.3). Therefore, I propose to reinterpret the syntax *law fa'ala . . . (fa-)sa-yaf'alu* of examples (1) and (2) as Present Counterfactual, as we shall see. I translate *wa-**law** sa'alta aḥada-hum min ayna atayta bi-hāḏā l-ḥaqqi . . . **fa**-lan taǧida raddan*, not as 'and **if** you ask one of them where did he get this truth from . . . [**then**] you will not find an answer' but as 'and if you asked one of them where did he get this truth from . . . [then] you would not find an answer'; and likewise I translate ***law** daḫalnā sibāqa tasalluḥin nawawiyyin fī l-minṭaqati **lan** yantahiya* not as '**if** we enter a nuclear arms race in the region it **will never** [lit. "**will not**"] end' but as '**if** we entered a nuclear arms race in the region it **would never** [lit. "**would not**"] end' (both examples from Badawi et al. 2004: 647).

Badawi et al. only distinguish between Factual (Temporal), Potential (Conditional), and Past Counterfactual (Counterfactual). They are therefore led, in their example (4), to classify as Conditional, 'with an unlikely future sense, retaining the syntax used in counterfactual sentences' (Badawi et al. 2004: 647), a sentence like ***law** utīḥa li-l-šu'ūbi l-'arabiyyati an tusammiya l-za'īma l-akṯara ša'biyyatan fī hāḏihi l-āwinati **la**-aǧābat* . . ., which they translate as a Present Counterfactual '**if** the Arab people were given [the opportunity] to name the most popular leader during these times, [**then**] they would answer . . .' (Badawi et al. 2004: 648; however, given the syntactic regularities observed in my corpus, it may be inferred that this sentence, whose structure is *law fa'ala . . . la-fa'ala*, is a Past Counterfactual (and not a Present) and therefore means 'if the Arab people had been given [the opportunity] to name the most popular leader during these times, [then] they would have answered . . .'; see below).

This leaves then only one example that Badawi et al. classify as Conditional, which I believe is actually a Potential, both syntactically and semantically, but which Badawi et al. translate as if it were an Present Counterfactual. This example is ***law** 'alimat bi-l-amri **yumkinu** an taṭluba min-hu an yuṭalliqa-hā*, '**if** she were to find out about the matter she could [lit. "**it would be possible** that"] ask him to divorce her', which I translate as a Potential: '**if** she finds out about the matter she will [lit. "**it will be**

possible that"] ask him to divorce her'. Let me now give a few examples from the corpus:

(28) ***law wuǧida*** *bayna l-ḥabībi wa-mubtaġā-hu ʿaqābātun yaʾmulu hadma-hā,* ***aǧʿalu*** *min-hā mustaḥīlan lā yumkinu taḫaṭṭī-hi* (*Al-Zaynī*: 287)

'**If there should occur** between the lover and his desire obstacles which he hopes to destroy, **I'll create** an obstacle that cannot be overcome'

(29) ***law naẓarnā*** *ilā dāʾirati l-mašriqi l-ʿarabiyyi l-muntiǧati l-raʾīsiyyati li-l-bitrūli, wa-llatī bi-hā 60 bi-l-miʾati min kulli mā ladā l-ʿālami mina l-bitrūli* ***naǧidu*** *anna asāsan raʾīsiyyan min istrātīǧiyyati-hā huwa . . .* (*Ḏāt*: 32)

'**If you look** at the Arab East, the leading oil producer and holder of 60 per cent of the world reserves, **we see** that the foundation of its strategy is . . .'

(30) ***law qaṭaʿnā*** *l-šaǧarata wa-dafannā raʾsa l-waliyyi* ***fa-laʿalla-nā nastariddu*** *abṣāra-nā wa-asmāʿa-nā* (*Al-ʿĀšiq*: 92)

'**If we cut down** the tree and bury the saint's head, **then maybe we will regain** our vision and our hearing'

In example (30), *laʿalla* ('maybe'), which marks the modality of possibility, confirms that *law* does mark the Potential.

(31) ***law ṯabata*** *hāḏā* ***taqaʿu*** *kāriṯatun* (*Warda*: 112)

'**If it** actually **happens, it will be** a disaster'

(32) ***law kāna*** *raʾsu l-ǧanīni fī l-aysari* ***yakūnu*** *waladan* (*Warda*: 361)

'**If** the head of the foetus **is** on the left side, **it will be** a boy'

4.3 The Counterfactual

The Past Counterfactual is classically expressed by *law* (98.9 per cent of the time). The Present Counterfactual is primarily and classically expressed using its historic operator *law* (40.7 per cent), but is also expressed using *iḏā (mā)*, which appears prominently in this hypothetical category (59.3 per cent), as Badawi et al. (2004: 656) tentatively note. Badawi et al. mention equally tentatively the existence of a structure in *law faʿala . . . (fa-)-sa-yafʿalu*, which they interpret in the same way as *law faʿala . . . yafʿalu*, whereas we see a difference (see above). Moreover, it appears that of the 47 examples in *iḏā faʿala . . . faʿala*, which are classically linked to Factual and Potential, only 8 really belong there, and then only in the Potential. Therefore only 17.0 per cent of examples with *iḏā faʿala . . . faʿala* actually express a hypothetical category conforming with that described in the Classical Arabic grammars, while 83.0 per cent express the Present Counterfactual – which does not conform to the classical account! Furthermore, as reported earlier, *la-* is not found systematically with *iḏā*, appearing in only 4.2 per cent of cases, in which it serves only to emphasise the beginning of the apodosis. On the other hand, *la-* appears much more regularly in the Past Counterfactual with *law*, in fact in 87.4 per cent of instances.

4.3.1 Present Counterfactual: iḏā faʿala . . . (la-) faʿala and law faʿala . . . (fa-) sa-yafʿalu

Iḏā

Of the examples given by Badawi et al., I argue that three should be reinterpreted as Present Counterfactual. Let us look at one example to show this: ***iḏā kāna*** *kātibu l-inšāʾi mulimman bi-miṯli haḏihi* (*sic*) *l-luġāti* ***kāna*** *aqdara ʿalā murāsalati-him*, '**if** the secretary of the chancellery **was** conversant with such languages as these he **was** more able to correspond with them [namely, foreign people]' (Badawi et al. 2004: 653). This evidently makes no sense. The translation given by Badawi et al. does not work, partly due to semantics (and common sense, because what the secretary of the chancellery has been reproached about is precisely his lack of any foreign language . . .) and partly due to syntax. For the second *kāna* to be interpretable as an imperfect or preterite, *fa-* would have had to be prefixed to it, since in examples like this *fa-* never fails to distinguish a formally perfect/jussive verb introduced by *lam* from a verb that is perfect in both form and sense. Thus, this sentence can only be understood as 'If the secretary of the chancellery were more conversant with such languages [but this is not the case], he would be more able to correspond with them'. There follow some more examples of this Present Counterfactual syntax with *iḏā*:

(33) *al-wāḥidu hunā lā yarā zawǧata ṣadīqi-hi lākin* ***iḏā qābala****-hā fī Lunduna* ***saharū*** *maʿan* (*Warda*: 241)

'Here, a man does not see the wife of his friend, but **if he met** her in London, **they would go out** together'

In example (33), the restriction implied by *lākin* ('but'), that is, the refutation of a present or future reality, indicates the interpretation as a Counterfactual.

(34) ***iḏā waḍaʿta*** *fī-hā ǧamalan* ***taḥawwala*** *ilā ṭayrin min maʿdinin yaṭīru afḍala min ayyi ṭayrin* (*Al-Numūr*: 60)

'**If you put** a camel there, **it would turn** into an iron bird flying better than any bird'

In example (34), it is the absurdity that proves the Counterfactual status of the sentence.

(35) *fa-****iḏā aḍafnā*** *ilā ḏālika anna l-duwala l-ʿarabiyyata bi-ḥukmi īmāni-hā bi-l-risālāti l-samāwiyyati wa-l-adyāni yaǧʿalu-hā aqraba ilā l-ġarbi mina l-šarqi* ***la-waǧadnā*** *anna ǧamīʿa hāḏihi l-asbābi tanfī . . .* (*Ḏāt*: 32)

'**If we added** that the Arab States, by virtue of their attachment to the revealed [Abrahamic] religions, feel closer to the West than the East, **we would see** that all of that would completely deny . . .'

The syntax of example (35) is not clear. In particular, we do not know what the subject of *yağ'alu-hā* is. Maybe there is a misprint here, and an indefinite relative pronoun *mā* is missing ('what makes them closer to West than to East . . .'). But it is clearly here the presence of the *lām* in imitation of the syntax of *law* which allows this to be interpreted as a Counterfactual, and specifically, because of *iḏā*, as a Present Counterfactual.

(36) ***iḏā sā'ada**-hu Zakariyā **kāna** ḏālika afḍala* (*Riğāl*: 46)

'**If** Zakariyā **helped** him, **it would be** better'

(37) *fa-**iḏā ḏakarta** la-nā asmā'a-hum, rubba-mā **kāna** li-ḏālika aṯarun fī taḫfīfi l-amri bi-l-nisbati la-ka* (*Al-Lağna*: 94)

'**If you told** us their names, maybe **it would** mitigate your situation'

(38) ***iḏā ḏahabtumā** li-taḫrībi qabri l-waliyyi wa-šağarati-hi **aḫaḏtu** 'alā 'ātiqī iblāğa l-šurṭati* (*Al-'Āšiq*: 92)

'**If you two were going** tonight to destroy the tomb of the saint and his tree, **I would take** upon myself the responsibility of contacting the police'

(39) *fī waqtin ṭawīlin ra'ā nafsa-hu ḥāmila l-ṯaqli l-fādiḥi, lā aḥada yu'īnu-hu 'alay-hi, ḥattā Manṣūrun ṣāḥibu-hu, **iḏā su'ila** 'an aṣḥābi-hi wa-zumalā'i-hi **qāla** lā fā'idata min-hum turğā* (*Al-Zaynī*: 259)

'For a long time he watched himself bearing the crushing weight. Nobody helped him, not even his friend Manṣūr. **If** anyone **asked** him what he thought about his friends and colleagues, **he would say** that there was nothing to be expecting from them'

(40) *fa-fāḍa qalbu l-abi bi-l-fuḍūli fa-tasā'ala 'an sirri 'abaṯi l-aqdāri dūna an yadiya, fa-ağāba-hu l-ḫafā'u: sirru 'abaṯi l-aqdāri laysa hawan wa-lākinna-hu ğadalun lan ya'mala-hu illā ṣuḥbānu l-ḫāfiyati, li-anna l-aqdāra **iḏā arādat** bi-maḫlūqin šarran **aḥyat-hu** wa-**iḏā šā'ati** l-aqdāru bi-maḫlūqin ḫayran **amātat-hu*** (*Malakūt*: 79)

'The father's heart was then filled with curiosity and he questioned himself about the secret of the absurdity of fate, which he did not know. The secret then answered him: "The secret of the absurdity of fate is not a caprice but a debate that only companions of the secret will know; because fate, **if it wanted** to hurt a creature, **would make it live**, and if it wished it well, **would make it die**"'

(41) *inna-hu yā Kahlānu **iḏā kariha** l-mar'u l-ḥaṣra wa-l-qaṣra **ṭalaba** kaṯrata l-yawmi wa-**štāqa** l-'adada* (*Ḥaddaṯa*: 150–1)

'Kahlān! **If** Man **hated** confinement and restriction, **he would ask** for abundance of the sea and **would rejoice** in such plentitude'

Law

(42) *yā Sa ʿīdu anā maqṭū ʿu l-amali mina l-mahdiyyi l-muntaẓari,* ***law qāma*** *nāṭiqu l-zamāmi,* ***law ẓahara, law ǧā ʾa*** *mina l-ka ʿbati yušhiru sayfa-hu l-ḏahabiyya,* ***sa-yataṣaddā*** *la-hu Zakariyā,* ***sa-yuḥarrimu****-hu duḫūla l-diyāri* (*Al-Zaynī*: 256)

'Sa ʿīd, I lost hope of seeing the Messiah. **If he rose, if he appeared, if he came** from the Ka ʿaba, brandishing his gold sabre, Zakariyā **would oppose** him, **he would prevent** him from coming to us'

(43) ***law i-stimarrat sa-yastaḥīlu*** *ʿalay-nā muġādarati l-makāni* (*Warda*: 134)

'**If it** [the bombing] **continued, it would be impossible** to go out'

Example (43) could have a Potential interpretation, if there were not an implicit *but*: 'but it will not continue' (in the following context: the heroine, writing her diary at the end of the day, knows that she will succeed in stopping the bombing).

(44) ***law ḍaraba****-nī* ***fa-sa-aqūlu*** *li-abī fa-ya ʾtī wa-yaḍribu-hu* (*Al-Numūr*: 26)

'**If he hit** me, **I would tell** my father who would beat him'

The same remark applies in example (44) as for example (43); compare again this structure with the preceding example; compare also example (46).

4.3.2 Past Counterfactual

Law fa ʿala . . . (la-)(mā) fa ʿala

La- is semi-systematically found at the beginning of the apodosis, and even if the apodosis is negated (as conventional, using *mā fa ʿala*), resulting in structures of the form *la-mā fa ʿala*. The context given by the following example shows that although this syntax is linked to the Past Counterfactual, *lākin(na)*, 'but' + *perfect verb* leaves no doubt about the interpretation:

(45) ***law sa ʾalta****-nī ʿan ḏālika* ***la-dalaltu****-ka ʿalā ṭarīqatin ǧiddi sahlatin, lā tukallifu ṯamanan!* ***lākinna-ka fakkarta*** *bi-ṭarīqati-ka* (*Al-Ǧāziya*: 133)

'**If you had asked** me about this, **I would have indicated** to you a very easy method, which costs nothing! **But you thought** according to your method'

In the same manner as above, in example (45) *lākinna* ('but') forces a Counterfactual reading; as it is associated with a past tense verb (*fakkarta*), the sense is Past Counterfactual.

(46) *wa-rakaḍa l-awlādu bi-aqṣā quwwatin wa-lammā bta'adū waqafū lāhiṯīna muḥmarri l-wuǧūhi. qāla Muḥammadun:* ***law amsaka-nā la-ašba'a-nā*** *ḍarban* (*Al-Numūr*: 62)

'The children ran as fast as they could. When they were far away, they stopped, panting, faces reddened. Muḥammad said: **if he had caught** us, **he would have beaten** us'

The context in example (46) shows that the only possible interpretation is that of the Past Counterfactual.

(47) *wa-**law kāna** mu'aqqadan bi-sababi lawni-hi ka-mā qāla Haykalun **mā ǧalasa** bi-l-sā'āti kulla yawmin fī -šamsi* (*Ḏāt*: 38)

'**If he** [Anwar al-Sadāt] **had had** a lot of hang ups about the colour [of his skin], as Haykal said, **he would not have spent** hours in the sun every day'

(48) *la-qad fakkara wālidī bi-l-amri:* ***law aǧǧara*** *ġurfatayni wa-**sakana** ma'a zawǧati-hi l-kasḥā'i fī l-ṯāliṯati iḏan **la-'āša** mā tabaqqā la-hu mina l-ḥayāti mustaqirran* (*Riǧāl*: 41)

'My father had thought about it: **if he had rented** two rooms and **lived** with his lame wife in the third, **then he would have lived** out what remained of his life well-situated'

(49) *wa-**law ǧā'a** aḥadu-humā qabla l-āḫari aw ba'da-hu, **la-marrati** l-umūru fawqa saṭḥi ayyāmī miṯla-mā nzalaqa ālāfu l-awliyā'i ilā nisyāni wa-lākinna-humā ǧā'ā ma'an* (*Al-'Āšiq*: 77)

'**If** one of the two **had come** before the other, or after him, things **would have moved** on just as thousands of saints have slipped into oblivion; but they came together'

(50) ***law saqaṭat*** *Raḫyūtu **ḍā'ati** l-minṭaqatu l-muḥarraratu* (*Warda*: 315)

'**If** ever Raḫyūt **had fallen**, the liberated area **would have been lost**'

(51) *wa-lākin **law ra'aytumū**-hum wa-ta'ammaltum waǧūha-humu llatī tanḍaǧu bi-mā tusammūna-hu fī mu'ǧami-kum sa'ādatan **la-ayqantum** bi-ǧadwā riḥlati-him wa-āmantum bi-risālati* (*Malakūt*: 128)

'But **if you had seen** them and had seen their faces which were perspiring with what you call happiness in your language, **you would have been assured** of the success of your journey, you would have believed in the prophecy'

(52) *wa-**law šā'a la-amkana-hu** an yuqaddima qiṣṣata-hu bi-miṯli mā qaddama bi-hi masrḥiyyata-hu l-Sudd* (*Ḥaddaṯa*: 32)

'**If only he had wanted, it would have been possible for him** to present his story as he presented his play *al-Sudd* [*The Dam*]'

(53) *wa-**law lam takun** qābilatan li-l-zawāği fī naẓari l-qaryati, la-mā aqdama l-šambīṭu ʿalā ḫiṭbati-hi li-bni-hi* (*Al-Ğāziya*: 28)

'And **if she had not been** fit for marriage in the eyes of the village, the constable would not have undertaken to engage her to his son'

(54) *wa-**law taraka**-hum **la-ğāʾū**-hu bi-suyūfi-him* (*Al-Zayni*: 299)

'**If he had let** them **be, they would have come** to him with their swords'

Law faʿala . . . kāna yafʿalu

Finally, we find in the literature an alternative to *faʿala* for the Past Counterfactual, *kāna sa-yafʿalu*, as Badawi et al. (2004: 645–6) note. However, there are only three occurrences of this structure in my corpus:

(55) *ʿiqābun āḫaru **law kāna ʿtāda**-hu munḏu ṯalāṯi sanawātin **la-mā kāna**, al-āna ʿalā l-aqalli, **yaktariṯu** bi-hi, miṯla-mā yafʿalu hāḏihi l-laḥẓata* (*Al-ʿĀšiq*: 28)

'Another punishment: **if he had not got used** to him over three years, **then he would not have been**, now at least, **preoccupied** by him, as he is at the moment'

5. Analysis

The data above suggests that a new characterisation of MSA's hypothetical clauses is needed, quite different from that found in the published grammars of the language of the contemporary period.

Classically, there existed two particles used to mark conditional clauses, *in* and *law* (see al-Zamaḫšarī 1999: 416; regarding the semantic and not merely syntactic identification of *law* with *in* in the conditional clause, see Versteegh 1991). Later, the adverbial *iḏā*, initially reserved for the Factual, gradually supplanted *in* in the expression of the Potential, to the point where *in* is now used only residually (only 16 examples in my data, 5.7 per cent), and is mostly confined to a few idioms like *in šāʾa llah*, 'if God wills' or, in the form *wa-in*, to the expression of concessive clauses (which are outside the scope of this chapter). The classic distinction between operators *iḏā* and *law* allowed the verbs used in the main and conditional clauses to be interpreted as neutral from a temporal point of view regardless of the verb form used, which was generally a perfect. Some exceptions to this are examples given by al-Zamaḫšarī (1999: 416), of clauses with *in*, specified as being used in the sense of the future (*'in' tağʿalu l-fiʿla li-l-istiqbāli wa-in kāna māḍiyan*), where the verbs are jussives (i.e. *muḍāriʿ*) perfects: *in taḍrib-nī aḍrib-ka* ('if you hit me I'll hit you'). Similarly al-Zamaḫšarī presents examples with perfects in clauses with *law*, specifying *a contrario* that these are used to express a condition in the past (*wa-'law' tagʿalu-hu li-l-māḍī wa-in kāna mustaqbilan*): *law ğiʾta-nī la-akramtu-ka* ('if you came/had come, I honoured you/would have honoured you'). In doing so, he still seems to retain for these so-called neutral verbal forms a certain tense value. Moreover, Ayoub (2003) notes the semantic implication of the speaker attached to *mağzūm* contrasting with the neutral utterance value of *māḍī*.

As noted, the verb form used was generally perfect although it appears that the primary form used in *in* clauses was the *muḍāriʿ maǧzūm* (jussive/imperfect apocopate), as the first two examples given by al-Zamaḫšarī (1999: 416) tend to show. Moreover, Larcher seems to favour a jussive origin of the hypothetical *in* clauses, noting that one finds in fact very few examples of the form *in faʿala . . . faʿala* in Qurʾanic Arabic, and actually none of *in faʿala . . . lam yafʿal* nor *in lam yafʿal . . . faʿala*; and the only denial of jussive *yafʿal* is *lā yafʿal*, the only negative example present in the Qurʾan being *illā [< in + lā] yafʿal . . . lā yafʿal*; see Larcher (2003a, 2008). All the current literature on MSA surveyed here continues to reproduce the strict dichotomy between *iḏā*-Potential and *law*-Counterfactual. Buckley puts it as follows: 'The temporal meaning of the verb will depend on the meaning of the condition' (Buckley 2004: 739). To that solely semantic criterion, we oppose the following syntactic criterion which is expressed thus: 'The meaning of the condition depends *both* on the temporal form of the verb in the apodosis (and therefore on its meaning) *and* on the conditional particle.'

The most important new observation about Modern Arabic's hypothetical clauses is that, probably under the influence of languages with only one *if* (*si* in French, *if* in English), the Classical Arabic conditional operators have become synonymous (see Sartori 2009 for a demonstration of the reality and syntactic implications of this synonymisation in one colloquial Arabic, namely Egyptian). In addition to its traditional function marking the Potential, *iḏā* has come to mark the Counterfactual (Present), alongside *law* which had historically had that function; meanwhile *law*, in turn, now also marks the Potential as well as the Counterfactual.

The result of this synonymisation is necessarily an upheaval of the traditional system in which only the operators carried the meaning and allowed the type of conditional to be identified (Factual/Potential, Counterfactual). This upheaval has resulted in the introduction of a kind of sequence of tenses, where the modern apodosis now gains a tense value. We can see that a system similar to the sequence of tenses seen in English or French has come into use (see Table 8.2; for the French, see Grévisse 2001 or Riegel et al. 2004: 509).

It is probably under the influence of European languages like French and English that the Arabic conditional system has changed.

The different categories of the conditional seem now to be distinguished by means of contrastive syntax, shifting the Arabic system closer to a 'sequence of tenses' system like that in Table 8.2. However, this sequence is not perfect (i.e. not a perfect imitation of the English or French system), since the verb of the protasis retains its neutral temporal value: it is almost always a perfect (except for a very few cases of *law yafʿalu*, the imperfect indicating here a Present Counterfactual) governed by a conditional operator, indicating only that the clause is part of a hypothetical clause. It is then the verb of the apodosis, the form of which is very different from that of the hypothetical clause of Classical Arabic, which has a tense value that distinguishes among the hypothetical categories, as in languages like French or English. Thus it is no longer the operator alone that marks the meaning of a conditional clause, but rather the *relationship* between the operator and the verbal form in the apodosis. This is therefore no longer an *essentialist* system as in Classical Arabic, but a *relational* one.

Table 8.2 English sequence of tenses

<table>
<tr><th colspan="2">Protasis</th><th>Apodosis</th><th>Meaning</th><th>Known as</th><th>Meaning group</th></tr>
<tr><td>if/when</td><td>Preterite/Past Continuous</td><td>Preterite/Past Continuous</td><td>Past Factual</td><td rowspan="2">'zero conditional'</td><td rowspan="4">Factual</td></tr>
<tr><td>if/when</td><td>Present</td><td>Present</td><td>Present Factual</td></tr>
<tr><td>if</td><td rowspan="2">Present (Simple or Continuous)</td><td>Present/Future (Simple or Continuous)</td><td rowspan="2">Potential</td><td rowspan="2">'first conditional'</td></tr>
<tr><td>if</td><td>Future (Simple or Continuous)</td></tr>
<tr><td>if</td><td rowspan="2">Preterite/Past Continuous</td><td>Conditional Present/ Conditional Present Continuous</td><td>Present Counterfactual[a]</td><td>'second conditional'</td><td rowspan="3">Counterfactual</td></tr>
<tr><td>if</td><td rowspan="2">Conditional Perfect/ Conditional Perfect Continuous</td><td rowspan="2">Past Counterfactual</td><td rowspan="2">'third conditional'</td></tr>
<tr><td>if</td><td>Pluperfect/ Pluperfect Continuous</td></tr>
</table>

Note: [a] Ambiguous between the Potential and the Present Counterfactual. See above.

Iḏā has retained a Factual sense, so used as such, and in imitation of European languages, it has become natural to use an imperfect verb for the Present Factual (equivalent to French's present indicative in *si/quand il fait beau, je* ***sors*** and the English present in 'if/when the weather is nice I **go** out'), and a perfect verb for the Past Factual (equivalent in French to the imperfect past as in *quand il faisait beau, je* ***sortais***, or in English either to the *used to* semi-modal or to *would* in the habitual sense, as in 'when the weather was nice I {used to/would} go out').

Similarly, for the Potential it was perhaps seen as more natural now to have, instead of and in contrast to the classic *faʿala* with its non-temporal value, a semantic and syntactic future (*sa-yafʿalu*), which is the Arabic equivalent of the French future in *s'il fait beau je* ***sortirai*** and of the English future in 'if the weather is nice I **will go** out'.

Iḏā with a perfect (*faʿala*) in the apodosis, formerly non-temporal, could then come to mark the Present Counterfactual, with context distinguishing this from the Past Factual.

Law still expresses the Counterfactual. In imitation of European languages, the Present Counterfactual acquires a meaning equivalent to the French conditional in *s'il faisait beau (mais il ne fait pas beau) je* ***sortirais*** or the English modal *would* in 'if the weather was nice (but it is not) I **would go** out', both of which conditional forms are obviously related to the corresponding (indicative) future forms. The form of the Arabic future *sa-yafʿalu*, equivalent to that English/French *future* (respectively *-rais/would*, which forms are obviously linked to the regular future *-rai/will*), thus becomes conditional as the apodosis of *law*.

The Past Counterfactual could therefore only be marked by an apodosis of a past verbal form (*faʿala* or *kāna sa-yafʿalu*) in a sentence marked by *law*.

Table 8.3 Verbal forms in the apodosis of the hypothetical clause of Modern Literary Arabic

	Factual	Potential	Present Counterfactual	Past Counterfactual
iḏā	*(fa-)yafʿalu*[a]	*(fa-(inna-hu)) sa-yafʿalu*	*faʿala*[b]	non-existent
law	non-existent	*yafʿalu*	*(fa-(inna-hu)) sa-yafʿalu*[c]	*(la-)faʿala*

Notes: [a] Ambiguous between the Present Factual and the Potential.
[b] Ambiguous between the Past Factual and the Present Counterfactual.
[c] ambiguous between the Present Counterfactual and the Potential.

It thus became possible for a structure with *law* to express, on the model of *iḏā*, a third hypothetical status, the Potential, through the use of the last verbal form not yet used in apodosis, the imperfect indicative (*yafʿalu*). Badawi et al. have noted this (2004: 636, 647–8), although, as mentioned, I do not fully agree with their analysis of the data they present.

I therefore arrive at the system outlined in Table 8.3 in terms of the combinations of operator and apodosis verb form.

6. Conclusion

The emergence of new usages in Modern Arabic does not necessarily invalidate the previous ones, which makes data interpretation difficult. It seems, however, that it is no longer only the operator that determines the meaning of the conditional clause, but the operator in *conjunction* with the verbal form of the apodosis. This verb expresses the temporal value of the conditional, where classically (and as is still the case today for the sole verb in the protasis) it was a usually perfect verbal form that was interpreted as temporally neutral. However, this upheaval seems not to have allowed the system to regain full coherence, as the three major cases of ambiguity reflect: *iḏā faʿala . . . faʿala* (Past Factual and Present Counterfactual), *iḏā faʿala . . . yafʿalu* (Present Factual and, less often, Potential), and *law faʿala . . . (fa-(inna-hu))sa-yafʿalu* (Present Counterfactual and, less often, Potential). These ambiguous structures, as we see, relate essentially to *iḏā*, which, moreover, does not cover the whole of the core conditional functions (Potential and Counterfactual); in contrast to *law*, around which exists, it seems, a more stable system. It is therefore possible that we find ourselves in an intermediate phase between two states of the language. Ultimately, *iḏā* could return to its pre-classical and classical domain, the Factual, and then *law* would supplant it in the core conditional functions (Potential and Counterfactual), as can be observed in some dialects, especially Egyptian. This possibility would be realised in the standard language only if the development in question were not perceived as too colloquial by speakers inclined to over-correction. In any case, it is already possible to hear on the airwaves usage conforming to that observable in the literary works in the corpus used here. Thus, in a newsletter broadcast by BBC Arabic on 4 April 2009, in connection with elections to be held in Eastern Europe, the journalist, speaking of a woman standing for election, said: *law untuḫibat . . . sa-takūn awwala -mraʿa . . .* This we cannot translate in any way other than 'if she is/was elected . . . she will be/would be the first woman . . .'. We find in this example both the absence of the *fa-* that should have been used according to classical rules, and the use of *law* to express a *future* and/or *possible* fact, that is, a Potential.[1] There is one constant point: the language, as practised today, and for at least the past forty years, does not match the characterisations given by the vast majority of descriptive works published about it. We must, then, ask ourselves what we are teaching . . .

Acknowledgements

This chapter is a translation from my French article 'Pour une approche *relationnelle* de la conditionnelle en arabe littéraire moderne' published in *Arabica*, 2010, 57, pp. 68–98. I dedicate it to ʿĀdil and Muḥammad, for them to understand a little bit more what I do with their language. Special thanks go to Hannah Scottdeuchar, who has gently read and corrected this English version, with patience and accuracy.

Note

1. More recently, *Al-ʿArabiyya* channel, on 2 March 2011, was reproducing and summarising Muʿammar al-Qaḏḏāfī's speech twenty days into the Libyan revolution. The script was as follows: *iḏā lam tastaqirr Lībiyā sa-yataḥawwalu l-baḥru al-mutawassiṭu ilā qarṣanatin* ('If Libya does not remain stable, the Mediterranean Sea will turn to piracy'). Here we see once more the same syntax we showed in our literary corpus, and where only a Potential interpretation is possible, due to the threatening tone used by the leader of the Great Ǧamāhiriyya.

References

Arabic grammars and novels

al-Ġalāyīnī, Muṣṭafā b. Muḥammad Salīm [1912] (2000), *Ǧāmiʿ al-Durūs al-ʿArabiyya*, ed. ʿAbd al-Munʿim Ḫalīl Ibrāhīm, Beirut: Dār al-kutub al-ʿilmiyya.

al-Ġiṭānī, Ǧamāl (1974), *Al-Zaynī Barakāt*, Damascus: Manšūrāt wizārat al-ṯaqāfa wa-l-iršād al-qawmī.

al-Zamaḫšarī, *Mufaṣṣal* = Maḥmūd b. ʿUmar b. Muḥammad b. Aḥmad, Abū al-Qāsim, Ǧār Allāh, al-Ḫawārizmī al-Zamaḫšarī (1999), *Al-Mufaṣṣal*, ed. Émile Badīʿ Yaʿqūb, Beirut: Dār al-kutub al-ʿilmiyya.

Ben Haddūqa, ʿAbd al-Ḥamīd (1991), *Al-Ǧāziya wa-l-Darāwīš*, 3rd edn, Beirut: Dār al-adab.

Ibn Hišām, *Awḍaḥ* = ʿAbd Allāh b. Yūsuf b. Aḥmad b. ʿAbd Allāh b. Yūsuf, Abū Muḥammad, Ǧamāl al-Dīn, al-Anṣārī, Ibn Hišām (1989), *Awḍaḥ al-Masālik ilā Alfiyyat ibn Mālik*, ed. H. al-Fāḫūrī, 4 vols, Beirut: Dār al-ǧīl.

Ibrāhīm, Ṣunʿ Allāh (1997), *Al-Lağna*, 7th edn, Cairo: Dār al-mustaqbal al-ʿarabī.
Ibrāhīm, Ṣunʿ Allāh (1998), *Ḏāt*, 3rd edn, Cairo: Dār al-mustaqbal al-ʿarabī.
Ibrāhīm, Ṣunʿ Allāh (2000), *Warda*, Cairo: Dār al-mustaqbal al-ʿarabī.
Kanafānī, Ġassān (1987), *Al-ʿĀšiq*, 3rd edn, Beirut: Muʾassasat al-Abḥāṯ al-ʿArabiyya, Muaʾassasat Ġassān Kanafānī al-Ṯaqāfiyya.
Kanafānī, Ġassān (2002), *Riğāl fī al-Šams*, 5th edn, Beirut: Muʾassasat al-Abḥāṯ al-ʿArabiyya, Muaʾassasat Ġassān Kanafānī al-Ṯaqāfiyya.
Kūnī (Al-), Ibrāhīm (2005), *Malakūt Ṭiflat al-Rabb*, Beirut: Al-Muʾassasa al-ʿarabiyya li-l-dirāsāt wa-l-našr.
Misʿidī, Maḥmūd (1997), *Ḥaddaṯa Abū Hurayra qāla . . .*, 4th edn, Tunis: Dār al-ğanūb li-l-našr.
Tāmir, Zakariyā (1981), *Al-Numūr fī al-Yawm al-ʿĀšir*, 2nd edn, Beirut: Manšūrāt dār al-ādāb.
Zafzāf, Muḥammad (1970), *Ḥiwār Layl Mutaʾaḫḫir*, Damascus: Manšūrāt wizārat al-ṯaqāfa.

Other secondary sources

Abi Aad, A. (2001), *Le système verbal de l'arabe comparé au français*, Paris: Maisonneuve et Larose.
Alosh, M. (2005), *Using Arabic: A Guide to Contemporary Usage*, Cambridge: Cambridge University Press.
Ayoub, G. (2003), 'Corrélation et rupture modales. Formes verbales et particules énonciatives dans les hypothétiques en arabe littéraire', in *Mélanges David Cohen*, Paris: Maisonneuve et Larose, pp. 29–45.
Badawi, E.-S., M. G. Carter and A. Gully (2004), *Modern Written Arabic: A Comprehensive Grammar*, London: Routledge.
Beeston, A. F. L. (2006), *The Arabic Language Today*, Washington, DC: Georgetown University Press.
Blachère, R. and M. Gaudefroy-Demombynes (1975), *Grammaire de l'arabe classique (Morphologie et syntaxe)*, Paris: Maisonneuve et Larose.
Buckley, R. P. (2004), *Modern Literary Arabic: A Reference Grammar*, Beirut: Librairie du Liban.
Fischer, W. (1987), *Grammatik des Klassischen Arabisch*, 2nd rev. edn, Wiesbaden: Harrassowitz.
Ghitani, J. (1985), *Zayni Barakat*, trans. J.-F. Fourcade, Paris: Le Seuil.
Grévisse, M. (2001), *Le bon usage*, 13th edn, ed. A. Goosse, Paris: DeBoeck et Duculot.
Hassanein, A. (2006), *Modern Standard Arabic Grammar: A Concise Guide*, Cairo and New York: The American University Press in Cairo.
Haywood, J. A. and H. M. Nahmad (2001), *A New Arabic Grammar of the Written Language*, 2nd edn, London: Lund Humphries.
Holes, C. (2004), *Modern Arabic: Structures, Functions and Varieties*, rev. edn, Washington, DC: Georgetown University Press.
Ibrahim, S. (1993), *Les années de Zeth*, trans. R. Jacquemond, Paris: Actes Sud.
Ibrahim, S. (2005), *Warda*, trans. R. Jacquemond, Paris: Actes Sud.

Kouloughli, D. E. (1994), *Grammaire de l'arabe d'aujourd'hui*, Paris: Pocket.
Larcher, P. (2000), 'Subordination *vs* coordination "sémantiques". L'exemple des systèmes hypothétiques de l'arabe classique', *Annales Islamologiques*, 34: 193–207.
Larcher, P. (2003a), 'Du jussif au conditionnel en arabe classique: une hypothèse dérivationnelle', *Romano-Arabica*, 3: 185–97.
Larcher, P. (2003b), 'Les systèmes hypothétiques en *law* de l'arabe classique', *Bulletin d'Études Orientales*, 55: 265–85.
Larcher, P. (2006), 'Le "segmentateur" *fa-(inna)* en arabe classique et moderne', *Kervan-Rivista internazionale di studi afroasiatici*, 3: 51–63.
Larcher, P. (2008), 'Les "complexes de phrases" de l'arabe classique', *Kervan-Rivista internazionale di studi afroasiatici*, 6: 29–45.
McCarus, E. N. (2007), *English Grammar for Students of Arabic: The Study Guide for Those Learning Arabic*, Ann Arbor, MI: Olivia and Hill Press.
Moïnfar, D. M. (1973), *Grammaire de l'arabe*, Paris: Saint-Sulpice Favière.
Neyreneuf, M. and G. Al-Hakkak (1996), *Grammaire active de l'arabe*, Paris: Livre de Poche.
Peled, Y. (1992), *Conditional Structures in Classical Arabic*, Wiesbaden: Otto Harrassowitz.
Riegel, M., J.-C. Pellat and R. Rioul (2004), *Grammaire méthodique du français*, 3rd edn, Paris: Presses Universitaires de France.
Ryding, K. C. (2005), *A Reference Grammar of Modern Arabic*, Cambridge: Cambridge University Press.
Sartori, M. (2009), 'L'évolution des conditionnelles en arabe égyptien contemporain', *Bulletin d'Études Orientales*, 58: 233–57.
Schulz, E., G. Krahl and W. Reuschel (2008), *Standard Arabic: An Elementary-Intermediate Course*, Berlin and Munich: Langescheidt KG.
Taha, Z. (1995), 'The grammar controversy: What to teach and why?', in M. Al-Batal (ed.), *The Teaching of Arabic as a Foreign Language*, Provo, UT: American Association of Teachers of Arabic, pp. 175–84.
Tahhan, B. (2007), *Kullo Tamâm. Arabe tome 2*, Paris: Delagrave.
Versteegh, K. (1991), 'Two conceptions of irreality in Arabic Grammar: Ibn Hišām and Ibn al-Hāğib on the particle *law*', *Bulletin d'Études Orientales*, 43: 77–92.

9

Quantitative Approaches to Analysing COME Constructions in Modern Standard Arabic

Dana Abdulrahim

1. Introduction

The fundamental tenet of constructionist theories of language is that the basic unit of linguistic organisation is a *construction*. According to Croft and Cruse (2004: 257), constructions 'consist of pairings of form and meaning that are at least partially arbitrary', where 'meaning' is basically defined as the conventionalised function of a construction. This conventionalisation of a construction's meaning/function not only includes the literal meaning of an expression, but also properties of the discourse situation in which an expression occurs (e.g. use of spatial deictic terms, such as *here* or *there*, that signal a reference point in a speech event) as well as the pragmatic implications of an expression (e.g. use of a yes/no question to request information, as in *Do you have the time?*) (Croft and Cruse 2004). The term 'constructions', therefore, covers both (1) the idiomatic portions of language – where the morphosyntactic structure of the expression may, in some cases, be idiosyncratic and where the meaning of an expression is not predictable from the component parts that make up the expression (e.g. *raining cats and dogs*) – as well as (2) any combination of two or more morphemes where only general morphosyntactic structures are utilised and where the meaning of an expression is fully predictable from its component parts (e.g. *I want to go*). This view of grammar postulates that 'the interaction of syntax and lexicon is much wider and deeper than the associations of certain verbs with certain complements' (Bybee 2010: 77), and that a considerable part of our linguistic knowledge consists of conventionalised expressions, or constructions (Langacker 1987).

According to any constructionist framework, therefore, the behaviour of a lexical item is best understood in its context of use and not in isolation. The syntactic structures in which it appears, the morphological inflections associated with it, its lexical collocates, and so on, all contribute to the (conventionalised) meaning or function expressed by this linguistic item. Such an approach calls for moving beyond single semantic, morphological, or syntactic properties of an individual lexical item to scrutinise the entire lexico-syntactic frame in which it appears. The availability of corpora caters to this analytical approach due to the fact that corpora provide a large amount of naturally occurring, contextualised usage, facilitating the investigation of the behaviour of lexical items or phrases in their natural discourse environment (as opposed to their behaviour in isolated examples, produced via introspection or elicitation, which may not reflect actual language usage). Moreover, corpora provide large amounts of linguistic data that permit a quantitative treatment of the phenomena under investigation. Corpus data can therefore ideally undergo various statistical analyses that can provide more insight than intuition and casual introspection (or even inspection) of data are ever able to achieve.

The existence of more than one verb denoting COME in Modern Standard Arabic (MSA), as we will see in section 1.2, provides an excellent case study for a constructionist, usage-based examination of the features that characterise the usage of supposedly synonymous lexical items. COME (and GO) verbs belong to a set of verbs referred to as 'basic verbs'. Verbs in this category correspond to concepts related to our everyday activities as human beings – such as going, coming, sitting, standing, lying, eating, drinking, seeing, hearing, thinking, and so on – and are therefore represented across all human languages. Basic verbs (and other linguistic units related to these fundamental human activities) are, therefore, high-frequency linguistic items that tend to be part of the early vocabulary acquired by children. The high frequency of basic verbs is not necessarily tied to their occurrences in their literal senses, but also reflects the fact that, across languages, these verbs tend to grammaticalise, in that they gradually become associated with grammatical functions such as tense or aspect marking. An example is the use of GO in English as a future tense marker (*I'm going to be in my office all day long*). In addition to that, basic verbs can have multiple idiomatic and metaphorical uses.

COME and GO verbs, in particular, are widely viewed as simple verbs of motion that do not encode manner or path in their lexical semantics, the way verbs such as *run*, *crawl*, *swim*, *fly*, *ascend*, *descend*, *fall*, *rise*, *enter*, or *exit* do (Talmy 2000; Slobin 1996). Along with simple motion, it has been routinely argued that *deixis* is one inherent feature that characterises, if not distinguishes, the semantics of this pair of verbs (Fillmore 1966, 1972; Sinha 1972; Gathercole 1977; among others). The basic assumption is that COME and GO are in deictic opposition, where COME is typically viewed as motion towards the speaker (or the deictic centre) and GO is associated with motion away from or typically *not* towards the deictic centre. However, languages do not seem to be consistent in their assignment of a deictic value to this pair of verbs (Wilkins and Hill 1995).

The vast majority of previous studies of COME and GO have tended to be (1) concerned with an individual feature or a very small number of features, usually pertaining to the lexical semantics of these verbs (e.g. deixis), and (2) qualitative in nature, with free data elicitation and experimental elicitation (e.g. Wilkins and Hill 1995), along with introspection (e.g. Fillmore 1966; and many others), being the major methods of data collection. A very few studies on GO and COME (e.g. Di Meola 1994; Newman and Lin 2007) have attempted to incorporate corpus data as a means of presenting contextualised usages of these lexical items, as well as adding a quantitative dimension to the study of GO and COME.

The presence of not one but four highly frequent COME verbs in MSA should therefore signal a proliferation of usage and meaning extensions that go beyond the physical motion of concrete entities. This suggests that there should also be divergent morphosyntactic behavioural patterns among these verbs. In order to examine the different lexico-syntactic constructions associated with COME verbs in MSA, I adopt the methodological approach outlined in Gries (2006), Gries and Divjak (2009), and Gries and Otani (2010) for arriving at a constructionist description of the Behavioural Profile of a lexical item. Gries and collaborators' quantitative approach involves constructing a data frame for every lexical item under study, in which a large number of corpus concordance lines are individually marked up for an extensive set of linguistic features (morphological, syntactic, semantic, and lexical). This includes, for example, specific features pertaining to verb morphology and phrase structure, as well as to the different elements that co-occur with the verb in specific constructions, including lexical collocates. Such a data frame can be approached via numerous mono-factorial and multifactorial statistical analyses as a means of exploring the kinds of constructions associated with the verbs in question.

In this chapter, I am particularly interested in multifactorial analyses of MSA COME verbs and will therefore subject the data frame outlined in section 3.1 to two multifactorial statistical analyses, namely Hierarchical Agglomerative Cluster Analysis and Hierarchical Configural Frequency Analysis. The latter statistical analysis will especially help identify the sets of constructions that typically characterise the use of each COME verb.

1.2 COME verbs in MSA

In Modern Standard Arabic, four verbs can signal a COME event: *atā*, *ǧā'a*, *ḥaḍara*, and *qadima*. According to Buckwalter and Parkinson's *Frequency Dictionary of Arabic* (2011), these verbs are among the 5,000 most highly frequent words in (different varieties of) Arabic, with the following rankings: *ǧā'a* (109), *atā* (343), *ḥaḍara* (809), and *qadima* (3,121). Some modern and classical dictionaries consider these lexical items to be synonymous, since they can be interchangeably used in a context such as example (1). In this sentence, we have a human agent moving towards a destination (one that is collapsible with the deictic centre), and the event is expressed in a past tense or perfective construction:

(1) أَتَت / جاءَت / حَضَرَت / قَدِمَت جدّتي إلى المَطار لِتُوَدّعَني

atat / ǧā'at / ḥaḍarat / qadimat	*ǧadda-ti*	*ila*
atā / ǧā'a / ḥaḍara / qadima.PERF.3SG.F	grandmother-CL.1SG.GEN	ALL
came	my grandmother	to

al=maṭār	*li=tuwaddi'a-ni*
ART=airport	PURP=say.goodbye.SUBJN-1SG.ACC
the airport	to say goodbye to me

'My grandmother came to the airport to say goodbye to me'

Modifying some particular contextual features would nevertheless trigger selectional restrictions on the verbs that are allowed in a certain context of use. For instance, in example (2), holding all constructional features constant and changing the verb inflection from perfective to jussive results in native speakers of Arabic favouring *atā* and *ḥaḍara* and dispreferring *ğā'a* or *qadima*. Changing the semantic category of the sentential subject from human to non-human, as in example (3), results in *ḥaḍara* and *qadima* being ruled out as possible means of expressing COME. (These findings arise both from native-speaker introspection and from examination of corpus data.)

(2) لَم تَأتِ / ؟تَجيء / تَحْضُر / ؟تَقْدُم جدّتي إلى المَطار لِتُوَدّعَني

lam	*ta'ti / ?tağī' / taḥḍur / ?taqdum*	*ğadda-ti*	*ila*
NEG	***atā / ğā'a / ḥaḍara / qadima***.JUSS.3SG.F	grandmother-CL.1SG.GEN	ALL
did not	come	my grandmother	to

al=maṭār	*li=tuwaddi'a-ni*
ART=airport	PURP=say.goodbye.SUBJN-1SG.ACC
the airport	to say goodbye to me

'My grandmother did not come to the airport to say goodbye to me'

(3) أتَت / جاءَت / *حَضَرَت / *قَدِمَت رَغْبَتُهُم في رؤيتِها بعدَ سماعِهِم بِخَبَر فوزِها بِجائزة اليانَصيب

*atat / ğā'at / *ḥaḍarat / *qadimat*	*rağbatu-hum*	*fi*	*ru'yati-ha*	*ba'da*
atā / ğā'a / *ḥaḍara /* qadima.PERF.3SG.F	desire-CL.3PL.M.GEN	LOC	seeing-CL.3SG.F.ACC	ADV
came	their desire	in	seeing her	after

samā'i-him	*bi-ḫabar*	*fawzi-ha*	*bi-ğa'izat*	*al=yānaṣib*
hearing-CL.3PL.M.GEN	INST-news	win.VN-CL.3SG.F.GEN	INST-award	ART=lottery
their hearing	of news	her winning	of award	the lottery

'Their desire to see her came after they heard the news regarding her winning the lottery'

Clearly, each of these four verbs must be associated with a cohort of meaning extension and usages and, most importantly, specific constructional elements. These (constructed) examples emphasise the fact that while the four COME verbs share certain contextual features, as evident in example (1), we can see that in examples (2) and (3) different elements, such as the verb inflection and the semantic category of the sentential subject, impose selectional restrictions on the verbs allowed in particular constructions.

2. Corpus-based analysis of MSA COME verbs

2.1 Corpus data and constructing the data frame

arabiCorpus (see Parkinson, this volume) is the source of the MSA COME data analysed in this study. This corpus contains about 130,000,000 words and consists of a number of subcorpora, belonging to different written genres such as newspaper articles, novels, nonfiction, the Qur'an, pre-modern, medieval science, and modern literature. arabiCorpus also contains a small subcorpus of colloquial spoken Egyptian. These subcorpora vary in size, with the newspaper genre being the largest. Since this corpus is not tagged for part of speech, regular expressions capable of capturing all finite forms of all four COME verbs were generated and fed into arabiCorpus in order to extract examples of these verbs from the Newspaper, Modern Literature, and Non-Fiction MSA subcorpora. All hits were downloaded for all four verbs; the concordances were subsequently randomly sorted in order to extract a sample of 500 examples of each verb as used in context from the corpus.

For the MSA COME verbs under study, the construction of my multivariate data frame involved annotating these 500 lines of corpus hits per verb for a large spectrum of morphosyntactic and semantic features. Along the lines of studies conducted by Gries and collaborators (e.g. Divjak and Gries 2006; Gries and Otani 2010) on the synonymy and polysemy of related lexical items, I developed a large set of morphological, syntactic, and semantic features that are potentially relevant to the phenomenon at hand, which are listed in Table 9.1. The data frame was coded for more variables than the set laid out in Table 9.1, such as the different morphosyntactic realisations of the semantic roles of GOAL, SOURCE, MANNER, and so on, which will be discussed in section 3.2.4. But only the variables listed in Table 9.1 were subjected to multivariate statistical analysis. The binary variables YES and NO refer to the presence or the absence of a given feature, respectively.

This set of 22 linguistic features, or variables, was motivated primarily by certain lexico-syntactic properties that pertain to a COME event schema, such as phrases specifying a GOAL and/or a SOURCE of the motion event, in addition to a MANNER phrase and the inclusion of a COMITATIVE phrase (i.e. a phrase expressing accompaniment by an object/individual in the COME event). Each verb token was also coded for the semantic category of the subject or the entity involved in the motion event. The semantic categories utilised include HUMAN, OBJECT, and more abstract/non-physical categories such as EVENT, COMMUNICATION (e.g. a statement), COGNITION (e.g. an idea), and so on. The morphosyntactic component of the list of features had to reflect the specific elements that are associated with the verb and the verb phrase in Arabic, such as verb inflection (MORPHOLOGICAL ASPECT AND MOOD, NUMBER, PERSON, and GENDER) as well as the TENSE and ASPECT of the phrase hosting the COME verb. In addition, TRANSITIVITY was used as a feature, since as well as appearing in the expected intransitive constructions, COME verbs in Arabic can appear in transitive constructions in which the direct object is the GOAL of the motion event, as in example (4):

(4) كانَت البِداية صَعبة اذْ لَم يَأتِها أيُّ زَبون

kānat	*al=bidaya*	*ṣa'ba*	*iḏ*	*lam*	*ya'ti-ha*
be.PERF.3SG.F	ART=beginning	hard	ADV	NEG	*atā*.JUSS.3SG.M-CL.3SG.F.ACC
was	the beginning	hard	since	did not	come to her

ayyu zabun
any customer
any customer
'the beginning was hard, since no customer came to her'

The text genre was not considered for use as a variable, since the majority of the corpus hits annotated in this random sample of 2,000 examples came from newspaper writing. The following results, then, should be considered as mostly reflective of the usage of COME verbs in newspaper writing. Table 9.2 shows a sample of annotated corpus hits

Table 9.1 A selection of the variables for which the concordance lines of the COME verbs were coded

Category of feature	Feature	Levels
Morphological	tense	present, past, future, irrealis (non-finite forms)
	aspect	simple, habitual, progressive, perfect, non-fin (non-finite forms)
	morphological aspect and mood of the verb	imperfective, perfective, subjunctive, jussive
	subject person	1st, 2nd, 3rd
	subject number	singular, dual, plural
	subject gender	feminine, masculine, nil (for 1st person inflections)
Syntactic	transitivity	yes, no
	interrogative	yes, no
	negative	yes, no
	prepositional phrases	yes, no
	locative adverb phrases	yes, no
	adverbial phrases	yes, no
Semantic	subject category	activity, animal, attribute, body, cognition, communication, content (of a document/speech), demonstrative, dummy subject, event, group, human, location, notion, object, sense, state, substance, time
	goal phrase	yes, no
	source phrase	yes, no
	manner phrase	yes, no
	setting phrase	yes, no
	path phrase	yes, no
	purposive phrase	yes, no
	comitative phrase	yes, no
	temporal phrase	yes, no
	degree phrase	yes, no

Table 9.2 Sample of annotation from the data frame for selected variables (for the instances shown in examples (5) and (6))

	VERB	TENSE	MORPH_ASP/MOOD	SUBJ_NUM	SUBJ_CAT	PP	ADVERBIAL	SOURCE	MANNER
5	*atā*	PRESENT	IMPERFECTIVE	SINGULAR	COMMUNICATION	NO	YES	NO	YES
6	*qadima*	PAST	PERFECTIVE	PLURAL	HUMAN	YES	NO	YES	NO

from the 2,000-line data frame. The variables that examples (5) and (6) are coded for here are only a subset of the larger set of variables listed in Table 9.1:

(5) ويأتي الرّدُ سَريعاً وبِنَبرةٍ عالية

wa=ya'ti	*al=radd*	*sari'an*	*wa=bi=nabra*	*'āliya*
CONJ=***atā***.IMPF.3SG.M	ART=response	quickly	CONJ=INST=pitch	high
and comes	the response	quickly	and with pitch	high

'and the response comes quickly in a high pitch'

(6) وكذلك تَحَدّثَت عن مَدرَسَتِهِ ومَكتَبَتِها التي عَمِل فيها عُلماء قَدِموا من أماكِن مُختَلِفة

wa=kadalik	*taḥaddatat*	*'an*	*madrasati-h*	*wa=maktabati-ha*	*allati*
CONJ=also	talk.PERF.3SG.F	about	school-CL.3SG.M	CONJ=library-CL.3SG.F	RP
and also	talked	about	his school	and its library	that

'amila	*fi-ha*	*'ulamā'*	*qadimu*	*min*	*amākin*	*muḫtalifa*
work.PERF.3SG.M	LOC-CL.3SG.F	scholars	***qadima***.PERF.3PL.M	ABL	places	different
worked	in it	scholars	came	from	places	different

'it also talked about its school and its library where scholars who came from different places have worked'

This multifactorial data frame can be explored via various statistical analyses. For instance, we could examine the contribution of individual constructional elements to explaining the behaviour of a certain COME verb using one-way (or 'goodness of fit') chi-square tests or other monofactorial tests. We could also examine the interaction between pairs of variables, in order to discern patterns of high co-occurrence of constructional elements, such as whether or not PAST tense correlates highly with PERFECTIVE morphological aspect, and so on. However, in this chapter, I will mainly focus on examining patterns of interaction between *multiple* variables at a time, as a means of zeroing in on the larger lexico-syntactic frames, that is, constructions, that host these four COME verbs. This analysis will help us establish the prototypical uses of these verbs in MSA (see Abdulrahim 2013 for further discussion of the methodology deployed here).

In the following section, I will be implementing the Behavioural Profiles method of analysis proposed by Gries and colleagues, as well as Hierarchical Configural Frequency Analysis (Gries 2004).

3. Analysing the COME data frame

3.1 Behavioural Profiles

The term *Behavioral Profiles* was introduced by Hanks (1996) in his investigation of *urge*, looking at patterns of collocations (the co-occurrence of lexical items with other lexical items) and colligations (the co-occurrence of lexical items with grammatical elements). His claim was that 'the semantics of a verb are determined by the totality of its complementation patterns' (Hanks 1996: 77). The Behavioural Profile of a lexical item is, therefore, determined by these co-occurrence patterns. Gries and colleagues elaborate on this analytical approach in their corpus-based examination of various semantic phenomena, such as the polysemy of the verb *run* in English (Gries 2006), the near-synonymy of Russian *try* verbs (Divjak and Gries 2006), and the synonymy and antonymy of size adjectives in English (Gries and Otani 2010), among others.

The Behavioural Profiles methodology employed in these studies relies on generating a table that lists relative frequencies, or proportions, of co-occurrence between the lexical items under investigation and each level of every variable it was coded for. Table 9.3 shows an excerpt of the co-occurrence table generated by the BP 1.01 script, a program written by Stefan Gries (2009) for the R statistical computing environment.[1] Table 9.3 displays the co-occurrence proportions of the different levels of the 'ID tags' (variables) with each of our COME verbs, such that the sum of proportions for a certain ID tag for each verb is 1.0 (since when all the levels of a variable are added together, 100 per cent of the examples are necessarily accounted for). The Behavioural Profile of a verb in this table is, therefore, the vector of co-occurrence proportions for all ID tag levels for that verb.

The matrix in Table 9.3 enables us to take a quick look at the distribution of variables across the lexical items under study. We can see, for instance, that IMPERFECTIVE aspect co-occurs frequently with the verb *atā*, while the other verbs appear to be more often inflected as PERFECTIVE. I will examine patterns of interaction between TENSE, ASPECT, and MOOD in section 3.2.2, where I discuss the implementation of Hierarchical Configural Frequency Analysis (HCFA).

Table 9.3 can now be subjected to a number of exploratory statistical analyses. I begin with Hierarchical Agglomerative Cluster Analysis (HACA). This method of analysis can handle a large number of variables at a time (unlike HCFA, as we will see in section 3.2), and each of the resulting clusters groups together items that are similar to one another and dissimilar to items in other clusters (for additional background, see Mohamed and Hardie, this volume). In the case of my COME data set, it is interesting to see which verbs cluster together, based on all 20+ variables and their 70+ levels. I decided to follow earlier Behavioural Profiles studies in which the (dis)similarity metric used is 'Canberra', and the amalgamation rule that computes

Table 9.3 Sample of co-occurrence table generated by the BP 1.01 script

IDTAG	IDTAG-LEVEL	ata	hadara	ga'a	qadima	
MORPH_ASP.MOOD	IMPF	0.752	0.208	0.006	0.014	columns sum to 1.0
	JUSS	0.042	0.042	0	0	
	PERF	0.126	0.692	0.992	0.984	
	SUBJN	0.08	0.058	0.002	0.002	
SUBJ_NUM	DUAL	0.002	0.004	0.002	0.04	columns sum to 1.0
	PL	0.062	0.07	0.03	0.486	
	SING	0.936	0.926	0.968	0.474	

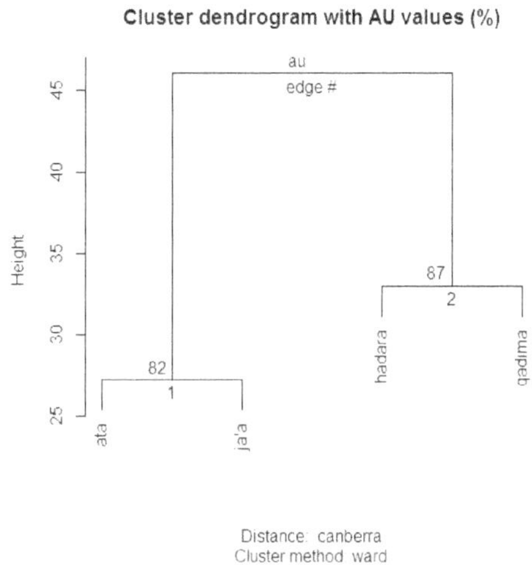

Figure 9.1 Dendrogram generated from the COME multifactorial data frame

a cluster structure is 'Ward' (for a detailed description of HACA, see Gries 2009a: 306–19).

The dendrogram in Figure 9.1 shows that the Hierarchical Agglomerative Cluster Analysis has identified two major divisions between the four verbs. The first cluster formed in this analysis appears to group the verbs *atā* and *ǧā'a* together, while the other cluster groups *ḥaḍara* and *qadima* together. The BP 1.01 script employs the *pvclust* statistical package (Suzuki and Shimodaira 2006) which assigns Approximately Unbiased (AU) values to each cluster as a measure of uncertainty in a hierarchical cluster analysis. This particular measure is based on performing multiscale bootstrap resampling in order to calculate the *p*-values we find for each cluster in this dendrogram. We can see here that *ḥaḍara* and *qadima* appear to be more strongly associated with one another – the cluster that groups them has an AU value of 87 per cent – than are the other two COME verbs. This does not necessarily imply a high level of similarity between these two verbs, but rather that they are more similar to one another than they are to either *atā* or *ǧa'a*.

3.2 Hierarchical Configural Frequency Analysis

The Behavioral Profiles, in the form of vectors of proportions, provided us with distributional statistics for the values of each variable for each verb. Yet with a multifactorial data frame like the one we have in hand, we can gain more insight by examining patterns of correlation among the different levels of variables. There is a wide variety of multifactorial statistical tests that can be applied to this kind of data frame, such as linear regression, principal component analysis, polytomous logistic regression, and so on. In this chapter I examine Hierarchical Configural Frequency Analysis as a tool for finding patterns within a large body of data. What I am currently interested in, and what HCFA would help us find out, is this: what kinds of patterns emerge if we examine the interaction between, for instance, VERB X TENSE X ASPECT?

One of the virtues of HCFA is its relative (conceptual) simplicity compared with more complex multivariate statistical analyses such as regression modelling. HCFA is an exhaustive, 'hierarchical' variant of Configural Frequency Analysis (CFA, von Eye 1990). The basic procedure in both HCFA and CFA includes the following steps: (1) tabulating the observed frequencies; (2) calculating the contributions to chi-square of the different observed frequencies; and (3) testing these latter values for significance through the calculation of $p_{corrected}$-values for the contribution to chi-square for $df = 1$ (Gries 2009b).

We could compute these significance values manually for multiple combinations of variables such as:

- VERB X TENSE *or* VERB X ASPECT *or* VERB X MORPHOLOGICAL ASPECT AND MOOD
- VERB X TENSE X ASPECT
- VERB X TENSE X ASPECT X MORPHOLOGICAL ASPECT/MOOD
- . . . and so on.

Running such a series of CFA tests manually could work on a small data frame with a very limited set of variables, but with a data frame like the one we have, with 20+ variables, running each analysis manually would end up being an extremely tedious job. HCFA 3.2 is an interactive script developed for R by Stefan Gries (2004), and is designed to save us the trouble of running individual CFA tests for every conceivable combination of variables. The HCFA 3.2 script can basically go through all possible combinations of the different levels of multiple variables and conduct a CFA test on each combination. An example of part of an output table generated by the HCFA script is shown in Table 9.4.

The first few columns in an HCFA output table contain the variables for which interactions between the different levels are being evaluated. For every interaction of levels – known as a *configuration* – the actual frequency of occurrence is reported in the fourth column, and the expected frequency is given in the fifth column (the expected frequency is how often this configuration of levels would occur by chance alone). In the next column the contribution to chi-square is calculated, as well as the adjusted Holm p-value (in the column 'P.ADJ.HOLM'); the intervening column, labelled 'OBS(ERVED)-EXP(ECTED)', indicates whether the observed frequencies are higher or lower than expected, while the 'DEC' column provides decisions regarding the statistical

Table 9.4 A sample output hierarchy table generated by the HCFA script

VERB	TENSE	ASPECT	MORPH_ ASP.MOOD	FREQ	EXP	CONT. CHISQ	OBS-EXP	P.ADJ. HOLM	DEC	Q
ǧa'a	PAST	SIMPLE	PERF	484	201.6032	395.569	>	2.91E-71	***	0.157
qadima	PAST	SIMPLE	IMPF	0	70.7126	70.7126	<	2.02E-29	***	0.037

significance of each configuration, based on the adjusted Holm *p*-value. The level of statistical significance is represented either by one to three asterisks (indicating how significant the variable interaction is, with more asterisks indicating a higher significance level), or by 'ms' (mildly significant) or 'ns' (non-significant). For instance, we see in Table 9.4 that the configuration *ǧa'a* x PAST x SIMPLE x PERFECTIVE occurs significantly more than expected, and is therefore considered a *type*. On the other hand, the configuration *qadima* x PAST x SIMPLE x IMPERFECTIVE occurs significantly less often than expected, and is thus considered an *antitype*. The *Q* value reported in the HCFA output table (rightmost column) expresses the 'degree of pronouncedness' or significance of the configurations of values. This value is independent of sample size, and varies from 0 to 1 (with a higher value indicating a higher degree of pronouncedness). In the following HCFA analysis of MSA COME verbs, I will take into account only the significant *types* and will therefore report only the 'DEC' and 'Q' columns to assess the significance and entrenchment of configurations.

Even though HCFA 3.2 can process an unlimited number of variables at one time, I decided to break down the entire variable set into different subgroups of variables, and subsequently regroup certain variables from one set with another set of variables. This method of reporting on HCFA findings proved to be consistent with the assumption that the different constructional elements associated with each verb are interlinked rather than working individually, and that in order to understand the distributional pattern of one variable per given verb, we have to explain that variable's distribution with regards to other variables. For practical reasons, breaking down the entire variable set into subgroups yielded rather interpretable results.

3.2.1 Morphological types and antitypes

Prior to examining different interactions between variables, I decided to investigate the most significant morphological features that characterise the use of MSA COME verbs (mostly in newspaper writing) as well as the morphological features that MSA COME verbs appear hardly ever to associate with. The idea behind this test is to provide evidence for the idea that elements within an inflectional paradigm are not evenly distributed in actual usage. For instance, I was interested to see which elements from inflectional categories of TENSE, ASPECT, MORPHOLOGICAL ASPECT AND MOOD, SUBJECT NUMBER, PERSON, and GENDER occur most often with MSA COME verbs in usage (not distinguishing among the four verbs at this point). I ran an HCFA test including all six inflectional variables, and ended up with *types* listed in Table 9.5 and *antitypes* listed in Table 9.6.

Irrespective of verb, and taking into account all the 2,000 annotated corpus hits represented in this data frame, it seems that the major trend with respect to TENSE, ASPECT, MORPHOLOGICAL ASPECT/MOOD marking is PAST, SIMPLE, PERFECTIVE. We can also see that the verbs seem to be typically inflected for 3RD PERSON, SINGULAR, MASCULINE. Again, this may well be a property of the usage of COME verbs specific to newspaper writing; these findings are reminiscent of Biber's (1988) observations regarding newspaper reportage writing in English (this and other narrative genres being characterised by a high frequency of 3RD PERSON pronouns and PAST TENSE verbs). On the other hand,

Table 9.5 Most significant univariate *types* for TENSE, ASPECT, MORPHOLOGICAL ASPECT/MOOD, SUBJECT NUMBER, PERSON, and GENDER

TENSE	ASPECT	MORPH_ASP.MOOD	SUBJ_NUM	SUBJ_PER	SUBJ_GEN	FREQ	EXP	OBS–EXP	DEC	Q
.	.	.	.	3RD	.	1926	666.6667	>	***	0.944
.	SIMPLE	.	.	.	.	1654	333.3333	>	***	0.792
.	.	.	SING	.	.	1652	666.6667	>	***	0.739
.	.	.	.	.	MASC	1501	666.6667	>	***	0.626
.	.	PERF	.	.	.	1397	500	>	***	0.598
PAST	.	.	.	.	.	1396	500	>	***	0.597

Table 9.6 Most significant univariate ***antitypes*** for TENSE, ASPECT, MORPHOLOGICAL ASPECT/MOOD, SUBJECT NUMBER, PERSON, and GENDER

TENSE	ASPECT	MORPH_ASP.MOOD	SUBJ_NUM	SUBJ_PER	SUBJ_GEN	FREQ	EXP	OBS–EXP	DEC	Q
.	.	.	.	2ND	.	15	666.6667	<	***	0.489
.	.	.	DUAL	.	.	24	666.6667	<	***	0.482
.	.	.	.	.	NIL	49	666.6667	<	***	0.463
.	.	.	.	1ST	.	59	666.6667	<	***	0.456
.	.	JUSS	.	.	.	42	500	<	***	0.305
FUT	.	.	.	.	.	53	500	<	***	0.298
.	.	SUBJN	.	.	.	71	500	<	***	0.286
.	.	.	PL	.	.	324	666.6667	<	***	0.257
IRR	.	.	.	.	.	179	500	<	***	0.214

Table 9.6 lists a number of inflectional elements that MSA COME verbs typically do *not* associate with.

Tables 9.5 and 9.6 show that, for instance, PERSON inflection on the verb is highly skewed towards 3RD PERSON, while 1ST and 2ND PERSON inflections are quite infrequent in this data frame. The same applies to NUMBER inflection, where SINGULAR accounts of a large proportion of NUMBER agreement on COME verbs while PLURAL and, especially, DUAL inflections occur significantly less often. As expected, these findings show strong evidence for the notion of 'inflectional islands' (Rice and Newman 2005), that is, that inflected forms in a paradigm are distributionally skewed and not equally represented in the usage of a certain lexical item. These findings also provide further evidence that 1ST and 2ND PERSON inflections seldom appear in written corpus data (c.f. Biber 1988), being more typically common in interactive conversation.

In the following multifactorial HCFA analysis, I will examine significant combinations between these morphological variables and the other kinds of variables the corpus data was coded for. The overall objective of the analysis is to show that examining a combination of variables at one time, rather than single variables, can provide a better understanding of the larger morphosyntactic frames – or *constructions* – hosting the lexical items under study. This analysis will also show that the four COME verbs have different preferences with regards to the morphosyntactic features they typically associate with.

3.2.2 VERB X TENSE X ASPECT X MORPHOLOGICAL ASPECT/MOOD

Table 9.7 shows the most significant configurations for VERB X TAM – or TENSE, ASPECT, and MOOD (in the case of Arabic morphosyntax, MORPHOLOGICAL ASPECT and MOOD form a single variable, as each aspect–mood combination has a different inflectional form in the paradigm). In this table we are only concerned with *types* or configurations that occur significantly more times than expected, since these would constitute the most prototypical TAM markings that characterise the inflected forms of COME verbs.

We can see in Table 9.7 that the verb *atā* is mostly used in the PRESENT, SIMPLE, IMPERFECTIVE, and to a lesser degree in the HABITUAL. We also find that *atā* appears, a lot of the time, in a non-finite form (cases where TENSE = IRREALIS and ASPECT marking = NON-FINITE). Non-finite uses of *atā* paired with the SUBJUNCTIVE or the JUSSIVE mood can be reflective of a negative construction. *Ǧa'a*, *ḥaḍara*, and *qadima*, on the other hand, all seem to appear almost exclusively in the PAST, SIMPLE, PERFECTIVE. Table 9.7 also shows that only *atā* and *ḥaḍara* appear in FUTURE constructions.

3.2.3 VERB X SUBJECT NUMBER X PERSON X GENDER X SEMANTIC CATEGORY

Earlier, the variables SUBJECT NUMBER, PERSON, and GENDER were grouped together with the TAM variables (in Tables 9.5 and 9.6 above) as a means of examining the general patterns of morphological behaviour of the four COME verbs in the data frame. However, each individual verb's preferences with respect to the SUBJECT NUMBER, PERSON, and GENDER variables are better explained by combining these with variables

Table 9.7 VERB X TAM configurations

VERB	TENSE	ASPECT	MORPH_ASP.MOOD	FREQ	EXP	OBS-EXP	DEC	Q
atā	PRES	SIMPLE	IMPF	206	18.8432	>	***	0.094
atā	PRES	HAB	IMPF	105	1.5722	>	***	0.052
atā	IRR	NON-FIN	SUBJN	40	0.1239	>	***	0.02
atā	IRR	NON-FIN	IMPF	32	0.8552	>	***	0.016
atā	IRR	NON-FIN	JUSS	17	0.0733	>	***	0.008
atā	FUT	SIMPLE	IMPF	14	2.6846	>	***	0.006
ḥaḍara	PAST	SIMPLE	PERF	339	201.6032	>	***	0.076
ḥaḍara	FUT	SIMPLE	IMPF	38	2.6846	>	***	0.018
ḥaḍara	IRR	NON-FIN	SUBJN	29	0.1239	>	***	0.014
ḥaḍara	IRR	NON-FIN	JUSS	20	0.0733	>	***	0.01
ḥaḍara	PRES	HAB	IMPF	11	1.5722	>	***	0.005
ǧa'a	PAST	SIMPLE	PERF	484	201.6032	>	***	0.157
qadima	PAST	SIMPLE	PERF	467	201.6032	>	***	0.148
qadima	PAST	PERFECT	PERF	15	2.0721	>	***	0.006

related to the semantic properties of the sentential subject in the analysis. I therefore re-ran those three variables in the HCFA script together with the variable SUBJECT SEMANTIC CATEGORY. Table 9.8 shows the most significant configurations of values found between VERB and these four variables.

We can see here that 3RD SINGULAR is the most prominent subject-related marking on each verb except for *qadima*. *Qadima* deviates from the general pattern in that it is mostly marked in the PLURAL. It was also found to be marked in the DUAL at least 19 out of the 24 times this NUMBER inflection appears in the data frame. As I will explain shortly, this appears to be closely tied to the fact that *qadima* is primarily used to talk about the physical motion of HUMAN agents. As far as GENDER marking goes, Table 9.8 does not show a striking pattern of distribution except that the significant *atā* configurations reported in this table are more likely to include FEMININE marking on the verb.

The four COME verbs also vary with respect to the types of sentential subjects they each associate with. Non-human entities such as ACTIVITY, EVENT, NOTION, and COMMUNICATION seem to be the most frequent types of subjects in *atā* sentences (typically with 3RD, SINGULAR, FEMININE agreement on the verb). Again we must not forget that this property of verb usage likely reflects the newspaper writing genre specifically rather than MSA writing in general. The pattern observed above, therefore, might change slightly if there had been more modern literature in the corpus underlying the annotated data frame. These instances of *atā* usage show that this verb is mostly used to talk about the metaphorical motion of inanimate, non-physical entities.

Like *atā*, *ǧā'a* seems also to associate with a wider range of sentential subjects than *ḥaḍara* or *qadima*. More specifically, however, it seems mostly to be used in certain fixed expressions that are very characteristic of newspaper writing. These include, for instance, constructions involving the use either of a demonstrative as a sentential

Table 9.8 VERB X SUBJECT NUMBER X PERSON X GENDER X SEMANTIC CATEGORY configurations

VERB	SUBJ_NUM	SUBJ_PER	SUBJ_GEN	SUBJ_CAT	FREQ	EXP	OBS–EXP	DEC	Q
atā	SING	3RD	FEM	ACTIVITY	43	8.2328	>	***	0.017
atā	SING	3RD	FEM	EVENT	32	2.5951	>	***	0.015
atā	SING	3RD	FEM	NOTION	33	6.1298	>	***	0.013
atā	SING	3RD	FEM	COMMUNICATION	24	4.9665	>	***	0.01
atā	SING	3RD	FEM	OBJECT	14	1.1633	>	***	0.006
ḥaḍara	SING	3RD	MASC	HUMAN	369	164.6162	>	***	0.111
ḥaḍara	SING	3RD	FEM	GROUP	25	5.2797	>	***	0.01
ǧa'a	SING	3RD	MASC	CONTENT	92	14.4767	>	***	0.039
ǧa'a	SING	3RD	FEM	ACTIVITY	42	8.2328	>	***	0.017
ǧa'a	SING	3RD	MASC	DEMONSTRATIVE	34	7.1637	>	***	0.013
ǧa'a	SING	3RD	MASC	ACTIVITY	52	27.4609	>	*	0.012
ǧa'a	SING	3RD	FEM	COMMUNICATION	24	4.9665	>	***	0.01
qadima	PL	3RD	MASC	HUMAN	238	32.2855	>	***	0.105
qadima	DUAL	3RD	MASC	HUMAN	19	2.3915	>	***	0.008
qadima	SING	3RD	FEM	GROUP	18	5.2797	>	*	0.006

subject, or of what I identified in my coding as the CONTENT of a document, that is, usually, a noun phrase referring to the text of the document or highlights thereof (see example (12) below, for instance). As well as co-occurring with significant configurations involving ACTIVITY and COMMUNICATION, *ǧā'a* can be seen in Table 9.8 to be mostly used to talk about the figurative motion of entities. *Ḥaḍara* and *qadima*, on the other hand, seem to be more restricted to sentential subjects denoting HUMAN agents and GROUPS (e.g. countries, news agencies, organisations).

3.2.4 VERB X SUBJECT SEMANTIC CATEGORY X PHRASAL SEMANTIC CATEGORY

The distribution of the semantic categories of subjects can be further interpreted in relation to the larger conceptual event frames associated with a COME motion event. As mentioned earlier, I coded the verb examples for the presence of semantic properties of additional (non-subject) phrasal constituents that specify the SOURCE and GOAL of the motion event, the MANNER and PATH (or trajectory) of motion, and the larger context in which the motion event takes place (SETTING), in addition to phrases signalling the involvement of other participants in the motion event (COMITATIVE), the explicit PURPOSE of the motion event, as well as adjuncts specifying the time frame (TEMPORAL) and frequency of occurrence (DEGREE). In the following analysis, I decided to exclude DEGREE from the set of variables included in HCFA, since the overall frequency of this variable in the 2,000-line data frame was relatively low (>20).

Since the Behavioural Profiles analysis above grouped two pairs of verbs together, I decided to examine the similarities and differences between the pairs of verbs that share a cluster in the dendrogram shown in Figure 9.1. Therefore, I split my data frame into two sets (*atā* and *ǧa'a* in one set and *ḥaḍara* and *qadima* in another set), each containing 1,000 examples of two verbs. These two data frames were then subjected to an HCFA test looking at the following set of variables: VERB X SUBJECT SEMANTIC CATEGORY X GOAL X SOURCE X MANNER X SETTING X PURPOSIVE X PATH X COMITATIVE X TEMPORAL. The analysis below aims to bring together the morphological patterns previously observed with the larger event schemas which characterise the use of each COME verb and which count as the most prototypical uses for each verb.

Atā and *ǧā'a*

Atā and *ǧa'a* appear to share a lot of the larger conceptual frames in which the COME event occurs as well as the types of sentential subjects they collocate with. It is therefore useful to run an HCFA test that involves only those two verbs in order to distinguish their different uses. Table 9.9 shows configurations considered to be *types* (where the observed frequencies are significantly higher than the expected frequencies) involving the two COME verbs and the other nine variables.

We can see that the verb *atā* takes on a relatively wider range of sentential subjects than does *ǧā'a*. *Atā* can appear with EVENT, NOTION, HUMAN, GROUP, and ACTIVITY subjects, while *ǧā'a* seems to have more specialised uses (at least as far as newspaper writing is concerned). In addition to collocating with subjects denoting ACTIVITY, *ǧā'a*

Table 9.9 SUBJECT SEMANTIC CATEGORY X SEMANTIC PROPOSITIONS configurations for the verbs *atā* and *ǧā'a*

VERB	SUBJ_CAT	GOAL	SOURCE	MANNER	SETTING	PATH	PURPOSIVE	COMITATIVE	TEMPORAL	FREQ	EXP	DEC	Q
atā	EVENT	NO	NO	NO	YES	NO	NO	NO	NO	20	2.4983	***	0.018
atā	NOTION	NO	YES	NO	NO	NO	NO	NO	NO	15	2.4979	***	0.013
atā	HUMAN	YES	NO	NO	NO	NO	NO	NO	NO	24	6.6215	**	0.017
atā	GROUP	YES	NO	NO	NO	NO	NO	NO	NO	11	1.6062	*	0.009
atā	ACTIVITY	NO	NO	NO	YES	NO	NO	NO	NO	23	7.8018	ms	0.015
ǧa'a	CONTENT	NO	NO	NO	YES	NO	NO	NO	NO	88	4.2516	***	0.084
ǧa'a	ACTIVITY	NO	NO	YES	NO	NO	NO	NO	NO	30	5.9623	***	0.024
ǧa'a	DEMONSTRATIVE	NO	NO	NO	YES	NO	NO	NO	NO	22	2.1039	***	0.02
ǧa'a	ACTIVITY	NO	NO	NO	NO	NO	NO	NO	YES	22	6.0478	**	0.016
ǧa'a	DEMONSTRATIVE	NO	NO	NO	NO	NO	NO	NO	YES	11	1.6309	*	0.009

features mostly as part of news reporting-related fixed expressions that involve the use of a demonstrative as a subject or would collocate with what I coded as 'content' of a document/speech/etc.

With regards to the larger event frames hosting VERB X SUBJECT CATEGORY, we can see that an ACTIVITY collocating with *atā* is mostly presented alongside a certain setting/context, as in example (7), while an ACTIVITY collocating with *ǧā'a* is mostly presented alongside a certain manner, as in example (8), and/or a certain time, as in example (9). Syntactically, these event frames are realised either as prepositional phrases, as adverbial phrases, or as locative adverb phrases:

(7) وقالَ المُحافِظ أنّ المَشروع يأتي ضِمنَ عِدّة قَرارات لِتَحقيق سُيولة مُرورية

wa=qāla	*al=muḥafeẓ*	*anna*	*al=mašru'*	*ya'ti*	*ḍimna*	*'iddat*
CONJ=say.PERF.3SG.M	ART=mayor	TOP	ART=project	***atā***.IMPF.3SG.M	ADV	several
and said	the mayor	that	the project	came	within	several

qarar-āt	*li=taḥqiq*	*suyula*	*mururiyya*
decision-PL	PURP=achieve	fluidity	traffic.ADJ
decisions	to achieve	flow	traffic

'And the mayor said that the project comes as part of a number of decisions taken to achieve traffic flow'

(8) وجاء الفَوزُ الهِلالي مُستَحَقاً بَعد انْ قَدَّمَ مُباراةٍ اَذهَلَت المُتابِعين

wa=ǧā'a	*al=fawz*	*al=hilali*	*mustaḥaqqan*	*ba'da*	*an*
CONJ=***ǧa'a***.PERF.3SG.M	ART=success	CONJ=Hilal.ADV	well earned	LOC	TOP
and came	the success	the Hilali	well earned	after	that

qaddama	*mubāratan*	*'aḏhalat*	*al=mutabe'-in*
present.PERF.3SG.M	game	astonish.PERF.3SG.F	ART=follower-PL
presented	game	astonished	the followers

'And the Hilal's [soccer team] victory came well-earned after having played a match that astonished the audience'

(9) وجاء هذا التوضيحُ بعد مَقال نَشَرتهُ أوّل من امس جَريدةُ «الجُمهورية»

wa=ǧā'a	*haḏa*	*al=tawḍiḥ*	*ba'da*	*maqal*	*našarat-hu*
CONJ=***ǧa'a***.PERF.3SG.M	DEM	ART=clarification	LOC	article	publish.PERF.3SG.F-CL.3SG.M.ACC
and came	this	the clarification	after	article	published it

'awwal	*min*	*'ams*	*ǧaridat*	*al ǧumhuriyya*
first	ABL	yesterday	newspaper	Al Jumhuriyya
first	from	yesterday	newspaper	Al Jumhuriyya

'And this clarification came after an article that the Jumyoriya newspaper published the day before yesterday'

Where the verb *ğā'a* appears in fixed expressions involving the use of a demonstrative as a subject, most of the time this construction is accompanied by clauses that situate the entity that 'comes' in a certain setting/context, as in example (10), or at a certain point in time, as in example (11):

(10) جاء هذا في رِسالةٍ وَجّهَها ميجور الى اعضاء الحَملة

ğā'a	*hada*	*fi*	*risala*	*waǧǧaha-ha*	*meğor*
ğa'a.PERF.3SG.M	DEM	LOC	letter	direct.PERF.3SG.M-CL.3SG.F.ACC	Major
came	this	in	letter	directed it	Major

ila	*'a'ḍā'*	*al=ḥamla*
ALL	member.PL	ART=campain
to	members	the campaign

'This came in a letter that Major addressed to campaign members'

(11) وجاء ذلك في وقتٍ استَمَرّت المَعارك في شَمال كابول

wa=ğā'a	*ḏālika*	*fi*	*waqt*	*istamarrat*	*al=ma'arek*
CONJ=***ğa'a***.PERF.3SG.M	DEM	LOC	time	continue.PERF.3SG.F	ART=battle.PL
and came	that	at	time	continued	the battles

fi	*šamāl*	*kābul*
LOC	north	Kabul
in	north	Kabul

'And that came at a time when the battles continued in northern Kabul'

We can see, however, in Table 9.9 that the bulk of instances of *ğā'a* are in constructions in which the verb collocates with subjects that denote some 'content' of a document or speech that has appeared a certain setting, as in example (12):

(12) فقد قَرَأتُ بعناية ما جاء في مَقالِكم تَحت عُنوان رسالةٌ الى شَيخ الأزهر

faqad	*qara'tu*	*bi='inaye*	*mā*	*ğā'a*	*fi*	*maqāli-kum*
DM	read.PERF.1SG	INST=care	RP	***ğa'a***.PERF.3SG.M	LOC	article-CL.2PL.GEN
already	I read	with care	what	came	in	your article

taḥta	*'inwāan*	*risala*	*ila*	*šayḫ*	*al=azhar*
LOC	title	letter	ALL	sheikh	ART=Azhar
under	title	letter	to	sheikh	the Azhar

'I have carefully read what appeared in your article under the title "a letter to the sheikh of Azhar"'

Atā, on the other hand, associates with a more diverse set of event frames. Like the highly frequent ACTIVITY in SETTING construction, it is mostly used to talk about an EVENT in a certain setting, as in example (13):

(13) مُشيراً الى أنّ الزيارة تأتي ضِمن الجُهود الفَرَنسية لِدَعم مُكافَحَة الإرهاب

muširan	*ila*	*anna*	*al=ziyara*	*ta'ti*	*ḍimna*
point.out.AP.3SG.M	ALL	TOP	ART=visit	***atā***.IMPF.3SG.F	ADV
pointing out	to	that	the visit	comes	among

al=ğuhud	*al=faransiyya*	*li=mukāfaḥat*	*al='irhāb*
ART=effort.PL	ART=French	PURP=fighting	ART=terrorism
the efforts	the French	to fighting	the terrorism

'pointing out that the visit comes as part of the French efforts to support fighting terrorism'

Atā does still to some degree associate with HUMAN agents, more than *ğā'a* does, in newspaper writing. Most frequently, HUMANs come to a destination, as in example (14). GROUPs, such as organisations and institutions, also come to a (less physical) destination, as in example (15), which may be syntactically realised as a prepositional phrase or as the object of a transitive construction:

(14) وكُنتُ أحضُرُ الحَفلات التي كان يُقيمُها، كما كان، من جِهَتِهِ، يأتي الى حَفلاتي

wa=kuntu	*aḥḍuru*	*al=ḥafal-āt-i*	*allati*	*kāna*
CONJ=AUX	***ḥaḍara***.IMPF.1SG	ART=party-PL-ACC	RP	be.PERF.3SG.M
and I was	attend	the parties	that	he was

yuqimu-ha	*kama*	*kāna*	*min*	*ğihati-h*
organise.IMPF.3SG.M-CL.3SG.F.ACC	CONJ	be.PERF.3SG.M	ABL	side-CL.3SG.M.GEN
organise it	also	he was	from	his side

ya'ti	*ila*	*ḥafal-āt-i*
atā.IMPF.3SG.M	ALL	party-PL-CL.1SG.GEN
comes	to	my parties

'And I used to attend the parties that he threw, just as he, on his part, used to come to my parties'

(15) وتأتي الوِلايات المُتحدة في مُقَدّم الدُّول الأجنَبية غير العَرَبية إستِثماراً في السُّعودية

wa=ta'ti	*al=wilay-āt*	*al=muttaḥida*	*fi*	*muqaddam*	*al=duwal*
CONJ=***atā***.IMPF.3SG.F	ART=State-PL	ART=united	LOC	forefront	ART=country.PL
and comes	the States	The United	in	forefront	the countries

al='ağnabiyya	*ġayr*	*al='arabiyya*	*'istiṯmaran*	*fī*	*al=sa'udiyya*
ART=foreign	NEG	ART=arab	investing.ADV	LOC	ART=Saudi
the foreign	non-	the Arab	investing wise	in	the Saudi

'And the United States comes at the forefront of foreign, non-Arab countries that invest in Saudi Arabia'

On a more figurative level, a NOTION collocating with *atā* is usually presented as coming from a particular SOURCE, as in example (16):

(16) ولَعَلَّ الأمل بإحياءِ روسيا يأتي من قُدرَتِها على الغُفران

wa=la'alla	*al='amal*	*bi='iḥyā'*	*rusya*	*ya'ti*	*min*
CONJ=MOD	ART=hope	INST=revive.VN	Russia	***atā***.IMPF.3SG.M	ABL
and maybe	the hope	with reviving	Russia	comes	from

qudrati-ha	*'ala*	*al=ġufrān*
ability-CL.3SG.F	LOC	ART=forgiveness
its ability	on	the forgiveness

'The hope to revive Russia might come from its ability to forgive'

Ḥaḍara and *qadima*

Another HCFA test was run for the verbs *ḥaḍara* and *qadima*, with the same set of variables that was explored for the previous pair of verbs. For this test I decided to exclude PATH from the previous set of variables since levels of this variable did not co-occur with either verb in the data frame, and adding this variable, therefore, would not contribute anything to the analysis. Table 9.10 shows the most significant *type* configurations found for these two verbs.

Table 9.10 shows that the most predominant use of *ḥaḍara* involves a HUMAN agent arriving at a GOAL. That particular construction accounts for more than 60 per cent of the examples. For the verb *ḥaḍara*, an EVENT is by far the most frequent kind of destination of the motion event (372/500), followed by (GEOGRAPHICAL) LOCATION (31/500), and HUMAN (10/500). Typically, constructions associated with *ḥaḍara* alongside GOAL are transitive. The trilateral root *ḥḍr* underlying the verb *ḥaḍara* has the meaning extension of 'to be present'; the verb can therefore refer to 'attending' or 'being present', mostly at an EVENT, which is then its object. Example (17) is an example of the typical usage *ḥaḍara*, with verb in a past simple perfective transitive construction, and a HUMAN agent arriving or being present at a destination (an EVENT):

(17) وحَضَرَ الاجتِماع ايضاً السّفير الاميركي في دِمَشق كريستوفر روس

wa=ḥaḍara	*al=iğtima'-a*	*ayḍan*	*al=safīr-u*
CONJ=***ḥaḍara***.PERF.3SG.M	ART=meeting-ACC	also	ART=ambassador-NOM
and attended	the meeting	also	the ambassador

Table 9.10 SUBJECT SEMANTIC CATEGORY x SEMANTIC PROPOSITIONS configurations for the verbs *ḥaḍara* and *qadima*

VERB	SUBJ_CAT	GOAL	SOURCE	MANNER	SETTING	PURPOSIVE	COMITATIVE	TEMPORAL	FREQ	EXP	DEC	Q
ḥaḍara	HUMAN	YES	NO	NO	NO	NO	NO	NO	321	142.6842	***	0.208
qadima	HUMAN	NO	YES	NO	NO	NO	NO	NO	136	27.1637	***	0.112
qadima	HUMAN	NO	NO	NO	NO	YES	NO	NO	41	15.2935	***	0.026
qadima	HUMAN	NO	YES	NO	NO	YES	NO	NO	30	5.2899	***	0.025
qadima	GROUP	NO	YES	NO	NO	NO	NO	NO	12	2.0802	**	0.01

al=amriki	*fi*	*dimašq*	*Christopher Ross*
ART=American	LOC	Damascus	Christopher Ross
the American	in	Damascus	Christopher Ross

'And the American ambassador in Damascus, Christopher Ross, also attended the meeting'

Like *ḥaḍara*, *qadima* also collocates mostly with HUMAN agents (and to a lesser degree subjects denoting GROUPS, e.g. organisations and institutions). With regards to the dominant conceptual frames hosting the COME event in *qadima* constructions, we can see that a lot of the configurations reported in Table 9.10 include the SOURCE as well as the PURPOSE of the motion event. The most frequent and robust configuration in Table 9.10 involves HUMANS coming from a certain SOURCE (in most cases a GEOGRAPHICAL LOCATION), as exemplified in example (18), and to a much lesser degree GROUPS coming from a SOURCE as well. What also appears to motivate the use of the verb *qadima* is a frame in which the motion of HUMAN agents, in many cases, involves a reason for coming (to or from a certain location), as we can see in example (19):

(18) الأمر الذي لَم يحدُث اللّا في دَولة قَطَر التي قَدِمَ منها

al='amr	*allaḏi*	*lam*	*yaḥduṯ*	*illa*	*fi*	*dawlat*	*qaṭar*
ART=matter	RP	NEG	happen.JUSS.3SG.M	ADV	LOC	country	Qatar
the matter	which	did not	happen	except	in	country	Qatar

allati	*qadima*	*min=ha*
RP	***qadima***.PERF.3SG.M	ABL=CL.3SG.F
which	came	from it

'which did not happen except for in Qatar, the country where he came from'

(19) استَقطَبَت عَدداً كَبيراَ من الزُّوار قَدِموا خصيصاً من مُختَلَف أنحاء العالَم لِشِراء الذّهب

istaqṭabat	*'adad-an*	*kabir-an*	*min*	*al=zuwwar*	*qadimu*
attract.PERF.3SG.F	number-ACC	big-ACC	ABL	ART=visitor.PL	***qadima***.PERF.3PL.M
attracted	number	big	from	the visitors	came

ḫiṣṣiṣan	*min*	*muxtalaf*	*'anḥā'*	*al='ālam*	*li=širā'*	*al=ḏahab*
ADV	ABL	various	part.PL	ART=world	PURP=buy.VN	ART=gold
especially	from	various	parts	the world	to buying	the gold

'It attracted a large number of visitors who came from different parts of the world especially to buy gold'

4. Summary and discussion

Both the Behavioural Profiles and the Hierarchical Configural Frequency Analysis methods proved to be powerful statistical tools for highlighting the constructional features (morphological, syntactic, semantic, etc.) that characterise the use of *atā*, *ǧa'a*, *ḥaḍara*, and *qadima*. HCFA, in particular, helped identify not only single variables but also configurations of variables that show affinity towards one particular COME verb, and which could therefore be considered the prototypical constructions that host each of these verbs. The findings from the two analyses are summarised below.

4.1 *Atā* and *ǧā'a*

Atā appears in a wide range of constructions and uses, and collocates with a number of types of sentential subjects. It *can* be used to express physical motion, but most of the *atā* uses I encountered in this data frame are figurative uses. As far as physical motion is concerned, the verb *atā* is still used to talk about a COME event in its basic senses: manner-free motion towards a deictic centre or a destination proximal to the deictic centre. Unsurprisingly, this usage mostly involves human agents or, more generally, animate objects moving in space, towards a goal or from a source. This pattern of use may be found more frequently in literary and spoken genres than in the news reportage genre which was prominent in my data.

Like *atā*, the verb *ǧā'a* is used to talk mostly about metaphorical motion and, to a much lesser degree, physical motion of animate agents. With regards to metaphorical uses of *ǧā'a*, I found that the majority of examples occur within fixed phrases that get used over and over again in news reportage, such as instances in which COME collocates with demonstratives or sentential subjects denoting the content of a document or speech.

In the metaphorical uses of *atā* and *ǧa'a*, specifically those constructions where an EVENT/ACTIVITY is presented in a certain MANNER, SETTING, and TIME, the 'motion' aspect inherent in a COME event seems to be heavily downplayed. What appears to be more salient here is the notion of 'taking place' or 'happening', which might reflect the deictic nature of COME verbs. For instance, we saw that EVENTS/ACTIVITIES come within a social/political/intellectual/etc. setting, or take place at a certain time, or occur in a certain manner. The same applies where *ǧa'a* collocates with demonstratives that refer to a non-physical entity, typically in constructions meaning something like 'this/that came in the context of/at a time when . . .'. There is much less focus on 'motion' and more emphasis on the final stage of a COME event – the state of being present at the deictic centre. It would be interesting to examine the level of interchangeability of *atā* and *ǧa'a* with verbs of happening and occurring in MSA in these contexts of use.

Interestingly, in constructions where *atā* collocates with NOTIONS 'coming' from a SOURCE, we can see a clear instance of a metaphorical usage of COME that exploits its core literal meaning of 'motion'. In this particular usage, we have an abstract notion construed as coming/moving from a source which is usually an individual or collective reasoning or action.

4.2 *Ḥaḍara*

The verb *ḥaḍara* combines with different constructional elements for different purposes. The most frequent use of the verb expresses the meaning 'to attend/ to be present at'. I pointed out earlier that *ḥaḍara* is mainly used in a transitive construction, where the direct object in most cases is an event or an activity. This particular use of *ḥaḍara* emphasises the final stage of a COME event. In contrast to *atā* and *ǧa'a*, *ḥaḍara* is more likely to express the notion of 'being present' at the deictic centre.

4.3 *Qadima*

The bulk of *qadima* uses appear to be associated with physical motion of human agents towards a destination. The data frame showed that the predominant type of destination in a *qadima* motion event is a physical location, be it a geographical location such as a city or country, or any other type of physical location. What seems also to set the use of this verb apart from the other verbs is the (statistically significant) presence of a purpose of the motion event. In other words, *qadima* appears to be the COME verb that is preferred when talking about the motion (coming) of individuals, or groups of individuals towards a certain destination to fulfil a particular purpose.

5. Conclusions

In this chapter I have presented a corpus-based constructionist analysis of four high-frequency lexical items in MSA. The statistical analyses I conducted on the MSA COME verbs are but a subset of the different varieties of statistical procedures that have been designed to explore multivariate data frames of the sort utilised here. The two analyses discussed in this chapter have succeeded in explaining the different behavioural patterns of the four MSA COME verbs. This highlights the multifaceted nature of deictic motion events, and the fact that, in MSA, the different aspects of a COME event are conveyed by a number of verbs instead of a single COME verb.

While the four COME verbs *can* be used interchangeably in certain contexts – mostly contexts expressing a human agent physically moving towards an end point – each verb has a life of its own. Each COME verb showed clear preferences with respect to the morphosyntactic and semantic elements it typically associates with, which reflects a divergence in the kinds of constructions that characterise the usage and the meaning extensions of these verbs. As I pointed out at the beginning of the chapter, tweaking different aspects of the construction hosting a COME verb (e.g. tense, subject semantic category, etc.) triggers restrictions regarding the MSA COME verbs that can fit into the resulting context. The analysis above has successfully shown that the behaviour of the four verbs is explained via a combination of multiple morphosyntactic and semantic features – rather than by single features. This leads us to the conclusion that the lexical choices made by native speakers of the language – in this case, as to which COME verb to use in what context – are probabilistic in nature rather than categorical. Evidence from a synonymy study by Arppe (2009) supports this view. An analysis, which for reasons of space cannot be discussed in detail here, of the COME data frame using polytomous logistic regression (Arppe 2008, 2012) yielded similar findings: while certain contexts of use favour one verb over the others 100 per cent of the time, other contexts vary in the degrees to which some or all of the verbs can be used interchangeably (Abdulrahim 2013). In other subsequent research, undertaken along the lines of the experimental work outlined in Arppe and Järvikivi (2007), these corpus-based findings have also been paired with experimental data from a forced-choice task that was completed by literate Bahraini native speakers of Arabic (Abdulrahim and Arppe 2013). Participants read fifty sentences in MSA and selected the missing verb from a given list of verbs. The stimulus items were chosen to represent the full breadth of contextual richness apparent in the corpus data and the entire diversity of probability distributions given in a context. Analysis of the data showed that the collective intuitions of the native Bahraini speakers of Arabic concerning the context-based associations governing the selection of the four COME verbs correspond to a great extent with verb selections predicted by the model, which was based on the MSA written corpus. Comparing these two sources of data (the corpus and the collective intuition of native speakers) has helped examine the extent to which literate Arabic speakers (from a certain dialectal background) have internalised the rules and conventions of lexical usage in MSA.

The data frame explored in this study is limited with regards to the number and range of variables it was coded for. For instance, I did not code for word order (SV or VS), or clause type (main, subordinate, relative, etc.), or the different types of adverbial phrases. Nevertheless, the range of variables can always be expanded and modified to arrive at a more finely tuned analysis of COME verbs in MSA. The construction of this kind of multivariate data frame to explore multiple levels of morphosyntactic, semantic, and lexical features offers a rather comprehensive methodology for detailed examination of synonymous and polysemous high-frequency linguistic items.

Acknowledgements

I would like to thank Professors John Newman and Sally Rice at the University of Alberta for their continuous guidance and feedback throughout the various stages of this research. I am also grateful to Professor Dilworth Parkinson at Brigham Young University for introducing me to arabiCorpus and for his tremendous help with corpus queries.

Abbreviations

1	1ST PERSON	IRR	IRREGULAR
2	2ND PERSON	JUSS	JUSSIVE
3	3RD PERSON	LOC	LOCATIVE
ABL	ABLATIVE	M	MASCULINE
ACC	ACCUSATIVE	MASC	MASCULINE
ADJ	ADJECTIVE	MOD	MODAL
ADV	ADVERB	MORPH_ASP	MORPHOLOGICAL ASPECT
ALL	ALLATIVE	NEG	NEGATION
AP	ACTIVE PARTICIPLE	NON-FIN	NON-FINITE
ART	ARTICLE	OBS-EXP	OBSERVED–EXPECTED
AUX	AUXILIARY	P.ADJ.HOLM	ADJUSTED HOLM P-VALUE
CL	CLITIC	PERF	PERFECTIVE
CONJ	CONJUNCTION	PL	PLURAL
CONT.CHISQ	CONTRIBUTION TO CHI-SQUARE	PP	PERSONAL PRONOUN
DEC	DECISION	PURP	PURPOSIVE
DEM	DEMONSTRATIVE	Q	QUESTION PARTICLE
DM	DISCOURSE MARKER	RP	RELATIVE PRONOUN
DUAL	DUAL	SG	SINGULAR
F	FEMININE	SING	SINGULAR
FEM	FEMININE	SUBJ_CAT	SUBJECT CATEGORY
FUT	FUTURE	SUBJN	SUBJUNCTIVE
GEN	GENITIVE	SUBJ_NUM	SUBJECT NUMBER
HAB	HABITUAL	TOP	TOPIC
IMPF	IMPERFECTIVE	VN	VERBAL NOUN
INST	INSTRUMENTAL		

Note

1. See ‘The R Project for Statistical Computing’, available at <http://www.r-project.org> (last accessed 24 May 2018).

References

Abdulrahim, D. (2013), ‘A Corpus Study of Basic Motion Events in Modern Standard Arabic’, unpublished doctoral dissertation, University of Alberta.

Abdulrahim, D. and A. Arppe (2013), ‘Converging linguistic evidence: The synonymy of Arabic COME verbs’, paper presented at the 27th Annual Symposium on Arabic Linguistics (ALS), Indiana University, Bloomington, 28 February–2 March 2013.

Arppe, A. (2008), *Univariate, Bivariate and Multivariate Methods in Corpus-Based Lexicography – A Study of Synonyms*, PhD thesis, University of Helsinki, *Publications of the Department of General Linguistics* 44.

Arppe, A. (2009), 'Linguistic choices vs. probabilities – how much and what can linguistic theory explain?', in S. Featherston and S. Winkler (eds), *The Fruits of Empirical Linguistics 1*, Berlin: de Gruyter, pp. 1–24.

Arppe, A. and J. Järvikivi (2007), 'Take empiricism seriously! – In support of methodological diversity in linguistics', *Corpus Linguistics and Linguistic Theory*, 3(1): 99–109.

Biber, D. (1988), *Variation Across Speech and Writing*, Cambridge: Cambridge University Press.

Buckwalter, T. and D. Parkinson (2011), *A Frequency Dictionary of Arabic*, New York: Routledge.

Bybee, J. (2010), *Language, Usage and Cognition*, Cambridge: Cambridge University Press.

Croft, W. and A. D. Cruse (2004), *Cognitive Linguistics*, Cambridge: Cambridge University Press.

Di Meola, C. (1994), *'Kommen' und 'gehen'. Eine kognitiv-linguistische Untersuchung der Polysemie deiktischer Bewegungsverben*, Tübingen: Max Niemeyer.

Divjak, D. S. and S. Th. Gries (2006), 'Ways of trying in Russian: Clustering behavioral profiles', *Corpus Linguistics and Linguistic Theory*, 2(1): 23–60.

Fillmore, C. (1966), 'Deictic categories in the semantic of "come"', *Foundations of Language*, 2: 219–27.

Fillmore, C. (1972), 'How to know whether you are coming or going', *Studies in Descriptive and Applied Linguistics*, 5: 3–17.

Gathercole, V. (1977), 'A study of the comings and goings of the speakers of four languages: Spanish, Japanese, English, and Turkish', *Kansas Working Papers in Linguistics*, 2: 61–94.

Gries, S. Th. (2006), 'Corpus-based methods and cognitive semantics: The many meanings of *to run*', in S. Th. Gries and A. Stefanowitsch (eds), *Corpora in Cognitive Linguistics: Corpus-Based Approaches to Syntax and Lexis*, Berlin and New York: Mouton de Gruyter, pp. 57–99.

Gries, S. Th. (2009a), *Statistics for Linguistics with R: A Practical Introduction*, Berlin: Mouton de Gruyter.

Gries, S. Th. and D. S. Divjak (2009), 'Behavioral profiles: A corpus-based approach towards cognitive semantic analysis', in V. Evans and S. S. Pourcel (eds), *New Directions in Cognitive Linguistics*, Amsterdam and Philadelphia: John Benjamins, pp. 57–75.

Gries, S. Th. and N. Otani (2010), 'Behavioral profiles: A corpus-based perspective on synonymy and antonymy', *ICAME Journal*, 34: 121–50.

Hanks, P. (1996), 'Contextual dependency and lexical sets', *International Journal of Corpus Linguistics*, 1(1): 75–98.

Langacker, R. (1987), *Foundations of Cognitive Grammar, Vol. I: Theoretical Prerequisites*, Stanford, CA: Stanford University Press.

Newman, J. and J. Lin (2007), 'The purposefulness of going: A corpus-linguistic study', in J. Walinski, K. Kredens and S. Gozdz-Roszkowski (eds), *Corpora and ICT in Language Studies*, Frankfurt am Main: Peter Lang, pp. 293–308.

Rice, S. and J. Newman (2005), 'Inflectional islands', presentation at the 9th

International Cognitive Linguistics Conference, 17–22 July, Yonsei University, Korea.
Sinha, A. K. (1972), 'On the deictic use of "coming" and "going" in Hindi', in *Papers from the Eighth Regional Meeting of the Chicago Linguistic Society*, Chicago: University of Chicago, Department of Linguistics, pp. 351–8.
Slobin, D. I. (1996), 'Two ways to travel: Verbs of motion in English and Spanish', in M. S. Shibatani and S. A. Thompson (eds), *Grammatical Constructions: Their Form and Meaning*, Oxford: Clarendon Press, pp. 195–220.
Suzuki, R. and H. Shimodaira (2006), 'Pvclust: An R package for assessing the uncertainty in hierarchical clustering', *Bioinformatics*, 22(12): 1540–2.
Talmy, L. (2000), *Toward a Cognitive Semantics*, Cambridge, MA: MIT Press.
von Eye, A. (1990), *Introduction to Configural Frequency Analysis: The Search for Types and Antitypes in Cross-Classification*, Cambridge: Cambridge University Press.
Wilkins, D. P. and D. Hill (1995), 'When "go" means "come": Questioning the basicness of basic motion verbs', *Cognitive Linguistics*, 6(2/3): 209–60.

R scripts

Arppe, A. (2012), *polytomous: Polytomous Logistic Regression for Fixed and Mixed Effects. R Package Version 0.1.4.*
Gries, S. Th. (2004), *HCFA 3.2 – A Program for Hierarchical Configural Frequency Analysis for R for Windows.*
Gries, S. Th. (2009b), *BehavioralProfiles 1.01. A Program for R 2.7.1 and Higher.*

10

Approaching Text Typology through Cluster Analysis in Arabic

Ghada Mohamed and Andrew Hardie

1. Background: classifying texts on external and internal criteria

Although there exist many different approaches to the classification of texts into categories, most such work can be considered *functional* in orientation, being based on features external to the text such as its purpose, the discourse context, and the medium of communication. Kinneavy (1971), for instance, provides a comprehensive framework for establishing text categories, using elements of the communicative situation to develop a philosophy of the aims of discourse. Those elements are: the person encoding a message; the signal (language) through which the message is communicated; the reality to which the message refers; and the receiver of the message (Kinneavy 1971: 19). According to Kinneavy, one of these elements could be the primary focus that distinguishes a specific discourse in a given situation, while the other elements have a subordinate role. On this basis, Kinneavy (1971) identifies four types of discourse: *reference*, *persuasive*, *literary*, and *expressive*.

De Beaugrande and Dressler (1981: 184) also use text-external features to classify texts into categories, stating that the main feature defining a text-type is the communicative function of the text. Accordingly, they identify eight text-types: *descriptive*, *narrative*, *argumentative*, *literary*, *poetic*, *scientific*, *didactic*, and *conversational* texts. Because of the diversity of text functions, de Beaugrande and Dressler (1981: 186) conclude that this typology does not result in absolutely distinct text-types; rather, some texts may overlap, moving from one text-type to another.

Werlich (1982) presents a typology which draws heavily on the description of text categories proposed by de Beaugrande and Dressler. On the basis of contextual factors such as persons with intentions, reactions, presuppositions, and status; objects; relations, and so on, Werlich establishes five text-types: *description*, *narration*, *exposition*, *argumentation*, and *instruction*. On similar lines, Hatim and Mason (1990) base their typology on what they call *dominant contextual focus*, identifying three text-types: *argumentative*, *expository*, and *instructional* – conflating three of Werlich's categories (*description*, *narration*, and *exposition*) into one, *exposition*.

As the cited studies exemplify, most research in text typology favours the same approach to text classification; one which is theory-heavy. That is, the contribution of the theory is central to the establishment of text categories. A typology so developed would be more or less similar to existing typologies with either some more distinctive traits of each type, few additional types, or conflated types, but overall they can be described as static. Further, the process of assigning a given text to a specific type is not systematic and the text categories that emerge are not linguistically motivated; in consequence, texts that belong to the same category are not necessarily similar in their linguistic forms. Such approaches must, therefore, be complemented by *bottom-up* approaches where categorisation is based on features internal to the language of the texts. The most widely known approach of this kind is Biber's (1988) *multi-dimensional* (MD) analysis of English, extended to cross-linguistic text typology by Biber (1995).

Biber's (1988) study implements an innovative and complex approach to the investigation of language variation, the *multi-feature/multi-dimensional* (MF/MD or just MD) approach. In Biber's work, a *dimension* is a group of linguistic features that consistently co-occur in texts, which can then be interpreted functionally. Each dimension has both linguistic and functional content (Biber 1989: 7). Biber's (1988) study of English uses a multivariate analysis called factor analysis, applied to the co-occurrence distributions of 67 linguistic features in a corpus of 481 written and spoken texts, to identify the patterns of co-variation which are functionally interpreted as dimensions. Each dimension emerging from the statistical analysis is marked by a group of linguistic features that co-vary consistently from text to text and from genre to genre, some with a positive weighting, some negative. Notably, Biber's dimensions are thus derived from a dataset in which externally defined genres are assumed (the LOB Corpus, augmented with some personal letters and spoken texts). Biber's (1988) model of variation consists of seven dimensions, of which the first five – summarised in Table 10.1 – were deemed statistically strong enough for inclusion in Biber's later work.

Biber (1989) uses another statistical tool, namely cluster analysis, to develop his typology further. This multivariate technique groups texts that are similar according to a set of features into unique clusters. Biber (1989: 13) analyses the similarities and differences across the clusters with respect to the five dimensions and identifies eight text-types: *intimate interpersonal interaction*, *informational interaction*, *scientific exposition*, *learned exposition*, *imaginative narrative*, *general narrative exposition*, *situated reportage*, and *involved persuasion*.

However, since Biber's method for identifying the dimensions in the first place takes into consideration externally defined genres, this means that his approach to text classification is not entirely bottom-up. An alternative methodology for establishing text-type categories that does not require this advance grouping of texts into registers is presented by Mohamed (2011). In this approach, a text typology based on similarities in linguistic form is derived systematically using cluster analysis, which has the distinctive feature of placing objects algorithmically into distinct groupings based on their overall similarities across multiple variables (Romesburg 1984: 27; Baayen 2008: 138). Mohamed uses cluster analysis to group the written texts in the British National

Table 10.1 A summary of Biber's (1988) model of variation

Dimension	Positive weight features	Negative weight features
Dimension 1: **Involved vs informal production**	Private verbs THAT deletion Contractions Present tense 2nd person pronouns DO as pro-verb Analytic negation Demonstrative pronouns General emphatics 1st person pronouns Pronoun IT Causative subordination Discourse particles Indefinite pronouns General hedges Amplifiers Sentence relatives Possibility modals Non-phrasal coordination WH clauses Final prepositions Adverbs	Nouns Word length Prepositions Type/token ratio Attributive adjectives Place adverbials
Dimension 2: **Narrative vs non-narrative concerns**	Past tense 3rd person pronouns Perfect aspect Public verbs Synthetic negation Present participial clauses	Present tense Attributive adjectives
Dimension 3: **Explicit vs situation-dependent reference**	WH relative clauses on object positions Pied piping relative clauses WH relative clauses on subject positions Phrasal coordination Nominalisations	Time adverbials Place adverbials Adverbs
Dimension 4: **Overt expression of persuasion**	Infinitives Prediction modals Suasive verbs Conditional subordination Necessity modals Split auxiliaries Possibility modals	None
Dimension 5: **Abstract vs non-abstract style**	Conjuncts Agentless passives Past participial clauses BY passives WHIZ deletion Other adverbial subordinators	None

Corpus (BNC) on the basis of 76 linguistic features, without any advance grouping of texts into registers. The resulting typology contains six major text-types: *persuasion*, *narration*, *informational narration*, *exposition*, *scientific exposition*, and *literary exposition*. These labels are assigned based on the analysis of prominent text-internal and text-external features across the members of the clusters.

Given the utility of a method based on cluster analysis demonstrated by Biber (1989) and Mohamed (2011) for systematising the diversity of English texts, it is reasonable to adopt the same methodology to examine the efficiency of cluster analysis to classify texts of other languages, in this case Arabic.

2. Why a typology of Arabic texts?

It can be noted from the studies reviewed above that English has received the greatest attention in text typology. Most work on text classification has focused on providing a comprehensive description of the English language, except for some few attempts which consider other languages for the study of register variation (see Biber 1995). This may be due to the large number of easily accessible English corpora, many of which contain representative samples of English texts and are moreover tagged for linguistic analyses, with, for instance, part-of-speech (POS) tags. Thus, the level of attention devoted to English is understandable.

In recent years, however, there has been an upsurge of interest in Arabic, which like English clearly has the status of an international language (Al-Sulaiti and Atwell 2006). Many corpora have been built (e.g. the Leeds Corpus of Contemporary Arabic) as well as tools for analysis (see Atwell, this volume, *inter alia*). Despite the growing number of studies on Arabic, efforts in the field of text linguistics are still limited. This could be due to two reasons. On the one hand, the morphological structure of Arabic is tremendously complex; thus, highly accurate tokenisers and taggers are required for comprehensively exploiting an Arabic corpus on a large scale (Atwell et al. 2004). Thus, most work on Arabic focuses on one particular aspect of Arabic in a specific, pre-defined genre (see, for instance, Gully 1996; Mohamed and Omer 2000). In consequence, broad-purview text-typological studies aiming at comprehensive description of the language are widely neglected in Arabic.

On the other hand, scholars who are interested in Arabic, and more specifically Arab scholars, have devoted much of their effort to the study of literary texts, most notably Classical Arabic literature, classifying these texts into groups such as pre- and post-Islamic poetry, historical writing, philosophy, and pre-modern and modern literary texts (Somekh 1991). The literature in Arabic is massive, and scholarly interest in the Arabic-speaking world seems to be directed towards a typology of literary texts that is *chronological* and *functional* in orientation. Other types of texts than the literary thus are in consequence marginalised, resulting in a huge gap in the field of Arabic text typology. Thus, this study aims to address this gap. We illustrate a plausible approach to systematising the diversity of Arabic texts by means of automatic classification.

3. Corpus selection and measuring linguistic features

For the purpose of developing a model of Arabic text-types defined by text-internal features, we must (1) select a large set of texts, and (2) compile a list of linguistic features which can be quantified in those texts (producing feature counts which can subsequently be used as input to the statistical method, i.e. cluster analysis).

3.1 Data

Establishing categories within a text typology should involve the investigation of actual language systems in which selections and decisions regarding grammatical forms have been made (de Beaugrande 2000: 161). Investigating recurrent patterns in authentic texts to establish text categories may be best approached by considering a relatively large dataset.

The Leeds Corpus of Contemporary Arabic (CCA, Al-Sulaiti and Atwell 2006) can be regarded as a good source for the purpose of establishing text categories. The CCA is a well-balanced corpus consisting of 1 million words of largely written language with a small spoken element (Al-Sulaiti and Atwell 2006: 27). The design of the CCA is inspired by existing corpora such as Brown/LOB, ICE, and the BNC, in which a wide range of genres are included (Al-Sulaiti and Atwell 2006: 12). Explicating their compilation of the CCA, Al-Sulaiti and Atwell say:

> Our main focus is to represent the standard form, written and spoken, as well as some regional varieties, for example as reflected in a range of Arabic broadcast media. The corpus will be a rich resource for learners to explore, compare and learn about the present Standard Arabic with its new vocabulary and its different regional varieties. (Al-Sulaiti and Atwell 2006: 16)

The classification of texts in the structure of the CCA follows Sharoff's (2004: 1745) classification scheme for internet-sourced corpora across a wide range of languages.

Table 10.2 shows that the categories are based on domain, that is, content, and hence are considered to be external divisions. The CCA contains 415 texts and 1 million words; it is therefore likely to be useful for the same kinds of applications that the similarly sized Brown and LOB corpora of English have been applied to – especially, the study of grammar and/or lexico-grammar, as LOB was used in Biber's (1988) study discussed above. In that it contains written texts from a wide variety of registers, the CCA can be considered to represent a broad cross-section of the contemporary language. Along these lines, Al-Sulaiti and Atwell state that:

> a 1-million-word corpus is still a potentially useful resource. Although Brown and LOB were collected about 30 years ago, they are still used in current research . . . Similarly, 1-million-word corpora have proven useful for comparative studies in the ICE project . . . (Al-Sulaiti and Atwell 2006: 17)

We work with a version of the CCA that has been annotated along the lines indicated by Ibrahim and Hardie (this volume), that is, using the MADA system

Table 10.2 The CCA text-types classified using Sharoff's domains (adapted from Al-Sulaiti and Atwell 2006)

Domains	Text types
NatSci	Scientific doc.
ApplSci	Scientific doc., ecology, instruction manuals, geography, technical doc., user manuals, internet comp.doc., health and medicine
SocSci	Education, academic papers, sociology, legal doc., religion
Politics	Politics
Commerce	Business letters, financial doc., application forms, economics, call for tender, patents, memos
Life	Conversation, formal letters, interviews, advertisements, recipes, rest. menus
Arts	Poetry, short stories, children's stories, autobiography, plays
Leisure	Entertainments, tourist/travel, sports, fashion

(Habash and Rambow 2005) for disambiguation of output from the Buckwalter Arabic Morphological Analyzer (Buckwalter 2004). This is particularly useful when searching for linguistic features in the CCA texts which can be directly quantified using the categories annotated in the MADA output.

3.2 Selection of linguistic features

The next preparatory step is to compile a list of linguistic features which can be quantified in the corpus. Biber and Conrad (2009: 63) suggest three approaches to deciding on a list of linguistic features for studying text variation. The first is to consult a comprehensive reference grammar (for Arabic, an example would be Ryding 2005). The second is to consider a single aspect of language use and identify linguistic features related to this aspect (e.g. referring expressions: nouns, pronouns, demonstrative pronouns, etc.). The third is to include as many different kinds of language features as possible, motivated by previous research on register analysis. Biber (1988), for instance, includes on his list any linguistic feature with a functional association, and also takes into consideration features identified in previous research as distinguishing between spoken and written discourse. We compiled a list of Arabic features inspired by the example of Biber (1988); as the analysis presented here is merely a first attempt to address text-typology in Arabic, however, our list of linguistic features for Arabic is not as detailed as Biber's list for English.

We proceeded by identifying Arabic grammatical elements which (1) parallel some feature of English found to be relevant by Biber – not difficult, since Biber's list approaches a comprehensive listing of English grammatical devices; and (2) can be retrieved by an automated corpus query with very high precision and recall. Some linguistic features which we might otherwise have included could not be retrieved accurately using automatic queries. At this early stage of our investigation, we thought it better to demonstrate the validity of the approach with a smaller, sounder set of features than to potentially include unreliable frequency data for 'difficult' features. Thus, we limited our list to features of Arabic grammar which can be searched for automatically and which can be directly quantified from the raw word forms in the corpus or from the MADA output. Our list consists of ten features, aligned under seven headings according to the area of the grammar that they relate to:

a. Nominal forms
   1. Nouns
   2. Independent pronouns

   ʾanā, *ʾantumā*, *naḥnu*, *ʾanta*, *ʾanti*, *humā*, *ʾantum*, *ʾantunna*, *huwa*, *hiya*, *hum*, and *hunna*.

b. Verb forms
   3. Past tense[1]
   4. Present tense
   5. Passive voice

c. Prepositions
   6. True prepositions

   There are only ten true prepositions in Modern Standard Arabic, but they are very frequent with a wide range of meanings (Ryding 2005: 367). These include: *bi-*, *li-*, *ka-*, *fī*, *min*, *'an*, *ʾilā*, *'alā*, *ḥattā*, and *munḏu*.

d. Post-modifying clauses
   7. Definite relative pronouns (*allatī*, *allaḏī*) equivalent to *which*, *that*, and *who*

e. Adjectives
   8. Attributive adjectives

f. Adverbs
   9. General adverbs

g. Conjunctions
   10. Connectives

wa- ‘and’ is the most frequent connective. Others include, for example: *fa-*, ‘and so, and then, yet, and thus’; *bal*, ‘rather, but actually’; *'innamā*, ‘but, but moreover, but also, rather’; *'ay*, ‘that is’; *'iḏ*, ‘since, inasmuch as’; *'iḏan*, ‘therefore, then, so, thus, in that case’; *ḥattā*, ‘until’; *ḥayṯu*, ‘where’.

To retrieve counts of instances for each linguistic feature selected for this study, we developed automatic corpus queries. Since our data was indexed using Corpus Workbench (Evert and Hardie 2011), we express the queries in that system’s *CQP syntax* (i.e. the syntax of the Corpus Query Processor program).[2] The queries were based on POS tags which abbreviate strings of MADA output features (an early version of the POS tags described by Ibrahim and Hardie, this volume). For instance, to search for the past tense, the following query was used:

```
[pos="VPV.*"]
```

in which the initial ‘VPV’ abbreviates ‘verb, perfective’ (i.e. past tense).

Using these queries, each linguistic feature was quantified in each text of the CCA. The step that follows then is to identify texts that are similar in their linguistic features and place them into unique groups using a multivariate statistical analysis.

4. The statistical method

4.1 Cluster analysis

The linguistic features identified in the previous section will act as variables for text classification in this study. What is needed next is a statistical method to identify sets of texts in the CCA which have a sufficient degree of similarity in their linguistic features and group those similar texts together, without any pre-assumed knowledge of groupings. The purpose of identifying these groups is to reveal *unnoticed* patterns that may exist in the data. Finding these patterns calls for the use of an exploratory multivariate technique.

There are many multivariate analyses, and the general view of statisticians is that the choice of method should be made in light of the research aim and of whether the investigation is into patterns between objects, between variables, or both. For our purposes, cluster analysis (specifically, *hierarchical agglomerative cluster analysis*) is the most appropriate multivariate technique, because it is directly applicable to searching for patterns among objects in a dataset based on their overall similarity across multiple variables – which is what the bottom-up establishment of a typology on the basis of a feature list demands. Cluster analysis is a method which assesses 'the similarities and dissimilarities between pairs of objects in a set' (Romesburg 1984: 27). Its purpose is to arrange a number of objects into meaningful groups, so that objects resembling each other belong to the same group and objects that are dissimilar belong to different groups (Crawley 2007: 738). The description of similarities of patterns in cluster analysis is based on standard statistical algorithms, and thus the groups/clusters are derived systematically and algorithmically without advance grouping of the data objects (in our case, no advance grouping of texts into registers).

There are three steps in cluster analysis; within each step there are many alternative procedures. The steps are: (1) obtaining a data matrix; (2) computing the proximity matrix; and (3) performing linkage.

4.2 Obtaining a data matrix

As with all multivariate methods, the starting point is a data matrix. The objects in the data matrix are chosen from a known *taxon* (Romesburg 1984: 204). The data matrix comprises the measurements of all variables for each object. In preparing the data matrix, some options are available. It is possible to maintain the original data and proceed with the clustering using the raw measurements of the variables. Alternatively, the original data can be treated to avoid weighting of variables (Everitt 1993: 39; Romesburg 1984: 89). Transforming the data to avoid unequally weighted variables may involve dropping some variables, reducing the number of variables, or applying some standardising function to each variable. There are various standardising functions that can be applied to the data matrix; they all involve expressing each value in terms of some statistic that characterises the variable that value occurs on. The most common standardising functions discussed in the literature are listed in Table 10.3.

4.3 Computing the proximity matrix

The data matrix is used to compute a proximity matrix, which measures the distance between each pair of objects. The distance between two objects can be measured in terms of similarity, or in terms of dissimilarity: in either case, multiple different measures are available. Table 10.3 summarises the most common alternatives in this step.

4.4 Performing linkage

The third step involves transforming the proximity matrix into a hierarchy of nested groups which can be depicted in a *dendrogram* (tree diagram) using a clustering method (Aldenderfer and Blashfield 1984: 36). The clustering method assimilates the mass of numbers produced in the previous step, reducing the proximity matrix to a tree of clusters-within-clusters.

Table 10.3 lists the alternative procedures for each step of the hierarchical cluster analysis (we do not consider non-hierarchical clustering here, but see Mohamed 2011).

5. Applying cluster analysis to the Arabic feature data

The general procedure of cluster analysis is conceptually simple. However, the number of possible combinations of alternative procedures is large, and it is a hard task to find

Table 10.3 A summary of clustering algorithm options

Obtaining the data matrix	Computing the proximity matrix	Linkage method
1. Original data 2. Transforming the data: a. Standardising functions: – The z-score – The range between maximum and minimum values – Standardising function based on ranking b. Applying an R-analysis c. Deleting some of the variables	1. Dissimilarity measures: a. The Euclidean distance measure b. Canberra distance measure c. Bray-Curtis dissimilarity measure d. Manhattan dissimilarity measure 2. Similarity measures: a. Correlation coefficient b. Cosine coefficient	1. SLINK 2. CLINK 3. Average 4. Ward's method 5. The weighted average group 6. The centroid

the combination(s) of techniques that deal optimally with particular datasets. Despite extensive research comparing clustering procedures, the majority of studies applying clustering to empirical data draw on the interaction between the method and the type of data. Moreover, clustering has been applied in different disciplines, and each discipline has its preferred methodological combinations (Aldenderfer and Blashfield 1984: 14).

In the field of text typology, cluster analysis has not been widely utilised. It is used by Biber (1989) to classify English texts; however, Biber did not explicitly state which clustering techniques were implemented, and whether alternative combinations of procedures were tested to determine which performed better for his dataset. More recently, Mohamed (2011, forthcoming) implements cluster analysis for English text typology using an *experimental* approach. That is, various alternatives at each step are tried out, in different combinations. The purpose of this experimental process is to determine which techniques are robust and best exhibit the natural groupings in the data. The experimental process reveals six stable and consistent clustering combinations for the classification of English texts (i.e. they robustly produce the same general results as one another):

- original data – Manhattan – complete method
- original data – Canberra – average method
- original data – correlation – complete method
- original data – correlation – average method
- max – Canberra – average method
- normalise – Canberra – complete method.

These successful clustering alternatives are also among the most commonly used in the literature, recommended by reviews of cluster analysis in most disciplines (see Faith et al. 1987; Fowlkes and Mallows 1983; Costa et al. 2003; Adamson and Bawden 1981).

In this study, we apply the stable *original data – Canberra – average method* combination. As noted earlier, statisticians recommend that the choice of a particular combination of procedures should be guided by the type of data and the goal of the research. In the field of English text typology, this combination has been assessed and found superior to other combinations; hence, we make the working assumption that it will be likewise efficacious for Arabic text typology. In a future extension of this research, we will test this assumption empirically. Figure 10.1 shows the dendrogram which emerged from the cluster analysis of the Arabic data.

The dendrogram is 'a visual representation of the distance at which clusters are combined' (Norušis 1996: 370). Objects are plotted as nodes across the bottom; the *y*-axis denotes the linkage distance (similarity/dissimilarity) between objects/clusters. The dendrogram's vertical lines are directed upwards from each object/cluster, while its horizontal lines represent points of similarity at which objects are merged. The vertical length of a branch indicates the distance between the subgroups (clusters).

Figure 10.1 shows the dendrogram after it has been 'cut', chopping off the fine details (object nodes) at the bottom. When analysing a corpus of hundreds or thousands

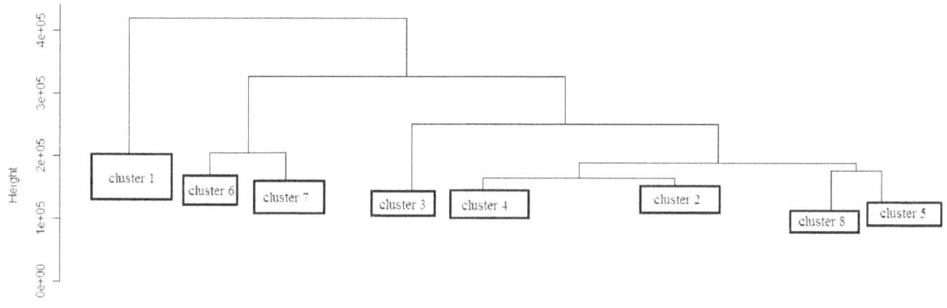

Figure 10.1 A simplified version of the dendrogram

of texts, the original dendrogram is not amenable to visual inspection, due to the very large number of nodes at the lowest levels. To get around this problem, we replace each grouping of objects/clusters at a certain level of similarity, that is, 'height' (in this case pragmatic motivations led to the choice of 106,024 as the cut-off point) with a labelled box representing the grouping that exists at that 'height'. Figure 10.1 shows the reference numbers assigned to the clusters at that level, and our analysis will refer to them. However, this initial determination will not be considered as necessarily an optimal estimator of the similarity level. The groupings *above* the cut-off point, that is, the higher-level groupings that indicate relationships among the clusters that exist at the cut-off point, will still be part of the analysis. This initial 'cut' generated eight clusters for further analysis and interpretation.

6. Interpretation of the cluster analysis

The cluster analysis groups texts with similar linguistic features into unique algorithmically derived clusters, so that texts within each cluster share an overall similarity according to the full set of internal features. Using an ad hoc procedure, described in detail below, it is possible to identify the most interesting and relevant linguistic features that contribute to the description of each cluster as a particular text-type. It is also crucial to see whether texts within a cluster are also similar in some way *externally* (i.e. in terms of genre/register), and whether this similarity is important to the description of the text-type.

6.1 Analytical techniques for cluster interpretation – internal features

We first utilise a heuristic procedure to identify prominent linguistic features in each cluster. This heuristic is to consider the proportion of texts in a cluster that are in the upper quartile of the whole corpus for that feature. This is emphatically *not* meant to be a statistically rigorous characterisation of the distribution of features across clusters; it is the cluster analysis that fulfils that purpose. Rather, this heuristic is a means of

Table 10.4 Determining the texts with high frequencies of the nouns

Text ID	Cluster	Nouns	H/L
AUT01	1	210025.4	L
AUT02	2	363930.2	
AUT03	2	409859.2	
AUT04	3	357346.7	
AUT05	2	436184.2	H
AUT06	2	432913.3	H

Table 10.5 Calculating the percentages of texts in each cluster with high frequencies of nouns

Cluster	Number of texts in cluster	Number of texts with H	Percentage
1	21	0	0
2	117	8	7
3	47	0	0
4	70	16	23
5	21	66	88

focusing discussion and manual analysis on features that are likely to be interesting in a given cluster.

We will illustrate this heuristic procedure in detail for one linguistic feature, nouns. First, the upper quartile (UQ) and lower quartile (LQ) values for the per-text frequency of nouns are calculated across the corpus.

The frequency of this feature in each individual text is then compared with the upper and lower quartile values. If it is equal to or higher than the upper quartile, the text will be considered *High* for this feature, while if it is equal to or lower than the lower quartile, it will be considered *Low*; the middle 50 per cent of texts receive no special flag. Table 10.4 illustrates this procedure for the first six texts in the CCA.

Then for each cluster, the number of H texts is summed, and a percentage calculated, as shown for the first five clusters in Table 10.5.

For a given cluster, a linguistic feature is described as:

- *highly prominent* if 30 per cent or more of texts are in the upper quartile for that feature
- *moderately prominent* if 15–29 per cent of texts are in the upper quartile for that feature.

So we say that nouns are moderately prominent in cluster 4 and highly prominent in cluster 5.

This approach is not exhaustive, because it points to especially frequent features only, whereas the clustering method has also taken into account features that are *infrequent*. However, since the aim is to identify features that we can productively examine in concordances, it is more useful to pull out frequent features rather than infrequent features.

This method is an ad hoc technique to focus attention on linguistic features that are likely to be relevant to accounting for the patterns in the cluster analysis. Those patterns are interpreted in functional terms to provide a foundation for identifying the functions underlying the overall prominent features in each cluster. Our interpretations of the functional associations of the linguistic features are based on previous descriptive grammars of Modern Standard Arabic, for instance Ryding (2005), and on prior quantitative studies on register variation of English texts, for instance Biber (1988) and Biber et al. (1999), given the presumable (near-)universality of the discourse functions that the linguistic features appear to embody. The interpretation of linguistic features is backed up by investigating (randomly sampled) concordances of the linguistic feature in context, to determine whether the function identified is actually evident in the underlying text.

6.2 Analytical techniques for cluster interpretation – external features

The second step in the cluster interpretation is to look for similarities of text-external features among the texts, if any exist. External features shared by a set of texts may include functional unity (e.g. overall communicative purpose), audience, domain, or subject matter. However, the CCA metadata is limited; our investigation of text-external features depended mostly on genre codes or surveying randomly selected individual texts to seek similar situational characteristics. In some cases, we could identify shared text-external features in a given cluster straightforwardly: for instance, if more than half of the texts in a cluster had the same CCA genre code, we could identify that genre easily as dominant for that text-type. In such a case, there was no need to look at individual texts' metadata for the dominant genre, and instead we have considered how the less dominant genres might be related to the dominant one. For instance, if a cluster is found to contain many fiction texts in addition to some texts from other genres, we might conclude that this cluster has the function of telling a story with sequential events. The texts from other genres in the same cluster are then examined to cross-compare their functions with the narrative function of fiction, to identify functional similarities that might account for the likeness in their language use identified by the clustering technique. We followed the same procedure when there were two or three dominant genres in a given cluster. However, if *none* of the genre codes could be seen to dominate a cluster then we had actually to read through (a random selection of) the individual texts.

7. Interpretation of the clusters as text-types

Since our technique for text classification was based on text-internal features, the resulting (initially eight) clusters are effectively text-types. However, the clustering that happens at a higher level is also interesting. We initially made the analysis of the dendrogram manageable by excluding the fine detail at the bottom. But the eight clusters are not free-floating units: they merge into broader groups at higher points in the tree. These interrelationships between clusters that are joined higher up in the branching dendrogram are also relevant to the analysis, if neighbouring clusters represent similar text-types. The numbers of the clusters (1 to 8) are an artefact of the clustering algorithm and are just labels. Thus, we will not present clusters in numerical order, but rather according to their interrelationships in the dendrogram – summarising similarities and differences among closely related clusters.

Overall, we arrive at a typology of three main text-types: *narration*, *exposition*, and *scientific exposition*, as outlined below.

7.1 Narration

Clusters 6 and 7 are close neighbours in the dendrogram. The majority of the texts in these clusters are fictional, but they also contain some non-fictional narratives. Their shared function is telling a story with sequential events and reporting on the activities, feelings, and thoughts of the characters involved.

7.1.1 Internal features

These clusters' prominent linguistic features relate to the function of narration, and are similar to the features underlying dimension 2 *Narrative vs Non-narrative concerns* in Biber (1988) at the narrative end. According to Biber (1988: 109), narrative discourse in English depends heavily on features such as past tense, perfect aspect, animate third person pronouns, and present participial clauses. Arabic equivalents of some of these primary markers of narration are highly prominent in these two clusters (see Table 10.6).

According to Biber et al. (1999: 371), narrative texts possess a verbal style (more occurrences of verbs). Biber (1988: 109) states that narrative English texts depend heavily on the past tense, as narration involves relating a series of events in the past. Likewise, the past tense in Arabic expresses completed states or actions in anterior time (Ryding 2005: 435), and hence is also prominently associated with the function of narration.

The simultaneous prominence of the present tense in these clusters is initially surprising. However, investigating some random concordance lines from both clusters

Table 10.6 Prominent linguistic features in clusters 6 and 7

Cluster 6		Cluster 7	
Features	Percentage of texts in upper quartile	Features	Percentage of texts in upper quartile
Pronouns	57	Pronouns	55
Past tense	50	Past tense	68
Present tense	100	Present tense	58
Prepositions	50		
Conjunctions	22	Conjunctions	39

shows that they occur in direct speech, or more commonly, they are part of compound verbs, for instance *mundu qalīl* ***kān y'batu*** *hunā*, 'He **was playing around** a while ago' (CCA: S08). Compound verbs, according to Ryding (2005: 446), are tenses 'that consist of the verb *kāna* plus a main verb', that is, they are what we might more generally call complex tense-aspect constructions. Auxiliary *kāna*, '(s/he) was', with the present tense of the main verb, is used 'to express a concept of an action that took place in the past, but extended or endured over a period of time . . .' (Ryding 2005: 447), that is, past tense plus durative or progressive aspect. This structure is often used in Arabic with verbs of cognition, where English would use the simple past tense (Ryding 2005: 447).

Table 10.6 also shows that pronouns are highly prominent features in these clusters. Pronouns in Arabic have a wide range of roles and traditionally are described as being used for emphasis (Eid 1983: 287). However, in a wider sense, pronouns are used in conversation to refer to participants/characters involved in a specific situation establishing an interactive, involved discourse. Without distinguishing third person and first/second person pronouns, however, there is a risk of inadequately distinguishing the narrative function and the function of interactive/involved discourse, respectively.

Another highly prominent feature in both clusters 6 and 7 is conjunctions. According to Ryding (2005: 407), conjunctions and other connectives are highly frequent in Arabic writing (more so than in English writing), and the role of these elements in structuring written narratives in Arabic is a common topic of study. In light of this, it is interesting to see that these elements – while of course frequent everywhere – are especially prominent in these narrative clusters in our analysis.

A linguistic feature which is highly prominent in cluster 6 but less prominent in cluster 7 is prepositions. A clear explanation of this difference awaits a more detailed analysis.

7.1.2 External features

Cluster 6 has 14 members; 9 (64 per cent) are fiction, as illustrated in Table 10.7. Cluster 7 has 31 members, 24 (78 per cent) of which are fiction.

Fictional prose is generally defined in the first place as having a narrative function. So it seems superfluous to investigate individual fiction texts to identify the functions they share. We see that the genre of Autobiography is strongly associated with fiction

Table 10.7 Genre classification in clusters 6 and 7

Cluster 6		Cluster 7	
Genre classification	Number of texts	Genre classification	Number of texts
AUT: Autobiography	2	Sc: Science	6
CH: Children stories	5	CH: Children stories	12
S: Short stories	4	S: Short stories	12
Int: Interviews	3	Ent: Entertainment	1
		Re: Religion	1

in terms of the linguistic features. Indeed, autobiography may only be distinguishable from fiction on the language-external basis of the story's truth or falsehood.

Interestingly, a number of science texts appear in cluster 7. These particular texts seem to be ones that incorporate the function of reporting sequential events. For instance, Sc11 talks about the history of medicine (specifically surgery); the description in this text is chronological.

Given the evidence for narrative reference as reflected in the internal linguistic features of the two clusters, it is not surprising to find spoken texts, that is, interviews, in cluster 6. As noted above, ideally we would make a more detailed distinction between third person pronouns and first/second person pronouns; doing so might provide a basis for spoken interviews to cluster more clearly apart from typical narratives.

In sum, clusters 6 and 7 clearly represent a specific type of text, that is, narration, albeit with some potential admixture of involved/interactive discourse. Although texts from other genres (not just fiction) appear in these two clusters, the majority seem to have a specific function, namely, telling a story with sequential events. This ties together very well with the highly prominent internal features – associated with the narrative function – noted above. Thus, we consider these two clusters to constitute the text-type of *narration*.

7.2 Exposition

Clusters 5 and 8 are close neighbours in the dendrogram. Most of the texts in both clusters are drawn from the CCA genres of Economics, and Tourist and Travel; both share highly prominent linguistic features reflecting an informational focus.

7.2.1 Internal features

The highly prominent linguistic features in clusters 5 and 8 express informational density (see Table 10.8).

Features such as nouns, relative clauses, and adjectives are all highly prominent in the two clusters. Those features, according to Biber (1988: 105) and Gumperz et al. (1984: 4), express informational and elaborated discourse. Rayson et al.

Table 10.8 Prominent features in clusters 5 and 8

Cluster 5		Cluster 8	
Features	Percentage of texts in upper quartile	Features	Percentage of texts in upper quartile
Nouns	88	Nouns	63
Relative clauses	39	Relative clauses	36
Adjectives	65	Adjectives	100
Passives	20	Adverbs	26
		Conjunctions	26

(2002) concur. That more informationally dense text should rely more on nouns is the kind of trend that we should anticipate holding constant across languages, since the very nature of the noun category is that it carries the lion's share of the information.

In Ec25, we can notice the density of nominal forms:

(1) wa-yasʿā almaǧlis ʾilā taʿzīz qudarātih ʿalā tawfīr ʾaḥdaṯ almaʿlūmāt alʾistiṯmāriyyah ad-daqīqah ʿan almamlakah alʿarabiyyah as-saʿudiyyah wa-alwilāyāt almuttaḥidah alʾamrīkiyyah
'And the council seeks to strengthen its capability to provide the most updated, accurate investment information about the Kingdom of Saudi Arabia and the United States of America'

Example (1) has six nominal forms: *almaǧlis* (the council), *qudarātih* (its capabilities), *tawfīr* (providing), *almaʿlūmāt* (information), *almamlakah* (the kingdom), and *alwilāyāt* (the States), while having one verb only, namely, *yasʿā* (seeks).

Other highly prominent features that clusters 5 and 8 share are adjectives and relative clauses. According to Ryding (2005: 322), in Arabic 'relative pronouns relate an element in a subordinate relative clause . . . to a noun or noun phrase in the main clause of a sentence', and hence can be considered as a technique of idea integration, which enhances informational density. Henry and Roseberry (1997: 492) state that relative clauses play an essential role in the move of expansion in expository writing. Temperley (2003: 482) also states that relative pronouns are commonly used to add elaboration and avoid ambiguity. Adjectives play a similar role to relative clauses in texts, that is, integration of ideas; thus, they too reflect informational density. Adjectives in Arabic are traditionally considered to be subclasses of nouns (Abboud et al. 1997: 67; Hobi 2011: 269), and in this light the extent to which the information-density functions of nouns and adjectives are actually separable phenomena may not be great.

Conjunctions are moderately prominent in cluster 8 but less prominent in cluster 5; they may thus also be a feature of idea expansion.

In Pol06, four conjunctions are used to expand the idea:

(2) **wa-**ʾaḍāfa ʾanna ʿalā alraʾīs alʿirāqī « ʾ**ammā** ʾan yuġayyir ṭarīqat wuǧūdih ʾ**aw** mawḍiʿih ». **wa-**ʾakkada bāwtšar ʾanna . . .
'**And** he added that the Iraqi President **either** has to change the way he exists **or** change his position. **And** Baucher also emphasised that . . .'

Numerous similar examples may be found in the concordance.

It is worth mentioning that the term *idea expansion* seems to be a wide cover term. In the Pol06 example, **wa-** seems to be used to indicate a sequence of additions (clausal coordination), whereas ʾ**ammā**/ʾ**aw** is a list of options, which is also covered by the term *idea expansion*.

Cluster 5 differs slightly from cluster 8 as it is moderately abstract in style, evidenced by the moderate prominence of the passive in cluster 5.

7.2.2 External features

Most texts in clusters 5 and 8 belong to the CCA genres of Tourist and Travel, and Economics (see Table 10.9); there are also some from Science and Politics in cluster 5, which seems to reflect (or cause) the abstractness in this text-type, noted above.

Examining the Tourist and Travel texts reveals that most provide information on services available for travellers. For instance, text To57 describes a new lost-luggage-tracking service available to travellers on Saudi Airline. Similarly, To35 is an announcement from a large construction company in the Middle East of its intention to build the highest tower in the world in Dubai.

Of the many texts from the Economics genre in these clusters, interestingly, the majority *also* include an announcement and description of some new service in the field of finance or economics. For instance, Ec1 is an announcement by Samba Bank, a leading bank in Saudi Arabia, of the launch of a new secured e-commerce service for its clients. Other examples are Ec22, Ec25, Ec5, and Ec14.

In sum, the texts in clusters 5 and 8 are highly similar in function and content. Genre-wise, they are predominantly announcements/descriptions of commercial ventures or services. The functions prominent in these texts are reflected by the prominent linguistic features of elaboration and integration, including nouns, relative clauses, adjectives, and conjunctions, all features whose frequency rises to reflect informational density and elaboration. Given the informational density features shared by these clusters, this text-type invites the provisional label of *exposition.*

7.3 Scientific exposition

Clusters 2 and 4 are neighbours in the dendrogram; their highly prominent linguistic features are largely similar (reflecting detached style plus informational focus). However, it is hard to identify shared external features in terms of genre between

Table 10.9 Genre classification in clusters 5 and 8

Cluster 5		Cluster 8	
Genre classification	Number of texts	Genre classification	Number of texts
Ec: Economics	15	Ec: Economics	4
AUT: Autobiography	2	Edu: Education	2
Edu: Education	2	HM: Health and Medicine	1
HM: Health and Medicine	2	Int: Interviews	1
Int: Interviews	2	Soc: Sociology	2
Pol: Politics	5	To: Tourist and Travel	9
Sc: Science	3		
Soc: Sociology	3		
Spo: Sports	3		
To: Tourist and Travel	38		

clusters 2 and 4. For this reason the label for this text-type is based solely on highly prominent features of these two clusters: *scientific exposition*.

7.3.1 Internal features

The highly prominent linguistic features in clusters 2 and 4 mainly reflect a detached, formal style (the passive) with informational focus (prepositions, relative clauses, and conjunctions) (see Table 10.10).

The passive, according to Biber (1988: 228), conveys highly abstract information as the agent in passive constructions is normally demoted or omitted. This generates a detachment between the events as described and the (presumably human) agents responsible. As in English, the passive in Arabic is used to put the patient of the action into subject (i.e. topic) position in the clause, while the agent is normally omitted, whether because it is unknown, or because it need not be mentioned. Ryding (2005: 659) notes that 'if the agent is to be mentioned, the passive is not normally used; the active verb is then the preferred option'; a preference for passives without agents over passives with agents has been noted in many languages.

The two clusters also share similar prominent features of information density and elaboration, which have been discussed earlier. These include relative clauses, adjectives, and conjunctions. Prepositions and adverbs are also highly prominent features in clusters 2 and 4. As markers of spatio-temporal (and other) relations between entities, a high frequency of prepositions, like a high frequency of relative clauses, is a clue that more information is being packed into the noun phrases of the text.

Another prominent feature in both clusters is pronouns. In this context it is worth noting that the majority of texts in cluster 2 are autobiographies (see further below), and thus the prominence of the first person is not unexpected.

A clear difference between the two clusters is the verb tense; in cluster 2 the past tense is moderately prominent, whereas in cluster 4 the present tense is highly

Table 10.10 Prominent linguistic features in clusters 2 and 4

Cluster 2		Cluster 4	
Features	Percentage of texts in upper quartile	Features	Percentage of texts in upper quartile
Prepositions	35	Prepositions	33
Passive	40	Passive	36
Pronouns	28	Pronouns	21
Relative clauses	37	Relative clauses	32
Past tense	26	Present tense	46
Adjectives	21	Adjectives	22
Conjunctions	28	Conjunctions	46
Adverbs	38	Adverbs	27
		Nouns	19

prominent. This difference between the two clusters may arise from differences in the two clusters' external features.

7.3.2 External features

Table 10.11 shows that on the one hand, the most dominant genres in cluster 2 are Autobiography, Science, and Sociology. On the other hand, the most dominant genres in cluster 4 are Health and Medicine, and Sociology. It is not entirely clear what external features these genres might share that bring them together. It is also not clear how the autobiographies in question are different from those found in the narrative text-type and discussed earlier. Given the data at hand, it is hard to arrive at answers by manual examination of text, given the very large number of documents involved, but resolving this point must be a clear priority for future research.

In sum, Clusters 2 and 4 share linguistic features expressing detached style and informational focus. The main difference between the two clusters is the contrast in prominent verb tense, which could be related to the genres which are dominant in each of these clusters. However, the genre mix of these two clusters is particularly difficult to interpret. Since it is difficult to identify the link between text-internal and text-external features here, the overall label for this text-type is given based on the highly prominent features only. As the two clusters share highly prominent features of detached, formal style which may reflect academic (scientific) writing, and others reflecting informational focus, we therefore apply the label *scientific exposition*. This is, however, only a preliminary analysis, suggested in part by the parallel English text-type identified by Mohamed (2011).

Table 10.11 Genre classification in clusters 2 and 4

Cluster 2		Cluster 4	
Genre classification	Number of texts	Genre classification	Number of texts
AUT: Autobiography	39	AUT: Autobiography	4
Sc: Science	22	Sc: Science	7
S: Short stories	1	S: Short stories	5
Int: Interviews	8	Int: Interviews	3
Soc: Sociology	14	Soc: Sociology	10
Ec: Economy	7	Ec: Economy	3
Edu: Education	4	Edu: Education	4
HM: Health and Medicine	3	HM: Health and Medicine	25
Pol: Politics	4	Pol: Politics	1
Re: Religion	7	Re: Religion	5
To: Tourist and Travel	7	To: Tourist and Travel	6
Spo: Sports	1	Spo: Sports	1
		Rec: Recipes	8

7.4 Other clusters

7.4.1 Cluster 1

Internal features
Cluster 1 merges with all the other clusters at a very great height, indicating that its texts are linguistically very distinct from all others. The only moderately prominent feature in cluster 1 is the past tense (see Table 10.12).

External features
The genre mix in cluster 1 is not amenable to easy interpretation. The most dominant genres are Science and Short stories (see Table 10.13); but it is not entirely clear what brings texts from these two rather disparate genres together in one type.

7.4.2 Cluster 3

Internal features
Cluster 3 merges higher up in the dendrogram with the clusters of *exposition* and of *scientific exposition*. Cluster 3 seems likely then to represent some other type of expository prose. However, the height of this merge indicates that the text-type must also be clearly distinct. Table 10.14 shows that the prominent linguistic features in cluster 3 are highly similar to those of *exposition* and *scientific exposition*, except that some

Table 10.12 Prominent linguistic features in cluster 1

	Cluster 1
Features	Percentage of texts in upper quartile
Passive	10
Pronouns	5
Relative clauses	10
Past tense	29
Adverbs	10

Table 10.13 Genre classification in cluster 1

	Cluster 1
Genre classification	Number of texts
AUT: Autobiography	3
CHD: Children stories	1
Int: Interviews	3
Sc: Science	8
S: Short stories	6

Table 10.14 Prominent linguistic features in cluster 3

	Cluster 3
Features	Percentage of texts in upper quartile
Prepositions	49
Passive	32
Pronouns	43
Relative clauses	37
Past tense	64
Present tense	34

Table 10.15 Genre classification in cluster 3

	Cluster 3
Genre classification	Number of texts
AUT: Autobiography	23
CHD: Children stories	9
Int: Interviews	3
HM: Health and Medicine	1
S: Short stories	2
Rel: Religion	7
Soc: Sociology	1
Spo: Sports	1

features which are highly prominent in cluster 3, past tense and pronouns, are moderately prominent in clusters 2 and 4 (*scientific exposition*).

In general, cluster 3 and the clusters of *scientific exposition* and *exposition* seem to be quite similar text-types based on their highly prominent features. However, the differences between them cannot be established clearly on the basis of the heuristic statistics we use here. It is possible that the differences among the clusters do not affect features for which we find many types in the upper quartile.

External features

The dominant genres in cluster 3 are Autobiography, Children's fiction and Religion (see Table 10.15). As with cluster 1, it is hard to state confidently what external features texts in these genres may have in common.

8. A summary of the analysis: a typology of texts

The analysis of the corpus in this study was initially based on overall similarities in text-internal features followed by an investigation of text-external features to identify major or typical text-types. The interpretation of the clusters showed that some pairs of clusters form quite similar text-types and are close neighbours in the dendrogram.

Table 10.16 A summary of the clusters presented as text-types

Cluster	General text type heading
Cluster 6 Cluster 7	Narration
Cluster 5 Cluster 8	Exposition
Cluster 2 Cluster 4	Scientific exposition

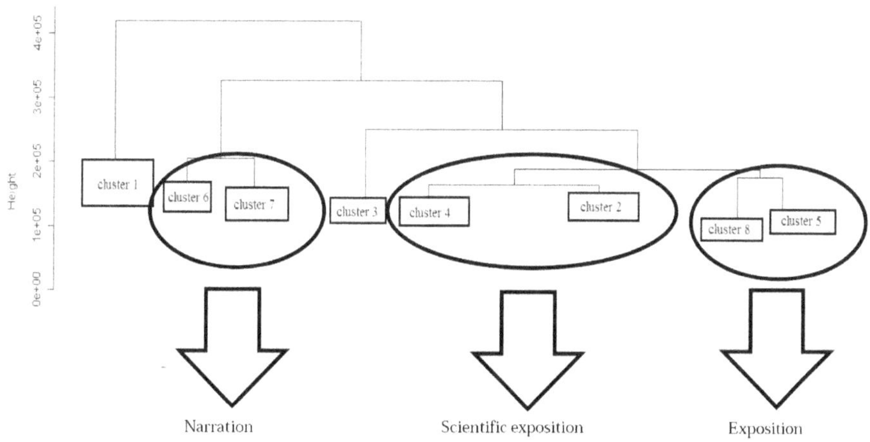

Figure 10.2 A model of text-types

It was thus possible to establish overall labels for these pairs of neighbouring types, reflecting their shared linguistic features. Table 10.16 summarises the clusters analysed in our study with their general text-type heading, while Figure 10.2 shows the model of text-types visually on the dendrogram.

9. Observations

Establishing a typology of texts is a complex process. Our analysis suggests that the clusters that emerged actually represent fuzzy categories, as the same features were critical to the definitions of multiple types. For instance, features of elaboration and integration are highly prominent in *exposition* (clusters 5 and 8), but are not exclusively frequent in this text-type; some of those features are also highly prominent in *scientific exposition*. Thus, text-types should be viewed as prototypical agglomerations of linguistic behaviours, rather than absolutely distinct entities. This conclusion regarding the nature of text-types is in line with previous work on English text typology, for instance Biber (1989) and Mohamed (2011, forthcoming). In addition, our general findings provide, to some extent, a cross-linguistic parallel to these two English text typologies. The three major text-types in this study were also identified by both Biber and Mohamed. Our *narration* type is consistent with Biber's text-type 5 (*imaginative narrative*) and Mohamed's *narration* type, in that all contain a majority of fictional texts and employ similar linguistic features serving the function of narration. Our *scientific exposition* type is similarly consistent with Biber's text-type 3 (*scientific exposition*) and Mohamed's *scientific exposition* type, in that all display a preference for the presentation of information in abstract, decontextualised style. Likewise, the highly prominent linguistic features marking our *exposition* type are similar to the features characterising Biber's text-type 4 and Mohamed's *exposition* type. Thus, the three text-types that emerged in this study seem likely to be stable cross-linguistically, in many languages if not all. Notably, the most prominent linguistic features characterising those three text-types are primarily similar across the two languages. For example, the past tense is a highly prominent feature in narrative texts in both English and Arabic, despite the substantial differences between the two languages' overall verbal conjugation systems. Biber (1988: 109) states that narrative English texts depend heavily on features such as the past tense, as narration involves relating a series of events in the past. Likewise, the past tense in Arabic expresses completed states or actions in anterior time (Ryding 2005: 435), and hence is also prominently associated with the function of narration.

Another cross-linguistic consistency is the clear split between literature and exposition at an upper level of the dendrogram, where general exposition and scientific exposition are much closer to one another than either is to the (generally literary) narrative text-type. This is also a prominent aspect of Mohamed's (2011) English text typology.

10. Conclusion

This study constitutes an initial attempt to develop a typology of Arabic texts based on text-internal features. In our approach, each category of texts that emerges from a cluster analysis based on a list per text of linguistic feature frequencies is then characterised by considering that category's overall similarities in terms of prominent linguistic features. Using the CCA, we extracted frequency data for ten features and applied cluster analysis to identify eight clusters, among which three pairs of clusters appear to form four identifiable text-types. We assigned overall functional labels to these pairs of clusters, reflecting their shared linguistic features: *narration*, *exposition*, and *scientific exposition*. As these text-types were also identified in a parallel study of the BNC (Mohamed 2011), it would seem that at least some major aspects of the 'textual landscape' have cross-linguistic consistency, for written prose in any case.

The limitations of this study are obvious if we consider it in comparison with Mohamed's analysis. For English, Mohamed used a list of 76 lexico-grammatical features, building in large part on Biber's (1988) classic list of 67 features. Here, we were able to define only ten features for Arabic – principally the frequencies of major part-of-speech categories and single-word grammatical phenomena (such as the passive, which in Arabic is inflectional rather than periphrastic as in English). This was in part because of the limited scope of this preliminary study – devising a full, comprehensive feature list is a very substantial undertaking, even without considering the subsequent analysis. However, it was also because, for a first experiment in quantifying the relevant features, we relied on categories directly annotated in the output from the MADA Arabic POS tagging and morphological analysis system. This was partly in the interests of simplicity and partly because, for Arabic, much less prior literature is available from which to draw ideas regarding linguistic features than was available on English for Biber in the 1980s. Traditional Arabic grammatical works focus very heavily on (inflectional and derivational) morphology as opposed to syntax, and thus can furnish only a partial guide here. As we saw in our discussion of *narration*, phenomena such as complex tense-aspect constructions combining auxiliary *kāna* with a main verb emerge as important in the characterisation of text-types even in a preliminary-level analysis. These constructions are obvious candidates to be added to the list of features for a fuller analysis; however, for this to be accomplished, they must be catalogued and classified – no small task. Other possible candidates for inclusion in our envisioned comprehensive Arabic feature set include: pronouns broken down according to person (third vs first/second), number, and gender; encliticised object pronouns; SVO and VSO word orders; frequency of genitive construct; predicative vs attributive adjective use; nominal definiteness; morphological nominalisations of verbal predicates (easily identified in the output of an Arabic morphological analyser); broad semantic categories of verbal predicates; and a more detailed breakdown of markers of interclausal connections according to the precise kind of connection that they indicate. We might also add less obvious but perhaps important features such as recent loan-vocabulary from English (easily identifiable by its script) or the presence of explicit vowel diacritics. The use of a more detailed feature list will have two beneficial effects. First, it will provide a 'toolkit' of much greater discriminatory power for the qualitative analysis of clusters. Many of the points regarding the nature of particular clusters that remain uncertain when we have only ten features in our armoury are likely to find resolution with this improved feature list. Second, and perhaps more centrally, the cluster analysis itself will have greater resolution, and thus produce stronger, more clearly differentiated text clusters, with a more detailed list.

It might be argued that the need to move to an improved feature list to better the work we present here actually undermines the results we have presented – since the three text-types whose existence in Arabic we argue for might disappear the next time the cluster analysis is done. This is of course possible. However, the centrality of considerations of narration and exposition, and of abstract, technical 'scientific' discourse, to nearly all empirical studies to date of text typology – not only their appearance as English text-types in Mohamed (2011) but also their presence among Biber's (1988) functional dimensions – as well as their apparent cross-linguistic stability would suggest that it is unlikely. We eagerly anticipate our preliminary findings on these three Arabic text-types being extended, refined, and improved in future work; we do not expect them to be entirely overturned (albeit it would certainly be *extremely* interesting if they were).

However, despite their preliminary nature, the findings of the present study on their own do represent a plausibly effective attempt to systematise the study of the diversity of Arabic texts by means of automatic classification. Cluster analysis proves to be a powerful tool for structuring this kind of frequency data, if its output is interpreted with care. Quantitative approaches such as the one implemented in our study have been to date largely neglected in Arabic text linguistics, and it is thus our hope that this initial exploration of Arabic text typology through cluster analysis will point the way to a substantive advance in the field.

Notes

1. We take no position on whether the primary contrast in the Arabic verbal system is one of tense or one of aspect, and use the terms *past tense* and *present tense* as labels of convenience only.
2. For details on the search syntax, see <http://cwb.sourceforge.net/documentation.php> (last accessed 25 May 2018).

References

Abboud, P., A. Attieh, E. McCarus and R. Rammuny (1997), *Intermediate Modern Standard Arabic*, Ann Arbor, MI: Center for Middle Eastern and North African Studies.

Adamson, G. W. and D. Bawden (1981), 'Comparison of hierarchical cluster analysis techniques for automatic classification of chemical structures', *Journal of Chemical Information and Computer Sciences*, 21: 204–9.

Aldenderfer, M. S. and R. K. Blashfield (1984), *Cluster Analysis*, Beverly Hills, CA: Sage.

Al-Sulaiti, L. and E. Atwell (2006), 'The design of a corpus of contemporary Arabic', *International Journal of Corpus Linguistics*, 11(1): 1–36.

Atwell, E., L. Al-Sulaiti, S. Al-Osaimi and B. Abu-Shawar (2004), 'A review of corpus analysis tools', in *Proceedings of TALN '04*, University of Mohamed bin Abdullah, Fez, Morocco, pp. 229–34, <https://www.researchgate.net/publication/268522847_A_review_of_Arabic_corpus_analysis_tools_-_Un_Examen_d'Outils_pour_l'Analyse_de_Corpus_Arabes> (last accessed 29 June 2018).

Baayen, H. (2008), *Analyzing Linguistic Data: A Practical Introduction to Statistics Using R*, Cambridge: Cambridge University Press.

Biber, D. (1988), *Variation Across Speech and Writing*, Cambridge: Cambridge University Press.

Biber, D. (1989), 'A typology of English texts', *Linguistics*, 27(1): 3–43.

Biber, D. (1995), *Dimensions of Register Variation: A Cross-Linguistic Comparison*, Cambridge: Cambridge University Press.

Biber, D. and S. Conrad (2009), *Register, Genre, and Style*, Cambridge: Cambridge University Press.

Biber, D., S. Johansson, G. Leech, S. Conrad and E. Finegan (1999), *Longman Grammar of Spoken and Written English*, London: Longman.

Buckwalter, T. (2004), *Buckwalter Arabic Morphological Analyzer Version 2.0*, LDC catalog no.: LDC2004L02, Philadelphia: University of Pennsylvania, Linguistic Data Consortium.

Costa, I. G., F. A. T. de Carvalho and M. C. P. de Souto (2003), 'Comparative study on proximity indices for cluster analysis of gene expression time', *Journal of Intelligent and Fuzzy Systems*, 13(2–4): 133–42.

Crawley, M. J. (2007), *The R Book*, New York: John Wiley.

de Beaugrande, R. (2000), 'Text linguistics at the millennium: Corpus data and missing links', *Text*, 20(2): 153–95.

de Beaugrande, R. and W. Dressler (1981), *Introduction to Text Linguistics*, Austin, TX: University of Texas Press.

Eid, M. (1983), 'On the communicative function of subject pronouns in Arabic', *Journal of Linguistics*, 19(2): 287–303.

Everitt, B. S. (1993), *Cluster Analysis*, 3rd edn, London: Edward Arnold.

Evert, S. and A. Hardie (2011), 'Twenty-first century Corpus Workbench: Updating a query architecture for the new millennium', in *Proceedings of the Corpus Linguistics 2011 Conference*, University of Birmingham, <http://www.birmingham.ac.uk/documents/college-artslaw/corpus/conference-archives/2011/Paper-153.pdf> (last accessed 29 June 2018).

Faith, D. P., P. R. Minchin and L. Belbin (1987), 'Compositional dissimilarity as a robust measure of ecological distance', *Vegetatio*, 69(1–3): 57–68.

Fowlkes, E. B. and C. L. Mallows (1983), 'A method for comparing two hierarchical clusterings', *Journal of American Statistical Association*, 78: 553–69.

Gully, A. (1996), 'The discourse of Arabic advertising: Preliminary investigations', *Journal of Arabic and Islamic Studies*, 1: 1–49.

Gumperz, J., H. Kaltman and M. O'Connor (1984), 'Cohesion in spoken and written discourse', in D. Tannen (ed.), *Coherence in Spoken and Written Discourse*, Norwood, NJ: Albex, pp. 3–20.

Habash, N. and O. Rambow (2005), 'Arabic tokenization, part-of-speech tagging and morphological disambiguation in one fell swoop', in K. Knight (ed.), *Proceedings of the 43rd Annual Meeting of the ACL*, Ann Arbor, June 2005, pp. 573–80.

Hatim, B. and I. Mason (1990), *Discourse and the Translator*, New York: Longman.

Henry, A. and R. L. Roseberry (1997), 'An investigation of the functions, strategies and linguistic features of the introductions and conclusions of essays', *System*, 25(4): 479–95.

Hobi, E. (2011), 'A contrastive study of attributive adjectives in English and Arabic', *mağalat kulliyat almaʾmūn alğāmiʿah*, 17: 264–74.

Kinneavy, J. (1971), *A Theory of Discourse*, Toronto: Prentice-Hall.

Mohamed, A. and M. Omer (2000), 'Texture and culture: Cohesion as a marker of rhetorical organisation in Arabic and English narrative texts', *RELC Journal*, 31(2): 45–75.

Mohamed, G. (2011), 'Text Classification in the BNC Using Corpus and Statistical Methods', unpublished PhD thesis, Lancaster University.

Mohamed, G. (forthcoming), *Text Typology in the British National Corpus (BNC)*.

Norušis, M. (1996), *SPSS 17.0 Guide to Data Analysis*, Harlow: Pearson.

Rayson, P., A. Wilson and G. Leech (2002), 'Grammatical word class variation within the British National Corpus sampler', in P. Peters, P. Collin and A. Smith (eds), *New Frontiers of Corpus Research: Papers from the Twenty First International Conference on English Language Research on Computerised Corpora, Sydney 2000*, Amsterdam: Rodopi, pp. 295–336.

Romesburg, H. C. (1984), *Cluster Analysis for Researchers*, Belmont, CA: Wadsworth.

Ryding, K. (2005), *A Reference Grammar of Modern Standard Arabic*, Cambridge: Cambridge University Press.

Sharoff, S. (2004), 'Towards basic categories for describing properties of texts in a corpus', in M. T. Lino, M. F. Xavier, F. Ferreira, R. Costa, R. Silva, C. Pereira, F. Carvalho, M. Lopes, M. Catarino and S. Barros (eds), *Proceedings of LREC 2004*, Paris: ELRA, vol. V, pp. 1743–6.

Somekh, S. (1991), *Genre and Language in Modern Arabic Literature*, Wiesbaden: Harrasowitz.

Temperley, D. (2003), 'Ambiguity avoidance in English relative clauses', *Language*, 79(3): 464–84.

Werlich, E. (1982), *A Text Grammar of English*, Heidelberg: Quelle und Meyer.

Appendix
Arabic Transliteration Systems Used in This Book

As explained in Chapter 1, the main Arabic transliteration system used in this book is the standardised DIN 31635, but for certain specialised purposes, the computer-oriented Buckwalter transliteration is used instead. This appendix gives (1) a parallel table of the two systems, listed along with (and in order of) the Unicode representations of the Arabic letters they transliterate; and (2) a short list of additional notes and exceptions that apply in DIN 31635 (the Buckwalter system has no such exceptions, being a direct one-to-one representation in ASCII of the original sequence of Arabic characters).

Not included here are letters used only for languages other than Arabic (e.g. Persian, Urdu), or the Arabic punctuation marks and numerals, whose relationship to the equivalent Latin punctuation and numerals is straightforward.

Readers unfamiliar with Arabic script should note that any given character can have multiple graphical forms depending on whether it is initial, medial, or final within a word. The list that follows uses the form taken by each character when it appears independently.

List of Arabic characters with Buckwalter and DIN 31635 equivalents

<table>
<tr><th>Unicode</th><th>Arabic character</th><th>Buckwalter</th><th>DIN 31635</th></tr>
<tr><td>U+0621</td><td>ء</td><td>'</td><td>ʾ</td></tr>
<tr><td>U+0622</td><td>آ</td><td>|</td><td>ʾā</td></tr>
<tr><td>U+0623</td><td>أ</td><td>></td><td rowspan="4">ʾ</td></tr>
<tr><td>U+0624</td><td>ؤ</td><td>&</td></tr>
<tr><td>U+0625</td><td>إ</td><td><</td></tr>
<tr><td>U+0626</td><td>ئ</td><td>}</td></tr>
</table>

Unicode	Arabic character	Buckwalter	DIN 31635
U+0627	ا	A	ā
U+0628	ب	b	b
U+0629	ة	p	h, t
U+062A	ت	t	t
U+062B	ث	v	ṯ
U+062C	ج	j	ǧ
U+062D	ح	H	ḥ
U+062E	خ	x	ḫ
U+062F	د	d	d
U+0630	ذ	*	ḏ
U+0631	ر	r	r
U+0632	ز	z	z
U+0633	س	s	s
U+0634	ش	$	š
U+0635	ص	S	ṣ
U+0636	ض	D	ḍ
U+0637	ط	T	ṭ
U+0638	ظ	Z	ẓ
U+0639	ع	E	ʿ
U+063A	غ	g	ġ
U+0641	ف	f	f
U+0642	ق	q	q
U+0643	ك	k	k
U+0644	ل	l	l
U+0645	م	m	m
U+0646	ن	n	n
U+0647	ه	h	h
U+0648	و	w	w, ū
U+0649	ى	Y	ā

Unicode	Arabic character	Buckwalter	DIN 31635
U+064A	ي	y	y, ī
U+064B	ً	F	an
U+064C	ٌ	N	un
U+064D	ٍ	K	in
U+064E	َ	a	a
U+064F	ُ	u	u
U+0650	ِ	i	i
U+0651	ّ	~	*n/a*
U+0652	ْ	o	*n/a*
U+0670	ٰ	`	ā
U+0671	ٱ	{	’

Notes and exceptions for DIN 31635

- Characters U+0651 and U+0652 are not directly represented. The former (a diacritic indicating consonant gemination) is transliterated by doubling of the consonant letter that it modifies. The latter (a diacritic indicating that no short vowel follows a consonant) is implied by the absence of any short vowel at the corresponding point in the word.
- In some cases, an orthographic letter which is phonologically redundant is omitted. Examples: (1) where a long /aː/ is indicated by a sequence of two characters which would *both* be transliterated as <ā> (e.g. U+0649 and U+0670), the <ā> is given once rather than twice; (2) where the presence of an (unwritten) initial short vowel at the beginning of a word is indicated by use of the letter *ʾālif*, character U+0627, the short vowel is written and the usual transliteration of *ʾālif*, which is <ā>, is omitted.
- The /l/ consonant of the Arabic definite prefix, *al-*, assimilates to a following coronal consonant (other than /dʒ/); the letters that represent such consonants are traditionally called *sun letters*, as opposed to all other *moon letter* consonants. This assimilation is, however, not reflected in the Arabic writing system, which always writes the definite prefix with U+0644, nor, thus, in the Buckwalter transliteration; but in DIN 31635 the <l> is replaced by the consonant to which it has assimilated.
- The definite prefix is joined to the base it modifies by a hyphen in DIN 31635; this hyphen does not correspond to anything in the original Arabic script. Other morpheme boundaries may be, but are not always, shown via hyphens as well.

Index

aConCorde, 105, 110
Alkulil Morpho Sys, 97
American English, 34, 35, 36, 105
annotation
  annotator/annotators, 11, 78, 79, 82, 85, 88, 89, 91, 92, 97, 102, 109
  discourse, 11, 76, 77, 78, 89, 92
  error, 107
  morphological, 76, 108
  morphosyntactic, 11, 56, 60, 108
  online, 108
  phonetic, 108
  prosodic, 108
  syntactic, 11, 12, 108
  treebank, 65
Arabic grammar and morphology
  accusative, 3, 4, 9, 61, 68, 198
  adjective/s, 22, 23, 44, 48, 58, 59, 60, 62, 64, 65, 68, 82, 178, 198, 203, 207, 216, 217, 218, 219, 225
  adverb/s, 23, 64, 65, 68, 84, 198, 203, 207, 216, 219, 221
  adverbial/s, 77, 78, 80, 94, 96, 124, 144, 163, 175, 176, 189, 197, 203
  affix/es, 3, 4, 48, 49, 59, 61, 62, 64, 68, 69
  apodosis, 12, 143, 144, 146, 147, 148, 149, 150, 152, 153, 154, 157, 159, 161, 164, 165, 166
  argument/s, 11, 76, 77, 78, 80, 81, 82, 83, 84, 86, 97, 89, 91, 92, 125
  auxiliary verb/s, 11, 57, 61, 67, 69, 70, 152, 153, 198, 203, 215, 225
  circumfix, 36
  clitics, 3, 58, 59, 61, 62, 64, 69, 70, 71, 80
conjunction/s, 3, 21, 23, 44, 59, 65, 68, 70, 71, 77, 78, 79, 80, 82, 84, 85, 88, 90, 93, 96, 156, 166, 198, 203, 207, 214, 215, 216, 217, 218, 219
connective/s, 11, 57, 61, 67, 69, 70, 152, 153, 198, 203, 215, 225
coordination, 77, 78, 93, 156, 203, 217
definiteness, 3, 58, 61, 65, 68, 225
discourse connectives, 11, 76, 77–92, 93, 94, 95, 96, 107, 111
frame/s, 13, 170, 177, 184–97
genitive/s, 3, 4, 53, 58, 59, 61, 125, 198, 225
grammarians, 8, 9, 31, 57, 107, 120, 122, 125
grammars, 2, 6, 8, 12, 32, 80, 143, 144, 146, 147, 148, 150, 158, 163, 167, 213
imperfect/imperfective, 23, 27, 53, 58, 60, 61, 69, 146, 147, 149, 159, 164, 165, 166, 175, 176, 178, 181, 184, 198
infix, 3, 155
inflection, 3, 36, 44, 46, 48, 49, 60, 61, 62, 63, 65, 67, 68, 69, 70, 170, 173, 174, 75, 178, 181, 184, 185, 224, 225
interrogative, 42, 53, 68, 144, 175
intransitive, 129, 174
mood, 3, 58, 61, 62, 63, 64, 69, 174, 175, 176, 178, 180, 181, 182, 183, 184, 185
morpheme/s, 3, 53, 59, 60, 61, 62, 66, 70, 71, 78, 170, 213
morphosyntax, 11, 13, 56, 57, 58, 60, 62, 64, 65, 67, 179, 172, 174, 184, 196, 197
negation, 36, 44, 149, 150, 198, 203
noun/s, 3, 18, 20, 21, 22, 23, 44, 46, 48,

49, 57, 58, 59, 60, 61, 62, 64, 65, 68, 70, 71, 80, 81, 82, 93, 84, 92, 93, 94, 95, 97, 121, 125, 132, 137, 144, 187, 198, 203, 206, 207, 212, 216, 217, 218, 219
object, 70, 71, 77, 78, 80, 87, 90, 130, 131, 132, 137, 138, 174, 175, 186, 191, 192, 195, 196, 201, 203
particle/s, 3, 23, 53, 57, 58, 60, 65, 68, 71, 95, 144, 147, 148, 149, 155, 156, 163, 164, 198, 203
plural, 53, 60, 68, 70, 175, 176, 184, 185, 198
prefixes, 3, 23, 44, 45, 46, 49, 59, 60, 61, 69, 70, 71, 144, 145, 156, 159, 231
preposition/s, 3, 12, 21, 23, 44, 64, 70, 71, 80, 84, 94, 95, 96, 120–5, 126, 127–39, 140, 141, 203, 207, 214, 215, 219, 222
proclitics, 3, 71
pronoun/s, 3, 9, 21, 23, 36, 42, 44, 50, 60, 62, 70, 71, 80, 82, 94, 95, 109, 111, 132, 137, 141, 160, 181, 198, 203, 206, 207, 214, 215–19, 221, 222, 225
protasis, 12, 144, 146, 148, 149, 150, 154, 164, 165, 166
root, 3, 4, 6, 8, 48, 49, 57, 61, 67, 71, 83, 84, 110, 122, 192
subcategory/ies, 3, 59, 60, 62, 65, 67, 68, 69, 70
subordination, 70, 77, 78, 79, 80, 93, 96, 148, 197, 203, 217
suffixes, 3, 4, 23, 44, 45, 46, 48, 59, 60, 61, 69, 84
tense, 3, 12, 14, 20, 21, 46, 49, 56, 58, 59, 61, 64, 69, 70, 83, 145, 149, 156, 163, 164, 165, 171, 174, 175, 176, 177, 178, 180, 181, 182, 183, 184, 185, 196, 203, 207, 214, 215, 219, 220, 221, 222, 224, 225, 226
transitive, 128, 129, 130, 138, 174, 191, 192, 196
verb/s, 3, 12, 13, 14, 18, 20, 21, 22, 23, 27, 36, 44, 46, 49, 50, 57, 58, 59, 60, 61, 62, 64, 65, 67–71, 73, 80, 84, 94, 120, 121–5, 126–41, 144–7, 147–50, 152–63, 163–6, 170–3, 173–94, 195–8, 203, 207, 214, 215, 217, 219, 220, 221, 224, 225, 226
Arabic sound system
consonant/s, 3, 4, 5, 36, 41, 57, 61, 84, 230, 231
pronunciation, 4, 34, 108, 110
prosody, 108
vowel/s, 3, 4, 5, 21, 23, 36, 41, 42, 45, 57, 59, 64, 68, 70, 71, 84, 105, 225, 230, 231
Arabic varieties
Algerian, 32
Cairene, 35, 36
Classical, 2, 3, 4, 12, 14, 31, 61, 62, 76, 100, 102, 103, 104, 108, 109, 110, 111, 143–7, 148, 149, 152, 154, 158, 164, 204
Colloquial, 2, 3, 4, 10, 18, 68, 164
Egyptian, 2, 18, 30, 32, 34, 35, 36, 37, 164, 166, 174
Iraqi, 35, 36, 37
Lebanese, 35, 40
Levantine, 37
Modern Standard (MSA), 2, 4, 11, 12, 13, 18, 30, 34, 35, 36, 37, 38, 39, 43, 61, 68, 73, 79, 81, 96, 100, 103, 104, 107, 108, 143, 148, 149, 150, 163, 164, 170, 171, 172, 173, 174, 177, 181, 184, 185, 195, 196, 197, 207, 213
Moroccan, 32, 35, 36, 41
Tunisian, 10, 30, 32, 35, 36, 37, 39, 40, 41, 42, 45, 46, 52, 53
vernacular, 32, 36, 37, 39, 53, 148
Arabic writing system
diacritic/s, 4, 5, 59, 70, 84, 225, 230
spelling, 34, 42–3, 49, 50, 52, 105, 107
writing, 3, 4, 8, 38, 42, 215, 231
artificial intelligence (AI), 12, 100, 101–2, 104, 111, 112

Biber, Douglas, 7, 13, 181, 184, 202–6, 210, 213, 214, 216, 219, 223–5
BootCaT, 41, 102, 106
Buckwalter Arabic Morphological Analyser (BAMA), 5, 11, 44, 58, 59, 63, 64, 67, 68, 69, 71, 79, 206

clustering
agglomerative, 13, 172, 178, 179, 208
dendrogram, 179, 187, 209, 210, 211, 213, 214, 216, 218, 221, 222, 223, 224
hierarchical, 172, 177, 178, 179, 180, 195, 209
collocation, 7, 25, 26, 28, 48, 50, 102, 106, 110, 120, 126, 139, 140, 177
computational linguistics, 1, 5, 42, 57, 63, 76, 77, 79, 102, 111
concordancing, 5, 6, 7, 12, 24, 33, 50, 51, 52, 66, 102, 105, 106, 110, 111, 121, 126, 127, 128, 129, 130, 131, 132, 133, 135, 139, 140, 172, 174, 175, 213, 214, 217
connotation, 121, 122, 123, 128, 130

construction/s, 10, 11, 12, 13, 69, 76, 97, 120–1, 124, 126, 127, 130, 132, 135, 137, 138, 140, 145, 152, 154, 170–3, 173, 174, 177, 181, 184, 185, 190–2, 194, 195–7, 215, 218, 219, 225
corpora
  arabiCorpus, 10, 18–22, 28, 103, 121, 126, 127, 131, 132, 133, 135, 173, 174, 197
  Arabic Gigaword Corpus, 33
  Arabic Internet Corpus, 102, 106, 107, 111
  Arabic Learner Corpus (ALC), 107, 111
  Arabic Treebank, 76
  Babylon Levantine Arabic Speech and Transcripts, 37
  Boundary Annotated Qur'an Corpus, 108
  British National Corpus (BNC), 18, 65, 71, 73, 106, 110, 204, 205, 224
  Brown Corpus, 104
  CALLFRIEND Egyptian Arabic Corpus, 37
  CALLHOME Egyptian Arabic Speech Corpus, 37
  Chinese Treebank, 79
  Collins COBUILD Corpus, 126, 129, 130, 141
  Columbia Arabic Treebank (CATiB), 64, 65
  Dark Web Terrorism Corpus, 103
  Fisher Levantine Arabic Conversational Telephony Speech Corpus, 37
  Gulf Arabic Conversational Telephone Speech Corpus, 37
  Hindi Discourse Relation Treebank, 79
  International Corpus of Arabic (ICA), 33
  Iraqi Arabic Conversational Telephone Speech Corpus, 37
  King Saud University Corpus of Classical Arabic (KSUCCA), 76, 110, 111
  Lancaster-Oslo-Bergen (LOB) Corpus, 104, 105, 106, 202, 205
  Leeds Arabic Discourse Treebank (LDATB), 11, 72, 76, 77, 78, 79, 81, 82, 85, 86, 89, 91, 92, 93, 94, 95, 97, 107, 111
  Leeds Corpus of Contemporary Arabic (CCA), 12, 13, 102, 104–5, 111, 204, 205, 206, 208, 212, 213, 215, 216, 218, 224
  Levantine Arabic Conversational Telephone Speech Corpus, 37
  Levantine Arabic QT Training Data Set, 37
  Oxford University Press Arabic Corpus, 44–5
  Penn Arabic Treebank (ATB), 44, 59, 64, 65, 79, 80, 92, 93, 94, 95, 96
  Penn Discourse Treebank (PDTB/PDTB2), 78, 79, 80, 82, 85, 87, 92, 97
  Prague Arabic Dependency Treebank, 65
  QurAna, 109
  Qur'anic Arabic Corpus, 12, 62, 65, 102, 103, 108–9, 112, 126, 129, 132, 134, 136, 137, 139, 141
  Qurany, 110
  QurSim, 109
  Tunisian Arabic Corpus (TAC), 10, 37–53
  Turkish Discourse Bank, 79
  Verbal Autopsy Corpus, 101
  World Wide Arabic Corpus, 106, 111
  World Wide English Corpus, 106
Corpus Query Processor Language (CQP), 72, 207
Corpus Work Bench (CWB), 66, 67, 71, 207
Correlation, 179, 209, 210
CQPweb, 56, 66, 67, 71, 72

dialect/s, 10, 31–43, 53, 76, 100, 103, 106, 148, 166, 197
dictionary/ies, 6, 8, 17, 29, 32, 37, 44, 103, 107, 126, 138, 141, 172
diglossia, 2, 32, 34

English, 2, 6, 7, 8, 9, 11, 12, 13, 17, 18, 30, 31, 32, 34, 36, 37, 38, 39, 41, 42, 43, 44, 48, 56, 58, 61, 65, 68, 69, 71, 76–83, 85, 87, 89, 92, 102, 105, 106, 107, 108, 110, 111, 121, 124, 126, 127, 128, 130, 131, 132, 134, 135, 137, 138, 139, 140, 155, 164, 164, 165, 171, 178, 181, 202, 204, 205, 206, 210, 213, 214, 215, 219, 220, 223, 224, 225
European Language Resources Association (ELRA), 103

French, 6, 9, 12, 31, 32, 42, 45, 53, 102, 106, 145, 147, 164, 165, 167, 191

genre/genres, 7, 18, 19, 23, 28, 33, 50, 92, 102, 103, 105, 121, 174, 175, 181, 185, 195, 202, 204, 205, 211, 213, 215, 216, 218, 220, 221, 222

International Computer Archive of Modern and Medieval English (ICAME), 103
Islam, 2, 31, 103, 106, 111–12

Lancaster University, 72, 141
language teaching, 104–7
Linguistic Data Consortium (LDC), 33, 37, 44, 58, 59, 103
logistic regression, 179, 197

machine learning, 11, 100–4, 112
Mechanical Turk, 39, 40, 41, 53, 102
Morphological Analysis and Disambiguation for Arabic (MADA), 11, 44, 56, 63–72, 205, 206, 207, 225
multivariate analysis, 13, 174, 180, 196, 197, 202, 208
Muslim/s, 2, 31, 100, 102, 103, 104, 105, 108, 111, 112, 133

ontology/ies, 107–11

parsing, 10, 44–7, 64, 77, 79
proximity, 208, 209

Quran/Qur'an, 2, 4, 12, 14, 18, 30, 32, 62, 65, 100, 102–12, 120–40, 141, 164, 174

register/s, 7, 8, 12, 13, 31, 39, 143, 150, 202, 204, 205, 206, 208, 211, 213

Sawalha Atwell Leeds Morphological Analysis (SALMA), 60, 62, 64, 65, 66, 69, 103, 106
schema/ta, 11, 56, 59, 62–6, 71, 77, 109, 174, 187
semantic prosody/prosodies, 12, 120–2, 126, 130, 132, 135, 136, 137, 139, 140, 141
Sībawayh, 8–10
Standard Arabic Morphological Analyzer (SAMA), 45, 59, 68, 144
subcorpus/ora, 7, 106, 174

tagset/s, 11, 56, 57–72, 106–8, 112
tajweed, 108, 110
text types/modes
  autobiography, 206, 215, 216, 218, 219, 220, 221, 222
  literature, 18, 19, 30, 31, 33, 174, 185, 204, 224
  medicine, 18, 206, 218, 220, 222
  narrative, 181, 201, 202, 203, 213, 214, 215, 216, 220, 224
  newspapers, 18, 19, 20, 23, 25, 31, 33, 34, 92, 105, 174, 175, 181, 185, 187, 190, 191
  sciences, 33, 174, 215, 216, 218, 220, 221
transcriber/s, 40–2, 50
transcription/s, 39, 40–2, 107–8, 111
  quality control, 41, 42
translation/s, 7, 12, 120–40
transliteration, 1, 4, 5, 14, 20, 21, 24, 42, 43, 45, 46, 52, 78, 229–31
  Buckwalter transliteration, 5, 20, 42, 45, 52, 229–31

Unicode, 5, 20, 89, 105, 229–31

visualisation, 12, 107, 108, 109, 110, 111

EU representative:
Easy Access System Europe
Mustamäe tee 50, 10621 Tallinn, Estonia
Gpsr.requests@easproject.com

www.ingramcontent.com/pod-product-compliance
Lightning Source LLC
Chambersburg PA
CBHW071838230426
43671CB00012B/1995
* 9 7 8 1 4 7 4 4 8 5 4 5 6 *